Approaches to Canadian Politics

Approaches to Canadian Politics

Second Edition

Editor

John H. Redekop

Department of Political Science
Wilfrid Laurier University

Prentice-Hall Canada Inc., Scarborough, Ontario

Canadian Cataloguing in Publication Data

Main entry under title:
Approaches to Canadian politics

Includes bibliographies and indexes.
ISBN 0-13-043745-X

1. Canada – Politics and government – Addresses,
essays, lectures.   I. Redekop, John H. (John Harold),
1932-

JL65 1978.A66 1983   320.971   C82-095311-3

42, 096

Prentice-Hall, Inc., Englewood Cliffs, New Jersey
Prentice-Hall International, Inc., London
Prentice-Hall of Australia, Pty., Ltd., Sydney
Prentice-Hall of India Pvt., Ltd., New Delhi
Prentice-Hall of Japan, Inc., Tokyo
Prentice-Hall of Southeast Asia (Pte.) Ltd., Singapore
Editora Prentice-Hall do Brasil Ltda., Rio de Janeiro

ISBN 0-13-043745-X

Production Editor: Heather Scott McClune
Production: Alan Terakawa
Cover Design: Fred Eskins
Typesetting: ART-U Graphics Ltd.
Printed and bound by Webcom
1   2   3   4   WC   86   85   84   83

Contents

Preface

This book is designed to fulfill four basic objectives: 1) to describe, illustrate and evaluate fifteen different ways of interpreting Canadian politics; 2) to stimulate interest in Canadian politics; 3) to enrich students' knowledge of Canadian politics by introducing them to new approaches; and 4) to demonstrate that no one approach can generate an adequate, let alone balanced, explanation of the subject. Additionally, reading this volume should help students to recognize and make allowance for biases and to understand the strengths and weaknesses, the potential and limitations, of each approach as they encounter it in their studies.

These fifteen original and generally brief essays should be of considerable help to those instructors and students who have spent tedious hours searching libraries and bookstores for suitable material to illustrate the large number of noteworthy approaches. My own students will, I trust, find this wide-ranging volume much more useful than the previous lists of scattered sections and first or last chapters. While each chapter is self-contained and can profitably be read by itself, the significant benefits of assessing the inter-author comments and of general comparison will be largely missed if the book is not read in its entirety.

The authors do not assume that readers come to this volume with substantial knowledge about Canadian politics; all chapters have been written with beginning students in mind. Our aim is to help students to understand and integrate the numerous ways in which substantive material is presented, be it in this book or elsewhere. Given this thrust and the usage of familiar categories, beginning students should have no difficulty in relating these chapters to their other readings in politics. While the book may have many uses, it is intended to be used primarily as a main or auxiliary text for courses in Canadian and introductory politics. The annotated bibliographies at the end of each chapter should be helpful for students as well as instructors.

It is with much pleasure that I thank the contributors for their diligence and cooperation in revising and updating their chapters, and the departmental secretaries, Joan M. Elvy and especially Arvis Oxland, for their many hours of typing and retyping. A special word of gratitude is extended to the numerous readers of the first edition who made suggestions for improvement; they will see that many of the desired changes have been made. Finally, it would be a serious omission not to mention the invaluable assistance of Barb Steel, Copy Editor, Heather Scott McClune, Production Editor, and Marta Tomins, Project Editor, all of Prentice-Hall.

John H. Redekop
December 7, 1982

Introduction

What is the best way of studying Canadian politics? Unfortunately there is no simple or straightforward answer to this question. As we shall see, the field of Canadian politics is torn between differing conceptions of what the study should encompass, what the really important questions are, and which approach is most useful.

Like so many terms in political science, the word "approach"—the generic term used in this book's title—has various meanings. As used here, it refers to a way of looking at and explaining politics, in this case, Canadian politics. An approach incorporates a logical framework for inquiry, and spells out what particular emphasis is considered important and, consequently, the criteria for deciding what data, questions, or problems are of greatest relevance. Every approach has a particular focus and scope, but not every one necessarily constitutes a full-fledged theory, be it descriptive, prescriptive or explanatory. While not all approaches come to grips with every aspect of Canadian politics, the fifteen selected for inclusion in this volume have all been described—if not here then elsewhere—either as explanations of the major features of Canadian politics, or as explanations of why some major component is critically important for a proper understanding of the whole.

The thrust of this book can perhaps be made even more explicit by suggesting some synonyms for the term "approach". Words such as orientation, interpretation and perspective come to mind. Perhaps one could even speak of an integrating focus.

Though there are references to "methodological approaches", this book reflects the assumption that there is a basic distinction between approach and method. If, as suggested above, approaches consist largely of convictions or assumptions concerning what is important and the attendant criteria for selecting problems and relevant data, then methods are the procedures for collecting and utilizing data. Given this distinction, it follows that methods are secondary and should be seen as instrumental to the larger and more fundamental questions of approaches. Accordingly, knowledge of approaches is both more important than, and should be antecedent to, knowledge of methods, significant though the latter is.

If the authors were addressing themselves primarily to questions of methodology within the discipline, then our first concern would be: "How should I study Canadian politics?" However, in the present volume the more inclusive and more basic questions to which all the authors address themselves are: "What should I study in Canadian politics in order to get at the heart of the matter?", "Which interpretation makes the most sense?" and "How useful is this particular approach?" Only incidentally do we concern ourselves with techniques and alternate methodologies. This book was not intended to deal with phenomena such as laws, scientific method, models, mid-range theories, behavioralism, structure-functionalism, game theory or inductive and deductive logic. Our purpose is neither to analyze techniques or methodologies, nor to develop broad theories about politics in general. Rather our aim is to present and assess alternative views of how we can acquire a broad and balanced knowledge about political affairs in Canada. Additionally, it should be emphasized that this book does not deal specifically with segments or divisions of Canadian politics, nor with problems or themes, although some of the topics treated here have often been dealt with in that manner.

Of course, the contributors, all experts in their areas, have not ignored the standard political science methodologies; they are discussed or even used in the various chapters but they are not analyzed as ends in themselves. In similar fashion, the writers use commonplace political science notions such as centrality of power, the significance of values, the nature of social cohesion and cleavages, the importance of decision-making, the dynamics of conflict resolution, and the role of influence and authority. Although we may use all these ideas and many more, we focus neither on their relative strengths or weaknesses nor on the scope of their utility. The point bears repetition: we are not as much concerned with the usual, broad methodological questions as with the much more specific question of what is really important in the study of Canadian politics.

Let me illustrate this point. The significance of environment, broadly defined, has been a major bone of contention among political scientists for a long time. In this book we do not debate the issue but acknowledge that in politics environment is consequential, at least to some degree. Accordingly, in Part One, four writers assess the significance of four different dimensions of the environment as keys to understanding Canadian politics. Similarly, without asserting exactly where any one of us stands in the continuing controversy about studying values, we note the obvious fact that ideas play a noteworthy part in Canadian politics. Thus, in Part Two, two scholars with related, though distinct, perspectives evaluate the extent to which such an emphasis can help us to understand the broader subject.

Part Three deals with structures. In ealier decades, the description of structures dominated the literature. Now the relevance of description is hotly debated; let the debate continue. In the meantime two contributors who believe that the study of structures is useful explain why they hold that view and draw our attention to the importance of certain structural arrangements.

Part Four treats processes, sometimes defined as the dynamics of the political system. We could have evaluated many processes, but we limited ourselves to three that are considered central in Canadian politics.

Part Five focuses mainly on political actors and their power. For centuries, political writers have debated the utility of the concepts of power and powerful groups. This volume does not join that ongoing debate. Rather, assuming that power is an important, if not basic, concept, we ask who actually exercises great or ultimate political power in Canada and to what extent an understanding of each of the four hypotheses provides us with knowledge about the entire political system.

The fifteen chapters all deal with Canadian politics, but they do not begin with the same set of assumptions, although every one of us has to begin with some. However, they all reflect the view that description by itself is inadequate and that not everything in a political system is of equal importance; but that is where the agreement ends. Different basic perspectives lead equally competent experts to give sharply different views of what belongs at the core of our study. But all contributors agree that no single approach is sufficient to explain all that we ought to know about the topic. There is some consensus that alternate, even competing, approaches complement each other and can be equally useful, although perhaps for different purposes. Students should recognize that each approach throws light on important insights. Readers will soon note the considerable overlap, expecially in certain sections; this is intentional and should serve to clarify differences in interpretation.

For our purposes we have defined politics very broadly. In its most comprehensive meaning it refers to the art and science of government as well as to those structures, organizations and activities through which individuals or groups of people seek to achieve power, freedom, economic rewards or other benefits. More than two thousand years ago, Aristotle defined politics as those arrangements and relationships found in more or less self-sufficient communities. Half a century ago, Max Weber said that politics involved the enforcement of law and order in a specific territory by a dominant authority employing coercion, threatening to do so, or at least capable fo doing so. More recently, Harold Lasswell has argued that politics involves the shaping and sharing of power with the purpose of determining who gets what, when and how. In similar vein, David Easton asserts that the essence of politics is the production and authoritative allocation of values, both tangible and intangible. For the present, we will include all the above emphases in our working definition of Canadian politics. As our study progresses we will probably want to reassess and revise certain aspects.

The approaches presented here were selected mainly because, either implicitly or explicitly, they are all found frequently in textbooks and scholarly articles dealng with Canadian politics. Doubtless, additional approaches might have been included to good advantage. For example, chapters dealing with communications theory, Freudian analysis, and the legal approach (which would have been included if this book dealt with American politics) would have added interesting perspectives but, given space limitations, a line had to be drawn somewhere. Several readers suggested that a chapter on quantification should be included but it seemed to me that quantification is not really an approach but a tool with which one may test certain kinds of approaches and theories.

It might be argued that the fifteen topics represent an arbitrary, not entirely logical, selection; I trust that this is not the case. They were chosen in the belief that they reflect usage and, as Vernon Van Dyke once put it, "that it is more significant to comment on usage than to devise an entirely logical classification scheme."

The theoretical coherence and unity of this volume derive from the fact that all the contributors address themselves to the same question: "How significant is the given approach in the study of Canadian politics?" They all delineate a specific approach; they all assess the strengths and weaknesses of their approach; most of them raise questions about other approaches and respond to questions raised about their particular approach; and generally their illustrations involve Canadian politics. Moreover, all contributors present a macro-perspective.

The variety of approaches presented in the following pages demonstrates once again the breadth, the rich diversity and the vitality found in the study of politics. However, it also reminds us of the absence of any general agreement on approaches or widespread acceptance of any single integrating or synthesizing theme.

In assessing the various approaches, readers may want to keep several questions in mind: Does the approach adequately explain the important changes and developments in Canadian politics? Does the approach deal with major questions or does it concentrate on details? Given the dynamic and changing nature of Canadian politics, is the approach becoming more useful or less useful? Is the scope and generality of the approach adequate? Is the approach compatible with existing knowledge and earlier approaches and, if not, then is the more recent approach clearly more useful and convincing? Does the approach allow for modification and reformulation in the light of new findings? Finally, and very subjectively, which approach provides the greatest enlightenment?

The revised edition incorporates several features not present in the first edition. In addition to clearer statements of chapter theme and purpose, each chapter has a point-form summary and ten study questions. All chapters have been substantially revised, some entirely rewritten. Throughout the volume we have sought to simplify and to clarify the analyses and to present as even a level of writing as possible. We have sought to be concise, direct, and to avoid scholarly jargon. Our hope is that you will derive as much satisfaction from reading these chapters as we experienced in writing them.

J.H.R.

Approaches to Canadian Politics

Part One

The Environment Shapes Canadian Politics

Environment, or setting, refers to the various forces that influence politics and the political system. These range from such tangible factors as geography to such intangible phenomena as historical development. In this section, four experts speculate on, or demonstrate how, certain environmental factors have affected Canadian politics.

Without suggesting that human decisions have been dictated or determined by inanimate nature—a naive dictum that must not be allowed to discredit a responsible geographic emphasis—the first chapter shows how Canadian politics has been affected by mountains, rivers, borders and anything else that can be depicted on a map. The vast reaches of the impenetrable and seemingly inexhaustible North, the crowded cities near the American border, and other geographical factors such as distance, watersheds and population clusters, play important roles. The discussion portrays the broad realities of the physical and human patterns which constitute Canada. Perhaps it is true that geography, more than anything else, has shaped Canadian politics. Professor Whebell raises many basic questions and makes many important observations.

The second chapter, while acknowledging the significance of geography, asserts that the truly important factor is not Canadian geography *per se* but the relationship with our giant neighbor to the south, the only country with which Canada shares a border. As the 1957 Fowler Report noted, "No other country is similarly helped and embarrassed by the close proximity of the United States." Maybe this American propinquity is the single most pervasive and influential fact for Canada. Professor Redekop suggests that whether we focus on geography or structures, on elites or culture, on economics or history, the continental fact is preeminent.

Chapter 3 demonstrates the great influence of economics. The productive capacity of the economy, the giant corporations which themselves have power

1

authoritatively to allocate "values" and manipulate consumption, the web of monetary and tax policies, the extensive labor-management regulation, the welfare state and the increasing governmental intervention in the free economy, all constitute part of a very complex relationship between economics and politics. But maybe it is not really a question of relationship. Could it be that Canadian politics is merely Canadian economics by another name? Professor McCready's analysis describes the close interrelationship.

Chapter 4 focuses on the past, stressing the importance of using chronology as both an ordering and an explanatory device. History is not only the main laboratory of political science but its basis. Perhaps Charles Beard was right: "Man speculates only in terms of the things he knows—things that have come out of the past." Professor McNaught asserts that "a command of our historical evolution is not only the best 'perspective' but is the *sine qua non* foundation of political perception." He explains why, without an assiduous study of the past, we cannot understand the present. Small wonder that many political scientists, not only in the area of theory, frequently write history though they may call it by another name.

1

Geography and Politics in Canada: Selected Aspects

C.F.J. Whebell*

"You cannot legislate against geography."
            Sir Wilfrid Laurier, 1887.

*"The present Dominion emerged not in spite
of geography but because of it."*
            H.A. Innis [attrib.]

INTRODUCTION

Two primary geographical facts about Canada directly underlie a great many political issues, past and present, national, regional and local. The first of these is Canada's enormous size. At nearly 10 million square kilometers, Canada is smaller than only the USSR and the People's Republic of China—at least in terms of a single coherent land area under a sovereign government. Physically, Canada is the world's largest polity with a democratic government—in the Western sense of the term. This alone makes it worth studying.

Without doubt, the tremendous distances within Canada would, regardless of other factors, have resulted in a marked tendency for the Canadian population to cluster into a number of regional communities—from sheer time and cost of travel and communication. One section, the Interior Plains, for example, though quite similar throughout in agricultural land resources has emerged as three major political units. But the second primary fact has had even more to do with the development and character of Canada's regional divisions: an immense

*Associate Professor, Department of Geography, University of Western Ontario.

3

diversity in the occurrence of natural resources—living, mineral, and energy-producing, both renewable and non-renewable.

This variety in the resource basis for social and economic life in Canada has given rise to a great diversity of regional communities, large and small, wealthy and poor, rural and urban-industrial. The resultant disparities in economic activity are of great and increasing political significance, especially in view of the universal desire for an ever-higher quality of living and for greater social security. Thus, some regions appear as "have" regions and others as "have-not". Some contribute more to the national treasury than they receive in benefits, while some are chronically "receivers" in this respect. Much of the internal political activity in Canada is powered by these disparities, and takes many forms, from party formation and allegiances to national energy questions.

Two other geographical facts need to be mentioned. Canada lies in a very northerly position, comparable with the USSR in this respect. Only a very tiny part of Canada extends south of 45°N latitude. This has great importance for agriculture, in terms of growing season, solar heat units, spring and fall frosts, and other vital factors. Though southwestern Ontario (which reaches as far south as 42°N) has solar input comparable to that of the French Riviera, agricultural possibilities dwindle rapidly with increasing latitude; fewer and fewer types of crops can be grown, the yields are poorer and the harvest increasingly uncertain. Only some 16% of all Canada is really fit for agriculture, and even this small fraction is distributed very irregularly across the southerly portions of the country.

The fourth basic fact is Canada's global/continental situation. The effects of situation on the internal politics of Canada are both direct and indirect. As a neighbor—indeed a Siamese twin—of the most powerful national economy in the world, Canada is immediately involved with and influenced by many environmental events in the United States, for example, a frost in the winter-vegetable producing areas, a drought in the livestock regions, acid rain blown across from the smoky northeastern industrial metropolises. With its three-ocean frontage, Canada is also a direct participant in the affairs and security of the world. Historically the Atlantic frontage has been of paramount importance in all ways—social, economic and political. But the Pacific frontage is becoming more significant (Japan is now Canada's second most important trading partner); and the Arctic is increasing in importance because of its energy prospects and its vital strategic role in the military security of North America.

Though the latter two geographic facts are of great and continuing significance for Canadian political affairs, this chapter will restrict itself to dealing mainly with the first two—size and regional disparity—in terms of their more direct and permanent effect on Canada's people and its political problems.

A geographer approaching a study of the politics of Canada must always keep these facts in mind, indeed, to begin with these facts as given. In general, geographers try to take realistic long-term views of the phenomena they study, and this is no less true of those who take a special interest in a study of political matters. The great geographical facts pertaining to any nation tend to have persistent effects on much of the political life of that nation, or, to put it in more humanistic terms, these great facts provide perennial or recurring problems to be solved and challenges to be met in the survival or development of that nation. Politically, the responses lie chiefly in political institutions and policies. Canada's form of federal government, for example, reflects the geographical distinctness of the political communities (then colonies) which, in 1867, attempted to gain the advantages of a larger-scale polity while yielding a minimum of their individual political characteristics. Nova Scotia, New Brunswick, Québec, Ontario (joined soon after 1867 by Prince Edward Island, Manitoba and British Columbia) comprised at the time a pretty mismatched set; significantly, since then many of the differences have become much greater.

On the whole, then, geographers studying the politics of Canada tend to start from the geographical facts and attempt to identify the influence these facts have on both political events and political processes. In a federal nation such as Canada, a special set of problems arises from the way in which constitutional authority is shared; this often means that the challenge posed by a geographical fact is not dealt with as a single problem but has to be solved on various levels according to the constitutional structure. For example, in a major river or lake, the water as a resource is a provincial responsibility; as a transport medium, it is usually a federal matter; but the most immediate problems of water management may need to be dealt with by some local authority on the waterway.

Three major concepts, or sets of concepts, are the foundation of a geographer's approach to the understanding of the complexities of Canadian politics or, more precisely, to the identification of realities of which the political system must always take account in some way. The first of these concepts is that of *resources*. Not all natural substances and processes are necessarily considered resources at any one time. Muskrats are a resource (fur) but field mice are not, at least in themselves. Winds blowing near the ground are an energy resource, though not much used at present; but the vast energies of upper altitude winds such as the jet stream are not.

The idea of utility to mankind, either immediate or potential, is thus included in the concept of resources. What people consider a resource is, therefore, variable, depending on its perceived utility. In turn, this perception varies with the state of technology as has, for example, the notion of exploiting petroleum deposits beneath the sea floor. This is now feasible but was almost unheard of a half-century ago. Even much more recently it was not considered practicable except in exceptional circumstances. This one change alone has had profound effects on the concept of national sovereignty over the oceans and has led to much political stress even within Canada over which level of government, federal or provincial, has primary jurisdiction in this new domain of sovereign claims. Disputes among adjacent sea-coast provinces over, for example, the resources of the bed of the Gulf of St. Lawrence might now be very acute, if there had not been a working agreement among the five in the early 1960s. As it is, the active issues are between Newfoundland, Nova Scotia and the federal government (with France added for good measure, as owner of two small islands off southern Newfoundland).

Distance, in addition to being itself a factor in the political events and processes, has a lot to do with the perception of how important a resource or potential resource is. For decades after the discovery of quality coal deposits in Alberta, very little of that coal could be mined profitably for shipment to Ontario, which consumed vast amounts for domestic and industrial purposes. Instead, the mines of Pennsylvania and West Virginia supplied the Ontario market. Only with political interference through massive subsidies could Alberta coal be transported 3000 km overland and still be available in the lower Great Lakes area at prices competitive with those from the much closer United States mines. The side effects of a high tariff charge, which in some respects is a subsidy, have made this tactic undesirable. Petroleum and natural gas are more easily transportable by pipeline, of course, but here political problems have arisen over the best routes, as there are a number of alternatives, each serving a somewhat different set of markets.

Some known substances and processes remain only potential resources because there is not yet an economically feasible method of transporting them great distances to the areas where they can be used to satisfy demand. This category includes coal deposits in the Arctic Archipelago, though the improved technology of pipeline transportation makes the oil and gas of the region of much more immediate interest.

This brings us to the second main concept that is part of the geographer's approach: the configuration of the population in relation to the territory, or, to put it more technically, the regional systems in which most of the important social and economic activity takes place and through which the political system is powered. It is a fact that people tend to cluster rather than spread themselves evenly over the earth's surface. They cluster in hamlets, villages, towns, cities, metropolises and certain linked sets of metropolitan urban complexes often called "megalopolises". One set of clusters and the associated rural dependencies forms a geographical entity termed a regional system, containing an urban "hierarchy". The relationships between regional systems and among the clusters of different rank within one system are very much involved in many political issues, especially those we shall consider later under the concept of centralization.

Each major population cluster with its dependent territory comprises what may be called in political terms a core-periphery system: the cluster comprises the core and the rest of the area the periphery. A city may be a sub-system within the periphery of a metropolis, while a village may be a sub-system within that of the city. The major aspect of the core-periphery concept that has relevance for the purpose of this book is that at each level the *core tends to provide the political leadership and local source of authority* for its dependent periphery. As a result, each regional system or sub-system has tended historically to function as a political community and to become formally delimited by boundaries as a political territory under the authority of its respective core.

The political functions of larger cores are to some extent stacked; thus greater

Halifax is the major city forming both the core of the province of Nova Scotia and also of Halifax County. But the constitutional levels of authority are of course quite different and involve different institutions and buildings.

Two major ideas must be included in the concept of a geographical core-periphery system. First, the rapidly increasing concentration of population and economic activity in the core clusters, and especially those of metropolitan rank, has led in this century to an increasing disparity between them and their dependent peripheral areas (provinces or counties, at least). The cities get bigger and more powerful politically as legislative constituencies are redistributed to keep the representation-population ratio within accepted limits. The rural and small-town peripheral communities stagnate or decline and so lose political strength. By 1976, for example, Montréal included 45% of the population of the province of Québec, 50% of its disposable income, 48% of its retail trade, 63% of its construction activity, and 85% of its head office employment.[1]

The second idea is that the meaning of geographical facts such as distance, implying economic cost, is undergoing constant change. While the physical distance between two towns, for example, remains the same, the social and economic meaning of that distance does not. The construction of a railway eases the communication difficulty and normally results in a greatly increased interchange of people, goods and messages between the towns; conversely, the closing of a railway may drastically reduce the level of communication and so foster alienation. This is one of the single most important facts in Canadian history and politics. Innovations in the technology of transportation and communication, such as telegraph, telephone, electronics, automobiles, airplanes, pipelines, containerization and computerization, have all had far-reaching effects. But when a link in some newly developing transportation or communications network is established between a large city and a smaller place, the advantage generally lies with the larger center which can, with each set of innovations, administratively dominate and commercially compete with the subsystems in its dependent periphery. Hence, for example, we see the disappearance of country stores, one-room schools, or small industries such as cheese factories from rural and smaller urban places.

The great size of Canada with its immense distances and energy requirements for surface travel has meant that through historical settlement processes, a number of distinct regional core-periphery systems have become established. The type of terrain and the pattern of land resources suitable for permanent agricultural settlement mean that some regional systems are large and some are small or fragmented. The northerly latitudes of Canada inhibit intensive settlement, so the major regional systems are in the south of the country, adjacent to the United States. Because none of the major regional systems of Canada is really immediately adjacent to shipping on either the Atlantic or the Pacific, the pull of the United States for commerce, migration and information flow is relatively strong for inland regions of Canada. Paradoxically, the pull of the United States is also strong for the smaller regions on the two coasts, since the distances to major US regional cores are much less than to any other country, or indeed than to any Canadian regional core, and the historic connections are well established through coastal shipping and kinship links resulting from migration. These geography-related north-south links have profound political significance.

The third main concept used by geographers studying political processes is that of the boundary. It is too frequently forgotten that a political boundary is an artifact, not formed by nature but by men, generally to resolve or prevent conflict between political communities. Where two such communities contend for territory lying between them, the conflict, which may even develop into armed encounters, is most often resolved by dividing the contentious zone and delimiting a formal boundary. When such a boundary is drawn through unsettled country it may be called an "antecedent" boundary. This type of boundary is very common in Canada at all levels of territorial unit, from the 49th Parallel, through the inter-provincial level, such as the Ontario-Québec boundary north of Lake Temiscaming, to the county and municipal district level where the phenomenon is common. Where rural townships are established, their boundaries are almost all highly arbitrary, though not usually formed to resolve local conflicts.

All antecedent boundaries lie across potential resources, dividing drainage basins, mineral-rich zones, forests, ecological habitats for fur-bearers and food fish, and so on, into the jurisdictions of different polities. Though often unrecognized or ignored as resources at the time the boundary was delimited, these geographical phenomena become very important later on: the growth of society and technological changes all too often make the conflict-resolving boundary of long ago a cause of conflict today. The current controversy over the boundary between Labrador and Québec is a classic example: the line of 1927 recognized by Newfoundland and the federal government cuts through an area of rich iron ore deposits and excludes from Québec an enormous hydroelectric development. Québec, perhaps understandably, is not in a hurry to concede that boundary as permanent. More will be said about boundaries later.

FUNDAMENTAL GEOGRAPHICAL PATTERNS

In the light of the foregoing discussion, let us now examine the salient geographical patterns of Canada as shown on the accompanying maps. Map 1 shows the major physical divisions of Canada. The southern part of the Interior Plains and the Great Lakes-St. Lawrence Lowlands are the best suited to commercial agriculture and therefore to continuous and extensive settlement, urban places and important regional systems. This is reflected in the composition of the Canadian parliament: of 282 members, 95 (34%) are from Ontario, 75 (27%) from Québec, and 49 (17%) from the three agricultural western provinces. On this fact alone turns a great deal of federal party politics, including the question of which party is the truly national one. Indeed, is it really possible for Canada

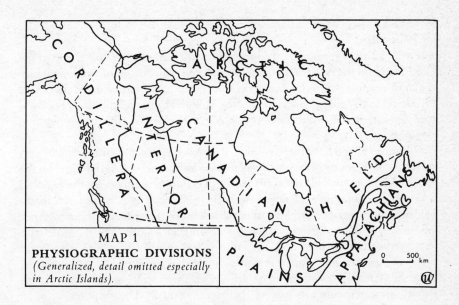

MAP 1
PHYSIOGRAPHIC DIVISIONS
(Generalized, detail omitted especially in Arctic Islands).

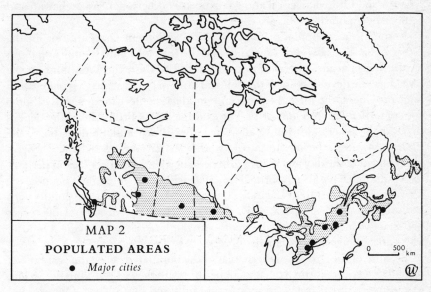

MAP 2
POPULATED AREAS
● *Major cities*

Compare these two maps carefully to note the following points: (1) the way in which the physiographic divisions are broken up by political boundaries, so that all major provinces contain at least two different land types; (2) the relationship between continuous settlement (mainly agricultural) and physiographic divisions — the northern limits of the main populated areas are generally associated with the climatic limits of grain farming; (3) the resulting political communities, the urban cores for which are shown, which differ widely in resources and economic potential. Much of Canada's political life turns on these geographical facts.

to have a party with nationwide strength sufficient to form a "national" government?

Other kinds of resources, of course, occur throughout the Shield and in the Cordillera and the Appalachian mountains and plateaux. Mineral deposits are the most notable, from the vast iron ore deposits in the easternmost portion of the Shield to the gold in the valleys of the Yukon. However large an ore or fossil fuel deposit, it will eventually be depleted; these are truly non-renewable resources.

But mineral and fossil fuel resources, if discovered in agricultural regions, can reinforce the farming economy by increasing local markets. Agriculture, on the other hand, can provide a second source of economic support for the regional sub-systems containing the non-renewable resource. The only part of Canada in which both agriculture and mineral resources (fossil fuels) occur together extensively is the southwestern part of the Interior Plains, mostly in Alberta. Any territorial unit with both agriculture and mineral resources has a good hedge against possible economic distress; it also has a political bargaining edge, since in Canada, resources *per se* are under provincial jurisdiction, though export arrangements are subject to federal control. The disputes between Alberta and Ottawa over oil and gas exports and between Saskatchewan and Ottawa over potash quotas are cases in point.

Map 2 shows population patterns. The settlement concentration in the Great Lakes-St. Lawrence Lowlands and the Interior Plains is quite apparent, as are the separate clusters of population in the East, the West, and on the Shield. In the development of the political units in the East, first as colonies and later provinces, the formal territorial boundaries reflect the interests of some core of settlement and authority. For example, New Brunswick is the dependency of the lower Saint John Valley, including the capital, Fredericton. In the Plains, however, the territorial units were in part imposed by the federal government of the day as a matter of expediency, and the cores, except perhaps for Manitoba, have largely formed *since* 1905 within the antecedent boundaries. The division of the Great Lakes-St. Lawrence Lowlands into two polities with no particular physical separation is a result of the well-known cultural differences between two incipient regional systems—anglophone Upper Canada (Ontario) and francophone Lower Canada (Québec).

Because of the strong southerly bias of the populated cores, the vast bulk of Canada's territory forms a dependent periphery to these cores. Thus the Shield, its resources and people, are mostly administered by Québec, Ontario and Manitoba; the Appalachian uplands by Québec and New Brunswick, with an extension to Newfoundland; the Cordillera by British Columbia; and the nonagricultural Interior Plains by Saskatchewan and Alberta. The North is largely administered federally. Both historically and at present this vast periphery has been seen as a zone of expansion, exploitation and investment by the respective provincial cores. But in the case of a really major find or development in some provincial peripheral area, the capability of the appropriate core to develop it without help from elsewhere, including federal grants or underwritings from "eastern" banks, may be very doubtful; in addition, there is the usual problem of the export market which involves the federal government.

THE POLITICS OF RESOURCES

Should a province derive all the financial benefits from a major resource within its territory or should some revenues be distributed in some way to less fortunate provinces and, if so, how? The "oil sands" problem of Alberta is a case in point. The cost of setting up and operating oil-extraction plants for this immense resource is so great that the firms proposing to make the investment require governmental guarantees and assurances that their pay-off will be adequate in amount and duration. But Alberta wants to ensure that the resources within its territory will benefit Albertans to the maximum extent, and this includes the right to sell the oil and gas in the most profitable markets. The federal government, on the other hand, wants to expropriate a portion of the revenues from Alberta's oil and gas for other parts of Canada, and to keep the cost of oil to all Canadians at the lowest practicable level. Alberta has withheld approval for oil sands production ("synthetic" oil) as part of its pressure tactics on Ottawa. But given the numerical control of parliament by oil-less Ontario and Québec, it is difficult to conceive how *any* party in power in Ottawa (even the Progressive Conservatives, had they remained) would find it expedient to concede *all* Alberta's demands. And so, in the impasse, all oil sands projects were suspended by mid-1981.

In the multiple-use category of resources such as high-quality land for which farming, forestry, wildlife conservation, water management and human recreation may all be in competition, ought the pattern and balance of use be determined by one local jurisdiction or by a set, or stack, of jurisdictions balancing the interests of both local and more distant regional systems of population and their political centers? A great deal of politics deals with these questions, involving pressure groups such as farmers, resource exploiters, urban land developers, sportsmen and citizen groups of many kinds. In resolving conflicting claims of these kinds—many, many examples exist—politics gains its epithet as "the art of the possible".

Problems involving water as a resource occur frequently. A user of river water, such as a factory or a city, may return raw effluent to the stream and impair the quality of the water for downstream users, such as farmers; this situation is more complicated if the offender is in one province and the affected area in another. A dam built for electrical energy may flood a tract of forest and cause great damage to hunting and other recreational activities. If a stream is to be tapped for irrigation, the apportioning of the available water upstream and downstream of the intakes must be determined. If an area is flooded for the construction of a dam for canalization, power, irrigation, or any combination of these, the question arises of whether compensation should be paid to those whose property is damaged and, if so, how damages should be assessed. These questions may seem to be legal issues, and they are, but only with respect to *existing* laws. The key questions are whether the laws should be changed and if so, what criteria politicians should use in changing them.

A special comment is required on the resources of Canada's oceans. The living resources are almost all mobile: fish and shellfish, whales, and seals. To harvest these resources, essentially hunting procedures must be employed. Regulation, conservation, jurisdiction and enforcement must therefore be based on broader criteria than those used to designate a timber berth or licensed trapline. Such waters are also used for Canada's foreign trade and exploited by fishermen, whalers and sealers from distant countries. The livelihood and prosperity of coastal Canadians may be threatened by these users of the oceans, so they express their concern politically, at both provincial and federal levels. Canada's unilateral extension of exclusive national control over fisheries in the early 1970s has had the effect of improving the economy of Newfoundland and Nova Scotia. The resulting prosperity, however, has provoked an issue between Nova Scotia and Newfoundland over exclusive *provincial* rights to certain fishing areas!

Land, living, mineral and water resources thus are rich sources of conflict and of issues that the political system at some level must try to resolve.[2] In some cases, such problems may be electoral issues, and become part of the campaign rhetoric of candidates; this was certainly the case in the 1979 general election, when the Progressive Conservatives espoused the cause of provincial control over energy resources. In others, the problem may be taken up by a bloc of legislators, or by a party, who want to resolve it by enacting laws, amendments or orders-in-council, as for example do the Ontario Liberals and NDP, both of whom wish to slow down the loss of good agricultural land to urban and other uses. Then again, some resources may be important enough that a whole bureaucratic department is assigned to oversee them and their exploitation. Thus many provincial and federal governments have or have had departments of mines, fisheries, forestry, wildlife, agriculture, water resources, electrical energy, conservation, irrigation, public parks, and so on. Such groupings of bureaucratic units are constantly changing, as a comparison of almost any two years of the *Canada Year Book* would show; in recent years, however, there has been a tendency for more comprehensive departments to be formed, under titles such as "Environment", to meet the need for more widely-integrated management of the increasingly complex relationships among resources and the activities of the voting public.

There has been a tendency, perhaps, to think of the utility of Canada's natural resources in terms of the "greatest good for the greatest number". But the urgent need for more and more natural resources for our high-technology society has driven the search far away from the urban-agricultural areas into the remote reaches of the Shield, the northernmost Interior Plains, and the Arctic Archipelago. The local populations in these areas are truly native— Amerind and Inuit—scattered in small clusters throughout almost the whole of

Canada's northern regions. In much of this area, the Canadian (or British) government acquired title to the land and resources by treaties concluded with native groups and nations—or so they thought.

Today a number of these treaties are being challenged, on various grounds, and native groups are adopting a position rather like that of Alberta's: this is *their* land, these are *their* resources; any would-be exploiter and exporter must gain *their* approval to do so. The most prominent example is that of the Dene Nation of the Mackenzie River valley, which has, as well as issuing a more general land claim, challenged the right of Canada to permit a pipeline to be built southwards from Norman Wells. (This challenge was denied by the Federal Court of Appeal in July 1981.)

Another kind of solution is exemplified by Québec's James Bay project.[3] In this case, the Cree people of the river valleys east of the bay agreed to sign over their land rights to Québec in return for monetary payments and other benefits, to clear the way for a massive hydroelectric project. Many other issues are arising, from the Atlantic to the Pacific, as native peoples gain a more acute awareness of the value to them of their land and its resources and begin to vocally oppose the impact of such things as salmon fishing quotas in the Gaspé, and pollution by mining of a British Columbia inlet or by paper mills of Ontario lakes.

Resources, then, will constantly provide new political issues for the geographer to study. There can be no final answers to the issues as the old Victorians, and maybe even their grandchildren, thought there could be. But there is another category of political issues that is best organized geographically by core-periphery concept, and it is to this that we should now return.

THE PROBLEM OF POPULATION DISTRIBUTION

The twentieth-century phenomenon of centralization has transformed the geographical patterns of Canada's regional systems and shows no sign of abating. The most obvious sign of this complex process is the explosive growth of the central core city or urban complex. This growth has in part resulted from immigration to Canada, most of which is destined for metropolitan centers. But there is also a very significant component from internal migration and this gives rise to a number of political issues.

Much internal migration to the large core cities is of young adults, who tend to be the most mobile and most attracted to the lifestyles of the big city. Their former home areas are thus left with a population of higher than average age, while that of the cities becomes younger than the national norm. This contrast has considerable significance for party platforms and campaign rhetoric, appealing to the young, lively voters in the urban ridings and the older, more sedate in the rural; issues such as law and order, de-criminalization of narcotics, unemployment benefits and housing are likely to be viewed very differently in the two kinds of riding. In the peripheral areas, moreover, the shrinkage of labor pools can detract from the economic well-being of communities, while local governments are faced with higher welfare costs (including those for the elderly) on a shrinking tax base. These are vital political issues both locally and provincially.

Many of the peripheral areas of the Canadian provinces, as has been shown, support only primary resource activities, often only one, such as fishing. When the resource is severely depleted, as in the case of the East Coast fisheries, or when lowered general price levels reduce production, as in the woodpulp industries of Québec and Ontario, the economic distress of such peripheral areas can intrude upon the national political scene. Creation of special welfare programs such as family allowances, of special rehabilitation agencies such as the PFRA (Prairie Farm Rehabilitation Agency) which was created as a result of the dustbowl disaster in the Prairies, and DREE (Department of Regional Economic Expansion) represent the implementation of policies intended to effect a more equitable distribution of economic growth. DREE has been especially concerned with peripheral areas in the various provinces which seem to have at least some natural potential for local growth: fisheries on Lake Winnipeg, tourist development in northern Ontario, and wood-processing industries in Québec and the Maritimes. The allocation of central funds to such projects and the designation of areas as eligible to receive funds are naturally matters for much political maneuvering, on a party or nonpartisan sectional basis, within federal and provincial parliaments.

A more direct political consequence of the geographical process of centralization is the steady accumulation of political power by the core cities and metropolises, and the weakening of such power or influence in the peripheral areas. Ironically, this is done in the name of democracy—the "representation by population" principle. Each redistribution of constituencies, for example, tends to allocate more members of a parliament or legislature to growing cities, and fewer in total to the peripheral areas. In practice this means that many constituencies in peripheral regions get larger and larger. The legislature in Manitoba, for example, had 16 members from Winnipeg metropolitan constituencies in 1951 and 41 from the rest of the province; in 1974 the numbers were 27 and 30 respectively.[4] The policy paper, *Design for Development*, published by the Ontario government in 1968, suggested that two major objectives of the provincial government ought to be the better equalization of economic growth throughout the province and improved access to government by the people. Improved access is hardly achieved by the creation of constituencies as much as 160 km in length, and remote from the capital at that.

Overwhelmingly the single most striking geographical change in Canada since Confederation has been the growth of urbanization in the lower Great Lakes-St. Lawrence region: Ontario and Québec. Each province has in general kept its regional structure of cities, towns and villages, but the chief cities have grown to enormous size. Toronto still represents the core of Ontario, and comprises about a third of the province's population; but while Ontario has generally gained in overall population, the northern part of the province actually lost people between 1971 and 1976. In Québec, Montréal has out-stripped its political superior and former economic peer, Québec City.[5]

The great concentration of the Canadian population along the Québec City-Windsor (Ontario) axis makes this truly the major national core of the country, containing the two largest cities as well as the national capital region. This area totals only some 100 000 square kilometers, only 1% of Canada; and yet it contains more than 53% of the population (1976), even more of the economic strength, and over half (about 55%) the seats in the House of Commons. Despite recent growth in the West, these proportions cannot change at all quickly. The rest of Canada is therefore clearly a dependency of this core in a number of ways, the major issues of politics and constitution turn on this fact.

GEOGRAPHY AND THE CANADIAN NATION

The most important of these issues derives from geographical distance, and involves the problems of national political integration. Political integration may be defined as the general acceptance of the norms of national political life such as laws, legislative procedures, sources of authority, and so on. Good communications are always essential to establish and maintain integration in a national territory, but clearly with Canada's great size the problem facing the political leaders in Ottawa was and is prodigious. The historical solution was to weld together the colonies on two oceans by railways—the Intercolonial and the Canadian Pacific. But in one form or another, the problem is still very much present, especially in view of the pulls to the south which are a feature of almost every region of Canada, especially of the West Coast. In the present days of mass transportation and affluence it is easier for a Vancouverite to drive to Seattle than to Calgary; for a Winnipegger to visit Minneapolis than Toronto; for a Torontonian to take a trip to New York than to Halifax; and for a Montrealer to fly to Florida or even to Paris than to Vancouver. In other words, the real cost of distance has become effectively less important, but not to the same extent in every region or in every direction.

One of the most salient consequences of the various shrinkages of distance has been the development, or at least the aggravation, of regional feelings of estrangement from or disaffection with the national core at both the official or bureaucratic level and at the commercial and popular one. An outstanding example of the official level of this problem was the Constitution debate. The staunchest (and almost the only) provincial supporter of the federal position of Mr. Trudeau was the Premier of Ontario; this is scarcely surprising given both the 95 members from Ontario in the House of Commons and the resources and energy features of the federal proposal, which protect the economy of the national core.[6] It is also scarcely surprising if the Atlantic and Western premiers take these features as proof of collusion between Toronto and Ottawa in other policy matters as well. (Québec ought to have been with Ontario as far as economic self-interest goes; but Mr. Lévesque's Parti Québécois follows a more culturally-orientated agenda which placed him in a position of dissent in the constitutional debates. Nevertheless the federal position does benefit the Québec portion of the national core). At the popular level there occur such expressions of regional disaffection as derogatory political cartoons depicting central Canadians (especially bankers) as rapacious buccaneers, and famous slogans such as "Let the Eastern ----- freeze in the dark!"[7]

This tendency to mythologize the relationships between the national core and the various sections of the periphery works against integration and in extreme cases may result in actual disintegration of the country through separatism. Some of this disaffection derives from resource management or revenue policies as was explained earlier. The province owning the resource objects to the degree of federal interference in exploiting the resource through taxation, export arrangements, output quotas, production subsidies, and so on.[8] Especially where the resource concerned is a primary foodstuff such as grain, livestock, dairy products or fish, producers presume the central federal authority does not appreciate their problems and their low income levels, which leads to particularist feelings. In extreme cases these feelings may lead to suggestions for a province such as Québec or a group of provinces such as those in Western Canada to separate from the federation.

Other forms of expressing disaffection have included the establishment of political parties of essentially regional origin and appeal. The primary producers of the plains region have organized several, two of which still exist: the CCF, an agrarian socialist party begun in Saskatchewan and now reconstituted as the NDP, and the Social Credit party, first prominent in Alberta. It is significant that attempts to transform both of these into national parties have been beset with difficulties; they have had to try to win members and establish a power base of voting strength in the populous Great Lakes-St. Lawrence Lowlands where interests and concerns are different. Reflecting the dominant views of a primary-producing region, their party platforms have had to be restructured to appeal to more urbanized voters. Such attempts have met with only limited success by the NDP, while even more drastic has been the fate of the "national" Social Credit party, which decided to raise its sights to the federal level. In a matter of a few years the widespread though relatively low-level support across the nation shrank to a small area in the East where the francophone supporters gave the party their own title, Créditiste, and then the party vanished almost completely.

Conversely, the old, established national parties headquartered in the Great Lakes-St. Lawrence Lowlands have lost ground in various regional areas, the Liberals in the West and the Conservatives in Québec, especially. The full reasons for this are complex, but several electoral considerations must be noted. First, the Québec portion of the national core has consistently seen the Liberal party as the one most congenial to its interests. On the other hand, the West has increasingly seen the Progressive Conservative party as its only hope. This leaves the Atlantic Provinces and Ontario, and given the parliamentary weight of Ontario, its support is much the more crucial. One very simple explanation for the results of the federal election of 1979, is that Ontario was persuaded away from the Liberals, helped in part by the separatist furor in Québec. In the ensuing election (1980), the bogey of Western oil prices drove Ontario back into its usual symbiotic relationship with Québec.

There seems little prospect that a national political party will be established, or re-established, capable of presenting one platform both credible and equally appealing to all sections of the nation, or at least having any chance of receiving a majority of votes in every section. Majorities, when they occur, will continue to rely on regional cooperation within a party, with all this implies in terms of deals, trade-offs, compromises and inconsistencies.

GEOGRAPHY AND LOCAL PROBLEMS

There exists a chronic but low-key movement to make northern Ontario a separate province (if not more than one). This is an example of core-periphery stress at the provincial level. Institutionally, such disaffection may also be expressed by localized political parties such as the United Farmers of Ontario and Progressive parties in the 1920s and 1930s. It is also apparent in peripheral municipalities' complaints over what they perceive as exploitation by the core, especially in resource development. Though the local population may indeed be interested in some sort of growth and increased income and municipal revenue, they are often completely shocked by the rapidity and scale of such development when it arrives. Since the transportation links to a peripheral area are commonly rather poor, the sudden arrival of a new railway, a full-scale highway, or a landing strip makes the area suddenly accessible, and the status of the resources there, whether timber, minerals or energy sources, immediately changes from potential to actual. Thus huge areas may be leased for pulpwood cutting, transforming comfortable small towns into roaring hives of economic activity and social stress, or startling somnolent villages into galvanic activity, to the discomfort and bewilderment of a population accustomed to a slower pace of life. Often the municipal councils are unable to cope with the pressures and ask for assistance from the province. Sometimes, as in the new Regional Municipality of Haldimand-Norfolk in Ontario, where a major industrial development occurred in an almost completely rural area, such assistance is thrust upon them without the asking—the British North America Act, and the new constitution, give provinces total authority over municipal government. There are numerous other examples of such sudden resource developments across Canada.[9]

A special case in point concerns recreation and tourism. Many small communities in the Canadian Shield and on the sea coasts and lakeshores had existed quietly for decades before the automobile explosion and road-building epidemic after World War I, and especially after World War II. As small remote

communities suddenly became easily accessible there was wholesale development of summer cottages, hunting and fishing lodges, ski resorts, and hotels/
motels, for example in the Muskoka Lakes area 160 km north of Toronto. With
municipal voting rights dependent on real property, local voting power became
dominated, at least potentially, by nonresidents. This was a windfall to the old
population as long as the nonresidents did not exercise these rights but could be
assessed for taxes to defray essential local services such as schools. But two factors
have changed all this. First, cottagers and lodge owners began to demand
higher levels of services, such as road maintenance, police and fire protection,
and even water and sewerage, commensurate with the level of services in their
city houses. Second, they began to make much more use of their properties on a
year-round basis as all-terrain vehicles and better winter snow clearance on
highways made areas accessible in winter. In a number of cases, the nonresidents'
majority vote has elected a council that will legislate to the advantage of the
cottagers and resort owners rather than the old permanent residents. Here is
core-periphery conflict in a municipal microcosm: the core population controls
the higher-order polity, the province, through their voting power at that level,
while also controlling local elective councils in the periphery through franchise
as nonresident property owners. It is small wonder that the permanent residents
of such outlying communities feel doubly threatened and sometimes find outlets
for their anxieties by forming regional separatist or at least particularist
movements.

THE SPECIAL PLACE OF QUEBEC

The integration of Québec into Canada and its converse require some special
comment. Because it is a French-speaking regional system, Québec has
remained distinct in two important ways. First, the life style (*genre de vie*) of the
Québécois developed in the context of the limited resource base of the region
largely in isolation from its parent country, France, and has therefore become
highly distinctive, if not unique. Second, many essential elements of the
Québécois life style did not spread into anglophone North America because of
the language barrier. This condition has not, however, prevented many aspects
of North American life, such as sports and the entire economic organization of
society, from penetrating Québec. Québec operates with a criminal code based
on Britain's, the one that applies federally to all Canada, but has its own civil
code based on the French model (the *Code Napoléon*).

The integration of Québec into the Canadian federation has, however, so far
been effected largely through anglophone links. This fact is, in turn, at the root
of the development of Québec City-Windsor as the federal core, with many
banks, insurance companies and other major corporations in finance, communications and manufacturing keeping their head offices in Montréal while

operating nationally. Because of this, the functional language of higher business in Québec has been English. Especially since the renaissance of the Québécois cultural identity in the early 1960s, this situation has seemed to many educated Québécois an unjust limitation on their upward social and economic mobility.

In a special sense, therefore, the rise of modern nationalism in Québec and its expression in particularist and separatist political movements, either within existing parties or through new ones such as the Parti Québécois, is also an example of core-periphery antipathy. The core, though *within* Québec, is not really *of* it, being properly of federal character. In contrast to this anglophone center of dominance, the entire province is seen to be a disadvantaged periphery, which extends to the very foundations of the Sun Life Building and Place Ville Marie, permanent symbols of subjection.

Québec as a provincial territory, then, has part of a federal-level core (Montréal) within it, as well as its historic provincial-level core (Québec City). It also has an enormous territory (1.5 million square kilometers) as periphery, not very much of which is either purely francophone or particularly closely integrated with the provincial core. One such area is the Ottawa Valley, which has much better communications with Ontario than with Québec City, and also has a large proportion of anglophone residents, especially in Pontiac County and near the federal capital city of Ottawa. The latter, designated by Québec as the Outaouais Region for local government purposes, has been undergoing something of a development boom because of federal office-building. A suggestion from the PQ government that the province liberate Outaouais from federal dominance was met with a rebuff by the mayor of Hull. Clearly the economic self-interest of that city and region seems to lie with the federal system. In an independent Québec, Hull would be very much a provincial peripheral area rather than part of a higher-order federal core. This section of Québec recorded a very heavy "no" vote in the referendum of 1980.

The northern portion, Nouveau Québec, which before transfer in 1912 was the Territory of Ungava, comprises nearly half the present province, and lies entirely within the Canadian Shield. It is populated mainly by Inuit and Amerindians whose early contact with Europeans was through the Hudson's Bay Company. Their usual language of communication with the core is, therefore, English and any connections they have had with European-style institutions such as a church are British-derived rather than French-derived. The integration of this vast tract with the core of Québec is an enormous challenge to the provincial (or national) government. That this will not be free from conflict is clear from statements of Inuit leaders, particularly on French-language school instruction, for some of these statements hint at separation from Québec. The mineral and energy resources of Nouveau Québec, however, are actually and potentially so valuable that integration policies are certain to be strongly and increasingly pursued. The development of the James Bay hydro-electric scheme is a clear indication of the provincial government's determination to keep control of this vast peripheral zone.

THE FAR NORTH—THE POLITICS OF THE FUTURE?

The far northern lands and waters of Canada also require some special comment. Though these immense tracts, well over a third of Canada's territory, are often referred to collectively as the North, they include different types of land in stark contrast to one another. The Yukon Territory, formed to provide an administrative framework during the Klondike gold rush, lies in the Cordilleran section. It is well forested and besides gold contains other metallic mineral resources. The Mackenzie District includes the northerly continuation of the Central Plains, drained by the Mackenzie River system and is quite well wooded; the eastern half of this territory, however, is largely barren Canadian Shield country, but contains large mineral deposits such as those at Echo Bay (Port Radium) and Yellowknife. To the east of this district, which is arbitrarily bounded by 102°W, is the District of Keewatin. As elsewhere in the Shield, the metallic mineral resources form the principal known economic base of this district. What may lie beneath the waters of Hudson Bay is open to speculation.

The final district, Franklin, is truly Arctic, consisting of all the islands north of Canada's mainland and Hudson Bay, together with the Melville Peninsula. These islands are not entirely in the Canadian Shield formation and so non-mineral resources such as fossil fuels occur. An exception is Baffin Island, which contains iron ore.

The whole northland is, of course, federally controlled. But the distances are so huge that integration is problematic and enormously costly. Resources, though known, are undeveloped because of the high costs of getting equipment in and material out. An exception may be allowed in the case of the District of Mackenzie, which is readily accessible from a main settled part of Canada, central Alberta, by road, rail and pipeline linked with seasonal traffic on the Mackenzie waterway and, of course, by air. Even so, only the Mackenzie Valley section of the district is served very well by surface communications. Before the airplane and radio were available, integration was rudimentary indeed.

Nowhere is there much concentration of population; the entire population of the North totals some 65 000, of which nearly half is in the Southern part of the Mackenzie District. In Franklin and Keewatin a very scanty population is scattered in extremely tiny clusters along the shorelines with very few inland settlements. In these two districts the people are mostly Inuit, but in Mackenzie there are some five or six tribal groups of Amerindians, who have recently formally termed themselves collectively the Dene Nation.

The normal integration of these northern Territories into the Canadian polity is beset with severe difficulties. The most obvious of these, as has been mentioned, is distance. Another is social, arising from the growing sense of community among the Dene and the Inuit; increasingly this difficulty is expressed in the rhetoric of national feelings and aspirations. Almost certainly this trend occurs because formerly widely separated groups can now communicate closely with each other by aircraft and radio and so begin to establish a common outlook.[10] This has reached the stage of legal opposition to the commercial groups in the developed provinces that, with federal government acquiescence, have undertaken major construction and exploitation of resources. There has been some talk about creating a new province in the North, but this movement does not yet appear to be well institutionalized. Nevertheless, it is similar, on a larger scale, to the case of the Muskoka area cited earlier, in that outsiders have had more power over local decisions than have local residents.

There is also the complex issue of the location of the main processing plants for the raw materials, plants which create employment and revenue where they are built. Ought they to be in the North, which is almost impossible; in the nearest populated and well-organized area, such as Alberta for the Mackenzie District; in the main markets in eastern Canada; or outside Canada altogether? The answers to these questions do not depend entirely on the economics of location, as specific location costs can be greatly affected by political action in awarding production subsidies, tax holidays, special depreciation allowances, direct land grants and transportation concessions such as freight-rate adjustments. The peripheral areas in provinces with substantial mining, pulpwood and energy developments are, of course, subject to the same sorts of constraints. The North is different, however, in that the federal government is directly involved in administration rather than indirectly involved through its transportation and foreign trade responsibilities.

CANADA'S BOUNDARIES

Most of the internal and external land boundaries of Canada were settled well in advance of colonization and are thus antecedent boundaries. Where these cut across terrain in a straight line, as the Saskatchewan-Alberta and northern Ontario-Québec boundaries do, they traverse land of differing suitability for settlement and transport development. In some areas along the boundary, such as swamps, rugged hills or barren soil, communication is difficult, while in others it is easier. In the latter the real meaning of the boundary is most evident; it clearly acts as an interface between two political systems with different laws, policies, social benefits, traditions and even language. These areas are therefore most likely to be theaters of conflict should the policies of the adjacent provinces be divergent from or even contrary to each other. If one province has a low charge on timber rights, while its neighbor has a higher one, the movement of timber across the provincial boundary (even surreptitiously) can be significant. Cross-boundary movement of other commodities such as wines and liquors is a well-known example of the same principle.

What is more important in this connection is the possibility that a part of one province may be more accessible to the core of another province than to its own core. In extreme cases this can result in a section of one province's periphery becoming socially and economically better integrated with the other province's core, though of course formal political control remains with its proper core. Such a condition exists in the Peace River section of British Columbia, the Kenora region of northwestern Ontario, the Clay Belt of northeastern Ontario (although here it is more the social connections with Québec that predominate) the middle Ottawa Valley portion of Québec, easternmost Ontario near Montréal, the Madawaska section of the Upper Saint John River which was once termed "La République de Madawaska", and the south shore of the Gaspé, to name some outstanding examples. It would be an exaggeration to say that such conditions must necessarily lead to disaffection and separatism, but they certainly challenge the respective provincial cores to devise and implement effective integrationist policies.

All the internal (interprovincial) boundaries in Canada are well-established and, discounting some very minor issues, agreed upon—except one. The Labrador portion of Newfoundland had for centuries an indeterminate inland limit. Since there was no pressing reason for Canada to exploit resources in that area, there was no urgency to formalize the boundary. An exception involved the coastal zone itself because of fisheries jurisdictions, especially over the tiny permanent and temporary settlements on the north shore of the Gulf of St. Lawrence. This boundary has lain just west of the Strait of Belle Isle since 1825. But the beginnings of timber exploitation in Labrador early in the twentieth century precipitated the issue of formal control between Canada, in right of Québec, and Newfoundland, a separate British colony at the time.

Eventually the Labrador boundary question was arbitrated in 1927 by the Privy Council of the United Kingdom which made extensive use of the watershed in its delimitation of the Labrador section. This sort of boundary, like that between southeastern Québec and the United States or that between southern British Columbia and Alberta, makes a great deal of sense in resolving issues over water, or timber which has historically been exploited by means of waterways. But such a boundary may be conspicuously unsuccessful in terms of land and mineral resources, and of the ability of the political systems it separates to integrate their peripheral sections effectively, through surface communications. The discovery and exploitation of the vast iron ore deposits in the geological structure known as the Labrador trough restarted the conflict, since the resource itself and the transport routes to exploit it cross the watershed defined as the boundary. The province of Québec has never been happy with the 1927 arbitration, and maps published in that province have for decades carefully omitted any boundary line except for a hint of one just inland of the Atlantic coast. The agreement over the Churchill Falls power scheme between Québec and Newfoundland highlights this issue, since in effect Newfoundland agreed to share benefits with Québec, and the agreement included a guaranteed price for the electricity, without prejudice to the boundary issue as such. But it is obvious from a map that the Churchill Falls area is more easily integrated into the Québec system than into that of Newfoundland proper, the capital core of which is just as far from Churchill Falls as is Québec City, but much more difficult to reach.

The geographical situation of this area was used by Québec to obtain a long-term contract for hydro power from Newfoundland at a low fixed price. This power has been sold (in effect) by Québec to United States utility companies at a large profit, to Newfoundland's great chagrin. Now the federal government has stepped in with legislation to allow a *federal* right of way across Québec for Newfoundland to use in exporting its own electrical power. This ploy has several important political aspects: it asserts federal supremacy over the transportation of all kinds of energy; it impairs the perfection (so to speak) of Québec's territorial integrity; and it may help to integrate Newfoundland with Canada.

CANADA'S OCEANIC BOUNDARIES

The St. Lawrence is the only coastal zone where several provinces border on a body of salt water but are *not* jurisdictionally excluded from its use, as is the case around Hudson Bay. Five provinces border the Gulf of St. Lawrence and extend into it. The advent of deep-sea mineral exploitation techniques such as drilling and dredging, has meant resources in the Gulf have had to be reappraised. Since the provinces have authority over natural resources, provincial authority was taken to extend over the sea floor and subsoil, as if it were submerged land. Since the early 1960s, the five Gulf provinces have agreed among themselves, without federal concurrence, to divide up the floor of the Gulf and have designated formal boundary lines to this effect (these are also antecedent boundaries). Québec obtained the greatest portion as it owned the tiny Magdalen Islands in the middle of the Gulf.

A special sort of federal-provincial conflict has occurred in the marine areas. When in 1966 the government of Canada proclaimed sovereign control over the sea floor and subsoil out to a depth of 200 meters of superjacent water, this was taken to mean that the coastal provinces could simultaneously extend their jurisdiction over the minerals and potential revenues from this zone. The federal government challenged this position and does not recognize the eastern provinces' own partition of the Gulf floor, holding that such new territory (which was in fact "created" by technological innovation) was federal land and not provincial, despite the allocation of resources to the provinces by the British North America Act. In 1967 the Supreme Court ruled in Ottawa's favor with respect to British Columbia's claim over the Pacific floor; but since the government of Canada has extended national jurisdiction into the ocean and air space (to 12 miles (19 km) from shore-tied baselines and not merely over the ocean floor), British Columbia appears to be trying to win some of this "lost" undersea area back.

The Progressive Conservative government of Mr. Joe Clark in late 1979 assured all coastal provinces that the federal government was prepared to let them control their own offshore areas—a policy position which was consistent with that on land-based resources, such as Alberta's oil and gas, and reflected the election platform of the party on which they gained (and retained) strong support in the West, particularly. This concession however did not acquire the force of law before Mr. Trudeau's Liberals swept back into power in 1980. The issue has reverted to one of federal-provincial confrontation, especially in the Atlantic region, and took a prominent place in the constitutional debates along with the provincial fisheries jurisdiction question. Newfoundland and Nova Scotia are especially vociferous in these matters, having very much to gain in revenues from exclusive control over ocean resources. Clearly, it would be of greatest advantage to the coastal provinces to have had these rights entrenched in Constitutional provisions. The government of Mr. Trudeau, however, mindful of the needs of the majority of Canadians in the national core, insisted on limiting the province's control to inshore areas, to maximize revenues to the national treasury. And since technological innovation "created" the 200-meter depth boundary and makes possible the enforcement of a 200-mile (320 km) (horizontal) fisheries boundary, it seems very likely to create jurisdictional problems over much deeper seabeds and possibly more distant fisheries. As it is, the Grand Banks off Newfoundland, one of the world's most prolific fishing areas, extend farther out to sea than 320 km, and highly promising geological structures occur in the seabed at depths of as much as 1500 meters. But, just as in the case of the Alberta tar sands, the huge investments needed for actual production of oil and gas are held back while the political squabble continues.

CONCLUSION

The discussion in this chapter about the geographical approach to Canadian politics has been highly selective. It has not dealt with external aspects, which involve foreign relations; it has not dealt with spatial patterns of voting, a subject commonly studied by geographers; nor has it dealt with *connectivity*, or the analysis of networks and flows, also a subject of geographical study, except very generally under the term "integration". Rather, the discussion has attempted to portray the broad realities of the physical and human patterns of Canada which must for a very long time be the theater and the basic stage on which our political drama is enacted. Some representative issues were included to show how important these basic geographical realities are in the scenarios of politics at federal, provincial and local levels.

The geographer's approach does not, however, have much to say about who the actors on this stage, the political elite, shall be, nor does it deal with personalities, family background, ideological slant, or intellectual taste. All these human qualities are very important to the kinds of institutional structures and policies designed to cope with the nation's problems. The political elite is concerned with devising strategies and long-term social and ideological goals, and it is against these goals that the geographical realities and patterns must be re-evaluated time and again and against which they take on new meaning.

Diefenbaker's "northern vision", Richard Rohmer's "mid-Canada corridor", Trudeau's "just society" are examples of imaginative concepts based on an existing geography, which give new meaning to the geographical patterns and prescribe new priorities for programs to achieve these goals. Such policy orientations often change quickly as politicians rise to and fall from power and as newcomers look for new concepts or at least slogans to help their rise to power. The same fact, for example rural economic decline, may be of little interest to one set of politicians but of fundamental concern to another; which set may be dominant at any time depends among other things on the principle of representation by population, on a driving need for political power in particular individuals, and on the leadership qualities of a few of them. None of these vital aspects of politics comes *inevitably* from the kind of reality geographers write about; but all have some connection with that reality in terms of an electoral power base, of the effective political expression of sectional interests, and of the careful balancing of sectional needs and aspirations to maintain an overarching concept of nation.

Almost every Canadian is at one and the same time subject to governance at local, provincial and national levels. At each level geographical realities provide both a framework for and fundamental constraints on policies in terms of the real costs of government, of resource development and management, and of integration. But if it is true that changing geographical realities can require adjustment of policies, of institutions and even of constitutions, then it is also true that policies can transform geography. Macdonald's concept of a nation from sea to sea was ultimately expressed in Confederation, in integrating railway systems, and in totally altered regional patterns of population and production. It could happen again that an important idea, translated through policies and programs, would change the total geography of Canada in significant ways.

If we want to understand Canadian politics we cannot ignore Canadian geography. From pre-Confederation days right down to the present, questions relating to geography have always been immensely important. In a fundamental sense, whether we think of 1867, or railway building, or resource development, or defense policies, or core dominance, or regionalism or separatism, geography holds center stage in the drama of Canadian politics. In the end, the geography of Canada provides both obstacles and opportunities, but it is within the framework of the political system that these must be identified if the obstacles are to be overcome and the opportunities realized. As Westfall (1980, p. 4) expresses the problem:

> "The rigidity of Canada's physical features and the relative constancy of her climate mean that the regional structure of Canada is also rigid and constant.... Consequently we have strong regional identities within a relatively weak nation-state".

.To build (or not to build) a strong nation state—that is the question for the next generation or two: to "legislate against geography". Only if this is done will the twenty-first century (finally) belong to Canada.

SUMMARY

1. Canada is a huge territory—third largest in the world. It is made up of a number of major physical divisions, and many subregions of these. Climatically, only the southernmost parts are good for agriculture and continuous settlement. These geographical facts have major political consequences.

2. Because of its geographical situation, Canada has developed as a set of political communities (at least ten major ones) which have chosen a federal system largely to avoid losing their individual political identities.

3. Much of current Canadian politics, including the Constitution issue, turns on the attempts of the provincial-level political communities to gain more power over their own economies, to gain more if not *all* the benefits from their natural resources.

4. The large number of people (over half of all Canada) in the Québec City-Windsor axis makes it, in effect, the core of the federal nation, and thus gives it much weight in the federal parliament and government.

5. Eastern and Western provinces stand as peripheral political dependencies of Central Canada (which however is divided on cultural grounds) and must struggle to obtain greater shares of national wealth and increased political autonomy; the most extreme form of this struggle is separatism.

6. Though it is one of the two political communities forming the national core, Québec has reacted culturally against the pre-dominance of anglophones in the economic and political activities of that core, so that its support for federalism is weakened.

7. Competitiveness *between* provinces over resource-based commerce occurs and has generated many major political problems. Peripheral portions of single provinces find themselves in similar difficulties with respect to the provincial urban core of economic strength and political authority, and express their disaffection through both provincial and municipal elections.

8. The Canadian North is a special case in that the local opposition to the policies of the federal government comes increasingly from native Amerindian and Inuit groups.

9. In the oceanic areas of eastern and western Canada, coastal provinces oppose the federal government and sometimes each other over control of fisheries and seabed resources.

10. The ways in which all these territorially-derived issues are resolved will be crucial to the kind of polity Canada will become. In the future, as in the

past, any balanced understanding of Canadian politics will require substantial knowledge of geographical reality.

STUDY QUESTIONS

1. Which of the prairie provinces has the smallest share of the Interior Plains agricultural land? What does this suggest to you—growing political power on the federal scene or otherwise?

2. Why is Edmonton called the "gateway to the North"? Is there a political dependency forming?

3. It has been suggested that a "political axis" is forming between Alberta and British Columbia. Explain this by reference to resources, communications and Canada's external trading patterns. Would the nature of the two political parties in power favor this happening or not?

4. The Peace River portion of British Columbia is the best multiple-resource part of that province. If you were Premier of British Columbia, what would you do to make this section feel that it would be better to stay in BC than to join Alberta?

5. Total the population of all cities along the route from Québec City to Windsor (500 miles or 800 km). Do the same along the route from Winnipeg to Calgary (800 miles or 1280 km). If you had to run a national (public) railway passenger system at an overall profit, would you run the same number of trains along each route? What political reactions would you expect from your decision?

6. If you were an old-time resident of a quiet farming or part-time farming/ forestry community which is suddenly invaded by summer cottages, power boaters and snowmobilers (and those who cater to them), how would you react politically?

7. Should the Yukon and Northwest Territories (including the Arctic Archipelago) be formed into one or more provinces under governments made up mostly of native peoples? Examine the *pros* and *cons* of this question.

8. There are three Maritime Provinces constitutionally. Is there really only one, *functionally?* Why is it unlikely that the three will unite politically?

9. Where are there French-speaking Canadians outside Québec? Why do these groups generally *not* identify with the nationalist/separatist viewpoint of many Québécois?

10. Why is Ontario strongly inclined to look to nuclear (fission) energy to assure its industrial future? What long-term political implications can you see in this (apparent) policy decision?

ENDNOTES

1. Department of Regional Economic Expansion, *Climate for Development* (Ottawa: Queen's Printer, 1976).
2. "Exogenous economic forces like the energy crisis have a highly differential regional impact. Because the domestic economy is so regionalized this impact sharpens internal divisions." R. Simeon, "Natural Resource Revenues and Canadian Federalism: A Survey of Issues," *Canadian Public Policy*, No. 6, 1980, Special Supplement, p. 182.
3. In the total land settlement of Nouveau-Québec, the Inuit were also involved. L.-E. Hamelin, *Canadian Nordicity: It's Your North, Too* (Montreal: Harvest House, 1979), Ch. 6.
4. In British Columbia, however, despite great increases in the metropolitan populations, rural voters are greatly over-represented by the continued provision of many rural constituencies with low numbers of voters; populations of the constituencies in the 1978 redistribution range from 5043 to 80 034. In this way a party with a power base in rural areas can help prolong its stay in office. David M. Greer, "Redistribution of Seats in the British Columbia Legislature, 1952-78," *B.C. Studies*, No. 38, 1978, pp. 24-46.
5. See M.H. Yeates, *Main Street, Windsor to Quebec City* (Toronto: Macmillan, 1975).
6. It is Section 92 of the Constitutional Act (The British North America Act of 1867) that Trudeau proposed to amend so as to restrict the powers of a province over the *export* of its resources, especially oil and gas, and the prices which it can charge other Canadians; the proposal would also provide for the supremacy of federal law over provincial in resource issues.
7. See L. Grossman, "Regionalism Run Amok: It's easier to trade with another country than with another province," *Canadian Business*, Vol. 53, No. 9 (September, 1980), p. 180. There is increasing interference by provinces in economic interactions among themselves, from "buy-at-home" bonuses to exclusion of other provinces' labor, commodities and even corporations.
8. Grabb has shown that the Atlantic provinces and the West have definite feelings of isolation from the federal government, though these findings are not couched in spatial terms. Ontario feels least "powerless". Edward G. Grabb, "Relative Centrality and Political Isolation," *Canadian Review of Sociology and Anthropology*, Vol. 16, 1979, pp. 343-55.
9. Weller stresses the fact that much of the local elite/leadership are expatriates from core cities. G.R. Weller, "Hinterland Politics: the Case of Northwestern Ontario," *Canadian Journal of Political Science*, Vol. 10, 1977, pp. 727-54, and G.R. Weller, "Local Government in the Canadian Provincial North," *Canadian Public Administration*, Vol. 24, 1981, pp. 44-72.
10. For the content and implications of the Drury report see G. Dacks, "The Drury Report: Constitutional Development for Whom?," *Canadian Public Policy*, Vol. 6, 1980, pp. 394-99.

SELECTED REFERENCES

IN ATLASES

A map is above all a device for displaying large amounts of information for rapid visual retrieval, and permits simultaneous analysis, on a spatial basis, of numerous categories of data, for example, political vs. population vs. transport. Careful comparisons between differently constructed maps of the same area can yield a great deal of insight into the relations between various geographic factors and politics, whether in terms of issues and policies or electoral questions.

Canada, Department of Energy, Mines and Resources. *The National Atlas of Canada*, 5th Edition. Ottawa: Canadian Government Publishing Centre. (1978). This edition of the national atlas is appearing in the form of individual thematic sheets. The best for the purposes of this book are: *Energy* (1978), *Agricultural Lands* (1980), *Indian and Inuit Population Distribution* (1981), and *Indian and Inuit Communities and Languages* (1981).

Canada, Department of Energy, Mines and Resources. *The National Atlas of Canada*. Toronto: Macmillan, 1974. A well-presented encyclopaedia of geographically displayed information about Canada as a whole and an essential source for data on population and resources.

Canada, Department of Energy, Mines and Resources, Policy Research and Coordination Branch. *Isodemographic Map of Canada*. Ottawa: Queen's Printer, 1971. A computer-transformed "map" that shows how the nation would look if mapped on the basis of units of population rather than units of land.

Canada. Department of the Environment. Lands Directorate. Map Folio No. 4 *Canada's Special Resource Lands* by W. Simpson-Lewis et al. Ottawa: Canadian Government Publishing Centre. 1979. A wide ranging and comprehensive compendium of maps, statistical data and bibliographic information on land uses for agriculture, wildlife, recreation and energy, including fossil fuels.

Dean, W.G., ed. *Economic Atlas of Ontario*. Toronto: University of Toronto Press, 1969. For Ontario's economic and social patterns this atlas is very useful.

Pleva, E.G., ed. *The Canadian Oxford School Atlas*. Toronto: Oxford University Press. 1957. Rev. ed., 1973. Though very selective, the thematic maps of Canadian geography are innovative and stimulating.

BOOKS

Berry, B.J.L., E.C. Conkling, and D.M. Ray. *The Geography of Economic Systems*. Englewood Cliffs: Prentice-Hall, 1976. Especially Part 5, "Regional Economic Structure", and Chapter 15, "Canada: The Challenge of Growth and Change". The two chapters indicated comprise a good discussion of the basic geographical structure and processes of Canada.

Cartwright, D.G. *Language Zones in Canada*. A reference supplement to the Report of the Second Bilingual Districts Advisory Board. Ottawa: Queen's Printer, 1976. The question of federal language policies is given a geographical dimension in this monograph.

Dacks, G. "The Drury Report: Constitutional Development for Whom?" *Canadian Public Policy* 6, 394-99, 1980. A brief critique of the report (1980) of a special investigation into the constitutional future of the Northwest Territories, Hon. C.M. Drury. This recommends that more powers be devolved onto the peoples of the territories; the critique states that the report does not go far enough in recognizing native claims.

Foster, H.D. and W.R.D. Sewell. *Water: the Emerging Crisis in Canada*. Toronto: Canadian Institute for Economic Policy/James Lorimer, 1981. A general popular overview of an approaching resource crisis of the first magnitude, including the continental as well as federal-provincial perspectives. The book argues for a national (*sic*) water policy.

Grabb, Edward G. "Relative Centrality and Political Isolation". *Canadian Review of Sociology and Anthropology* 16, 343-55, 1979. An investigation into the strength of the sense of isolation Canadians feel *vis-à-vis* the federal government. It must be said that the form of the questions posed probably aggravated any feelings of disaffection that may already have been present.

Greer, David M. "Redistribution of Seats in the British Columbia Legislature 1952-78". *B.C. Studies* 38: 24-46, 1978. A detailed account of the reluctance of an essentially rural-based party (Social Credit) to allocate seats to the burgeoning metropolitan areas of the province.

Grossman, L. "Regionalism Run Amok: it's easier to trade with another country than with another province". *Canadian Business* 53, No. 9, 180, Sept. 1980. Excerpts from a speech by the Ontario minister of Industry and Tourism in which he points out various ways in which provinces discriminate against other Canadians. For example, Petrosar Ltd. (an Ontario firm) is not approved by Alberta's Petroleum Marketing Commission as a purchaser.

Hamelin, L.-E. (tr. W. Barr). *Canadian Nordicity: It's Your North, Too.* Montreal: Harvest House, 1979. An immensely imaginative, creative analysis of all aspects of the Canadian north: a superview rather than merely an overview. Political, socio-cultural and economic issues are all discussed bluntly but with *panache*, in what is nothing less than a celebration of Canada's northernness.

Hare, F.K. "Does Nature Bind Canada Together"? Royal Society of Canada *Proceedings and Transactions* 4th Series, Vol. 16, 27-37, 1978. A non-technical discourse on the geographical patterns of Canada. Against the north-south trends of the physiography of North America stands the east-west expanse of the northern (boreal) forest—the one nation-wide resource of Canada's geography.

Moore, A.M. (et al.). "Fact and Fantasy in the Unity Debate". *Canadian Public Policy* 5: 206-22, 1979. What are the various aspects of the separatism of Québec and the consequences to the rest of Canada? This is a general review of the subject.

Nicholson, N.L. *The Boundaries of Canada, its Provinces and Territories.* Canada, Department of Mines and Technical Surveys, Geographical Branch, Memoir 2, 1954. Toronto: McClelland and Stewart, Carleton Library Series, 1977. This monograph is the standard work on the evolution of Canada's boundaries.

Olling, R.D. and M.W. Westmacott. "Canada and the Constitutional Question 1970-1980: themes and variations". *Business Quarterly* 45, No. 2, 41-48, 1980. This is a comprehensive, plain-language account of the development of the constitutional debate over a decade, and places the issue of resources in the context of the whole debate.

Ray, D.M. *Dimensions of Canadian Regionalism.* Canada, Department of Energy, Mines and Resources, Policy Research and Coordination Branch, Geographical Paper No. 49. Ottawa: Queen's Printer, 1971. A large number of social and economic variables are given detailed statistical and cartographic treatment.

Simeon, R. "Intergovernmental Relations and the Challenges to Canadian Federalism". *Canadian Public Administration* 23, 14-32, 1980. Pointing out the growth of regionalism (*qua* provincialism) and the breakdown of the federal party system into regional ones, the author discusses how interprovincial and federal-provincial conferences have emerged as a major innovation, not altogether a laudatory one, in the governance of Canada.

Simeon, R. "Natural Resource Revenues and Canadian Federalism: a Survey of the Issues". *Canadian Public Policy* 6 (Special Supplement) 182-91, 1980. A thorough review of the implications for provincial economies of the energy "crisis". Approaches to resolving the crisis depend on whether the concept of a single nation—Canada—is the ultimate goal of policy, or whether strong provinces (or regions) receive the highest priority.

Simmons, J. and R. Simmons. *Urban Canada* Toronto: Copp Clark, 1969. The phenomenon of Canadian urbanism is presented clearly and briefly. There are useful bibliographies after each chapter.

Smiley, D.V. "Territorialism and Canadian Political Institutions". *Canadian Public Policy* 3: 449-57, 1977. A fairly general comment on the problems of governing a Canada with strong territorially-based (i.e. provincial) interests, with some proposed reforms.

Trotier, L., gen. ed. *Studies in Canadian Geography*, 6 Vols. 22nd International Geographical Congress, Toronto: University of Toronto Press, 1972. Robinson, J.L., ed. *British Columbia*. Grenier, F., ed. *Quebec*. Smith, P.J., ed. *The Prairie Provinces*. Macpherson, A.G., ed. *The Atlantic Provinces*. Gentilcore, R.L., ed. *Ontario*. Wonders, W.C., ed. *The North*. A series of short monographs which together comprise probably the most comprehensive introduction to Canadian geographical topics. Each volume has a short bibliography.

Warkentin, J., ed. *Canada: A Geographic Interpretation*. Toronto: Methuen, 1968. The standard interpretive work on the geography of Canada.

Weller, G.R. "Hinterland Politics: the Case of Northwestern Ontario". *Canadian Journal of Political Science* 10: 727-54, 1977. Analyzes the specific problems of a provincial periphery, in terms of its economic base of extractive industries and urban industries, which are controlled, like the administration, from distant centers.

Weller, G.R. "Local government in the Canadian Provincial North". *Canadian Public Administration* 24, 1981, 44-72. A review of how the various provinces handle their northern areas in terms of municipal and other local administrations. The problems of distance, irregular economic development, native societies and local political tendencies are explored.

Westfall, W. "On the Concept of Region in Canadian History and Literature". *Journal of Canadian Studies* 15, No. 2, 3-15, 1980. This is one of a number of papers on regionalism in Canada from many aspects, in this single thematic issue of the journal.

Yeates, M.H. *Main Street, Windsor to Quebec City*. Toronto: Macmillan, 1975. This work deals in considerable detail with the most intensely occupied area of Canada, and includes some comments on projections into the future.

2

Continentalism:
The Key to Canadian Politics

John H. Redekop*

Geography has made us neighbors;
history has made us friends;
economics has made us partners
and necessity has made us allies.

> President John F. Kennedy
> addressing Members of Parliament,
> Ottawa, May 17, 1961

INTRODUCTION

As used in this chapter, the term "continentalism" has two meanings: on the one hand it refers to North American continental activities involving both the United States and Canada as a single region; on the other hand it describes Canadian-American relations, specifically the overwhelming American impact on Canada, involving both governmental and private sectors. As will shortly be evident, this chapter deals mainly with activities associated with the second definition. Canadian politics is given a broad definition, including not only public policy, policy makers, and the structures within which they operate but also the phenomena associated with political socialization.

My general hypothesis is that the overall American impact on Canada is the most important single fact for Canada and the main key to understanding Canada's emergence, development and current situation. In other words, it is not only a matter of Canada's only neighbor, the most powerful country in the world, permeating and influencing almost every aspect of Canadian life, but a matter of the Canadian experience and Canada itself being a response to the

*Professor of Political Science, Wilfrid Laurier University.

United States and American developments, both governmental and private. Thus, while an understanding of the great gamut of Canadian-American relations is not in itself sufficient to explain Canadian politics, it is absolutely necessary.

Given the magnitude and diversity of continentalist forces, J.M.S. Careless's observation seems appropriate: "To a large degree the American presence has shaped Canada.... One is tempted to conclude, in fact, that there could not be a Canada without the United States—and may not be a Canada with one."[1] In a similar vein, J.B. Brebner begins his last volume by asserting that "perhaps the most striking thing about Canada is that it is not part of the United States."[2] Sounding a more pessimistic note, Mel Watkins begins his introduction to Laxer's volume by stating that, "It has been our fate in this century to be absorbed increasingly into the American empire, to be dominated in virtually every aspect of our lives by giant American-based corporations."[3] Arguing that the American impact has already destroyed the basis of an independent Canada, the highly respected conservative philosopher, George Grant, expresses the most gloomy note of all: "Canada has ceased to be a nation, but its formal political existence will not end quickly."[4] Even as cautious a commentator as Mitchell Sharp, then Canada's Secretary of State for External Affairs, in his carefully considered statement on "Options for the Future,"[5] agreed that, "In a Canada undergoing profound and rapid changes...there has been a growing and widely felt concern about the extent of economic, military and cultural dependence on the United States."[6]

Why is it that such diverse observers, writing from various political perspectives, all stress a common theme? Let the evidence speak for itself. Given space limitations, I cannot describe the full scope and intricacies of North American continentalism with all its official and unofficial activities, but I shall present the most consequential aspects.

BOUNDARIES

Let us begin by considering Canada's formal boundaries. Since Canada has only one neighbor, all her boundary delineations, including the early ones negotiated by Great Britain, have involved only that neighbor. The Peace of Paris (1783) established the general line between the Atlantic and the western tip of Lake of the Woods with later adjustments spelled out in Jay's Treaty (1794) and the Webster-Ashburton Treaty in 1842.

The 1817 Rush-Bagot Convention for naval disarmament on the Great Lakes—the world's oldest disarmament treaty—stabilized relations in that region. Later the Treaty of London (1818) established the western border along the 49th parallel to the Rockies, and the Oregon Treaty (1846), despite the Democratic Party's 1844 campaign slogan of "54°40′ or fight" and President Polk's repeated threats, extended the line to the West Coast and around the southern tip of Vancouver Island. The San Juan Islands dispute was resolved in 1872 when the invited arbiter, the German Emperor, anxious to improve diplomatic and trade relations with the United States, awarded the bulk of those islands to the United States. The last segment of Canada's boundary was fixed in 1903 when the American government, amidst shouts, threats and bullying, managed to win almost all its demands on the Alaskan frontier with Canada. President Teddy Roosevelt's "big stick" policy had once again paid off handsomely. With the ratification of the Boundary Waters Treaty in 1909 and the concomitant establishment of the International Joint Commission, Canada's boundary arrangements were complete. The country's demarcation thus became fixed and acceptable to the United States but for Canada the price was high; thousands upon thousands of square kilometers that once were part of British North America, from the Aroostook Valley to the Upper Mississippi, and from the Oregon Territory to part of the Alaska panhandle, were permanently lost.

HISTORICAL DEVELOPMENTS

The gradual setting of boundaries, while politically significant in its own right, was, however, greatly overshadowed by other political developments. The noted historian, A.R.M. Lower, asserts that "Canada, from the British Conquest on, had always been under the influence of the southern god. In every year of her history she has been 'Americanized',"[7] American political designs on British North America were evident early. Already in the 1770s John Adams orated, "The Unanimous Voice of the Continent is Canada must be ours!"[8] A few decades later Thomas Jefferson, president from 1801 to 1809, declared the conquest of Canada "a mere matter of marching."[9]

With the outbreak of hostilities in 1812 the loosely associated Canadian provinces discovered a new sense of commonality—resistance to the United States—a recurring and frequent phenomenon ever since. Having frustrated the expansionist efforts of the bumptious southern giant, the emerging northern Dominion experienced its first clear sense of self-conscious nationhood. But Canadian anti-Americanism, triggered by the first colonial efforts at military conquest during the Revolutionary War and reinforced by the War of 1812, has always been tempered by widespread admiration, even envy. The attraction-rejection theme has been continuous. The positive sentiment was evident as early as 1837 when the militant Patriotes of Lower Canada included the actual words of the American Declaration of Independence in their own revolutionary resolutions: "In accordance with the example of the wise men and heroes of 1776, we hold as self-evident and repeat the following truths: That all men are created equal; that they are endowed by their Creator with certain inalienable rights; that among the number of these rights are life, liberty and the pursuit of happiness."[10] Canadian imitation of things American had an early start.

Canadian Confederation in 1867 was itself largely a response to the American presence; as a defense strategy, as imitation, and as a general alternative. When in 1866 the Americans ended the 1854 Reciprocity Treaty, the Canadian provinces found themselves in dire economic straits. To complicate matters, American commercial interests and settlers were rapidly encroaching on the western Prairies, American railroads were being extended into various Canadian regions, many Maritimers were looking enviously at the more prosperous New England states, and the victorious Northern Army stood poised for a possible march northwards. Granted, there were domestic French-English, economic, political, regional and imperial factors that also played various roles, but the truth remains that the major factors that brought about Canadian Confederation were American. "The fear of a slow death by absorption and a quick one by annexation hung over Canadian constitutional debates."[11]

The Fathers of Canadian Confederation were well aware of American notions of northern Manifest Destiny and of general American sensitivities. In order to avoid further irritation of the United States, the original name "The Kingdom of Canada" was changed to "The Dominion of Canada". But the Americans were not fully assuaged; when it became clear that Canadian Confederation was imminent, the US House of Representatives adopted a resolution expressing displeasure with such action. As P.B. Waite observes, "the American purchase of Alaska one day after the British North America Act was signed on March 29, 1867—three months before it was proclaimed—was no mere coincidence."[12] Significantly, many US maps of North America continued as late as 1888 to show Canada as an anticipated addition to the great republic.[13]

Not surprisingly, the Fathers of Confederation saw much of value in the American political system. After due consideration they adopted the US federal pattern—with slight modifications—as well as some constitutional guarantees, and a few years later established an American-style independent judiciary. Of course, I must hasten to add that these features were added to what remained, and evolved as, an essentially British parliamentary system.

Clearly the United States played a major and complex role in the whole Confederation phenomenon. Keeping in mind the events and pressures of 1867 and in view of the economic, defense and cultural situation a century later, some Canadians understandably wonder whether the very agent that made the creation of Canada possible, the one that pushed Canada from "Colony to Nation" in one empire, has not in recent decades pulled it from "Nation to Colony" in its own.

Throughout the intervening century the United States has constantly loomed large in Canadian political and diplomatic affairs. The entry of British Columbia into Confederation on July 20, 1871 was closely related to American penetration and blandishments. The final vote in the BC legislature favoring union with Canada rather than with the United States was carried with only a slim majority. Predictably, Canada's first venture into diplomacy, albeit as part of the British team, involved the United States and took place at the Washington

Conference of 1871. The extent to which Canada lost out in the ensuing treaty remains a significant question in its own right.

We have already noted the 1909 Boundary Waters Treaty which gave rise to the International Joint Commission with its wide range of judicial, administrative, investigative and arbitral functions. This continuing and very useful agency has facilitated close cooperation between the two countries in resolving a host of problems and disputes from navigation and fisheries to pollution, water diversion and hydroelectric power development.

A few years later, in 1911, a resurgence of Anti-Americanism generated widespread rejection of the Reciprocity Treaty which the American Congress had reluctantly approved. Chanting the slogan, "No truck nor trade with the Yankees," the Canadian electorate soundly defeated Prime Minister Laurier's government and thus rebuffed their powerful southern neighbor. The election of 1911, it should be noted, was only one of many in which Canadian-American relations played an important part.

Other major events and developments that demonstrated the dominant role the United States played in the evolution of the Canadian polity included the Canadian-American Halibut Fisheries Treaty of 1923, the first Canadian treaty that was not countersigned by a British representative; the 1927 establishment of Canada's first permanent diplomatic mission to a foreign country when Vincent Massey was sent to Washington; and Canadian emulation of American isolationism, and even neutralism, during the 1930s.

Throughout these years the close and intense Canadian interaction with the United States was counterbalanced by equally close ties with the United Kingdom and the Empire. But with the granting of full Canadian autonomy in the Statute of Westminster, 1931, the situation began to change. By 1940, with the establishment of the Ogdensburg Agreement between Prime Minister Mackenzie King and President Franklin Roosevelt, the traditional relationships had taken a new turn. In the words of Frank Underhill,

> All our Canadian experience since 1783 has depended upon our successful manipulation of our particular North Atlantic triangle — the triangle of Canada, Great Britain, and the United States. Until very recently our Canadian world has in effect consisted of this triangle.... We survive as a distinct individual Canadian entity by the feat of balancing ourselves in a triangle of forces in which Britain is at one corner and the United States at the other corner of the triangle....
>
> This British century of our history was a happy century for us. We achieved independence without separation....
>
> But now we have gone through the revolution of 1940. In that year we passed from the British century of our history to the American century. We became dependent upon the United States for our security. We have, therefore, no choice but to follow American leadership.[14]

The accuracy of Underhill's assessment was substantiated by subsequent events. Canada became caught up more and more in the American orbit. The 1956 House of Commons pipeline debate about an American-owned line drew attention to economic penetration. The Cuban crisis of 1962, the Bomarc missile crisis of 1963, the 1969 S.S. Manhattan voyage, and the long Canadian delay in recognizing Peking, which was caused partly by direct pressure from Washington but mainly by "Canadian uneasiness about provoking the wrath of the U.S. Congress,"[15] all illustrated the preponderant American role in Canadian foreign affairs and continental defense. The situation persists. Canada followed the US in boycotting the 1980 Moscow Olympics, in joining in a rather futile anti-Soviet grain embargo, and in cooperating fully with the American anti-Iranian policy following Ayatollah Khomeini's triumph, even to the point of hiding and eventually, at considerable risk, organizing the escape of six American officials. The "Iranian Escapade", as it came to be known, meant that Canadian officials also had to leave Iran, and the Canadian embassy had to be abandoned. But Ambassador Ken Taylor became a great American and Canadian hero!

Small wonder that many Canadians have been preoccupied with finding a counterbalance. John Diefenbaker, looking to the past, tried to revive Commonwealth ties but had little success. Although Pierre Trudeau later attempted to establish a counterbalance by broadening Canadian-European relations, with similar lack of success, his observations upon first entering federal politics are revealing. He commented that only about 30% of Canada's foreign policy was devised by the Department of External Affairs; the remaining 70% was "predetermined" by the Canadian-American relationship.[16]

Trudeau's concern was shared by others. The best-selling Canadian author, Farley Mowat, wrote about "the privileged position presently enjoyed by Canadians as 'most-favoured serfs',"[17] and even the sometimes continentalist head of the Canadian Institute of International Affairs, John Holmes, said that "The real nature of the alliance relationship is obscured by the rhetoric of 'free and equal partnership'.... We have bored the world too long with sermons about our unfortified frontier. In a nuclear age the unfortified frontier between a super-nuclear power and one which could not defend itself for five minutes is an irrelevant symbol."[18] The acute disparity between the political impact and military significance of the two countries could not and cannot be denied.

CONTINENTAL DEFENSE

The general thesis of this chapter, that knowledge of Canadian-American relations holds the key to an understanding of Canadian politics, broadly defined, is nowhere better illustrated than in the area of defense policy. The rather surprising fact that the government's 1970 restatement of foreign and defense policy[19] contained no analysis of Canadian-American relations does not alter that situation. Six brochures were issued; none dealt with the one country that is truly important for Canada, the one that has greater impact on Canada than all the others combined. The explanation may lie in the fact that the complex relationship cannot be easily summarized or perhaps the Trudeau government did not consider continental affairs to be foreign affairs. After all, when Canada was intimately tied to, and subordinate to, the United Kingdom, Canadian-UK relations were not thought of as foreign affairs either.

In a fundamental sense, Canada has never been master of her own defense. "Actually, if the criterion is the ability to defend oneself without outside help, Canada has never been a sovereign state."[20] As early as 1823 the American Monroe Doctrine already extended a form of security to Canada, a fact acknowledged by Prime Minister Laurier at the turn of the century when he asserted that "the Monroe Doctrine protects us against enemy aggression."[21] In a more substantive form, continental defense arrangements were initiated in the late 1930s and are thus relatively recent. It was at Kingston, Ontario, in 1938, that President Roosevelt first gave explicit assurances that the United States, despite its general isolationist stance, stood ready to protect Canada from external aggression: "I give you assurance that the people of the United States will not stand idly by if domination of Canadian soil is threatened by any other Empire."

On August 18, 1940, at a dark period during the Second World War, the new policy was formally enunciated. Meeting at Ogdensburg, New York, Franklin Roosevelt and Mackenzie King met to discuss continental defense. The Ogdensburg Agreement created a Canadian-American alliance and established the Permanent Joint Board on Defense, an organization still functioning, to "consider in the broad sense the defense of the north half of the Western Hemisphere."[22] The PJBD, in turn, soon recommended the construction of the Alaska Highway, various new military airfields in Canada, and other defense projects. The Hyde Park Agreement of April, 1941, further intertwined Canadian and American military and economic war efforts by coordinating the mobilization of resources in both countries. In actual fact, as defense integration proceeded, Canada increasingly became only a junior partner. Assessing those developments, George F.G. Stanley has written that "at times Canada was treated as a satellite rather than a willing partner."[23]

In November 1945, the American government requested that Canada extend the wartime alliance indefinitely; the Canadian government agreed. Shortly thereafter, in February 1946, the Joint Military Cooperation Committee was established to formulate further joint defense plans. In late 1946 the longstanding Rush-Bagot Agreement was amended to allow for naval training ships to operate on the Great Lakes. Many arrangements were undertaken in Canada via orders-in-council. Finally, on February 12, 1947, Prime Minister Mackenzie King rose in the House of Commons and described the Declaration on Defense Cooperation, which was simultaneously announced in the United States. This agreement, proposed by the PJBD, committed Canada to the exchange of observers, exchange of military personnel, the establishment of common standards for arms, equipment, training methods, etc., reciprocity of "military, naval, and air facilities," and much more.

As a result of the Korean military action in 1950, Canada and the United

States drew up a "New Hyde Park Agreement" in October of that year. The two countries agreed on detailed and close coordination involving military procurement, economic controls, use of raw materials and industrial mobilization. Increasingly Canada functioned as a region within American continental defense planning. Not surprisingly, C.D. Howe, speaking for the Canadian government, announced in Washington that "Canada and the United States march side by side in time of War."[24]

A part of this dual march involved the building of radar installations across Canada to detect possible Soviet approaches across the Arctic and thus give advance warning to the bombers and interceptors of the American Strategic Air Command. They were of very little use to Canada. In 1951 the governments of Canada and the United States agreed to build the first line, the Pinetree Line, across southern Canada. About two thirds of the total cost of $450 million was borne by Washington; the rest by Canada. The second line, the Mid-Canada Line, was begun even before the first was completed, apparently because experts agreed that the first line was already inadequate if not obsolete; it had been built too far south. This second line, recommended by the PJBD, was entirely Canadian in equipment and financing, at a cost exceeding $170 million. Even before this second line was completed, the United States had already begun construction of a third line, the Distant Early Warning (or DEW) Line. The cost, about $450 million, was borne entirely by the United States. The line was completed in 1957.

Much controversy developed over alleged surrender of Canadian sovereignty in the Arctic. "The Americans ran the DEW line as if the Arctic were part of the United States. The Liberal MP for Mackenzie River, Mervyn Hardie, objected to the fact that when he wanted to visit his constituents at the stations he had to obtain a permit from the American head office in Paramus, New Jersey."[25]

The next stage in the development of total American hegemony in continental defense was the creation of the North American Air Defense (NORAD) in 1958. This new air defense arrangement bound the security of the two countries together as nothing before had done, except wartime emergencies during World War II. The American assumption was that the security needs of the two countries were basically synonymous. A few Canadians objected to the close security embrace[26] but most, including both the Conservative Diefenbaker government and the Liberal Pearson government, agreed to the proposals, perhaps fearing that failure to do so would provoke Washington to ask for something even more difficult.

In financial terms, NORAD could be seen as a bargain for Canada; the Americans agreed to foot more than 90% of the cost of providing as complete a security blanket as possible for the continent. But in political terms the cost was formidable. Theoretically the two countries have joint command but the arrangement was that the commander-in-chief would always be an American while the deputy-commander would always be a Canadian. NORAD headquarters was located in Colorado Springs, Colorado. The major innovation was that there was now a peacetime organization, having weapons, facilities and a command structure which could operate at the outset of hostilities in accordance with a single air defense plan approved in advance by the governments of Canada and the United States. The real clincher, of course, was that the commander, always an American, would always be operating under the direction of the President of the United States.

The degree to which the NORAD arrangements placed Canadian defense policy and security matters under American control became evident in the early 1960s. The Cuban missile crisis of October 1962 was the acid test. As a result of President Kennedy's decision to challenge Soviet missile activity in Cuba, NORAD troops were alerted to be ready for immediate action. Prime Minister Diefenbaker was not consulted before the American decision. When he was eventually informed, he refused for forty-eight hours to sanction the alert but he was powerless to prevent it and against the explicit wishes of the Canadian Prime Minister, Canadian troops geared up for battle. The American authorities resented Diefenbaker's refusal to cooperate fully. Writing five years later, one of them observed that, "It wasn't as bad as it looked. This was because the Canadian forces went on full alert despite their government."[27]

The second crisis came the following year and may well have been related to the first. The Diefenbaker government, despite strong pressure from Washington, refused to arm its Bomarc missiles with nuclear warheads. Whether such a policy made military sense is still in dispute but in any event it was Canadian policy. The crisis escalated and in February 1963 the minority Diefenbaker government was defeated in a House of Commons confidence vote. The Conservatives alleged American interference, especially in the ensuing election campaign which produced a Liberal government headed by Lester Pearson. The nuclear warheads were soon installed on the Bomarc missiles. A statement by Tom Kent, a senior official in the Liberal party who was later to become Prime Minister Pearson's executive assistant, gives some indication of Liberal party policy: "The first essential interest of Canada in the world today is the security of the United States; that takes overwhelming priority over everything else in Canada's external relations."[28]

The NORAD treaties were accompanied by certain economic arrangements, most notably the 1959 Defense Production Sharing Agreement. Continentalism in defense production had been agreed to as early as 1941 in the Hyde Park Agreement, but that had been during wartime; now an even more far-reaching arrangement was agreed to in peacetime. One reason the Canadian government agreed to such a venture was that a large segment of its own fairly sophisticated defense industry collapsed in 1958-59 when production of the advanced, but costly, Arrow airplane had to be abandoned because the United States refused to purchase any of the planes. The Americans insisted on producing an acceptable alternative at home. Thereafter Canadian defense industries participated almost exclusively as subcontractors for the United States military-industrial complex, a relationship that persisted throughout the Indochina wars and continues today.

The key stipulation in the 1959 arrangement was that Canadian firms could henceforth bid on equal terms with American firms for US defense contracts. The arrangement proved to be relatively lucrative for Canadian industry. In one year alone, 1965, Canadian arms exports to the United States amounted to $260 million or 30% of all Canadian inedible end-product exports to the United States.[29] A corollary of these Canadian sales opportunities was that the Canadian government committed itself to purchase certain American war supplies for its own use. In 1966 such defense purchases in the United States amounted to $332.6 million.[30] The Canadian Minister of External Affairs could assert: "Think of the impossible position we would be in if the Defense Production Sharing Agreements were abrogated...to pull out would be to endanger our economy and safety."[31] However, the deal was at least as advantageous to the United States as to Canada.

Partly because of the booming trade in armaments and partly because of the resultant low defense costs for Canada—less than 14% of total national budget for Canada but well over 40% for the United States—subsequent Canadian governments have shown no reluctance in renewing the arrangements. Most recently, in 1980, the NORAD treaty was again renewed by the Canadian government. Of course, the NORAD treaty is only one part of a much larger whole; at present the total number of treaties between Canada and the United States exceeds 180, covering such diverse areas as "atomic energy, aviation, boundary waters, customs, defense, economics, extradition, finance, fisheries, health and sanitation, highways, maritime matters, migratory birds, military affairs, naval vessels, navigation, postal arrangements, hydroelectric power, tenure and disposition of property, smuggling, taxation, telecommunications, trade and commerce and others...."[32] Given such a context for formal defense treaties it is hardly surprising to have Canadian General Charles Foulkes assert that, "Canada has not always agreed with U.S. strategic policies, but it is usually frank enough to point out its views, and is staunch enough to support any challenge to our North American way of life."[33] The term "North American" is apt.

As Canada entered the last quarter of the twentieth century no one could seriously dispute the contention that Canadian security policies, Canadian defense production, perhaps even the bulk of overall Canadian foreign policy, can be understood only in the light of American hegemony in continental affairs.

CONTINENTAL ECONOMICS

We turn now to the second major area of American preeminence in the Canadian polity—the whole realm of economics. At the outset we need to emphasize two points; the awesome American economic influence on, and presence in, Canada, a sequel to historic British economic hegemony, has come almost entirely in response to Canadian desires, and, second, in large part the roots of this American economic penetration go back to Sir John A. Macdonald's 1879 tariff scheme, known as the National Policy. At first the National Policy seemed to be successful in that its aim of enticing foreign firms to establish branches in Canada was quickly realized. But in the longer term that kind of economic nationalism turned out to be self-defeating inasmuch as the Canadian government yielded control over large segments of economic decision-making and related public policy. Accordingly, American corporations, and to a lesser extent American governments, came to play an ever larger role in Canada. Of course, part of that situation was simply the result of the naturally ominous impact of a massive economy on a relatively small neighboring one.

Let us briefly analyze the diverse ways in which American economic activity has influenced Canadian politics, especially in recent years. While focusing on current affairs we should keep in mind that throughout Canada's first century the American economic reality, from the tariff policies of the 1880s to the reciprocity question of 1911, to the Wall Street crash of 1929 and to wartime cooperation, was always a major question in Canada and frequently a central issue in election campaigns. Many of these American-related issues did not, and do not, pertain only to Canada, but their larger significance in no way decreased their importance for the northern neighbor.

Perhaps the most publicized aspect of the American economic impact involves investment, both direct and indirect. Direct investment refers to acquisition of minority or majority ownership in refineries, factories, warehouses, sales offices, natural resources and so on. Such investment typically involves bringing in personnel, technology, machinery, brand names, and some measure of ownership and control. Much American money comes in as venture capital engaged in the discovery, refining and merchandising of mineral resources, the development of certain agricultural commodities, the manufacture and distribution of consumer goods, and the operation of utilities and miscellaneous other activities.

Indirect or portfolio investments include bank loans and other credits given to foreigners, as well as the purchase of foreign bonds and debentures. The purchase of small amounts of Canadian noncontrolling equity stock by American residents would also fit into this category. The point to bear in mind is that indirect investment is basically a financial transaction that can be paid off while direct investment involves at least partial ownership and control. The difference between the two types of investment is, of course, crucial. In the case of the indirect investment, control remains with the borrower; in the case of direct investment, it rests unequivocally with the lender and creates a liability that tends to be permanent and to grow.

As indicated in Figure 1, American investment has grown rapidly in recent decades, especially in the form of direct investment. By 1946 the US share of Canada's total foreign liabilities had risen to 72% with direct investment liabilities accounting for about 40% of all Canada's foreign indebtedness. By 1952 the American component of the total had reached 77% and American direct investment had surpassed American portfolio investment. By 1964

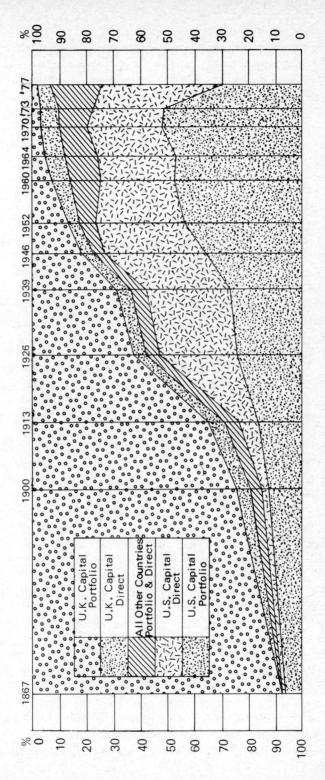

Figure 1
Foreign Investment in Canada

Legend:
U.K. Capital Portfolio
U.K. Capital Direct
All Other Countries Portfolio & Direct
U.S. Capital Direct
U.S. Capital Portfolio

Sources: Statistics Canada, *Canada's Investment Position*, 1971-1973, pp. 42, 86, 87; Statistics Canada, *Canada's International Investment Position*, 1977, p. 63-71.

approximately 80% of long-term foreign investment in Canada was American. The $12.9 billion that American firms had by that time invested in Canadian branch plants and subsidiaries accounted for 31% of all US direct foreign investments; US direct investment in the relatively small country of Canada was greater than the total of all US direct investment in all Europe or Latin America. By the end of 1973, total long-term foreign investment was $51.415 billion of which 78% was American, 9.2% British, and 12.8% came from other countries. American-controlled investment in Canadian companies, often wholly owned subsidiaries, had risen to $26.143 billion and constituted 79% of all foreign direct investment. By 1977 total long-term foreign investment had reached $86.116 billion of which 73.3% was American, 7.5% was British, and 19.2% was from other countries. Though the American percentage is down slightly, the actual figures for US direct investment in Canada rose from $26.143 billion in 1973 to $37.602 billion in 1977, while US portfolio investment in Canada rose from $13.984 billion in 1973 to $25.498 billion in 1977.

By the 1970s it was abundantly clear that, given the massive extent of American investment in Canada, the Canadian government was no longer in a position to spell out and enforce public economic policies on its own. Indeed numerous earlier task forces and royal commissions, most notably the 1957 Royal Commission on Canada's Economic Prospects, chaired by Walter Gordon, had already researched the dilemma. The Watkins Report in 1968 and the Wahn Report of 1970 had provided additional important information. In late 1971 the findings of the government review, *Foreign Direct Investment in Canada,* commonly referred to as the Gray Report, were released to the public. Most Canadians were surprised, some were shocked, and some were angry. The report opened with the statement: "The high and growing degree of foreign, and particularly U.S. control of Canadian business activity has led to a Canadian industrial structure which largely reflects the growth priorities of foreign corporations."[34] It continued, this has "led to the establishment of 'truncated' firms for which many important activities are performed abroad by the parent company, with the result that the development of Canadian capacities or activities in these areas is stultified."[35] Particularly significant, politically, was the further observation that "these developments have made it more difficult for the Government to control the domestic national economic environment. They have also influenced the development of the social, cultural and political environment in Canada."[36]

The foreign, mainly American, control of certain key sectors was indeed staggering: petroleum and coal products, 99.7%; rubber products, 93.1%; transportation equipment, 87%; chemicals and chemical products, 81.3%; machinery, 72.2%; and about 60% in all manufacturing. The list seemed endless. Partly because Canada had then and has now fewer restrictions on foreign investment than does any other major country in the world, and partly because of Canadian caution as well as American tax advantages, Americans had developed and continue to maintain a stranglehold on key segments of the Canadian economy: coal, gas, oil, iron, rubber and some major metals, to name a few.

Theoretically Canadian governments could, of course, nationalize all these foreign holdings but they have neither the capital nor the political support to undertake such a foolhardy task. Sir John A. Macdonald's National Policy had brought in infant industries but not infant firms. Over the years many of these infant industries had become giants and had squeezed out their host. Such was and remains the nature of the problem. The status of the American presence in Canada's petroleum industry, for example, was underscored by the howls of protest and calls for retaliation from American firms.when the Canadian government in 1980 and 1981 stated that by 1990 it wished to have half the industry Canadian-owned. Even with full compensation payments, the foreign multinationals were apparently not inclined to allow the Canadian government to make Canadian public policy.

What had happened over the years was that the massive American branch-plant economy in Canada had acquired a dynamic vitality of its own. Its expansion had been financed almost entirely by retained Canadian profits and Canadian borrowing which was often available at preferred rates of interest because of the additional security provided by large parent firms. Indeed, Kari Levitt has demonstrated convincingly that in the 1960s Canadians actually were losers in the matter of investment flow. "In the period 1960-67 remitted profits of American subsidiaries in Canada ($5.9 billion) exceeded new capital inflows ($4.1 billion) by $1.8 billion."[37] The sum is substantially larger if license and management fees and royalties are included. Today, despite the activity of Canada's Foreign Investment Review Agency, forty of Canada's hundred largest firms are American-controlled and the extension of American ownership in most sectors continues virtually unchecked. Between 1960 and 1969, 606 Canadian corporations were taken over by foreigners, mostly Americans;[38] the rate has hardly changed since that time.

There are many ways, almost all of great political consequence, in which branch-plant activity influences Canada. As already suggested in part, the establishment and growth of American branch plants almost always means the importation of American technology, management, product development, advertising, market access, market control, and research activity or lack of activity. At a time when product specialization has become critical, especially for exports, the Canadian government is almost helpless in shaping or promoting branch-plant research and development. Easy access to US technology and entrepreneurship discourages the development of domestic expertise in those areas. Also, given the common trading restrictions that parent firms place on foreign subsidiaries, Canadian governmental attempts to increase exports are seriously weakened. The case of the Ford Motor Company of Canada is a classic example. Its 1906 articles of incorporation give the Canadian firm market rights in all British Commonwealth countries (excluding the best, the United Kingdom), while the rest of the world is reserved for the US parent firm or its other subsidiaries. Additionally, branch-plant purchases are often not subject to market forces but to parent-firm directions which often weaken Canadian government attempts to build up certain Canadian industries, to lessen regional unemployment, and so on. Significantly, 50% of all export sales of subsidiaries are made to parent firms and 70% of their imports are procured from parent companies, often despite the fact that materials can be bought at lower prices within Canada. There is also the problem of tax loss. Long before President Nixon's 1971 DISC (Domestic International Sales Corporation) policy, which provided a 50% tax benefit if export sales were made from within the United States rather than by foreign-based subsidiaries, hundreds of major branch plants in Canada were avoiding Canadian taxes by various transfer payments to their parent firms. Much to the consternation of Canadian governments, or at least of some ministers, these "corporations have mastered the techniques of manipulating our personal and social requirements in the interests of their private imperatives of survival,"[39] or expansion or control.

A further complication arises from the pervasive "miniature replica" phenomenon. Many American firms, with their huge domestic base, simply spill over into Canada where, without undertaking any research or product development and capitalizing on massive transborder advertising, they can easily make considerable profit on relatively small sales. The resulting market fragmentation with too many firms producing much too wide a range of products for the smaller Canadian economy results in high unit costs, inefficiency, less success in exporting and instability in employment. Successive Canadian governments have found it increasingly difficult to develop public policies that can successfully control and redirect the activities of such a derivative and generally imitative Canadian industry. The Canadian government's frustrations in this regard have been complicated by the fact that most Canadians do not favor further governmental restriction on American investment in Canada if that would mean even a slight reduction in the Canadian standard of living.[40] The Canadian business community and the elite class generally are especially opposed to any further governmental intervention.[41]

In sum, the economic impact of burgeoning branch-plant activity—and there are now well over 8500 American-controlled factories in Canada—while very important is not necessarily advantageous. For example, between 1950 and 1960 the percentage of Canadian manufacturing output controlled by foreigners rose from 50% to over 60% but because of transfer payments to parent firms, inefficiency, and so on, the percentage of companies that lost money rose from 26% to 31% and the rate of profit after taxes fell from 9.5% to 4%.[42] Clearly, Canadian governments have a tailhold on a great monster.

Another aspect of economic continentalism is total industry integration. While several sectors are moving in this direction, the auto industry is the farthest advanced. The Automotive Agreement of 1965 created a single Canadian-American manufacturing and sales area, at the wholesale level, for virtually the entire automotive industry. However, given the fact that 95% of the Canadian automobile industry is American-owned, such integration did not change the Canadian segment very much. The two most important consequences were that the companies could rationalize production and thus increase their profits, and, second, with fewer lines produced in Canada but for the entire continental market, the Canadian industry could be very seriously disrupted by changes in American consumer preferences, American governmental policies dealing with gas consumption requirements, pollution standards, fuel prices and a host of other matters. Without doubt, the Canadian automobile industry is now controlled far more from the boardrooms of Detroit and the legislative halls in Washington than by the Canadian Parliament. It is of note that "in 1968 the Canadian government gave up $80 million in customs duties to the industry and made no effort to recover any part of the sum for fear that the parent companies would break the pact."[43] In the late seventies and early eighties a rather pathetic practice evolved. Canadian provincial governments, in seeking to bolster their industrial base, competed with each other in granting large tax concessions and huge outright grants to American auto firms if those firms would establish new plants in their provinces. Understandably, the American firms sometimes accepted these offers. However, more often than not, they soon closed down some of their older facilities, cut back production elsewhere in Canada, or simply sold out, taking their profits, including the Canadian public subsidy, with them.

Another important element of continental economics and politics involves trade, especially following the 1935 re-establishment of general Canadian-American trade reciprocity. From earliest times Canadian prosperity has depended on trade. The old staples—fur, fish, timber and wheat—given reasonable transportation systems, could and did develop east-west commerce. But the new staples—nickel, iron ore, lumber, newsprint, natural gas— generally destined for US markets have tended to develop north-south trade patterns, thus contributing to "the economic and political balkanization of Canada."[44]

Increasingly Canada has become dependent on trade with the United States. This fact was already evident in 1929 when the American Wall Street crash hit Canada particularly hard. By 1932 Canadian exports to the United States had declined to only 47% of their 1929 peak. Other countries, also hit hard, turned to alternative markets but given geographical and distance factors, Canadian options were severely limited.

Since the Second World War the Canadian-American situation has become far and away the world's largest bilateral trading relationship. In recent years almost 70% of Canadian exports have gone to the United States and about 70% of Canadian imports have come from the United States. In actual figures, Canada's 1973 imports from the United States were valued at $16.484 billion and her exports at $17.07 billion. For the United States the figures, while proportionately less significant, were also high. In 1970 exports to Canada were 27.8% of total US exports and imports from Canada were 21% of total US imports.[45] This trade is critical for Canada. Between one quarter and one third of all goods produced in Canada are exported to the United States.[46] Canada must trade, and must trade with the United States, in order to remain economically viable; in Canada 24% of gross national product comes from exports while for the United States the corresponding figure is only 4%. Such extensive trading with only one country produces not only viability but also vulnerability.

However, the scope and magnitude of continental trade does not tell the whole story; we must also look at the pattern and specific aspects of the transactions. Foreign, especially American, controlled industries in Canada tend to export raw materials or only semiprocessed goods. For example, in a study of thirteen industrialized Western countries it was found that labor-intensive end products accounted for 60% of exports but for Canada the comparable figure, despite government efforts to develop more secondary industry in Canada, was only 19%.[47]

A further complication in continental economics pertains to extraterritoriality, a term that means the extension and application of a state's laws and policies into foreign countries, in this case, US laws into Canada. When this happens, the political independence of the host country and its capacity to implement its own public policies are severely restricted. Space limitations do not permit detailed illustration of this phenomenon; suffice it to say that for many years such American ventures as the application of American antitrust legislation to subsidiaries in Canada, which prevents consolidation and rationalization of manufacturing in Canada, the application to Canadian subsidiaries of the US Trading with the Enemy Act, which prohibits certain exports, and the 1965 application to Canadian subsidiaries of American "voluntary guidelines", which severely restricted economic freedom, all create major economic and political costs for Canada, especially when they are in direct conflict with Canadian trade policies. Interestingly, and very consequentially for Canada, the United States is the only country that practises such extraterritorial application of law and public policy.[48] Of course, much of the importance of such extraterritoriality lies in subsidiary management's anticipation of effects and the desire to develop and retain good standing with the parent firm rather than in actual instances of blatant interference, thwarted exports, and so on.

There can be no doubt that continental economics weakens internal integration in Canada, strengthens the provinces *vis-à-vis* Ottawa, improves Canada's living standard but at a cost of decreased flexibility, and generally has transformed Canada into an industrialized country but one in a state of permanent economic adolescence with a branch-plant mentality resigned to perpetual reliance on external initiatives.

CONTINENTAL POLITICAL SOCIALIZATION

Political socialization plays a great role in any body politic; Canada is no exception. The key issue in this regard is the multifaceted and profound impact of the giant southern neighbor on Canada. Here again, as in the realm of economics, the bulk of the impact involves private rather than governmental activity and again the penetration is generally invited rather than imposed. Concerning expectations, mores, values, priorities and life styles, the United States, despite persistent national differences about sense of destiny, greater social agitation and more dynamic liberalism, depth of patriotism, and a general world view, has become the most important shaper of Canadian social and political values. The extent of commonality and American influence has struck many people. More than two decades ago that astute British observer, Dennis Brogan, wrote, "I do not know of any real parallel to this situation, in which two countries have had so much in common.... It is not a question in Canada of imitating some American ways of doing things. Canada is part of the American culture in most aspects of daily life."[49] Canadians, generally unwilling to initiate corrective policies, have, however, not been blind to either the extent or significance of developments. As early as 1929 Archibald MacMechan observed that the danger "lies in gradual assimilation, in peaceful penetration, in a spiritual bondage—the subjection of the Canadian nation's mind and soul to the mind and soul of the United States."[50] In the late 1960s John Kenneth Galbraith observed, "If I were still a practising as distinct from an advisory Canadian, I would be much more concerned about maintaining the cultural integrity of the broadcasting system and with making sure Canada has an active, independent theatre, book-publishing industry, newspapers, magazines and schools of poets and painters. I wouldn't worry for a moment about the differences between Canadian or American corporations."[51] And two days before his retirement Prime Minister Lester Pearson declared: "The industrial and economic and financial penetration from the south worries me, but less than the penetration of American ideas, of the flow of information about all things American; American thought and entertainment; the American approach to everything."[52]

Canadian governments have not been unaware or unconcerned about these trends. Numerous royal commissions, task forces, special senate committees and other bodies have looked into the matter. In 1951 the Massey Report noted that, "Our use of American institutions or our lazy, even abject, imitation of them has caused an uncritical acceptance of ideas and assumptions that are alien to our tradition."[53] The 1957 Fowler Report re-emphasized the point: "Can we resist the tidal wave of American cultural activity? Can we retain a Canadian identity, art and culture—a Canadian nationhood?"[54] But diagnosis has proved to be easier than remedy. Canadian leaders and spokesmen, stressing the cultural mosaic, glorifying multiculturalism, and shaping a society seemingly having little more in common than a lowest common denominator of ambivalent anti-Americanism, constantly lost out. The Canada that these elites constructed could not easily be held together or integrated into something positive and dynamic. In brief, since early times Canadian society has been vulnerable and permeable. American culture has always had easy and usually welcome access. Indeed, as early as the 1920s a public opinion survey found that in every area of communications the mass of Canadians preferred American culture to their own.[55] For this reason, the long-time trends have not been reversed.

The whole matter of border crossings—vacation travel, brief excursions, employment commuting and migration—has played an important part in the political socialization of Canadians, especially given the widespread Canadian border mentality derived from the fact that 80% of Canadians live within 160 km of the US border and 90% within 320 km. Given the historical migration trends, it is not surprising that many Canadians see themselves as possible future Americans and have numerous relatives and friends "across the line". Between 1850-1950 some 7.2 million people migrated to Canada but some 6.6 million emigrated, almost all to the United States. In two years, 1882 and 1961, Canada lost as many people as came in.[56] For most years during the first three quarters of this century Canadian migration to the United States ranged between 30 000 and 100 000 annually; only since 1966, because of new US regulations, has it declined significantly. Generally American migration to Canada has been low, with the exception of a few years in the early part of this century and to some extent during the Vietnam War. Tourism keeps booming. In 1971 there were more than 35 000 000 Canadian visits to the United States and about 38 000 000 American visits to Canada. Unofficial figures for more recent years are slightly higher. All this transborder movement is not without political and social consequence.

Hollywood and the entire American film industry constitutes another major shaper of Canadian ideas and values. Feature films are still the mainstay of the commercial cinemas and almost all the feature films shown in Canada are American. The establishment of the Canadian Film Board in 1939 and of the Canadian Film Development Corporation in 1968 have not changed things much. It has been impossible to beat American competition. In 1972 the CFDC helped to finance thirteen major films. Thereafter production declined rapidly. With the CFDC in mind, and considering also the shorter films and documentaries, one critic observed, "After seven years, 20 million tax dollars, and about 150 films, only about 6 percent of the Canadian theatregoing public were actually seeing any of the CFDC-backed films."[57]

The major problem has not been the quality of the Canadian productions but the stranglehold that certain American-controlled firms, such as Famous Players and Paramount, have on distribution and virtually all the big, money-making cinemas. In 1972, for example, fewer than 2% of the movies shown in Ontario were Canadian, in Québec fewer than 5%. Most of the others, in all provinces, were American.[58] In 1975 Canada achieved the dubious distinction of becoming Hollywood's biggest customer, surpassing Italy. From 1974 to 1975 the total amount Canadians paid to see American movies increased by 36% to reach $54.5 million. In that year the CFDC share of the box office revenue was about 4% or about $860 000.[59] In brief, Canadian films are not seen by many Canadians and for most Canadians are not even available. By the late 1970s and early 1980s, however, there was some evidence of a reverse trend.

Radio and television in Canada reflect similar trends; were it not for the Canadian Broadcasting Corporation which the Canadian government created in 1932, most of Canada might be only a region within the American networks' coverage area. As it is, even with massive governmental effort and expenditure, the current situation is certainly unique. Canadian nationalists would doubtless term it foreboding. As early as 1924 *Maclean's* magazine reported that "nine-tenths of the radio fans in the Dominion hear three to four times as many United States stations as Canadian."[60] The exposure to American programs was increased in 1936 when the CBC incorporated US programs into its schedules. About the same time Canadian stations started using the American chart or "hit parade" system. This venture had a double impact. Aside from the general importation of musical fare it also meant that any Canadian artists who hoped to become known across Canada could succeed only if they achieved national acceptance in the United States. Hence it is little wonder that as late as 1973 only 2% of all the records sold in Canada were produced by Canadian firms.[61] Record production and distribution are almost entirely continental, which is to say American. As a result of recent Canadian Radio-television and Telecommunications Commission directives that figure has now reached 8%.[62] Further improvement is anticipated.

But basic Canadian radio listening preferences have not changed. In early 1976 the CRTC ordered the FM cable systems in Canada to drop American stations and replace them with Canadian. The extent and depth of the angry response from the public shocked both the politicians and the bureaucrats and by fall, scarcely three months after the first phases of policy implementation, the CRTC was forced to cancel its FM Canadianization policy.

If radio and the record business are continental, television is even more so. Time after time the American norm becomes the Canadian norm. That axiom apparently held true even over the selection of a color television system. The technically better and cheaper SECAM III system was rejected in favor of the American NTSC system, mainly because of compatibility with American systems.[63]

The preferences for the US offerings which persist in radio, are equally true for TV. The 1970 Davey Committee Report lamented the fact that English-speaking Canadians favor American to Canadian programs, 71% to 24%. CRTC regulations have increased Canadian content in recent years but with little impact on viewer habits. For one thing, such totally American spectacles as baseball's World Series and Hollywood's Academy Awards have been classified by the CRTC as Canadian for purposes of content regulation. Then, too, the Canadian networks carry a large number of American programs and, in addition, American TV stations reach about 55% of all Canadian homes. Rapid development of cable systems is raising that percentage. By 1974 it had climbed to about 80% and the more than four hundred cable systems are constantly expanding. The effect is profound; cable systems have indeed moved the American border 300 km north. The result is that probably two thirds to three quarters of Canadian viewers are watching American programs. A 1973 survey revealed that in Toronto Canadian programs attracted only 13% of evening viewers and only 9% in the prime time period from 8 to 10 pm.[64] Here, as elsewhere, trends are crucial, and the trends are clearly continentalist.

Some Canadians blame the Canadian television networks for the fact of foreign domination but from a strictly financial point of view and considering viewer preferences and the all-important ratings, they are behaving quite rationally. For example, the CBC in 1975 paid only $2000 for each weekly episode of "All in the Family" for which it sold $24 000 in advertising. At the same time it paid out $65 000 a week to produce its own show, "The Beach-combers", which generated no more advertising revenue.[65] Little wonder that a generation of Canadians has grown up with basic political socialization derived from Sesame Street, Captain Kangaroo, Mary Tyler Moore, Archie Bunker, Walt Disney, Howard Cosell and Walter Cronkite. Over time the names may change, but the phenomenon seems to be fixed.

Official warnings about trends in the electronic media are also expressed over publications. In 1961 the Royal Commission on Publications observed that "communications are the thread which binds together the fibres of a nation.... The communications of a nation are as vital to its life as its defences, and should receive at least as great a measure of national protection."[66] The commission's fears were well-founded. In 1969, 95% of all the magazines available in Canadian retail outlets were American imports. About 80% of all magazines read were American. For decades the two American giants *TIME* and *Reader's Digest* took about 40% of total magazine advertising in Canada. The 1974 figures were $18.8 million for the two and $39 million for all the members of the Magazine Association of Canada. The *Reader's Digest* had a circulation of 1 250 000 monthly and *TIME* 550 000.[67] In 1969 *Maclean's* switched to the size and format used by *TIME* so that ads appearing in the giant operation could be reproduced in *Maclean's* at no additional preparation cost. Even so, *Maclean's* was still at a great disadvantage because it had to provide its own editorial copy while *TIME* used its American copy. *Maclean's* rates, therefore, had to be much higher than those of *TIME*, just to recover cost. In 1970 the respective rates were $4 600 and $2 700 for full page ads. In February 1976, the Canadian Parliament passed a bill whose requirements about Canadian content brought about the demise of the Canadian edition of *TIME*. But most Canadian *TIME* subscribers simply switched to the American edition and the basic problem remains unresolved. Illustrating the plight of Canadian magazines, the Davey Committee Report noted that "We spend more money buying American comic books than we do on seventeen leading Canadian-owned magazines."[68]

Largely because of continentalism Canadian authors and book publishers are also in dire straits. Throughout Canadian history the perennial Canadian theme of resistance to Americanization has been mirrored in actual fact; the parallel British influence has gradually weakened. Mark Twain, Hemingway, and a vast host of US novels and novelists have become dominant. In 1969 two thirds of the value of all books bought in Canada was accounted for by imports, 80% of which came from the United States. Surprisingly, almost half of all American book exports go to Canada. Publishing in Canada, in 1969, was as follows: 59% by US firms, 22% by British, and 19% by Canadian.[69] Of total

Canadian bookstore purchases in 1973 apparently only 20% involved Canadian material.[70]

If we look at the big educational market the situation is even more lopsided. American publishers, at relatively low retail prices, flood the Canadian market with low-cost run-ons of their own domestic editions, often without any adaptation. As recently as 1973 some 68% of all book purchases for Canadian classrooms were foreign books, mostly American, some with adaptation. An additional 29% were Canadian-authored but not published by Canadian firms and only 3% were Canadian-authored and Canadian-published.[71] The postsecondary situation was similar. A 1973 survey of 37 political science and sociology departments at Canadian universities showed that 55% of all prescribed texts were American-authored and American-published while only 13% were Canadian-authored and Canadian-published.[72] Wherever one looks the situation is the same. Only 7% of books sold through book clubs in Canada are Canadian and less than 2% of the 32 million paperbacks sold in Canada are Canadian-authored.[73] The figures are staggering. In 1970 Canada imported $245 million worth of printed material from the United States, more than the United States sold to all other countries combined. Canadian writers and publishers have come to understand the significance of a statement by Walter Wulff, a vice-president of McGraw-Hill International: "The prime objective of a foreign subsidiary is not its own publishing but the sale of the US product."[74] Canada is the only country in the industrialized world whose total print medium is overwhelmingly dominated by foreigners, and by foreigners from only one country at that.

The spillover effect of such a situation into curriculum and general value formation is predictable. American concepts, problems, heroes, mythology, fads, and American mass culture (as contrasted with the more elitist earlier Canadiana) have become preeminent. Many Canadians seem to know more about the United States than about their own country. But what else should one expect when, for example, an adapted standard Grade 6 history text used in Winnipeg in 1975, *Canada— The New Nation,* has not one word on the Winnipeg General Strike but has two full chapters on Abraham Lincoln![75] Unfortunately such instances are not rare. A major 1968 study revealed that American magazines outnumbered Canadian magazines three to one in Canadian school libraries. One secondary school principal acknowledged that of a thousand books purchased for the new school library, not a single one was Canadian.[76]

Continentalism prevails at the university level also. Most Canadian universities use the Graduate Record Exam, a totally American-oriented test, to evaluate applicants for graduate school. In 1974 the University of Windsor rejected four of its own graduates who had A standings because their American GRE marks were not high enough. Often such behavior is justified on grounds of cosmopolitanism and internationalism, but for Canada these terms are almost synonymous with Americanism. Space limitations do not permit a description of the American emphasis in university curricula, or of the profound effect of American specialized and scholarly journals, or the numbers of Americans on university faculties, an issue that has been explored elsewhere.[77]

American dominance in the Canadian labor force constitutes another important phase of continentalism. As early as 1911 the so-called "internationals" controlled 90% of union members in Canada. By the mid-1950s the percentage had dropped somewhat to about 70%. In 1965 some 110 international, or American, unions had a total of 1 125 000 members in Canada while 52 Canadian unions had a total of 390 000 members or about 26%. In no other industrial country of similar size does one find a situation even remotely similar. Of course, the arrangement merely parallels the continental situation as far as entrepreneurship and management are concerned. For many spokesmen on both sides of the bargaining table, the international boundary might as well not exist.

Several other aspects of continental socialization deserve at least a brief comment. The Canadian sports culture, but especially professional sports, has become continental. The National Hockey League ownership and location of franchises have for half a century been more American than Canadian and the most important people associated with the government-protected Canadian Football League are the imported American players and coaches. Given the great commercialization of sports in Canada, Americanization is inevitable. But even at amateur levels the trends are the same. For example, most members of Canada's 1968 Olympic team trained at American universities. In fact, American college sports of all kinds have a much greater following in Canada than do Canadian college sports.

Although the two countries have different religious traditions, the Americanization of Canadian religion is well-advanced. Most religious broadcasts on radio and TV are American, most religious books are American, and most of the dominant personalities are American. Billy Graham, Jerry Falwell, Oral Roberts, Rex Humbard, Cardinal Cushing, the Mormons, and countless others have cut a very wide swath. The Moral Majority of 1980-81 is a special case in point. Here, as elsewhere, the continental osmosis is almost entirely unilateral.

American service clubs from Rotary to Lions, youth organizations from 4H to Up With People, philanthropic foundations from the Ford Foundation to the Carnegie and Rockefeller Foundations, reformist organizations from the traditional Women's Christian Temperance Union to contemporary ecology groups, quasi-political groups from the Non-Partisan League to women's liberation, and countless commercial ventures from Colonel Sanders Kentucky Fried Chicken to Amway have spread across Canada. The dimensions of absorption, not to mention emulation, defy measurement. Naturally, all these aspects must be seen in association with economic and defense aspects of continentalism; it is the awesome and ominous cumulative effect that we are witnessing.

The policy problem for Canadian governments is truly staggering. American mass culture is sought after and enjoyed by the Canadian masses while a small minority, heavily subsidized by the Canadian government, attempts valiantly to retain or develop a culture uniquely Canadian. Its success is in doubt. In 1970

CRTC chairman Pierre Juneau concurred with the view that "Canada has one decade remaining in which its members have to make up their minds whether they want to remain a distinct political, cultural and geographical nationality."[78] His time frame may be in error but whether or not his basic pessimism is well-founded remains to be seen.

CONTINENTALISM: SCOPE AND CONSEQUENCES

The limits of continentalism are very broad. More than 180 formal treaties link the two countries. Together they have undertaken numerous major ventures from the International Joint Commission's activities to the St. Lawrence Seaway Project to the Columbia River Treaty to reclamation of the Great Lakes to NORAD and much more. In scores of major policy areas, Canadian governments have emulated the American; sometimes, as with pollution controls, because there was no other option. The New Deal, the War on Poverty, civil rights legislation, ecology programs, prohibition and electoral financing reforms are a few obvious examples. The Canadian public's emulation is equally diverse and extensive. Phenomena such as the Progressive movement, the civil rights movement, the antiwar movement, the Indian movement, and student activism in the 1960s all had mainly American roots. Indeed some movements, such as the New Left, petered out in Canada primarily because their roots and causes were alien.

The consequences of such extensive commonality can hardly be overstated. American influence on Canadian political practices and on the policies of the two major parties is great. Even greater is the impact on the lifestyle, values and attitudes of the average Canadian. To a total stranger the overall trends must surely seem to be fixed and irreversible. Canada stands alone as the country that seems to be losing political, economic and social autonomy as it becomes more urbanized, industrialized, educated and affluent. Scores of national and provincial Canadian commissions have studied the relationship, or problem, but given the general and deep Canadian desire for things American, continentalism will probably continue to flourish and Canadian autonomy weaken.

In 1967 Blair Fraser wrote that, "Without at least a touch of anti-Americanism, Canada would have no reason to exist."[79] But the anti-Americanism that Fraser perceived has for decades been overshadowed by a more deeply rooted acknowledgement of dependence coupled with a mixture of envy and admiration. The complex love-hate relationship is more love than hate. True, in continental affairs Canada is a permanent minority but when agreement in preferences and policies, however such agreement is achieved, vastly overshadows basic differences, such a status is not entirely disagreeable. For many Canadians, closer ties to the United States are no threat. And, of course, whether or not Canada should join the United States is always an issue in Canada; the debate is real but it evokes little fear, a fact that is understandable since only 9% of Canadians believe that "Americans have a markedly different way of life."[80] For George Ball the picture is quite clear; Canadian resistance to Canadian-American union is pointless, "a rearguard action against the inevitable."[81]

LIMITATIONS

Of course, continentalism cannot explain all aspects of Canadian politics. Such factors as the British and French roots, the current English-French controversy, the geographical setting, and the parliamentary system all play a part, but no other factor is as important as the proximity of and penetration by, the public and private sectors of the United States. For Canada, economics, culture, defense and development are continental and the focal point of each continental system lies south of the border.[82] A further limitation or weakness in the continentalist approach is that by becoming pre-occupied with the colossal American impact we tend, in a sense, to reinforce its significance.

CONCLUSION

In terms of the Eastonian systems approach we could describe the situation as follows: the Canadian sociopolitical environment includes the bulk of the American sociopolitical environment and the American political system, while the American environment includes virtually nothing of the Canadian. Similarly, American feedback plays a major role in Canadian inputs but Canadian feedback is virtually inconsequential for American inputs. Perhaps most importantly, as we have seen, a large percentage of Canadian demands and supports emanate from the American sector of the continental environment. That situation helps us to understand why many Canadians, and Canadian governments, look to American-dominated continental systems and subsystems for demand satisfaction and many other components of living in contemporary Canada.

In 1966 J.B. Brebner observed, "Any foreigner could tell them [Canadians] what they themselves felt compelled to deny—that the greatest force exerted on their development was the stimulating example of the people of the United States."[83] A few years later Prime Minister Trudeau made the same point more bluntly. During the 1968 national election campaign he stated that Canada is no more independent of the United States than is Poland of the Soviet Union; he then remarked that Canada has only 10% independence and can maneuver only within that degree of freedom.[84] In making that statement he both reflected and reinforced Canadian reality. The 1980-81 mushrooming of Polish

"Solidarity", suppressed in 1982, and the growing demands for Polish independence, make Trudeau's comparison particularly interesting.

After the British conquest of Québec in 1759, the bulk of settled North America flew one flag—until 1776. For Canada the intervening two centuries have been one long struggle for an autonomous destiny. Year by year the struggle becomes more complex and ominous; it is not yet clear whether the northern half of the continent has the capacity and will to exist independently or whether that early brief experience of "continental" unity under one flag will be reestablished but this time in a more encompassing and irreversible fashion under a different flag!

SUMMARY

1. The overall American impact on Canada is the most important single fact for Canada and the main key to understanding Canada's emergence, development and current situation.
2. Canadian Confederation in 1867 was largely a response to the American presence and threat. Confederation can be seen as a defense strategy, as imitation, and as a general political reaction to what was happening in the US.
3. Until 1931 (the Statute of Westminister), Canada was to a large extent in the British sphere; since 1940 (the Ogdensburg Agreement) Canada has been even more in the American sphere.
4. Since the Second World War, Canada has been dependent on the US for defense; simultaneously, Canada has followed the US in all major foreign policy stances.
5. For Canada, economics is largely a continentalist phenomenon. This situation holds true whether we focus on investment, foreign ownership, trade, development trends or the general economic situation.
6. Canadian political socialization involves a very high degree of American influence. This impact comes largely via television but radio, magazines, books, films, records and travel are also important.
7. Most of the American impact on Canada involves the private rather than the public sector.
8. In general, the Canadian public has welcomed instead of resisted the growing continentalization of Canada.
9. By and large, Canadian governments have not adopted major policies to counteract continentalization. Given the facts of geography, economics and Canadian public opinion, they may have no other option.
10. It is not yet clear whether the pessimists who predict the ultimate disappearance of Canada as a sovereign state will be proven right.

STUDY QUESTIONS

1. To what extent is it correct to say that Canadian Confederation was a grand political experiment which from the outset was doomed to fail?

2. Why do most Canadians not see continentalization, or Americanization, as a threat?

3. Do separatist tendencies in Québec strengthen or weaken the Canadian will to survive as an autonomous state?

4. What policies might the Canadian government undertake to reduce American control of the Canadian economy?

5. Should the Canadian government adopt coercive policies to prevent Canadians from watching mainly American television? What is your rationale for your view?

6. How can the Canadian government counteract the "miniature replica" phenomenon in Canadian industry?

7. In what ways was John A. Macdonald's National Policy a success and in what ways was it a failure?

8. Are there significant ways in which the Canadian government could reduce Canada's dependence on the US for defense?

9. What are the major arguments for either supporting or opposing Canadian unification with the US?

10. What recent developments in Canada suggest that the degree of Canadian autonomy from the US is increasing rather than decreasing?

ENDNOTES

1. J.M.S. Careless, "Hooray for the Scars and Gripes!" *The New Romans*, ed. Al Purdy (Edmonton: M.C. Hurtig, 1968), p. 134.

2. J.B. Brebner, *Canada* (Ann Arbor: University of Michigan Press, 1960).

3. James Laxer, *The Energy Poker Game* (Toronto: New Press, 1970), p. 1.

4. George Grant, *Lament for a Nation* (Toronto: McClelland and Stewart, 1965), p. 86.

5. Mitchell Sharp, "Canada-U.S. Relations: Options for the Future," *International Perspectives*, special issue (Autumn, 1972).

6. John Sloan Dickey, *Canada and the American Presence* (New York: New York University Press, 1975), p. 66.

7. A.R.M. Lower, *Canadians in the Making* (Toronto: Longmans, Green and Company, 1958), p. 441.

8. Janet Morchain, ed., *Sharing a Continent* (Toronto: McGraw-Hill Ryerson, 1973), p. 69.

9. *Ibid.*, p. 70.

10. S.D. Clark, *Movements of Political Protest in Canada* (Toronto: University of Toronto Press, 1959), p. 302.

11. Morchain, *op. cit.*, p. 108.

12. See P.B. Waite, *The Life and Times of Confederation 1864-1867* (Toronto: University of Toronto Press, 1962), pp. 304-05.

13. See, for example, Morchain, *op. cit.*, p. 124.

14. F.H. Underhill, *In Search of Canadian Liberalism* (Toronto: Macmillan, 1961), pp. 256-60.

15. Dickey, *op. cit.*, p. 142.

16. Morchain, *op. cit.*, p. 50.

17. Farley Mowat, "Letter to My Son," in Al Purdy, *op. cit.*, pp. 3-5.

18. J.W. Holmes, "The Relationship in Alliance and World Affairs," *The United States and Canada*, ed. J.S. Dickey (Englewood Cliffs, N.J.: Prentice-Hall, 1964), pp. 100, 131.

19. Department of External Affairs, *Foreign Policy for Canadians* (Ottawa: Queen's Printer, 1970).

20. Morchain, *op. cit.*, p. 68.

21. Quoted in Brebner, *North Atlantic Triangle*, Carleton Library Edition (Toronto: McClelland and Stewart, 1966), p. 277.

22. Quoted in Roger Swanson, *Canadian-American Summit Diplomacy, 1923-1973* (Toronto: McClelland and Stewart, 1975), p. 71.

23. Quoted in John W. Warnock, *Partner to Behemoth* (Toronto: New Press, 1970), p. 105.

24. "Mr. Howe's History," *Saturday Night*, LXVI (November 7, 1950), p. 6.

25. John W. Warnock, *op. cit.*, p. 114.

26. See, for example, James M. Minifie, *Peacemaker or Powder-Monkey; Canada's Role in a Revolutionary World* (Toronto: McClelland and Stewart, 1960).

27. Quoted in *Financial Post*, March 25, 1967.

28. Tom Kent, "The Changing Place of Canada," *Foreign Affairs*, 35 (July, 1957), p. 581.

29. Kari Levitt, *Silent Surrender* (Toronto: Macmillan, 1970), p. 129.

30. *Ibid.*, p. 129.

31. *Ibid.*, p. 129.

32. Green H. Hackworth, "General Aspects of Canadian-United States Treaty Relations and Their Import for the Conduct of Relations between Nations on the Basis of Respect for Law and Mutual Interests," *Canada-United States Treaty Relations*, ed. David R. Deener (Durham, N.C.: Duke University Press, 1963), p. 125.

33. Charles Foulkes, "The Complications of Continental Defence," *Neighbors Taken for Granted*, ed. L. Merchant (New York: Praeger, 1966), p. 120.

34. *A Citizen's Guide to the Gray Report* (Toronto: New Press, 1971), p. 11.

35. *Ibid.*, p. 11.

36. *Ibid.*, pp. 11-12.

37. Levitt, *op. cit.*, p. 94.

38. Laxer, *op. cit.*, p. 27.

39. Levitt, *op. cit.*, p. 29.

40. Morchain, *op. cit.*, p. 144.

41. Laxer, *op. cit.*, p. 45.
42. Levitt, *op. cit.*, p. 87.
43. C.W. Gonick, "Foreign Ownership and Political Decay," *Close the 49th Parallel, Etc.*, ed. Ian Lumsden (Toronto: University of Toronto Press, 1970), p. 65.
44. Laxer, *op. cit.*, p. 15.
45. Dickey, *op. cit.*, p. 22.
46. Gonick, *op. cit.*, p. 45.
47. Levitt, *op. cit.*, p. 127.
48. See Dave Godfrey and Mel Watkins, eds., *Gordon to Watkins to You* (Toronto: New Press, 1970), esp. pp. 204-19.
49. D.W. Brogan, "An Outsider Looking In," *Canada's Tomorrow*, ed. G.P. Gilmour (Toronto: Macmillan, 1954), pp. 271-3.
50. Archibald MacMechan, "Canada as a Vassal State," *Canadian Historical Review* (Toronto: University of Toronto Press, 1929), p. 347.
51. Quoted in the *Toronto Daily Star*, Sept. 14, 1968.
52. Quoted in the *Toronto Daily Star*, May 2, 1968.
53. Royal Commission on National Development in the Arts, Letters and Sciences, Vincent Massey, Chairman, *Report* (Ottawa: King's Printer, 1951), p. 15.
54. Royal Commission on Broadcasting, Keith Davey, Chairman, *Report* (Ottawa: Queen's Printer, 1957), Vol. I, p. 8.
55. Morchain, *op. cit.*, p. 190.
56. *Ibid.*, pp. 8, 138.
57. S.M.Crean, *Who's Afraid of Canadian Culture?* (Don Mills, Ontario: General Publishing, 1976), p. 72.
58. *Ibid.*, pp. 81-2.
59. *Ibid.*, p. 87.
60. Quoted in Crean, *op. cit.*, p. 29.
61. Crean, *op. cit.*, p. 17.
62. *Ibid.*, p. 54.
63. Lynn Trainor, "Science in Canada—American Style," in Lumsden, *op. cit.*, p. 247.
64. Dickey, *op. cit.*, p. 56.
65. Crean, *op. cit.*, p. 49.
66. Royal Commission on Publications, Grattan O'Leary, Chairman, *Report* (Ottawa: Queen's Printer, 1961), p. 4.
67. Crean, *op. cit.*, p. 224.
68. Special Senate Committee on the Mass Media, Keith Davey, Chairman, *Report* (Ottawa: Queen's Printer, 1970), Vol. I, p. 156.
69. Dickey, *op. cit.*, p. 51.
70. Crean, *op. cit.*, p. 182.
71. *Ibid.*, p. 189.
72. J.H. Redekop, "Authors and Publishers: An Analysis of Textbook Selection in Canadian Departments of Political Science and Sociology," *Canadian Journal of Political Science*, IX, No. 1 (March, 1976), p. 110.

73. Crean, *op. cit.*, pp. 208-9.
74. Quoted in S.M. Crean, *op. cit.*, p. 215.
75. Crean, *op. cit.*, p. 233.
76. *Ibid.*, p. 235.
77. See Robin Mathews and James Steele, eds., *The Struggle for Canadian Universities* (Toronto: New Press, 1969); and Wallace Gagne, ed., *Nationalism, Technology and the Future of Canada* (Toronto: Macmillan, 1976), esp. pp. 113-20.
78. Davey Committee, *Report, op. cit.*, p. 11.
79. Blair Fraser, *The Search for Identity: Canada, 1945-67* (Garden City: Doubleday, 1967), p. 301.
80. Morchain, *op. cit.*, 177.
81. George Ball, *The Discipline of Power* (Boston: Little, Brown, 1968), p. 113.
82. For a discussion of a systems interpretation of Canadian-American relations see J.H. Redekop, "A Reinterpretation of Canadian-American Relations," *Canadian Journal of Political Science*, IX, No. 2 (June, 1976), pp. 227-43.
83. Brebner, *North Atlantic Triangle, op. cit.*, p. 364.
84. See Lumsden, *op. cit.*, p. 71.

SELECTED REFERENCES

Axline, Andrew, et al., eds. *Continental Community? Independence and Integration in North America.* Toronto: McClelland and Stewart, 1974. The authors present a rigorous analysis of continentalism. Various aspects and components of North American integration are presented and important theoretical models discussed.

Bowles, Richard P., et al. *Canada and the U.S.: Continental Partners or Wary Neighbors?* Toronto: Prentice-Hall, 1973. This introductory volume consists of scores of short articles, excerpts of all sorts, and discussion questions as well as connecting and interpretive sections. Topics covered include economics, cultural affairs, domestic politics, foreign affairs, historical developments and prospects for the future.

Brossard, Philippe J. *Sold American!* Toronto: Peter Martin, 1971. A closely reasoned monograph that argues that the primary cause of "the erosion of Canada's independence is not to be found in Washington, but rather in the boardrooms of the economic and financial elite of Canada."

Canadian-American Committee. *The New Environment for Canadian-American Relations.* Montreal: Private Planning Association of Canada, 1972. A brief study by free enterprise spokesmen of the major problem areas in North American continentalism.

Carr, D.W. *Recovering Canada's Nationhood.* Ottawa: Canada Publishing Company, 1971. Written by a member of Canada's economic elite, this thoughtful book provides a frank examination of Canada's lack of national objectives, economic trends and policies, the inadequate performance of Canadian elites, and specific policy proposals.

Clement, Wallace. *Continental Corporate Power; Economic Linkages between Canada and the United States.* Toronto: McClelland and Stewart, 1977. An excellent account of

Canadian-American economic relations, past and present, with special emphasis on structures and elites.

Crean, S.M. *Who's Afraid of Canadian Culture?* Don Mills, Ontario: General Publishing Co., 1976. A hard-hitting, lucid analysis of virtually all components of Canadian culture; special emphasis is given to recent American influences.

Dickey, John Sloan. *Canada and the American Presence.* New York: New York University Press, 1975. Written by an American, this important book provides a balanced, yet penetrating account of all major aspects of the relationship.

Feldman, E.J., and Neil Nevitte, eds. *The Future of North America: Canada, the United States, and Quebec Nationalism.* Cambridge: Harvard University, 1979. This study published jointly by Montreal's Institute for Research on Public Policy and Harvard's Center for International Affairs deals with the major themes developed in this chapter with added attention given to Canadian unity.

Fox, Annette Baker, Alfredo O. Hero Jr., and Joseph S. Nye, Jr. eds. "Canada and the United States: Transnational and Transgovernmental Relations." *International Organization* 28, No. 4 (Autumn, 1974). Special isue. The seventeen chapters in this advanced study present recent findings in many areas of a complex relationship and spell out various theories and explanations; a balanced and intensive study.

Gagne, Wallace, ed. *Nationalism, Technology and the Future of Canada.* Toronto: Macmillan, 1976. Consists of seven essays each dealing with broad areas of Canadian independence and its relationship to technological change.

Godfrey, Dave and Mel Watkins, eds. *Gordon to Watkins to You; A Documentary: the Battle for Control of our Economy.* Toronto: New Press, 1970. A compilation of data, critical views, interpretive essays, and diverse excerpts set in a framework of socialist assumptions.

Grant, George. *Lament for a Nation.* Toronto: McClelland and Stewart, 1965. This penetrating and pessimistic analysis of Canadian nationalism and continentalism stands as a classic statement on the subject.

_____. *Technology and Empire: Perspectives on North America.* Toronto: Anansi, 1969. An agonized and grandly argued book that criticizes America's march to world empire, especially as that march has affected Canada.

Laxer, James. *The Energy Poker Game: The Politics of the Continental Resources Deal.* Toronto: New Press, 1970. A brief but powerful indictment reflecting a socialist orientation.

Laxer, Robert M., ed. *Canada Ltd., The Political Economy of Dependency.* Toronto: McClelland and Stewart, 1973. Written from a socialist perspective this volume analyzes various social and cultural aspects of dependency.

Levitt, Kari. *Silent Surrender.* Toronto: Macmillan, 1970. A carefully researched economic study of the American impact on Canada with special emphasis on the multinational corporation.

Litvak, I.A., C.J. Maule, and R.D. Robinson. *Dual Loyalty: Canadian-U.S. Business Arrangements.* Toronto: McGraw-Hill, 1971. This book describes the problems of continental business arrangements and Canadian policies adopted to deal with those problems. The bulk of the book consists of case studies.

Lumsden, Ian. ed. *Close the 49th Parallel Etc.: The Americanization of Canada.* Toronto: University of Toronto Press, 1970. The most wide-ranging survey of specific problem areas covering business, labor, media, resources, science, sports and much more; written, in the main, from a socialist perspective.

Mathews, Robin and James Steele, eds. *The Struggle for Canadian Universities.* Toronto: New Press, 1969. A collection of letters, speeches, memoranda and articles dealing with the alleged Americanization of Canadian universities.

Merchant, Livingston T., ed. *Neighbors Taken for Granted; Canada and the United States.* New York: Praeger, 1966. A former American ambassador to Canada and various experts discuss developments that "threaten the American-Canadian friendship"; written mainly from a continentalist perspective.

Minifie, James M. *Peacemaker or Powder-Monkey: Canada's Role in a Revolutionary World.* Toronto: McClelland and Stewart, 1960. This interesting and informative analysis makes a strong case for the view that Canada should adopt a neutralist stance in foreign affairs. Such a stance, the author argues, would be of great benefit to both Canada and the United States.

Moffett, Samuel E. *The Americanization of Canada.* Toronto: University of Toronto Press, 1972. When it first appeared in 1907 this study pioneered a new area of research. Many of Moffett's observations are still relevant. The introduction by Allan Smith adds substantially to the book's worth.

Morchain, Janet. ed. *Sharing a Continent.* Toronto: McGraw-Hill Ryerson, 1973. The beginning student will find this panoramic survey of virtually the entire gamut of Canadian-American relations very useful. The scores of excerpts, the skillful introductions and general commentary and the fine bibliographies combine to make this book one of the most important in the field, even for those students already knowledgeable concerning North America.

Pope, W.H. *The Elephant and the Mouse.* Toronto: McClelland and Stewart, 1971. Presented as "A Handbook for Regaining Control of Canada's Economy," this slim volume provides the basic background for understanding the workings and consequences of foreign investment.

Redekop, John H., ed. *The Star-Spangled Beaver; Twenty-four Canadians Look South.* Toronto: Peter Martin, 1971. A collection of diverse assessments of the American impact on Canada covering most of the major areas of transnational interaction.

Rotstein, Abraham and Gary Lax, eds. *Getting It Back; A Program for Canadian Independence.* Toronto: Clarke, Irwin, 1974. Presented by the Committee for an Independent Canada, this compilation of interpretive essays and case studies covers most of the important aspects of Canadian economy and culture, both defined broadly.

Safarian, A.E. *Foreign Ownership of Canadian Industry.* Toronto: University of Toronto Press, 1973. A sometimes sympathetic but still eminently thorough study of the behavior of branch-plant firms in Canada.

Swanson, Roger Frank. ed. *Canadian-American Summit Diplomacy, 1923-1973: Selected Speeches and Documents.* Toronto: McClelland and Stewart, 1975. An excellent collection of major documents that convey a sense of immediacy. The introductory chapter and the summaries at the beginning of each chapter provide helpful interpretation.

Sykes, Philip. *Sellout: The Giveaway of Canada's Energy Resources.* Edmonton: Hurtig, 1973. Focusing mainly on petroleum policies, the author presents a hard-hitting examination of the big energy deals since 1950.

Tupper, Stanley R. and Douglas L. Bailey. *One Continent—Two Voices: The Future of Canada-U.S. Relations.* Toronto: Clarke, Irwin, 1967. In this very useful introduction to the topic the authors argue that if Canadians wish to have Americans become more aware of them, they must resolve the continuing problem of Canadian identity and purpose.

Warnock, John W. *Partner to Behemoth*. Toronto: New Press, 1970. This book presents a challenging, left-of-center reinterpretation of Canadian military policy, especially with reference to Canadian-American relations since 1945.

3

Canadian Political Economy

Douglas J. McCready*

> The ideas of economists and political philosophers, both when they are right
> and when they are wrong, are more powerful than is commonly understood.
> Indeed the world is ruled by little else. Practical men, who believe themselves to
> be quite exempt from any intellectual influences are usually the slaves of some
> defunct economists.[1]

Keynes, when he wrote these words, perceived that economics and economists
had had a profound influence on people's ideas, the policies favored by voters,
and the determination of the mix of policies offered within the public sector.
Canadian politics, it is argued here, is very much affected by economics—
indeed, Canadian politics is in reality Canadian political economy.

The relationship between economics and politics is long-standing and extensive. Canada's political structure evolved from and reflects the pre-Confederation economy. Political parties and voting behavior are both expressions of
economic reality. Most public policies involve economic decisions; even the
1981 restructuring of Confederation involved basic economic considerations.
Economics has had a pervasive and profound influence on Canadian politics;
thus a basic knowledge of the economics of Canada is essential for a clear
understanding of Canadian political affairs.

Economics is the science of allocating resources.[2] Economists talk about
producing goods and services with labor, machines, raw materials and technology, and then of allocating those goods among competing consumers. Most
economists fix their sights on the market where consumers maximize their
satisfactions, producers maximize their profits, and where prices, because of
demand and supply, supposedly ensure that there are no excess inventories or

*Associate Professor of Economics, Wilfrid Laurier University.

unmet needs. This model allocates all resources. Economists who advocate a totally free market forget that there are some goods that cannot be priced because they are not consumables in the usual sense of the word; that production can be greatly affected by the ease or difficulty of obtaining raw materials; and that to some people the model is unsatisfactory because they do not feel that the market is fair or equitable to groups who cannot bring power to bear when they bargain. Thus a political system must develop to provide goods and services not provided equitably, or at all, by the private market.

THE NEED FOR GOVERNMENT

Even Adam Smith, the acknowledged advocate of a basically unregulated marketplace, recognized the need for government to provide some goods such as justice, defense and lighthouses.[3] These goods are not provided in the private marketplace. These so-called 'public goods' are indivisible[4] or exhibit externalities,[5] or are so important yet so scarce that the community recognizes the need for collective effort and responsibility.

Moreover, government is needed to help exploit resources. Access to raw materials and markets can be hampered by lack of government. Thus, in Canada, the orderly development of a trading system which would encompass all the British colonies required the establishment of a single government and we shall see that the structure and policies of the government were greatly influenced by the way entrepreneurs wished the development to take place.

Most people recognize that the initial misallocation of resources is often a circumstance over which there is little control. In the absence of government, the rich and powerful will get richer and more powerful, while the poor and disadvantaged will find their lot in life deteriorating.

This chapter focuses on several key issues: how economics influences the form that government takes, its policies, and the general political situation; how economics can "generate" a federal form of government; how it can be used to explain the dissimilarities of the political parties; and how economic issues play key roles as determinants of policy.

HISTORICAL REVIEW

In 1867, the long-term economic stability and prosperity of the Maritime provinces, given their interrelated fish, lumber, wooden shipbuilding and carrying trades, was very much in doubt. Although the Civil War in the United States had sustained exports in the early 1860s, the development of steam and steel were operating against the Maritimes. While in 1867 there was little obvious economic need, the Maritimes sought the economic prosperity that would result from the development of year-round ports for the Canadas.

In Upper and Lower Canada, manufacturing had grown and diversified after 1850. Large, readily available supplies of raw materials and natural protection arising from a lack of transportation facilities contributed to the growth of a local manufacturing sector. However, the need for larger markets became evident and acted as a stimulus in the push of the two Canadas—now Ontario and Québec—toward Confederation.

Confederation itself can thus be seen as largely an economic arrangement. The colonies were each looking for economic stability and growth. Ontario and Québec, which had not prospered to the same extent as the Maritime colonies, were searching for ways to expand. This economic difference explains the initial decision on the part of Prince Edward Island and Newfoundland to remain outside Confederation and the bargaining power held by Nova Scotia and New Brunswick in the early days of Confederation. [6]

Note the use of the term "Confederation". A centralized form of government was preferable to a federation of the colonies if the amalgamation took place for military purposes. Indeed, the Fathers of Confederation did frame the British North American Act in centralist terms. Control of the bulk of revenues and expenditures and residual powers was given to the central government. [7] This was, no doubt, influenced by the fact that the United States had just fought a civil war and was considered a military threat, particularly in the West.

However, the distribution of powers between the new federal government and the provinces entering the federation was mainly of an economic nature. Of the enumerated distribution of legislative powers in Sections 91 and 92 of the British North America Act, 56% can be classed as strictly economic. Indeed, beginning in 1867 and continuing to the present, the provinces have jealously guarded the economic powers granted to them.

Since the major source of revenue in pre-federation days had been the tariff and since a major task of the federation was to form common tariff barriers with the outside world while breaking down the existing barriers between provinces, it made the most sense to turn the tariff over to the central government. In return, the central government was to give the provinces per capita grants for their own operations. Other powers given to the central government in Section 91 of the BNA Act included external relations and the costly area of defense, both of which were subject to imperial control and assistance, and those most related to economic integration—trade and commerce, aspects of interprovincial transportation and communication, navigation and shipping, control of banking, currency, patents and copyrights, interest, bankruptcy, and so on. Control over agriculture and immigration was jointly shared and closely related to national economic development—but in both instances, a clash was to be resolved in favor of the central government.

In addition, the British North America Act explicitly stated that a railway between Halifax and the St. Lawrence should be built. This was mutually agreeable for it eased transportation of goods produced in Ontario and Québec and made the Maritime ports more important. There was also provision for the incorporation in Confederation of Hudson's Bay Company lands in the West, again a market for Ontario and Québec manufacturers and a source of raw materials, including land. The 1867 agreement to form one country can thus be seen as essentially an economic agreement; economics can be found throughout the document.

In contrast to the emphasis on economic matters, language and culture were given minor attention, being referred to only in Section 133 of the BNA Act.

Three issues having economic significance played a role in the political development in the late nineteenth century. The building of the transcontinental railway and the attendant "Pacific Scandal"; the execution of Louis Riel in 1885; and Macdonald's National Policy.

The construction of the CPR can be viewed as the result of British Columbia and Manitoba entering Confederation, which is the usual explanation; but it can also be interpreted as a result of pressure by interests in Ontario and Québec to develop natural resources; the desire of British Columbia for access to markets in the eastern colonies for fur and gold; and a desire to improve transportation for settlers.[8] The ensuing political difficulties, which came to be known as the Pacific Scandal, were very much economic in nature. The Pacific Scandal arose from competition between the Canadian Pacific Railway and the Grand Trunk Railway, the fact that the government of Sir John A. Macdonald wanted to keep taxes low and insisted on private enterprise constructing the railway, and the involvement of American versus British funds.[9] In August 1873, a Royal Commission was appointed to look into the financing of the Canadian Pacific Railway Company; the commission presented its report to Parliament on October 23 of that year. After a two-week debate Sir John A. Macdonald resigned on November 5, 1873, in part because of the commission's report.

Obviously, the development of the CPR was an economic and technological achievement with great political significance. It is clear that business interests pressed hard for the building of the railway. The question of multinational as opposed to purely national involvement in the financing was a major issue and here we see the onset of a historical trend of strong connections between businessmen and politicians in Canada.

The Riel rebellions involved some of the same economic issues as the building of the CPR. After the Canadian government purchased Hudson's Bay Company lands in the Red River Valley, the Métis led by Riel protested the potential loss of their own lands, and thus their livelihood, to new settlers. The fact that the Métis had not been consulted made them all the more angry. Riel fled to the United States but returned to Saskatchewan in 1885 to protest again the loss of lands to new settlers. This time Riel was captured, convicted and hanged for treason, an event that led to religious/racial division in Ontario and Québec and had long-term political consequences. Since 1885, the outlook for the Conservative Party in Québec, largely because of Riel's execution, has been bleak.[10]

Finally, Macdonald's National Policy, built squarely on a high tariff, was purely economic. Early in the history of the new Dominion, tariffs were raised, mainly to provide adequate revenue for the new government. Later, tariffs were used as the key instrument in a deliberate attempt to foster industrial development in Canada. Originally, Macdonald had advocated reciprocity with the United States but a policy of tariff protection became a second-best solution to Canada's trade problems. To this day, the Conservative party is represented as the party that stands for high tariffs.[11]

Each of the three policies has manifested itself in Canadian political life for nearly a century. Perhaps we can find some common thread in these early issues that could be instructive today. First, they all arose because of a push by some interests for expansion of trade and for economic growth. Second, each can be seen as involving a dichotomy of interests between big business and the small businessman, consumer and voter. The Canadian Pacific scandal arose, in part, because government was allowing one company to get larger with the aid of United States financiers while another company, the Grand Trunk, and the voters, were not willing to permit that to happen. The Riel rebellions can, to a considerable extent, be seen as a Métis backlash to the government's promotion of fast development of the West in the interests of Ontario businessmen. Québec voters, who themselves had only minor business interests, perceived that Ontario business interests were favored by the Conservative party. The National Policy can be seen as a tool for industrializing Canada and achieving future reciprocity in tariff policy but also as an attempt by government to establish the growth of the business rather than the farm sector. The cost of imported goods and services would rise, thereby permitting domestic firms to charge more, and encouraging foreign interests to jump the tariff barrier and invest directly in Canada.

ELECTIONS

Since the late nineteenth century, economic issues have determined the outcome of many elections: in 1911 reciprocity played a crucial role; in 1962 the value of the Canadian dollar was a major issue; in the 1974 election wage and price controls were the issue; in 1979 mortgage assistance was significant; and in 1980 oil and gas pricing promises returned the Liberal party to power. In addition, there is some suspicion that Mackenzie King threw the election of 1930 so that he would not be prime minister when the economy was weak.[12] The election result of 1935 was obviously associated with the lack of improvement in the economy.

Economic factors were important even in those elections ostensibly fought on other issues. For example, Diefenbaker's "National Dream" can be viewed in economic terms. Diefenbaker capitalized on a certain amount of humdrum economic existence in which people saw themselves as having jobs, paying taxes, but getting ahead only very slowly. He transformed that unexciting existence into a dream of rapid economic growth in which all would share. Instead of government budget surpluses, he promised to be daring in investing in the future and, more importantly, to start with additional payments to the disadvantaged old-age pensioners and the residents in the Atlantic Provinces. Thus, while some may classify the 1957 and 1958 elections as having been fought on closure used in the pipeline debate, the real issue in many minds was Diefenbaker's economic vision.

Consider the election of a separatist party in Québec in November 1976. Was there anything economic in that event? Clearly, Lévesque won that election because of an economic backlash against the Liberals, not because of separatism. A comparison of the results of the 1976 and 1981 elections to the results of the May 1980 referendum, show that a large number of non-separatists must have voted for the Parti Québécois. In 1976, that figure was estimated to be as high as 20%. Significantly, in a survey carried out in 1977 for the *Toronto Star* by Goldfarb Consultants Ltd., it was found that "jobs, not language, are the issue in Québec."[13] There had been strikes, taxes were increasing, unemployment was high and the Liberals could apparently offer only more of the same. Lévesque, besides being a separatist, was also associated with Québec's growth in the early sixties; he himself seemed to promise hope for a better economic future. By 1981, Lévesque was arguing for continued support of his economic package and at least one radio station indicated in its newscast on the election results that the results were a victory for Lévesque's economic policies.

Separatism itself is mainly an economic issue despite the fact that the Prime Minister prefers to interpret it otherwise. In the May 1980 Québec referendum, the 'no' vote was more an indication that the average Québec voter saw federation with Canada as providing greater economic benefits than costs. The figures released by Jacques Parizeau in 1977 purporting to show that Québec had paid more for federation with Canada than had been received were countered by the federal government, the province of Ontario, and private organizations such as the C.D. Howe Institute. Obviously, current economic arrangements play a greater role than those of the past and the vast majority of Québec residents are quite aware of the current benefits of subsidized oil, a subsidized textile industry, and huge equalization payments.

Recently, Western separatists have become more vocal. At a 1981 *Financial Post* Conference on Western Economic Development, Donald Johnston, President of the Treasury Board, stated that "The fundamental grievance of Western Canada is that there has been a very marked and important economic shift to the West—but there has not been a shift of political power."[14] The West, particularly Alberta, perceives the National Energy Policy introduced in October 1980, and the Constitutional "patriation" package which had initially been supported by Ottawa, as attempts by the federal government to reduce the economic power of the West. The resulting alienation is described by the *Financial Post* in the following sentence: "Oilmen do not need to go to separatist rallies to register their alienation ballot. Their votes show up in declining economic activity."[15] Significantly, the decline in economic activity showed up in the first-in-many-years deficit incurred by the Alberta government in the fiscal year ending March 1981.

Obviously, unemployment causes disenchantment among the electors even when the opposition does not use it specifically as an issue. Thus, all other things being equal, any prime minister choosing an election date will prefer to wait until the unemployment figures are low. It could be argued that elections are held in June, September, or October because the unemployment figures on an unadjusted basis are likely to be lowest.[16] A winter election catches many people seasonally unemployed and, therefore, much more likely to be disenchanted with the government.

Moreover, the economy can be artificially stimulated prior to an election by tax cuts and spending increases to further the political fortunes of the government. In the events of 1972 to 1975 there is some evidence to support this notion. At the time of the 1972 election, unemployment was very much an issue and the Liberal party gained a smaller percentage of the popular vote than in 1968 in every province except Newfoundland.[17] After the 1972 election many policies were introduced which either increased spending or decreased taxes and the 1974 election reestablished a Liberal majority.[18] Those policies of 1972-74 were not without cost, however. Inflation in Canada rose steadily after the 1974 general election so that on October 13, 1975 Prime Minister Trudeau announced wage and price controls effective as of midnight that night. While it may be, as Trudeau explained, that some of our inflation was imported from abroad, the introduction of wage and price controls was an admission that a large part of inflation was domestic. Thus, the government bought its own reelection in 1974 and made the voters pay for it after the election with wage and price controls.

Economists impute a motive to the government just as they impute the profit motive to producers or the satisfaction maximization motive to consumers. The motive attributed to government is that of maximizing chances of reelection.[19] Thus, a government will try to put together a program or combination of policies to satisfy the largest group of voters. In introducing any specific measure, it is aware that generally there are costs associated with compensating those who are against the measure. Those costs may be paid by direct monetary reimbursement or by implementing a measure specifically desired by the group that has been hurt. Resource allocation, then, takes place between elections, often with much success. As a result, voters are dissuaded from turning against the government and choosing a party which they feel would better reflect their preferences.[20]

POLITICAL PARTIES

In the last section we said that governments attempt to put together policies that maximize their chances of reelection. Of course, opposition parties attempt to do the same thing, to formulate policies that maximize their chances of forming the next government. In this section, the ways in which political parties act as mediators between competing interest groups in the political arena will be discussed. When examined carefully, this mediation is seen to occur between economic interests, and the different political parties tend to be identified with particular economic classes.[21]

Chi, in his analysis of class cleavage, dealt with the identification of union members and blue-collar workers with the four major Canadian parties. He found that the New Democrat and Social Credit parties have strong identification with blue-collar workers (54% of NDP voters and 47% of Social Credit voters are blue-collar workers). Even more important is the influence that direct union membership has in the party structure of the NDP for this represents a preference, at least in the eyes of some voters, for strong labor organization as a counterbalance to business.[22] The Social Credit party, on the other hand, may represent working-class voters but in a very different context. The working-class support for the Social Credit party is not nearly as well organized as NDP support (35% of Social Credit support is composed of organized labor as opposed to 45% for the NDP).

Social Credit is conventionally portrayed as right wing, which is consistent with its support from blue-collar workers who are less organized than those who support the NDP. The Social Credit solution to the economic disadvantages faced by its supporters is to advocate an economy in which free enterprise is dominant, in which large corporations are not powerful, and in which the individual has the power to become part of the economic elite. However, once in power provincially in Alberta and British Columbia, the Social Credit party has been pragmatic and has accommodated big business.

The NDP, which is socialist, favors control of big business including nationalizing some firms, and the balancing of big business by big unions and big government, as the solution to the economic ills of society. This orientation befits the large percentage of its supporters who have a union background. However, again, the NDP's rise to power in certain provinces has blunted its stated intentions, as it has in British Columbia, Saskatchewan and Manitoba where the NDP has at various times held office. Of course, the party rhetoric may well persist.[23]

The identification of union members and blue-collar workers with the NDP or Social Credit is not surprising since both parties started as protest movements founded during the Depression as responses to economic dislocations.

One aspect of class cleavage or economic scission that has not been dealt with by Chi or others is the voting behavior of professional, managerial or white-collar workers. The two major parties share similar voter profiles, but they advocate different policies. It is hypothesized here that these policies develop from the differences in the kind of white-collar workers who vote for one party versus another.

Meisel, in his book, *Working Papers on Canadian Politics*, was the first to provide occupational figures on voting.[24] More recently, occupational data have become available for the 1974 and 1979 elections, the latter being reported in Table 1. Comparison of the 1968 election with the 1979 election shows a shift of voters in the farmer, retired, management and professional categories towards the Pro-

Table 1

Occupational Breakdown of Voting in 1979 Election
(In Percentages)

Occupation	Liberal	P.C.	N.D.P.	S.C.
Professional	38.6	43.1	15.7	2.6
Semi-Professional	42.4	38.0	18.5	1.1
Proprietors, Managers or Officials, large	39.5	48.7	9.2	2.6
Proprietors, Managers or Officials, small	42.4	41.4	13.6	2.5
Clerical and Sales	49.2	37.5	11.7	1.5
Skilled Labor	43.5	32.6	18.8	5.1
Semi-skilled Labor	43.4	37.6	15.0	4.0
Unskilled Labor	40.9	27.7	25.8	5.7
Farmers and all farm occupations	23.4	59.4	15.6	1.6
Housewives	47.4	36.4	12.2	4.1
Retired	35.5	51.2	12.4	0.8
Unemployed	38.3	38.3	21.3	2.1
Students	52.7	20.9	23.1	3.3

Source: Computer printout of FED 79 supplied on April 28, 1981 by K. Hildebrandt of the University of Windsor.

gressive Conservatives while the Liberal Party maintained its support among housewives, clerical and sales people and skilled and unskilled laborers.[25] One is tempted to attribute the strong loss of support by the Liberal Party among the professional and management groups to the economic record of the government through the 1970s.[26]

At this point we need to clarify the implications of support by various economic groups for particular political parties. The mediation of economic questions undertaken by the Liberal party and the NDP is more in terms of bigness. Their model is very much business versus labor with government seen as a big balancing force. On the other hand, the Progressive Conservative and Social Credit parties are more inclined to smallness, from which a number of policies will naturally follow. Thus, the Progressive Conservative and Social Credit parties have tended to advocate policies to assist small business and individuals. A good case in point was the original proposal to index taxes—a Conservative proposal designed with the individual in mind. When the Liberal party leaked information that they were considering dropping personal income tax indexing in 1980, the Conservatives countered with full-page advertisements showing how lower income families would suffer more than high-income families. Even the wage and price advocacy of the PC party in 1974 can be seen in terms of support for the less powerful businesses which were less able to shift price increases onto consumers and against big businesses which were more able to shift price increases. Wage and price controls as proposed by the Progressive Conservatives were designed to assist those who are most hurt by inflation—the farmer, the pensioner and the consumer whose incomes are not rising as fast as are the incomes of unionized labor.

The Progressive Conservative party does not normally advertise its role as proponent of the little man. During its nine months in office the proposed mortgage deduction plan became a mortgage and property tax credit plan, more advantageous to lower-income families, and increasing oil and gas prices were accompanied by an oil tax credit scheme, something studiously avoided by the Liberals. Neither plan was explained very well to those who would benefit most. Indeed, the voter's perception of the Progressive Conservative Party is one that does not encompass its individualism and its championing of the "little man". In fact, of course, the 1979 election shows that proprietors of small businesses were not as favorable to the party as were proprietors of large businesses. Thus support for political parties is very much related to economic policies while in turn the policies advocated by the parties result from the perceived economic base of those parties.

PARLIAMENT: ECONOMICS IS THE BIG TOPIC

The operations of Parliament are, at the best of times, slow and the parliamentary process is poorly understood by many. Even so, the time allocation and the rules of Parliament give us some indication of the importance of issues.

The first major debate in any given session of Parliament is the Throne Speech in which broad guidelines for the government's program are set out. Normally, many announcements about economic measures are contained in the Throne Speech. The Throne Speech debate continues over eight sitting days and opposition leaders have an opportunity to move motions of want-of-confidence. Such motions provide an opportunity for areas of dissatisfaction to be publicized. The contents of these motions are usually economic.

Other opportunities for discussing the economy come in the debate on the budget speech when the same procedures apply as during the Throne Speech. Here, economic policy is *the* issue. The budget speech contains a review of the state of the economy and a statement about the general principles being applied to government spending and taxation. There are usually specific proposals for tax changes as was evidenced by the tabling of seven ways and means motions at the conclusion of the budget presented in October 1980. Two want-of-confidence motions followed the budget referring to the regressive nature of the budget, failure to reduce unemployment, failure to introduce a program of capital investment, a fair prices commission, or cost of living tax credits.

In January of each year the government tables a document in the House of Commons known as the estimates. Since 1968, all estimates are referred to functional standing committees of the House of Commons for deliberation. Thus, for example, the Standing Committee on Transport and Communications examines the estimates of the Ministry of Transport. The standing committees are given three months (March, April and May) to complete their examination while the House of Commons is given 25 days in which the opposition chooses to debate whatever it wishes. At the end of each time period allocated to opposition debate; if estimates and supply are debated, (five days in the fall, seven days before March 31, and thirteen days before the end of June), the House of Commons votes supply and appropriation (that is, gives authority to departments to spend) without further discussion.[27]

Following a fiscal year, it is the duty of the auditor-general to conduct a post-audit of financial transactions and to report his findings to the House of Commons. The auditor-general is to report misuse of funds, overexpenditure of appropriations, expenditures not authorized by Parliament, fraud and inefficiency in departmental operations. The Public Accounts Committee, a standing committee of the House of Commons, is charged with examining the report and calling on departmental officials to explain mismanagement. Over time, the auditor-general's report has revealed such gross irregularities as horses on Sable Island being paid as civil servants, the *Bonaventure* fiasco, in which an aircraft carrier was refitted for double the $8 million estimated but scrapped three years later, and the fact that many hundreds of thousands of square meters of office space were rented by the government but not used.

A great deal of time in the House of Commons and the standing committees is devoted to the estimates and the auditor-general's report. The Public Accounts Committee is so important in our political system that since 1958 the opposition has been allowed to designate the chairman, currently Mr. Bill Clarke (Vancouver Quadra) of the Progressive Conservatives.

Question Period, sometimes seen as the heart of parliamentary interaction, is an occasion for the opposition parties to raise issues of national significance. Obviously, the questions are often designed to gain information and/or to make the governing party appear incompetent. The vast majority of these questions deal with the economy.[28] Quite apart from Question Period, it would appear that more than half of all parliamentary time, including committee time, is spent on economic matters.

A government defeated on a money bill is considered defeated as if it had lost a non-confidence motion, as happened to the Liberals in 1974 and the Conservatives in 1979. An election followed in both instances. Parliamentary rules also preclude initiation of money bills from any other source than the government. In fact, the governing party is sometimes referred to as occupying the "treasury benches". Both these facts illustrate the pre-eminence of economic matters.

THE CIVIL SERVICE

One thesis about the public service is that it emerged to assist in the process of resource development. Thus, at the outset, canal and railway construction were primary. A long-term geological survey became the next important function. Gradually, the public service assumed a protective function and eventually a promotional function. Four of the original departments, all still important, were tied to Canada's staples, and Hodgetts has suggested that today the responsibilities of five departments are primarily staple-oriented.[29] Moreover, many of the Crown corporations and government boards deal with economic matters; for example, the setting of service rates, the regulation of natural resource development, and the marketing of various commodities.

Since the civil service is oriented toward serving the government of the day, it might be argued that its influence on decisions is not important and that policies adopted by government are established by the politicans. However, the civil service has a major influence over policy; indeed, its role is so significant that it warrants further analysis.

The civil service is a well-educated group of individuals who assist in planning and actualizing the hopes and wishes of the community. More and more the public service, with its experience, expertise and knowledge, advises and influences politicians. The advice of the civil service cannot easily be rejected.[30]

Because the civil service is highly educated and operates so that political firings are virtually impossible at the middle and lower levels, it does not matter much which party is in power. Nor does it matter very much what promises have been made to the electorate, for the implementation and ultimately the success of any policy hinges on the civil service's cooperation in planning and executing that policy. Once in power, all parties, whether provincial or federal, have tended to adopt similar policies, which doubtless bears some relation to the fact that the public service, at least at the decision-making level, is generally of one economic class and has a great deal of influence over policy.

Canada owns many economic enterprises either because the government believes that the undertaking is best handled as a monopoly or because it wishes to exercise a certain control over the economy. There are now 366 Crown Corporations[31] with undertakings varying from eleven different harbor commissions which facilitate the development of infrastructure, to subsidiaries of the Canada Development Corporation such as POP Shoppes of Canada. The latter is rarely thought of as being government-owned.

The Financial Administration Branch of the Treasury Board has divided the list of Crown Corporations into eight groups, but for our purposes they may be thought of as being in one of three categories. Departmental corporations such as the Agricultural Stabilization Board are responsible for administrative, supervisory or regulatory services and their transactions are included in budgetary revenues and expenditure. Agency corporations, responsible for trading and service operations, report through a minister and get parliamentary appropriations but their budgets are separate from the government accounts. The Canadian Mint is an example. Proprietary corporations, such as Air Canada, Petrocan and the Canadian Broadcasting Corporation enjoy a great deal of autonomy and carry on as any normal business would. Crown corporations can thus be viewed as regulatory bodies, supply bodies or operating corporations, but each is used by the government to affect the economy.

Many Crown Corporations are so imbedded in the voter's mind as being part of government that they inevitably become embroiled in influencing the vote. In 1972, the Unemployment Insurance Commission became a significant issue. Similarly, in the 1974 and 1979 elections, the Canadian Wheat Board was accused of making payments to farmers just prior to the vote. Petrocan became a symbol of the Progressive Conservative desire to privatize some Crown Corporations in 1979 but since the 1980 budget its role has been to buy up large portions of the oil and gas exploration and distribution system to make the industry at least 50% Canadian-owned. The latter is to be accomplished with tax funds.

ARE REGIONAL CLEAVAGES ECONOMIC?

There is a theory that Canadian politics can be explained as attempts to balance regional cleavages.[32] These regional cleavages are based on the idea that Ontario and Québec represent the core and the remainder of Canada is seen as the periphery. The core is dominant in the number of corporations registered in those two provinces (in 1973, 91% of corporations federally incorporated were in Ontario and Québec) and in corporate taxes collected (in 1978-79, 62.9% of corporate taxes were collected in Ontario and Québec). The political consequences of the core-periphery model are many. It has been suggested that the periphery will show its alienation in ideological polarization. In Canada, significantly, much of the support, and indeed the spawning, of the Social Credit and New Democratic parties involves the periphery.

Perhaps it would be best to examine a specific issue to determine whether regional cleavages are economic. It is sometimes difficult to understand what makes an Albertan join a separatist party. The basis of the argument is that Ontario (specifically Toronto) has controlled the economy to Alberta's detriment and that this can be redressed by making Ontario suffer. Indeed, Western separatists argue that Alberta has succeeded financially despite Ontario. They believe that national policies have been imposed over the years to keep markets secure for Ontario-manufactured products at the cost of making the West dependent on non-renewable natural resources. The end result will be an Alberta without diversification and without resources.

Such economic attitudes are widespread. In 1973 Prime Minister Trudeau, several cabinet colleagues, and some top civil servants met with a number of Prairie and BC civil servants and politicians at what was called a "western summit". Almost all the demands presented by the provinces at that time were economic in nature and arose from economic alienation. The demands of the Western Provinces included provincial control over monetary policy, adequate equalization payments and greater Ottawa support of grain farmers.

FEDERALISM: THE ONLY ECONOMICALLY VIABLE ARRANGEMENT

Canada is heterogeneous. The people in Québec are descended from the *habitants*, whose livelihood was not dependent on education or travel. The people in the Atlantic provinces are descended from United Empire Loyalists or are Acadians. Ontario has a base of descendants of United Empire Loyalists but has also absorbed, more than any other province, a large immigrant influx from Europe, the Caribbean and other areas of the world. In the Prairies, settled largely by East Europeans, the hard rugged winters, the dependence on agriculture and raw resources and the fact that the settlers were in many instances mobile entrepreneurs looking for land and opportunity have left a mark on the inhabitants. British Columbia, populated mainly by people of British descent, has the long spring, the influence of the sea, and the influence of the eastern lands bordering the Pacific Ocean.

This heterogeneity causes people to have different wants. A national government cannot understand, let alone begin to satisfy, the wants of such a heterogeneous people. Yet, a national government can supply defense, external relations, trade barriers and the like more efficiently than could a number of smaller countries. Thus, there is an economic justification for a federal form of government where the national government is given some exclusive powers such as defense, and where local governments provide the economic goods for which the demand is likely to vary.

In 1867, the Fathers of Confederation believed that Canada needed a strong central government for defense purposes. Again, during World War II, the central government was conceded many taxation and other powers that had earlier been administered by the provinces. Yet in other times, provincial powers have been on the ascendent.

In the discussions on "patriation" of the constitution which have taken place at various times, the provincial governments, reflecting the demands of their constituents, have asked for guarantees that they alone would be responsible for the provision of "local" goods and tax levels while the federal government has argued that to carry out its responsibilities, which include the national economy as well as defense, strong central powers are necessary.

It is clear that the discussions on federalism and the constitution have been and will continue to be discussions about the distribution of goods with the provinces wanting to retain the ability to provide the diversity demanded by their heterogeneous populations. Ontario's support for the federal stand stems from the fact that in recent years Ontario has lost some of its pre-eminence and sees itself as gaining from a redistribution, particularly in energy, that can only occur if the federal government is strong enough to carry out the redistribution.

NATIONALISM: ECONOMIC FORCES AT WORK?

Nationalism, it is generally argued, is a diversion from "economic rationality" and those politicians who are able to take people's attention away from economic reality are often rewarded by getting high ratings in public opinion polls and by winning at election time.

At this point we might ask how nationalism has affected Canada. Certainly, the very existence of Canada is partly the result of nationalistic influences. Prior to Confederation, the United Empire Loyalists had settled in parts of Ontario, New Brunswick and Nova Scotia and had brought with them a strong allegiance to the British Crown. They were not anxious to develop strong links with the United States and thus there was a need for rail lines and economic expansion to the West. This resulted in an economic policy based on tariff barriers and railway construction which contradicted natural north-south trade patterns.

Tariffs, which were mentioned earlier as part of the National Policy, resulted in a large amount of foreign investment. Initially, foreign investment was encouraged as a means of establishing manufacturing but later the Canadian government was keen to invite exploitation of raw materials. Even though foreign direct investment may have been a result of Canadian policies, foreign control eventually became the cause of further problems because, once established, foreign firms became a dominant force in the economic environment. For example, our educational system, our research efforts, our industrial structure and our balance between exports and imports all were largely shaped and became less changeable because of the number of branch plants that developed.

Traditional economics does not admit a problem of dependency. Each party, whether it be individuals or firms, tries to accrue a greater benefit to himself at the expense of the other. However, both enter into the market of their own free will, and because there are alternative buyers and sellers, an even-handed relationship between the traders is assumed. Thus, no theoretical recognition of a dependency problem is possible in traditional economics.

It is when Canadians begin to examine some of the intertwined political problems, many of them of an economic nature, that concern arises. Canadian exports dependent on components and technical data from the United States are subject to the Export Control Act of 1949, an act that emanates from the United States government. Further, the United States Trading with the Enemy Act, Foreign Assets Control Regulations and the Cuban Assets Control Regulations apply to goods exported by affiliates and subsidiaries of United States firms, even when they make no use of US components. Also, the United States Department of Justice has jurisdiction under the Sherman Act and the Clayton Act to scrutinize and prosecute when Canadian subsidiaries of US firms combine or are taken over.

Large multinational firms exert powerful political influence. Typically, those firms recognize the importance of being politically active. Taxes and regulations, export and import controls, and pricing policies are all of direct interest to these firms. Also, highly placed corporate individuals have moved into politics; a former vice-president of Imperial Oil, for instance, moved to a policy and research post in the office of the leader of the opposition.

There are, therefore, two types of consequences that arise from foreign direct investment. The first consequence is one that can be measured; we can calculate the economic costs of exports foregone, the costs of American control over Canadian industrial structure, and the amount of our gross national product that flows out of the country to pay for projects of parent companies in other countries. There has been much debate about the net costs to the Canadian economy of these matters.[33]

Far more subtle and, in the long run, more consequential is the participation by branch operations in Canadian political life, particularly concerning the Liberal party. Contributions to party coffers, advertising assistance, and ultimately a connection on a personal level between cabinet members and some of the directors of these foreign subsidiaries constitute, in many eyes, a threat to political sovereignty.

There can be little doubt that Canadian policy is dictated to some extent by direct foreign investment. Certainly, the fact that Canadians have not seemed inclined to make risk capital available privately in competition with foreign firms has caused the federal government to look more favorably at expansion of the government sector. Examples are numerous, one being the Canada Development Corporation. The Canada Development Corporation has as one of its directors the Deputy Minister of Industry, Trade, and Commerce, but has issued shares to the public through a massive campaign to get Canadians involved. Petrocan is currently buying multinational oil companies.

We fear that foreign ownership will lead us to an ultimate loss of wealth. While we would not lose our jobs, we would lose our ability to allocate resources and to develop in new areas so long as we pay out interest and dividends to others. Moreover, so long as monetary flows between countries are large, it is necessary to maintain an exchange rate policy thereby decreasing the government's ability to carry out fiscal and monetary policy (to fight inflation and unemployment). Thus, the political concern with nationalism is really an economic concern.

The government has created a Foreign Investment Review Agency (FIRA) to control the further erosion of Canadian ownership. As a regulatory body FIRA was initially quite strict, but recently there have been fewer attempts to stop foreign takeovers.[34]

Thus, today's political decisions are largely shaped by economic reality, shaped in turn by past political decisions which, when examined turn out to have been mainly economic decisions. It is a very basic cycle. Once the government decides to interfere in the marketplace, other decisions follow. For instance, the National Energy Policy of 1980 assumes the multinationals will agree to higher taxes. Instead they are leaving Canada because exploration costs are lower in the United States. That provides an excuse to further nationalize or governmentize the industry.

IS POLITICS REALLY ECONOMICS BY ANOTHER NAME?

The approach of economics assumes self-interest on the part of the voter and on the part of the policy-maker. Certainly, many voters and policy-makers fit this rational model but the world is not composed exclusively of rational human beings. It would be dull if it were.

The economic approach is only one of many. Moreover, it overlaps with the continental approach and the geographical approach as well as with others. However, as we have seen, the economic approach to Canadian politics makes a great deal of Canadian political activity comprehensible.

One phenomenon that seems to lie beyond the realm of economic explanation is charisma. Trudeau has used charisma to his advantage since 1968 but it will be noted that it is most effective when the economic issues are perplexing; least effective and least needed when, economically, times are good. The rise of the Liberal party in public opinion polls early in 1977, after a year of being below the Progressive Conservatives, demonstrates the diversion from economic issues that can be achieved. Pierre Trudeau, at about the same time as the polls showed an increase in Liberal popularity, began to focus on the issue of national unity and in particular carried that message to the US Congress where he made a widely televised speech. By implication, he let it be known that he was the only one who could keep Canada together. Thus, the heaviest unemployment since World War II and severe inflationary pressures no longer constituted the primary issue. Public attention was largely diverted from economic areas in which Trudeau and his government had done very badly and which had been the cause for the continually unfavorable polls during 1976.

One could argue that the Constitutional debates were ostensibly a diversion from economics. Support for Trudeau's package was at first limited to Ontario and New Brunswick, provinces that would benefit economically from the initial document. But the provinces which stood to lose economic power fought the document in the courts and protested to the federal Parliament in an attempt to maintain economic power.

CONCLUSION

It is no accident that the old name for economics was political economy. All the classical economists called it by that name....Indeed, at the present time there is some question as to whether the two sciences are not showing signs of amalgamating again, perhaps into economic politics rather than into political economy.[35]

In writing these lines, Kenneth Boulding confirms what we have noted in this chapter, namely, that one cannot separate an understanding of Canadian political reality from an understanding of economic problems. Politics has been, and will continue to be, a struggle for economic power.

Economics can explain much in Canadian politics; to a large extent it can account for regional voting patterns; it can help explain why sons follow their parents in voting behavior (social class tends to be transferred to the next generation). Many elections, many feelings, develop directly or indirectly from economic problems or issues.

To understand why we have a federal system of government; to understand why Canadians rely on government ownership of public enterprise; to understand why the political parties adopt the positions they do (particularly on issues such as foreign ownership, protection and support for small business and farmers); and to understand why governments in Canada tend to last for rather lengthy terms, it is necessary to have a knowledge of economics.

SUMMARY

1. When goods that cannot be produced in the marketplace profitably are needed it is necessary for government to interpret the need and either produce the good or ensure that the good is produced.

2. Confederation was an economic arrangement as the colonies recognized the benefits to be derived from increased markets and increased business through eastern ports.

3. The building of railways, the settlement of the West despite Riel, and the National Policy (high tariffs to the outside world), all demonstrate the economic nature of the major political decisions of the nineteenth century.

4. A number of elections have been won on economic issues. In 1911, reciprocity was an issue; in 1930 the economy was entering the Depression and five years later had not recovered; in 1962 the devalued and pegged Canadian dollar lost the Conservatives as many as thirty seats; in 1974 wage and price controls were an issue; in 1980 the proposed taxes on oil and gas lost the Conservatives many Ontario seats.

5. Separatism is an economic issue. The rejection of the separatist option in the Québec referendum in May 1980 is recognition that currently the Québec people receive more from the federal government than what they pay. Similarly the rise of western separatism is recognition that they pay more than they gain from remaining a part of Canada.

6. The political parties can be interpreted in light of the economic status of their membership. The Liberals tend to be closely allied to big business, the NDP to big unions, the Conservatives to small business, and the Social Credit to unorganized blue collar workers.

7. The policies advocated by the parties tend to be most appropriate to their own constituents—for example, the Progressive Conservative advocacy of mortgage assistance and income tax indexing.

8. Much time in Parliament is devoted to economic issues and over three quarters of the questions asked during Question Period are economically oriented.

9. The civil service is highly influential and tends to be of one economic class.

Thus, the policies of government tend to be similar regardless of governing party.

10. The core-periphery analysis of Canadian politics can be interpreted as an analysis of differences in economic power and an attempt to gain a redistribution of economic resources from the center to the periphery.

11. Federalism is an economically viable arrangement whereby the provinces can deal with the provision of 'public' goods to a heterogeneous population.

12. Nationalism and Canadianization can be seen as fundamentally economic in nature.

STUDY QUESTIONS

1. If economics is "the allocation of scarce resources", how is politics "the allocation of scarce resources"?

2. Is separatism, in Québec or the West, mainly cultural, mainly political, or mainly economic?

3. Are Canadian elections, federal or provincial, becoming less or more economically oriented?

4. Why does federalism satisfy the basic economic needs of Canadians better than a unitary government?

5. To what extent can personal charisma and party rhetoric overshadow economic reality?

6. Show how the argument that Petrocan must be used to Canadianize the petroleum industry is dependent on previous economic decisions by the government.

7. Is there any growth of Canadian government apart from economic activity?

8. In the National Energy Policy of 1980, the federal government argued for increased federal revenue from petroleum products. Was that argument, and was Alberta's response, entirely economic?

9. To what extent is economic reality weakening, or even undermining, party ideologies?

10. Is there any evidence that economic crises are becoming more important in Canadian politics?

ENDNOTES

1. John Maynard Keynes quoted by C.R. McDonnell, *Economics*, 6th ed. (New York: McGraw-Hill, 1975), p. 2.

2. Resources here refer to more than natural gas, coal, iron, ore, etc. There are

human resources and physical products as well as natural resources which must be allocated.

3. Adam Smith, *The Wealth of Nations* (London: Routledge, 1913), Book V, pp. 541-644.

4. An indivisible good is one that an individual cannot be excluded from consuming simply because he does not pay for it. An example is national defense. A missile in northern Canada fired to detonate an enemy's projectile benefits all people in southern Canada, whether they have paid or not. No private company will provide missiles in optimum quantity since it would have no way to force people to pay for these goods.

5. An externality arises when one or more economic units derives an economic gain or loss from an economic action initiated by another economic unit. For instance, a new technological process to produce pulp and paper is introduced by firm A. The effluent from this process does not affect firm A but rather firm B, a fishing enterprise, and thus the public generally. Since firm A does not derive any loss from the effluent, there will be no pollution control unless forced by collective action.

6. Although Section 118 of the British North America Act spoke of subsidies as a "final settlement", the federal government offset a determined bid for separation by Nova Scotia by increasing its subsidies. New Brunswick held out for a more favorable bargain upon finally surrendering its export duties in 1873. See J.A. Maxwell, *Federal Subsidies to the Provincial Governments in Canada* (Cambridge: Harvard University Press, 1937).

7. See *Report of the Royal Commission on Dominion-Provincial Relations* (Ottawa: Queen's Printer, 1940), Book 1.

8. See H.A. Innis, *Political Economy in the Modern State* (Toronto: Ryerson, 1946), pp. 251-6, and *A History of the Canadian Pacific Railway* (Toronto: University of Toronto Press, 1923).

9. Innis, *A History of the Canadian Pacific Railway*, op. cit., pp. 78-84.

10. In only two elections since that time have the Conservative party fortunes been good in that province. In 1930, with a depression having started under the Liberals, the Conservatives received 44.7% of the Québec vote. In 1958, when the rest of the country was clearly voting for Diefenbaker, Québec voted 49.6% for the Conservatives.

11. For a contrary and well-documented view see John Weir, "Trade and Resource Policies," *Political Parties in Canada*, ed. C. Winn and J. McMenemy (Toronto: McGraw-Hill Ryerson, 1976), pp. 228-49.

12. There is no doubt the economic situation played a role in the campaign. As well King confided to his diary on learning the results of the election, "I shall be glad to throw on to Bennett's shoulders the formation of a government and finding a solution for unemployment and other problems." See H.B. Neatby, *William Lyon Mackenzie King* (Toronto: University of Toronto Press, 1963), pp. 327-42.

13. *Toronto Star*, May 14, 1977, p. 1.

14. As quoted in the *Financial Post*, March 29, 1981, p. 23.

15. *Financial Post*, March 28, 1981, p. 23.

16. Canadian federal elections have been held between the middle of May and the

first week of November on twenty-three occasions. Since there have only been thirty-two elections, 72% of all elections have taken place in those months. July and August are not favored because of the number of people on holidays during those months.

17. In 1972, the percentage who voted for the Liberal party by province, changed from 1968 in the following manner: Newfoundland, +2.4; N.S., -4.1; N.B., -1.2; P.E.I., -4.4; Québec, -4.0; Ontario, -8.2; Manitoba, -10.5; Sask., -1.8; Alta., -10.7; and B.C., -12.8. Calculation made from Report of the Chief Electoral Officer.

18. In 1974, the Liberal party increased its seats in the House of Commons from 109 to 140. Policies introduced between 1972 and 1974 include: indexing personal taxes, old-age pensions, family allowances and civil service pensions. Also in this period family allowances were increased by more than 100%, New Horizon grants were started, LIP and OYP grants were fully utilized and parliamentary salaries were increased—all to gain parliamentary and electoral support.

19. Albert Breton, *The Economic Theory of Representative Government* (Chicago: Aldine, 1974).

20. For a full description of this topic, see Roland McKean, *Public Spending* (New York: McGraw-Hill, 1968), pp. 10-30.

21. N.H. Chi, "Class Cleavage," *Political Parties in Canada, op. cit.* Chi concludes that "there are class differences in access to income, but also there are class differences in party support."

22. The United Auto Workers and the Steel Workers have been central to the NDP's financial survival.

23. One only need refer to the nationalization of potash in Saskatchewan, car insurance in British Columbia, Saskatchewan and Manitoba, and the original medical care bill in Saskatchewan for proof of this statement.

24. John Meisel, *Working Papers on Canadian Politics* (Montreal: McGill-Queen's University Press, 1975), p. 291.

25. Mildred Schwartz, *Politics and Territory* (Montreal: McGill-Queen's University Press, 1974, p. xii) discusses the stability of voting behavior. The data presented here are not sufficient to contradict Schwartz's conclusions.

26. The evidence is mainly circumstantial. Previous cabinet members from the Liberal party have been favored with large numbers of board of directorship appointments on their retirement from politics. The movement in the opposite direction has been significant as well. Note the directorships currently held by Turner and MacDonald or the directorships held in the past by Harris, Sharp, Sinclair or Winters—all Liberals. All are with large corporations—some multinational. Previous PC cabinet members have been less favored. Even those who were considered to be good administrators have not moved freely between politics and big business, for example, Churchill, Alvin Hamilton, Fairclough, Fulton or Bill Hamilton. It is interesting that of the large number of defeated Liberal cabinet ministers in the 1979 election, none have received directorships of the type held by Turner, Sharp or Winters.

27. Donald S. MacDonald, "Changes in the House of Commons—New Rules," *Canadian Public Administration*, 13, No. 1 (Spring, 1970), 33-4.

28. Between March 9 and March 13, 1981 there were 72 oral questions, of which only 17 did not relate to the economy. No unemployment or inflation figures were

announced during the week and President Reagan visited Ottawa. Questions of a non-economic nature included those on the new appointments to the Status of Women Committee, Bilingualism, House of Commons Privileges, and El Salvador. Those dealing with the economy included questions on profits, banks, FIRA, Income Tax, National Energy Program, Fishing Treaties, pipeline construction, Treasury Board, grain and the Western Development Fund.

29. J.E. Hodgetts, *The Canadian Public Service: A Physiology of Government, 1867-1970* (Toronto: University of Toronto Press, 1973), p. 21.

30. For an interesting account of the policy influence, as well as the information control of civil servants, see: F. MacDonald, "The Minister and the Mandarins," *Policy Options*, 1, 3 (September/October, 1980), 29-31.

31. Clive Baxter, "What's at Stake in Canada's 366 Crown Corporations," *Financial Post,* May 14, 1977, p. 5.

32. See Douglas McCready and Conrad Winn, "Geographical Cleavage: Core vs. Periphery," in C. Winn and M. McMenemy, *op. cit.,* pp. 71-88.

33. See Kari Levitt, *Silent Surrender* (Toronto: Macmillan, 1970); *Eleventh Report of the Standing Committee on External Affairs and National Defence Respecting Canada-U.S. Relations,* Ian Wahn, Chairman (Ottawa: Queeen's Printer, 1970); *Foreign Ownership and the Structures of Industry,* M. Watkins, Chairman (Ottawa: Queen's Printer, 1968); Abraham Rotstein, "Development and Dependence: The Canadian Problem," *Economics: Contemporary Issues in Canada,* ed. D.A.L. Auld (Toronto: Holt, Rinehart and Winston, 1972); and Grant L. Reuber, "Foreign Investment in Canada: A Review," in D.A.L. Auld, *op cit.*

34. In one recent month, all applications submitted to FIRA were approved.

35. Kenneth E. Boulding, *Economics as a Science* (New York: McGraw-Hill, 1970), p. 77.

SELECTED REFERENCES

Auld, D.A.L. et al. *Canadian Confederation at the Crossroads.* Vancouver: The Fraser Institute, 1978. This book is a collection of articles about Canadian Confederation that is easily read by non-economists. It deals with many of the issues addressed by politicians in attempting to reach agreement over a patriated Constitution.

Bartlett, Randal. *Economic Foundations of Political Power.* New York: The Free Press, 1973. This book deals with three questions. First, how government decisions are made; second, how this allocation process affects the allocation of resources in the economy; and third, what are the relationships between economic and political power.

Breton, Albert. *The Economic Theory of Representative Government.* Chicago: Aldine Publishing Company, 1974. This short, theoretical work uses standard economic theory of supply and demand to analyze public spending. However, Breton, in his analysis of the market behavior that underlies public spending decisions, makes some very perceptive comments on the institutional framework. It is here he suggests that governments try to maximize their own probability of reelection — a special view of the unseen hand.

Breton, Albert and Anthony Scott. *The Design of Federations*. Montreal: The Institute for Research on Public Policy, 1980. This is a recent exploration of possible alternative constitutional arrangements. The authors argue that an extended constituent assembly would reduce the costs of federation by chanelling political behavior.

Boulding, Kenneth E. *Economics as a Science*. New York: McGraw-Hill, 1970. Boulding treats economics as part of a broader analysis in which the background of the discipline is most important. He treats economics as a social science, a behavioral science, a political science, and so on. If one reads the chapter on economics as a political science, one is struck by the fact that political science can be viewed as an economic science as well.

Buchanan, James M. and Richard E. Wagner. *Democracy in Deficit: The Political Legacy of Lord Keynes*. New York: Academic Press, 1977. A book in which two economists trace the impact of Keynesian economic theories on our political institutions, and the effects that these institutional changes have wrought on economic policy decisions. An excellent, although somewhat advanced, example of how economics creates political bias which in turn affects economic choices.

Carrigan, D. Owen. *Canadian Party Platforms: 1867-1968*. Toronto: Copp Clark, 1968. This book is a summary of each party platform in each of the twenty-eight elections between 1867 and 1968. A reading of this volume will impress the reader with the importance of economic issues in party policy in Canada.

Hodgetts, J.E. *The Canadian Public Service: A Physiology of Government, 1867-1970*. Toronto: University of Toronto Press, 1973. This book, sponsored by the Social Science Research Council of Canada to examine one aspect of the setting of decision-making in Canada, is a thorough analysis of the origins and sociology of the Canadian public service. The reader gets a feeling for the importance of the civil service as well as why decision-making has an economic bias.

Innis, H.A. *Political Economy in the Modern State*. Toronto: Ryerson, 1946. Harold Innis was an internationally known Canadian economist whose stress on political economy was extremely significant.

La Forest, Gerard V. *The Allocation of Taxing Power under the Canadian Constitution*. Toronto: Canadian Tax Foundation, 1967. This study is an account of the division of economic powers between the central government and the provinces. The first chapter on history is particularly important.

Levitt, Kari. *Silent Surrender*. Toronto: Macmillan, 1970. This book has had an influential impact on the nationalism of the 1970s. It deals with the influences of multinational corporations—a "slide into a position of economic, political and cultural dependence on the United States." Kari Levitt has written a plain and forceful book which shows how Canada's dependence has come about and suggests ways of changing that dependence.

Royal Commission on Dominion-Provincial Relations, *Report*. 1 vol. Ottawa: Queen's Printer, 1954. Commonly known as the report of the Rowell-Sirois Commission, the original document was published in May, 1940. The fact that it had to be reprinted attests to its importance as a document on Canadian federalism. In the *Report* and the studies commissioned by the investigators, a great deal of the history of Canada can be garnered, particularly as it relates to the economy and the influences that it has had on Canadian political life.

Simeon, Richard. *Federal-Provincial Diplomacy: The Making of Recent Policy in Canada.* Toronto: University of Toronto Press, 1972. This book was sponsored by the Social Science Research Council of Canada as part of a series on "Studies in the Structure of Power". Simeon examines three federal-provincial issues of the 1960s—the Canada Pension Plan, finances and the constitution—from the point of view of the participants. Because the focus is on decision-making, Simeon plays down the fact that all three issues were to a greater or lesser extent economic in nature.

Winn, C. and J. McMenemy, eds. *Political Parties in Canada.* Toronto: McGraw-Hill Ryerson, 1976. Although ostensibly about political parties, this book has much useful information on other topics as well. Some of the chapters deal with the economy directly or indirectly. For our purposes, the chapters on Geographical Cleavage, Class Cleavage, Redistributive Policy, and Trade and Resource Policies are particularly useful.

4

History and the Perception of Politics

Kenneth McNaught*

Lord Bolingbroke once remarked that history is "philosophy teaching by examples."[1] The "examples," of course, are all important for they are of necessity selective, yet universality is always claimed by those who make the selection. From the patriotic-narrative history of Thucydides and Herodotus, through the more analytical history of Vico to the extraordinary expansion of Clio's claims in the twentieth century, history has consistently embraced the totality of human experience. Clio has reached out promiscuously to artists of pen and brush, to princes and politicians, to theologians, merchants, and scholars, and even to the unpredictable progeny of the computer. Enriched by the methods and findings of the social sciences, the historical craft has remained the essential integrator of every study relating to man. Without knowledge of the details and patterns of the past a student of politics is like a man without a memory. He is the merest existentialist groping amongst the chimerical experiences of the present, which is, in any case, no longer existent. He will see warfare in Vietnam, terrorism in Québec, anglophone response to bilingualism in Calgary or Vancouver or to unilingualism in Québec, with about the same degree of understanding as the man who cuts off his finger to prove to himself that he is alive. The pain is present, the loss acute, but comprehension is absent. And already the loss is in the past.

Most social scientists would allow that historical knowledge enriches one's understanding of contemporary politics. Not so many, however, would go beyond endorsing the value of "perspective" and proclaim that a command of our historical evolution is not only the best, but is the *sine qua non* foundation of political perception. Such primacy is a very large claim; yet it is one which may be plausibly defended. One can, for example, test by poll and questionnaire the

*Professor of History, University of Toronto.

89

political behavior and opinion patterns of Canadians in a variety of contemporary situations. Thus we can, without the aid of history, delineate quite accurately the reactions to the 1970 FLQ crisis, to federal energy policies, to 'patriation' of the BNA Act, or to restrictive labor laws. But in each case, perception and understanding will be minimal without knowledge of the historical deposits of experience and thinking which, like geological activity, form a nation's political-social topography, its public philosophy.

Specifically, the terrorism of 1970, as well as the massive support for proclamation of the War Measures Act and the subsequent electoral success of the Parti Québécois cannot be understood in any satisfactory way by someone who knows little of the Papineau-Mackenzie era, of what Lord Durham did for French Canadian nationalism, or of the achievements of the great political partnerships of Baldwin and Lafontaine, Cartier and Macdonald or King and Lapointe. Nor can one apprehend or explain the curious mixture of apathy and passion which enveloped the effort to terminate clause seven of the Statute of Westminster and to entrench a charter of rights in our "new" constitution unless one knows quite a bit about the history of provincial and language rights and the deeply rooted Canadian suspicion of direct and majoritarian democracy. Again, the short fuse on labor militancy, when unions perceive any legislative reaction as a threat to their collective bargaining position or right to strike, cannot be fully explained without knowing something about the historic struggles of 1919, say, or the early 1940s. The present, in short, is inseparable from the past.

If all the facts that the political analyst-theorist has to consider lie in the past, even if he is only a pollster, a futurist, or utopian, in what way is he not a historian? The answer is that he is a historian whether he accepts the tag or not. And this being the case, it is to his advantage to know and become involved with the kaleidoscopic problems of writing, interpreting and using history. The very table of contents of this book underlines the indissoluble marriage of politics, or the understanding of politics, and the historical process. This fact is evident whether by history we mean what has actually happened or whether we mean the evolution of a discipline by which we may enhance our comprehension of the past. Environment, values, structures, processes, the exercise of power: historians and social scientists alike aspire to define, describe and assess the role of such "forces".

Increasingly it seems as if some supra-academic prism has been trained upon all this diligent endeavor. Amoeba-like splintering has always been an intellectual passion and the advent of counting has served, ironically, to inflame a proclivity to focus on ever smaller segments of any discipline. Historians have not been immune to this pervasive trend. Statistics, for long thought to be the means by which scholars might bring the facts of ever more complex social evolution under control and at the same time enrich and support their description of past politics, has exploded to include not only tax rolls and other state-kept records, but every conceivable collection of facts to be culled from church basements and newspaper files to trade unions and chambers of commerce membership records. We learn about voting patterns in and out of legislatures, about mobility and other social patterns (poor people have tended to take in more roomers and to move less frequently than rich people), about incidents of violence carefully categorized by class, region and decade. Patterns emerge and we discover that a lot of women have moved into the "work force", have been paid less than men, and have found the routes to the top somewhat tortuous. Even ideas are now counted, assigned numbers, and forced into computer-card holes. Their significance will then depend on how many holes catch the attention of the machine.

Aside from controversies about the value of mechanized quantification, the peculiar evolution through which historians have both broadened and narrowed their interests has enriched the historical process immensely. Yet no matter how specialized, methodical or even present-minded the historian becomes, his *essential* role is that of integrator. Sooner or later the "story" part of his function has to predominate; even Whig history is narrative. The detail and the analytical basis of fact may be endlessly enriched but sooner or later the historian has to put it all together, with or without a conclusion.

Those historians, such as A. J. Toynbee, who have minimized the importance of time in their comparative history become, in fact, social scientists. That is, like all scientists, they search for laws, or even *a* law, which is all explaining. I recall an evening spent several years ago with the American political scientist Louis Hartz and four Canadian historians. Only one of the historians agreed with Hartz that the purpose of historical research was to discover and define a law that could explain the development of new nations—particularly Canada and the United States. I was surprised on two counts: first, because we all assumed that Hartz knew something about history as such,[2] and second, because the historian who supported him is best known for well-crafted descriptive-analytical writing based solidly on primary sources. His history is concerned at least as much with personality and the discreet event as with determining forces, either ideological or physical. In short, while this pro-Hartzian academic is fascinated by patterns of thought, action and community he cannot help testing them in the white water of people and accidents. The fact that Macdonald was a dipsomaniac and, while bedded down in a bilious bout of recovery, could make remarkably vulgar suggestions to an emissary from Rideau Hall as to what the governor general could do with his vice-regal request for an immediate audience, is an angular datum that such a historian finds difficult to fit into an explanatory law.[3] Similar problems arise over Mitchell Hepburn maintaining a vibrant residence-cum-hospitality suite in Toronto's King Edward Hotel, the premature death of Sir G.E. Cartier, Count Frontenac's personal financial problems and vainglorious personality, or Mackenzie King's impenetrable foibles.

In Canada the relationship between social scientists and historians has been peculiarly close. The political economist, H.A. Innis, for example, emerges as historian par excellence in a recent book on Canadian historians;[4] Carl Berger depicts Innis's *The Fur Trade in Canada* as "one of the few books in Canadian historical literature that truly deserves to be described as seminal." Berger's almost hyperbolic assessment flows from the growing tendency of historians to ransack the evidence in search of patterns, laws or explanatory principles; that is, to use the conceptual approach of the sciences. This tendency can be seen not only in the new breed of quantifying historians[5] but also in social and intellectual historians who do not use the computer. Ideologies, Marxism or liberalism for example, become single-cause explanations of global evolution.[6] Yet history is not likely to fall completely prey to law-making any more than good scientists are likely to ignore the past. The interrelationship of the two approaches is, indeed, the mainspring of any university, a point made recently by a Canadian physical scientist. "The university is false to its calling if it does not declare that it is first concerned with the understanding through history of man and his imaginings, of life, of matter and materials and only consequentially with the instrumentalities, methodologies and techniques that arise out of this endeavour."[7]

The perception of politics must always originate with an attempt to understand "man and his imaginings" through history. But history is not only what has happened and the people or circumstances that made it happen. It is also the "instrumentalities, methodologies and techniques" employed by historians to delineate and analyze the past. I take it as *a priori* that a political scientist must be more or less aware of the origins and evolution of any institutions, behavior-belief patterns, or customs that he cares to study. Thus a noted British historian, who is putting what he preaches into practice as Dean of the School of Humanities and Social Science at the Massachusetts Institute of Technology, can refer to "...the distinctive contribution that history brings to the social sciences, because of its roots in the humanities. It is one of the tasks of historians to explain to their fellow social scientists that they must refresh their store of ideas by resort to history, literature, music and philosophy."[8] Cultural characteristics, along with social science concepts of class, economic systems, popular or working-class culture, social control, and other "one dimensional devices used to explain how societies hold themselves together" must be integrated by history.[9]

Let us examine a few concerns of Canadian political science in order to test the applicability of the foregoing general remarks: the nature of our constitution, our party system, our regionalism-federalism, and the economic and social bases of our political ideas.

I suppose the most common error to be found in undergraduate essays and examination answers is the assumption that until recently our constitution was the British North America Act. This is not surprising when one considers the popular usage in the media and even among our political leaders. The classic example of this was the reverberating demand that we must "repatriate our constitution." Apart from courtesy copies of the British statute, the BNA Act had never been "in Canada" (and there is no verb "to patriate"), and it was not our constitution. The pervasiveness of this error, and it is not confined to students alone, is similar to other total misconceptions that could be multiplied many times. The Proclamation "Act" was, almost without fail, "issued" in 1763—unless it was 1760 or 1774. That great charter of French-Canadian rights and the "fifth cause" of the American Revolution, the Quebec Act, was "passed" by George III in 1774—or thereabouts. Laurier lost the election of 1911 because of the Reciprocity "Treaty," and the Progressive "party" won sixty-five seats in the 1921 federal election and Pierre Trudeau "issued" the War Measures Act in 1970. The list is endless and many items will seem irrelevant or even pedantic to issue-oriented students. Yet pedantry, or precision, is the *sine qua non* of genuine political *or* historical understanding.

It is the historian who will insist most quickly on a sequential reading and understanding of the basic documents, including the primary evidence from which alone we may understand the significance of continuity. Thus, to the historian, the preamble to the BNA Act, which declares that Canada shall have "a constitution similar in principle to that of the United Kingdom" is probably the most revealing part of the Act. He will not only emphasize the failure of the Act to describe the powers of the executive, legislative and judicial branches of the various governments established and provided for by the Act, but also the consequent need to know the whole of British and colonial history in order to understand what the Act says. Throughout the Act continuity is of the essence: existing laws, powers and procedures all continue as before and until they are altered by the new governments. To understand the Act requires a thorough knowledge not only of pre-existing practices and laws but also of what was in the minds of the people who framed it. Look, for example, at Sections 58-68 which purport to describe the "provincial constitutions": the "Executive Council of Ontario and Quebec shall be composed of such persons as the Lieutenant-Governor from time to time thinks fit," and in Nova Scotia and New Brunswick the "Executive Authority" (why the different phraseology?) shall "continue as it exists at the Union, until altered under authority of this Act." The entire operation is *déjà vu* with the exception of the division of powers and revenues and within specifically political passages, such as the future acquisition of the North-West and the building of the Intercolonial Railroad, which were, as Macdonald noted, the consequences of a very political union.

These whimsical reflections on history and our 1867 "constitution" lead directly into the question of historical evidence and the perception of politics. Let us take a few specific subdivisions of this question to illustrate the general problem: the party system, political culture and regionalism. It is generally conceded that the achievement of responsible government in Canada was a function of the party system. But as that party system evolved through the spasms of confederation, expansion, schools, language crises, war and urbanization-industrialization, it took on deep-grained, specifically Canadian characteristics. These characteristics are the very ones most likely to be mini-mized, or even unknown, by law-making, model-oriented social scientists.

In early writing on the party system the model was usually British: parlia-mentary supremacy, a two-party structure based on a majority party and a loyal opposition, with Section 18 of the BNA Act endorsing the Westminster model. In the 1930s, 1940s, and 1950s a different, but equally law-making, model found favor and was thought to break fresh ground by anyone who had not read Goldwin Smith or Lord Bryce. Canada was a North American, continent-wide federal state. Therefore the political party requirements described by F.J. Turner, Charles Beard and Pendleton Herring in their analyses of the American political experience must also apply to Canada. Because of geography, extent, federalism and isolation from Europe, Canadian politics must be, and must have been, a brokerage mechanism, eschewing ideology. Like the American, the Canadian could only be a two-party system with each party offering a department store variety of goodies to regions, classes and interest groups. Thus, as prescribed by the American model, third or minor parties had as their principal function the preservation of the two-party system. They could force particularist issues upon the attention of one or another of the major parties but having thus "stung", as Richard Hofstadter summed it up, they must die. Their essential function was that of a safety valve to let off steam which might otherwise explode the great North American two-party system.

Well, it is the role of history to examine and, if necessary, explode just such myths or laws. In Canada the historical record demonstrates pretty conclusively that our federalism, our immigration patterns, our parliamentary rather than presidential-congressional constitution, our deeply rooted regional identities, our personal proclivities, our isothermal lines, our east-west waterways, and our other peculiarities have sustained something other than a two-party system. From the day of the "loose fish" who flip-flopped from vote to vote in the nascent stage of political parties through W.S. Fielding's Nova Scotian secessionist reformers, Mercier's Parti National, Ontario's Patrons, the Progressives, the CCF-NDP, Social Credit, and the Parti Québécois it is clear that those periods in which we have had a two-party system are indistinct and at best an exception rather than a rule. Even in the classic period of 1896-1917 the rumblings of labor, farmers and Henri Bourassa enter many codicils to a two-party model.

Although most political scientists now concede that since at least 1921 it is virtually impossible to descry a genuine two-party system in Canada, it is the historically oriented scholar who is most likely to identify and stress the flaws in the penumbra of that lingering model. He will be less inclined to view our increasing propensity for minority government as an aberration, or the disturbing tendency of minor parties to survive (even through metamorphosis) as something that has to be explained by reference to deviations from a North American norm. The Lipset-Hartz-Hofstadter parlor game of "whatever happened to populism and socialism" is historically irrelevant to the Canadian condition. Congealed liberalism and separation of powers no doubt explain something about American politics, but the steady withering of American social-democratic minor parties from the peak 1912 presidential vote of slightly more than 6% is not to be understood by reference to a law established in the 1770s or at any other time. In the perception of Canadian politics an acquaintance with history helps to avert surprise as we note that Lester Pearson never had a majority during his tenure as prime minister, that Edward Schreyer presided over a creative minority government for four years, and that Pierre Trudeau, after arriving in a similar position in 1972, remarked with wry intellectual honesty: "we are more forced to listen… probably as a result of that some of our legislation will be better… we'll have to compromise."

In that 1972-74 parliament the "compromises" were so significant that, among other things, they became the foundation of a major Liberal shift toward economic nationalism. The NDP balance of power produced not only substantial increases in old age pensions and an income tax revision favoring lower income-earners, but also a Foreign Investment Review Agency, an oil-pricing policy which sheltered Canadians from OPEC price hikes, and the decision to establish a national petroleum company. For this kind of 'third party' power there is no comparison in American history; nor, for that matter, in Britain or in the coalition systems of western Europe, where the political bargaining is within a contractual rather than a fluid parliamentary situation. Nor can this unique Canadian political procedure be explained only as a function of the "recent" history of the 1972 election results. Its origins lie in our exotic mixture of responsible cabinet government and federalism. Specific instances of the flexibility and responsiveness of the system suggest also the inadequacy of monocausal explanations as well as the cumulative process of precedents.

The first significant and precisely identifiable use by a legislative party of a balance of power situation was in 1903. In that year, J.H. Hawthornthwaite's tiny Socialist Party of Canada contingent in the British Columbia legislature agreed to save the Conservative government from defeat in return for mine safety legislation which had theretofore received very low priority. In 1926, the foundations of our modern social security system were laid when Mackenzie King agreed to enact the first old age pension law in return for the crucial votes of only two labor MPs, J.S. Woodsworth and A.A. Heaps. The further opportunities of influencing national policies that arise from our relatively ample provincial jurisdictions are best illustrated by the ripple effect of innovative regional legislation—seen, for example, in the emulation of Ontario's original forays into public ownership with the Temiskaming and Northern Ontario Railway and the hydroelectric power system, or in the inexorable spread of public health insurance which followed the successful struggles of the Douglas government in Saskatchewan. And no doubt Premier William Davis will be able to add revealing comments about the impact of 'minority government' when he finds time to pen his memoirs. Sooner or later, people come to understand that to vote for a 'third party' candidate, whether one is a socialist, or social creditor or a nationaliste, is not a formula for 'losing' one's vote. And this immensely important difference between the Canadian and American political systems can be understood only by comprehending the evolution, the history, of the two political traditions.

The interaction in Canada of an increasingly flexible federal structure with regional identities and a sense of continuity that has been sustained and enhanced by monarchy, empire, commonwealth and special relationships with the francophone world, one which never suffered the constrictions of a unifying and centralizing civil war, or of cumulative apprehension, has produced a unique sense of ideas, structure and custom that defies the model maker. The whole point is the uniqueness, and this can *only* be understood by the attitudinal moraines deposited by history. The largely unwritten customs of our 1867 constitution are clearly not to be understood by simplistic reference to a Westminster model or a Turner-Beard-Hofstadter model. Those customs, and therefore our whole political life, are to be understood by reading the lives, letters, speeches and actions of the people who established them. The liberal British aristocrats who goaded, guided and responded to our political evolution; the land-grabbers, railway promoters, grain speculators, timber and other merchants; the defenders of religion, language and schools; the anticonscriptionists, strikers and protesters of all sorts—without knowing something about all this glorious melange and the people who tried to articulate Canadian beliefs and aspirations, the contemporary analyst will be about as secure as a goose on shell ice.

A few examples will illustrate the above argument; they may seem idiosyncratic but that is the nature of history. How can the political scientist explain the persistence of a monarchical structure in Canadian law and politics without reference to history? According to opinion polls, most Canadians today are unaware of the fact that we live in a monarchy, let alone that Queen Elizabeth is the Queen of Canada. Yet there is clearly resident in Canada a deep understanding of the continuities represented by monarchy and all its forms. Talk to any of the thousands of lawyers who are admitted every year to the various Canadian bars and you will find no perplexity in distinguishing between federal and provincial Crowns; but you may find some difficulty in comprehending the apparent ease with which these young men and women accept and work within an "illogical" structure. Again, why did the *rouge* Wilfrid Laurier think it wise to leave the power to disallow Canadian legislation in London? Why did the radical republican Mackenzie recant completely and return happily under amnesty to a colony of the British Crown? Why does the Lévesque government, heir to generations of francophone condemnation of the Manitoba Schools Act, justify its own school legislation with the argument that it will do for Québec what the earlier law did for Manitoba? Why did massive majorities, French- and English-speaking, endorse the proclamation of the War Measures Act in 1970? Why did Laurier accept a knighthood and Trudeau exhibit a functional and even leadership interest in the Commonwealth?

Facile answers to such thorny questions are many. The domination of the charter groups that man our power elites, the pervasive legacy of John Locke, the co-optative power of continentalism, our colonial complex, the class relations inherent in capitalism, geographic and natural resource determinants—any and all of these facts give clues to the meaning of the story. But it is the task of the historian, while taking account of all these facts and their implied methodologies, to try to weave them into a balanced account. Since historians are no more likely than other scholars to achieve objectivity, whatever that may be, the balance will vary from pen to pen, but if there is no balance the product will not be history. It is the special responsibility of the historian to stir into his mix the accidents, the vagaries of personality, and the concurrence of propitious or disadvantageous circumstances. He must deal pertinaciously with the "ifs" of the past and present. *Would* there have been two western rebellions if Louis Riel had not been born, or if he had been "sane"? Would there have been the monumental shift of Québec from the Conservatives to the Liberals if Macdonald had not decided to let Riel hang, though every dog in Québec might bark in his favor? What would have been the fate of democratic socialism had Woodsworth not been the product of his background—a Canadian Savonarola; or if the Lewis family had not possessed or developed its special blend of social conscience and political shrewdness? And need one recount the staggering array of "improbabilities" that bedeck the life and diaries of Mackenzie King?

In the midst of all the "ifs" and idiosyncrasies of the historian's selective process he will endeavor to derive patterns from his research. Yet even if he decides that Rome fell because of the triumph of Christianity and barbarism or that Canada is defined by the dominance of metropolitanism, he must put in the shading of personality, doubt and cumulative loyalties. The historian or political analyst who omits these real, if amorphous, forces from consideration will be unduly surprised by the present, and ill-prepared to discuss policy for the future. This implies a utilitarian role for history, and not by accident. If history must deal in particularities and probabilities rather than in laws, it nevertheless is "philosophy teaching by examples". Thus a historian who knows something about the continuities of political attitudes and customs will not be surprised by the reassertion in every kind of social crisis of the belief that order underlies liberty; that apparently authoritarian measures can be justified in defense of this principle as long as their application is followed by lenience and compromise. This is not a Canadian law, but it is a general pattern of sorts and justifies certain assumptions when policy has to be made.

Lack of attention to historical continuities often leads even the most perceptive contemporary observers into surprisingly ahistorical positions. One example is the editorial campaign of the *Toronto Star* to turn Canada into an American-style republic. Despite diligent use of market research techniques, the *Star* is unlikely to win its war against Canadian history, even with the aid of painfully obvious slanting of its coverage of the royal family. Another example was supplied by the courageous, libertarian former editor of *Le Devoir*. Claude Ryan was probably the most sophisticated political editor in the country, yet his response to the Québec election of 1970 and the federal election of 1972 betrayed a startling disregard for the validity and vitality of certain kinds of *collectivités* which he usually stressed. The underrepresentation of the Parti Québécois, which was widely assumed to be one reason for the October Crisis of 1970 in Québec, and the minority government "mess" in Ottawa, led Ryan to conclude that we should abandon our single-member constituencies and adopt proportional representation and formal coalition governments as is done in much of Western Europe.[10] He seemed to ignore several historical forces. One is that minor parties support proportional representation only as long as they are not within sight of governmental or official opposition status. One hears little of proportional representation from Péquistes or NDPers today. Another factor is our cumulative suspicion of coalitions; the flexibility of our evolving parliamentary-party system is not something that any of our parties is likely to give up lightly, as has been demonstrated most recently in Ontario. Finally, most Canadians do not agree that an injustice is suffered when a particular party fails to get a number of seats in a legislature directly proportional to its share of the popular vote. The historical evolution of constituencies as collective identities and the electing of legislators to represent them are even more important than academic adjustments of the popular vote across the country or across individual provinces. A West German model or a Scandinavian model may be intellectually gratifying, but it does not conform to Canadian history. As Mackenzie King said of Earl Grey, who tried to promote proportional representation in 1909, the governor-general was a "faddist".

When all is said and done, it remains the job of the historian to prevent faddism. While making use of the methods and findings of the social sciences he will remain essentially a conservative within the academic fold. It is never wise to ignore a conservative—especially in Canada.

SUMMARY

1. Enriched by the methods and findings of the social sciences, the historical craft has remained the essential integrator of every study relating to man.

2. Present Canadian political practices, problems and policies can only be understood in the context of historical events.

3. Political analysts are also historians, whether they accept the tag or not.

4. The essential role of the historian is that of integrator.

5. History is not only what has happened and the people or circumstances that made it happen; it is also the instrumentalities, methodologies and techniques employed by historians to delineate and analyse the past.

6. A social science emphasis on laws or models tends to minimize the vitally important, often "unwritten", and peculiarly Canadian characteristics in the structures, processes and norms of Canadian politics.

7. It is the role of history to examine and, if necessary, explode certain kinds of myths or "laws".

8. The customs of our constitution, and therefore our whole political life, are to be understood by reading the lives, letters, speeches and actions of the people who established them.

9. Since historians are no more likely than other scholars to achieve objectivity, whatever that may be, the balance will vary from pen to pen, but if there is no balance the product will not be history.

10. Lack of attention to historical continuities often leads even the most perceptive contemporary observers into surprisingly ahistorical positions.

STUDY QUESTIONS

1. In what ways are all social scientists historians?
2. To what extent is it correct to describe history as "the laboratory of politics"?
3. What are the major meanings of the term "history"?
4. Why has the relationship between social scientists and historians been peculiarly close in Canada?
5. How would you distinguish between studying recent political affairs as politics and as modern history?
6. Which major components of our political system have their roots in British politics?
7. What contemporary myths about Canadian politics would be exploded if Canadians studied history?
8. In what ways is history "utilitarian"?
9. If it is the job of the historian to prevent faddism, which academic fads need to be resisted at present?
10. To what extent is it accurate to say that Canada's present political problems go back to the 1867 Confederation agreement?

ENDNOTES

1. Henry St. John, Viscount Bolingbroke, *On the Study and Use of History, Letter 2.*
2. L. Hartz, *The Liberal Tradition in America* (New York: Anchor Press/Doubleday and Co., 1955) is in many respects elaboration of a thesis advanced by H.G. Wells in *The Future in America* (New York: Anchor Press/Doubleday and Co. 1906) and either ignores or dismisses evidence that does not support the thesis, such as the political history of the South. See further my exchange with Hartz in J.M. Laslett and S.M. Lipset, eds., *Failure of a Dream* (New York: Anchor Press/Doubleday and Co. 1974), pp. 397-424.
3. The relationship between the existence of a members' bar in the House of Commons and the caliber of speakers in the chamber has been previously noticed by an astute observer of Canadian politics who, like all effective political scientists, is three quarters historian. See Norman Ward, "The Formative Years of the House of Commons, 1867-91," *Canadian Journal of Economics and Political Science.* Vol. XVIII. 1952.
4. Carl Berger, *The Writing of Canadian History* (Toronto: Oxford University Press, 1976).
5. Canadian examples would include J.P. Wallot (on early nineteenth century French Canada), E.L. Shorter (on social patterns in Western Europe), Michael Katz (on nineteenth century urban classes in Ontario), and J.M. Beattie (on crime in eighteenth century England).
6. See, for example, Gad Horowitz (like his mentor, Louis Hartz, historian-by-courtesy) *Canadian Labour in Politics* (Toronto: University of Toronto Press, 1968)

Ch. 1; or S.B. Ryerson, *Unequal Union; Confederation and the Roots of Conflict in the Canadas, 1815-73* (Toronto: Progress Books, 1968).

7. Dean James Ham, School of Graduate Studies, University of Toronto, Convocation address, December 3, 1976.

8. H.J. Hanham, review of *Perspectives on the Social Sciences in Canada, Canadian Historical Review*, LVIII, No. 1 (March, 1977): 86.

9. See R. Twomey's perceptive article, "Capitalism, Society and the Rule of Law," *Bulletin of the Committee on Canadian Labour History*, 3 (Spring, 1977): 10-19.

10. *Le Devoir*, November 25, 1972.

SELECTED REFERENCES

Berger, Carl. *The Writing of Canadian History: Aspects of English-Canadian Historical Writing: 1900-1970.* Toronto: Oxford University Press, 1976. A pioneer work of historiography and intellectual history.

Bothwell, R., I. Drummond, and J. English. *Canada Since 1945: Power, Politics and Provincialism.* Toronto: University of Toronto Press, 1981. A fine interweaving of history, economics and politics.

Cook, G.R. *Canada and the French Canadian Question.* Toronto: The Macmillan Co., 1966. Demonstrates the importance of the history of ideas in studying the political process.

Fox, Paul. *Politics Canada.* 5th edition, Toronto: McGraw-Hill, Ryerson, 1981. Indispensable essays with a strong historical flavor.

Granatstein, J.L., and Paul Stevens, eds. *Canada Since 1867: A Bibliographical Guide.* Toronto: A.M. Hakkert, 1974. This is the best concise critical bibliography for post-Confederation trends in historical literature.

McNaught, Kenneth. "The Multi-Party System in Canada," *Essays on the Left*, eds., L. LaPierre et al. Toronto: McClelland and Stewart, 1971. An attempt to explain the historical reasons for rejecting an American (or any other) model.

_____. "Political Trials and the Canadian Political Tradition," *Courts and Trials*, ed. M. Friedland. Toronto: University of Toronto Press, 1975. A discussion of historial patterns as opposed to laws.

Millburn, Geoffrey. *Teaching History in Canada.* Toronto: McGraw-Hill, Ryerson, 1972. A stimulating collection of commentaries on the nature of history, including the interpretation of Canadian history.

Silver, A.I. "Some Quebec attitudes in an Age of Imperialism and Ideological Conflict." *Canadian Historical Review*, LVII, No. 4 (December, 1976). One of the best examples of the significance of careful intellectual history for understanding the political present.

Stone, Laurence. "The Revival of Narrative: Reflections on a New Old History", *Past and Present*, No. 85, 1979. A brilliant article, critical of the recent, temporary, flight from history.

Trudeau, Pierre Elliott. "The Practice and Theory of Federalism," *Social Purpose for Canada*, ed. M. Oliver. Toronto: University of Toronto Press, 1961. Still one of the most interesting applications of a historical perspective by a practising politician.

Part Two

Values Form the Foundation of Canadian Politics

The two chapters in this section argue that unless we have some knowledge of Canada's dominant belief systems and how they have developed, we have not really understood Canadian politics. These systems are important not only for knowledge of the general political climate but for decision-making in various political arenas.

In the first chapter, Professor Christian demonstrates the extent to which ideology has been and continues to be important in Canadian politics. Since ideologies are simultaneously descriptive and normative, their significance is sure to continue. Moreover, since belief systems influence behavior, we can only answer the most basic questions about Canadian politics by studying those belief systems, even though they may be vague and not easily stated. Obviously, knowledge of political ideologies and principles, of political beliefs and orientations, is vitally important.

The second chapter tells us much about political socialization and political culture. Culture denotes learned behavior patterns shared by groups of people. What is our mode of thinking, acting, feeling; our way of life? How do we acquire it? How do we express it politically? Without answering these questions, or at least understanding them, we are unable to comprehend the ideological basis of our entire political system. Professor Whittington spells out clearly the significance of political values and attitudes for political behavior and contrasts parochial, subject and participant political cultures.

Both chapters remind us that politics is largely the expression of values, debates about values, implementation of values and reactions to values. They also remind us that in a healthy, vibrant society there must be no minimization of thought about thought, especially thought about political thought.

5

Ideology and Politics in Canada

William Christian*

INTRODUCTION

"Words, words, words," complained a freshman Member of Parliament, elected to the House of Commons in 1980, after a career completely unrelated to politics. "All they ever do up there in Ottawa is talk. I was elected to get things done, and I want to get on with it."

It is likely that many Canadians share the frustration felt by this political neophyte. Businessmen are often the most vocal in their complaints. Those guys in the federal government, they say, are messing up the country, and what's more, they're trying to tell us how to run our businesses. Just look at them. Trudeau has never worked a day in his life; Broadbent was just a university professor; and as for Clark, what has he ever done? None of them has ever had to meet a payroll.

Businessmen and political novices would not be so outraged if they thought about politics for a bit. Take the word Parliament. The dictionary tells us that it comes from the Old French word *parlement* which meant speaking; it is related to the French verb, *parler*, which means to speak. So gardeners garden, farmers farm and politicians talk.

What is so surprising about this? We all talk. Gardeners, it is said, talk to their plants, and farmers talk to their animals. We might make matters a little clearer, then, by suggesting that it is the subject matter about which politicians talk that makes all the difference. And what they talk about is politics.

We use this word regularly, and with little difficulty in everyday speech; but unfortunately, if we consult those who ought to know what it means, we come away more than a little confused. Politics, some have said, concerns the

*Associate Professor, Political Studies Department, University of Guelph

authoritative allocation of values; others, more simply, have claimed that politics determines who gets what, where, why and how, or who dominates whom. Mao Tse-Tung told his comrades that political power grew out of the barrel of a gun, but more recently we have heard that politics is really about people.

I have, certainly, no desire to add another definition to an already extremely lengthy list. Out of this apparent confusion comes a glimmer of light. Politicians have a special relationship with words. Unlike soldiers who fight with tanks and rifles, politicians battle with one another using words. These struggles can take many different forms. There can be disputes over facts: How many people are unemployed? Did the government make a secret undertaking with a foreign power? There can be disagreements concerning the effectiveness of policies: Will a restriction in the money supply lead to a decline in the rate of inflation? Will the creation of a national milk marketing board solve the problems of overproduction in the dairy industry? But the most fundamental questions about which politicians dispute usually involve principles, or, to be more precise, the relative importance of principles. Here then the dispute is not about such matters as welfare programs, foreign aid, regionalism, tariffs, multiculturalism, immigration, state insurance, public regulation, the proprietary state, foreign resource development, Canadian culture, national security or any other of a great host of issues. It is rather about the importance of such central values as liberty, equality, hierarchy and tradition.

POLITICAL WORDS

The central importance of political words was highlighted in the seventeenth century by Thomas Hobbes. The eighteenth century Scottish writer, David Hume, also placed this element at the center of his understanding of political life. He drew attention to the "empire of opinion" as the single most important factor in securing the obedience of the mass of the populace to their political regime. Even if the soldiers who follow their commanders in a military takeover can subjugate the majority of the citizenry through terror or the threat of terror, they themselves obey their commanders for some reason other than fear of punishment. Usually they believe in the rightness of the actions taken by their leaders and give voluntary, and often enthusiastic, assent.

Almost every adult has at least some opinions about politics. These may not be particularly profound or coherent and many consist of a series of beliefs, such as "we pay too much tax" or "the government cannot be trusted". Such beliefs might be quite fragmentary and indeed even inconsistent: for example, someone might oppose strikes in the public sector, but favor a particular strike by policemen, firemen or nurses, without ever thinking it inconsistent.

These simple opinions about politics can be of two kinds. They can refer to beliefs either about what is, or about what ought to be. For example, Mr.

Trudeau ran into considerable criticism when he mused after the imposition of wage and price controls in 1975 that the free-enterprise system no longer existed in Canada. The prime minister appears to have taken it for granted that his observation about the existing situation was not controversial. But the reaction from the Canadian business community was swift and vigorous. Not only did businessmen deny that the free-enterprise system was dead, they also vigorously repudiated the suggestion they took to be implicit in the prime minister's remarks; namely, that it was not a bad thing that it was. Thus they also disagreed with Mr. Trudeau's beliefs, or at least suggestions, of what ought to be.

It is these kinds of opinions that the eighteenth-century Anglo-Irish political writer, Edmund Burke, called prejudice, and which he characterized as the wisdom of unlettered men. He thought that it represented an important aspect of political life and one that every serious student of politics would want to take into account. But this simple kind of opinion or prejudice has two grave limitations. First, it is not systematic. Traditions arise at various times and reflect the concerns of diverse ages. For example, Canadians are quite capable of responding to appeals for vigorous leadership, while at the same time lamenting the erosion of the independence of the private member of the House of Commons. Second, prejudice is not comprehensive. It touches political life only here and there. It may, for instance, yield a strong response in favor of or against continued Canadian contribution to NATO, but not about an Alaska oil or gas pipeline.

The search for a simple but complete description and explanation of political life has become increasingly urgent since the period of the French Revolution in the late eighteenth century. In North America, the increasing democratization of politics has been the catalyst for the search. As politics has become less and less the concern of a small and relatively homogeneous elite, and has more and more come to involve millions of men and women, there has developed a pressing need for a way to explain and justify political actions in terms that are intelligible to, or at least acceptable to, an electorate that has often been told that theirs is the only opinion about political affairs that matters. Hence we have witnessed since the 1820s and 1830s the development of various explanatory and justifying theories that we now recognize easily by the suffix "-ism": liberalism, conservatism, anarchism, Marxism, Leninism, Stalinism, Maoism, nationalism, fascism, national socialism, and many, many more. Even the word ideology itself was coined fairly recently, at least in historical terms, during the French Revolution. With these dogmas, political leaders offer their followers relatively systematic insights into the nature of political life, present, past and future.

IDEOLOGY

"The philosophers have only interpreted the world in various ways. The point however is to change it." This maxim of Marx adorns his tomb in London's

Highgate Cemetery. It captures the essence of what ideologies seek to do: they all try to move men to action. The ideologist is always a rhetorician, an artist with words. But unlike the novelist, poet or playwright, whose words aim at amusement or insight, the ideologist always selects his words carefully with a view to urging his listeners or readers to act, and not merely to believe. The conservative wants to preserve the state as it is; the revolutionary wants to destroy it and create another. The anarchist proclaims a pox on all states, and wants to destroy all organized power so that the free creative individual can flourish. All share the common hope that their followers will heed their words and will act in an appropriate way.

Consider now the relationship between those who develop or use an ideology and those who listen to it or follow it. How do political leaders make use of words to move citizens and voters in a democracy to action, especially the action of casting a vote for a particular political candidate or, in the context of most modern Western democracies, on behalf of a particular political party, or even for a particular political leader? It is obvious that the political slogans and arguments a politician can use come from a relatively limited range of ideologies. Liberals, conservatives and social democrats can secure a hearing in a country such as Canada and can turn that hearing into votes. But communists and fascists have never commanded an attentive audience in this country, or succeeded in securing widespread popular support. At times doctrines like Social Credit have gained a limited popular following, generally regionally concentrated. For the most part, however, Canadians have preferred to choose their political candidates from parties whose leaders have espoused one of the three ideologies mentioned above. Why is this the case?

IDEOLOGIES IN CANADA

There are two important lines of explanation. One is that offered by Professor Louis Hartz and his collaborators in *The Founding of New Societies* (1964), later modified by Gad Horowitz in *Canadian Labour in Politics* (1968). The second follows the general argument of George Grant, especially in *Lament for a Nation* (1965).

For Hartz the decisive factor about North and South America, South Africa, Australia and New Zealand was that they were "fragment" societies. By this Hartz meant that the emigrants from Europe did not represent all elements of the society they left. By the time this emigration began in earnest, the old European societies had broken with their feudal past and had generated liberal or bourgeois strains. The feudal period had been noteworthy for its emphasis on hierarchy and on organic unity, or collective solidarity as it might also be called. A number of factors had shattered the unity of the old society and had brought forth the bourgeois man, the independent individual, seeking to make his own way in the world and trying to discard the fetters of the old society. Although ultimately victorious, the bourgeois did not eliminate all the old feudal strains. These coexisted into the nineteenth century when some of the limitations of the liberal vision became apparent. Then a new force, socialism, emerged from a synthesis of the previous two movements in European history. The socialist shared with the feudal or tory strain the longing for social or communal solidarity but accepted the liberal's notion of the importance of freedom. The socialist, then, advanced the ideal of collective freedom and combined this with a value that was implicit but subordinate in the liberal's vision, namely, equality. In Europe all three traditions survived, though the latter two, liberalism and socialism, became preeminent.

In North America, to concentrate on the aspect of Hartz's analysis that is of special importance for us, the situation was different. As fragment communities, the American colonies, New France and later Canada, did not receive the full measure of their European inheritance. The immigrants to North America tended to be preselected. Those who went to the American colonies were predominantly liberal, whereas those who went to New France came from France before the liberal spirit had yet penetrated with force; they represented a more feudal strain. The "process of contagion" that was at work in Europe by which "ideologies give birth to one another over time" did not occur in the New World.[1] Having lost close contact with the jostling ideologies in Europe, the ideologies in the New World lost some of their original richness. In the United States the liberalism of John Locke became the prevailing ideology, whereas in New France a kind of feudal catholicism prevailed. These monolithic ideologies reacted to rivals by trying to assimilate or expel them.

Gad Horowitz, a Canadian political scientist, was particularly struck with the explanatory power of Hartz's hypothesis for Canada. With some important modifications, he thought that it could be made to explain two troubling features about Canadian politics. First, he argued, if we recognized that Canada, unlike the United States, had a greater tradition of ideological diversity, we could account for many important differences in the political life of the two countries, one of the most salient of which is the existence in Canada of a socialist movement which had attained a respectable level of electoral support. Second, we could also understand some of the reasons for the failure of this socialist movement, relative to Europe.

In *Political Parties and Ideologies in Canada* (1964), Colin Campbell and I consolidated this position along lines first suggested by the great Canadian social scientist, Harold Innis. We agreed with Horowitz that the presence of an electorally successful Canadian socialist movement was a key difference between the United States and Canada; and we also agreed with Horowitz that Canadian Liberalism, Canadian Conservatism and Canadian Socialism differed from those ideologies with similar names to the south. The process of ideological development we had studied convinced us that the Canadian pattern was much closer to the European than it was to the American, or to fragment communities in general. Although we recognized that there has been a considerable debate about the ideological nature of the United Empire Loyalists, it struck us that it could be generally admitted that the tory strains among the Loyalists shifted the ideological images of the two North American English-speaking settlements in such a way as to affect subsequent settlement, with the more liberally inclined choosing the United States and the more conservative immigrants preferring to retain contact with the mother country. Subsequent cultural, economic and political links with the United Kingdom reinforced the strength of the tory segment in Canada and gave it a substantial, but by no means dominant, presence.

Thus the stage was set for the later reception of British socialist ideas because Canada already contained the seeds out of which socialism could be generated. Just as Liberalism and Conservatism had adapted themselves to their new environment, Canadian Socialism grew out of indigenous forces. With the transformation of the Canadian party system in the aftermath of the First World War, the stage was set for the creation of an electorally successful socialist party during the Great Depression. Although this process took place a good deal later than in Europe, it was more analogous to the pattern there than to ideological developments, or lack of them, in the United States. The Canadian ideological system, therefore, did not congeal, but developed into the open-ended process of mutual exchange and influence that leaves the way open for future modifications.

In *Lament for a Nation* (1965), George Grant argued that the most likely future development would be, ironically, the destruction of just those tory and socialist aspects of the Canadian political conversation that differentiated it from the ideological structure of the United States. Although fundamentally at odds with one another, socialism and toryism did share this one important belief: that there were public goals of more importance than the satisfaction of private desires. In itself this may not sound like a striking assertion, but it was Grant's claim that the liberalism that was unchallenged in the United States and was becoming increasingly dominant in Canada denied just that point, and held the satisfaction of private desires to be the highest and indeed the only valid social goal. This aim was inherent in the notion of maximizing individual freedom, the keystone of liberalism. It was possible for the first time in the history of the world because modern science in harmony with modern technology held open the possibility of a total conquest of nature, both non-human and human, and hence held out the dream of man the unlimited creator, of Prometheus unbound. It was for this reason that Grant lamented the defeat of Canadian nationalism. He reiterated the same position in his collection of essays, *Technology and Empire* (1969): namely, that the triumph of Canadian liberalism entails the destruction of an independent Canadian state.

Grant's argument and the earlier thesis by Hartz share this in common: they both agree that the ideology known as liberalism is widely diffused and strongly held by the preponderant majority of English-speaking North Americans. This forms what some political scientists call the ideological environment; others refer to it as the political culture. I prefer to describe it as the political tradition. It might, of course, be possible in principle to test these hypotheses through public opinion polls, which are often adequate guides to the state of popular prejudice at any given time. However, they would not be reliable tests of the almost ineluctable progress toward ubiquitous liberalism that Grant fears, or the dialectical interchanges that Hartz admires.

ORIGINS OF OUR POLITICAL IDEAS

Be that as it may, most ordinary citizens do not have a comprehensive and conscious view of politics that they could readily articulate. As children, they will learn something about politics from their parents, from their parents' friends, from school, and from playmates. It is not at all uncommon to hear eight-, nine-, and ten-year olds discussing contemporary political issues with great vehemence and even greater confidence. As children grow into adolescence, school becomes a more important source of their ideas. They also begin to absorb ideas from other sources, such as the news media; even popular radio stations usually devote a small portion of each hour's broadcasting to spot news reports. This latter impact continues through life and often creates political attitudes in quite subtle and unintended ways. Work, marriage and age will modify these attitudes, but usually not in any fundamental way. The child is father to the man.

For most people active involvement in politics is limited. The majority vote in federal or provincial general elections, though far fewer in municipal elections, and note with varying degrees of pleasure or dismay news reports of parliamentary and governmental activities. A few make personal contributions of money, services or time during election campaigns and even fewer display an enduring or abiding willingness to be active in political life. Most are anxious to get on with the business of living and are content to leave politics to others.

These others are the politicians. Canada has been among the few nations to have inherited and then successfully adapted the British model of representative parliamentary government. For the most part this method of government proved unsuited to the needs, desires or capacities of the nations in Africa and Asia to which it was exported, but it did thrive in New Zealand, Australia and Canada. For our purposes, its salient features are as follows: relatively frequent elections based on universal suffrage; a reasonably fair system of representation by population; secret ballots; news media with considerable liberty to support or condemn particular policies, parties and candidates; and political parties with designated leaders. It is these institutions and practices that allow our representative system to operate in a satisfactory manner. They allow a coherence to develop between the latent ideology of the governed and the more explicit positions of the political parties. Politicians grow from the same political tradition as the voters to whom they appeal. They are subject to the dreams, illusions and myths of the civilization whose values they share, but they also play a role in the unfolding and developing of ideological principles by deepening them here, broadening them there, and, most important of all, applying them to the shifting maze of changing circumstances. Completeness and coherence of ideological vision as well as skill in inducing others to act in accordance with its imperatives, are the true marks of a politician.

Were it true that Canadian politicians from the time of Confederation and beyond have engaged in an endless series of brokerage transactions, reconciling the conflicting interests of manufacturer, farmer and merchant; Protestant and Catholic; French and English; East and West; center and periphery; men and women; rich and poor, then one would expect the history of ideological development in Canada to present the aspect of "a tale told by an idiot, full of sound and fury, signifying nothing." Yet nothing could be farther from the truth. The history of the leading Canadian political parties has a consistency that can best be understood by recourse to an explanation that assumes that voters, parties and leaders guide their activities by reference to ideas and principles that they inherit from their political tradition.

Before sketching this development it is useful to summarize the argument. People are social animals; they are also animals who think. Therefore, they have ideas about the nature of the political community in which they live and, more important, often have strong opinions about the way that their community ought to be reordered to make it better. For the most part, however, Canadians have not been a particularly reflective people, and indeed Sir John A. Macdonald once expressed with curious enthusiasm the view that he thought it improper to "waste the time of the legislature and the money of the people in fruitless discussions on abstract and theoretical questions of government."

WHY WE SHOULD STUDY IDEOLOGIES

There is much to be learned about Canadian politics from a careful examination of the ideas that have been central to its political tradition. First, we will no longer live under a delusion that our own politics are an inferior copy of the real thing in the United States. The allure of that country under its recent succession of presidents has rather diminished in recent years. Nonetheless, there are still many Canadians, especially those living within the range of American television signals, who appear unable to distinguish American from Canadian political events, or who still are fascinated by the global problems of managing an imperial foreign policy.

Americans are divided into what they call liberals and conservatives. This division arose in response to the Great Depression, and particularly the question of Franklin Roosevelt's policies to combat the misery it wrought. Roosevelt created a corporatist welfare state in the United States with his New Deal policies. Those who supported this extension of the state's activities, and wished to see them further extended in such areas as the food stamp program, called themselves liberals; those who thought that such developments represented the destruction of the American tradition of thrift, initiative and private enterprise described themselves as conservatives.

In Canada the division was never as clear cut. By 1935 both Liberals and Conservatives agreed that the state must take steps to alleviate the hardship of economic dislocation; and ironically, it was the Liberals who were shocked by the dramatic interventionist measures proposed by Conservative Prime Minister R.B. Bennett. Both major Canadian political parties came to agree, though for different reasons, that our society and economy would function best if co-operation, rather than conflict, prevailed in the relationship between government, industry and the trade union movement.

Broadly speaking, the same approach was adopted by the mainstream of the Canadian Socialist movement. In the United States, socialism appeared in a Marxist guise, emphasizing the inevitability of conflict between the owning and the laboring classes, and pointing in the direction of a violent revolution as the only means of overcoming this division in society. Although Canadian socialism contained a Marxist element, its dominant tone was set by the great leader of the Canadian left in the 1920s and 1930s, J.S. Woodsworth. Woodsworth took the lead in 1932-33 in founding the Cooperative Commonwealth Federation (CCF), the party that was to carry the banner of Canadian Socialism until it was replaced by the New Democratic Party in 1961. As the party's name suggests, Woodsworth saw co-operation between all classes of Canadians as the future of the country; and he thought that the co-operative commonwealth should be established by a democratically elected government that had successfully persuaded the majority of the Canadian people of its inherent desirability.

Thinking about ideologies will help us to understand that Canada is not simply a poorer, generally inferior, version of the United States with a tenth of the population, lacking a nuclear arsenal and a space program. We live instead, in a country with a powerful political tradition all our own. There is another advantage that accrues to us by looking into the history of the ideologies of Canadian political parties. By accepting uncritically the analysis of most political scientists that there were no significant issues of principle that divided the Liberals and the Conservatives, we have ignored an extremely important analytical element in understanding the dynamics of Canadian political life.

Mackenzie King was often understood by his contemporaries to be the consummate manipulator of interests and interest groups, concerned only with what would bring partisan success to the Liberal Party. But King, and I am sure he was right about this, did not see his own career in this light. As he confided in his diary, "...Pasteur's Law of Peace, Work and Health...became the thesis of my *Industry and Humanity*. Indeed it has been the basis of most of my work since. A sort of star guiding along my work since."[2] King himself saw with extreme clarity what political scientists, historians, journalists and the general public have often misunderstood, namely, that political activity, when successful, is necessarily a blend of settled principles and changing circumstances. As King noted, "It was necessary to have fundamental principles but their application in relation to both time and space was the essence of politics."[3]

Many New Democrats chide what they call the old line parties with being as indistinguishable as Tweedledum and Tweedledee. However useful this caricature might be for electoral purposes, we can never understand the dynamics of political debate either within or between parties if we believe this charge. To be good political observers, we must make careful note of the stable principles that underlie the policies adopted by each of the major Canadian parties. These principles guide, but also limit, their capacity to respond to changing national problems. It is time to look at these principles and their embodiment in the concrete realities of political life.

CANADIAN LIBERALISM

The Liberal party in Canada has been the preeminent feature of federal electoral and parliamentary life in the twentieth century: Laurier was prime minister from 1896 to 1911; King from 1921 to 1930 and 1935 to 1948 with a brief break in 1926; St. Laurent from 1948 to 1957; Pearson from 1963 to 1968; and Trudeau from 1968 to 1979, and from 1980 to the present. In all the Liberal party has formed the government for about sixty of the first eighty-two years of this century.

As Canada's electorally most successful federal political party the Liberals have stood for an appropriately wide range of policies, many of which have shown little apparent relationship to the central tenets of Liberalism. But on issues that were to have a decisive effect on the nature of the Canadian polity, it can be demonstrated that Liberal policies have been remarkably consistent. The salient concerns have been twofold. In the first place, Liberals have taken as their major concern the condition of the individual. Put so starkly, this may seem like an odd principle, indeed one that was hardly likely to be opposed. But it must be remembered that organized society often puts forward claims on behavior and belief that seem oppressive. Subordinate groups, be they corporations or trade unions, often behave in an aggressive way to members and non-members alike. It is against the claims of social groups, including the nation, that Liberalism elevates the individual. Recent reforms of the laws governing abortion and divorce bear the imprint of this principle.

Second, Liberals have been concerned with enhancing freedom. Modern science allied with modern technology has opened up possibilities that are still being dreamed. The politician, of course, paints on a circumscribed canvas, but there can be little doubt that Canadian Liberalism has accepted in principle that more freedom is intrinsically desirable, as Pierre Trudeau's repeated and finally successful attempts to entrench a charter of rights and freedoms in the Canadian constitution clearly showed.

Within Canadian Liberalism, there have developed two conceptually distinct strands. Both share the fundamental concern for individual freedom, but they differ on how best to realize it. The first of these strains I shall call business liberalism because it is a doctrine that historically and at present has a strong appeal among businessmen and those who support business interests. This doctrine takes the view, so eloquently enunciated in the nineteenth century by writers such as John Stuart Mill, that the state is the institution most likely to restrict individual freedom. Although businessmen are most interested in avoiding restrictions on their own economic affairs, they also tend to be most suspicious of government initiatives generally.

The rival strain I call welfare liberalism. This traces its intellectual roots to the nineteenth-century English writer, T.H. Green. It took its original political inspiration from the British chancellor of the exchequer and subsequent prime minister, the Liberal Lloyd George, and later from the rhetoric and practice of the American President, Franklin Roosevelt. Rather than fearing the state, welfare liberals look to it as the most effective social institution available to free citizens from other forms of restrictions, including those imposed by large business organizations. Both business and welfare liberals talk the language of freedom, with its corollary, the language of rights. Their debate, though at times spirited, may sometimes become a dull and lifeless thing, because it is a debate within an ideology, not between ideologies. It involves men who are in fundamental agreement over basic values, and in disagreement only over the most appropriate means to achieve those ends.

These two strains came out clearly in the Liberal party platform of 1957: "The Liberal party believes in the minimum of interference and control by the state...and is opposed to any scheme of overall control of the economy; but it is in favour of intervention by the government when required to meet the needs of the people."[4] The welfare liberal element made its first major inroads into official Liberalism in the convention of 1919 that chose Mackenzie King as Sir Wilfrid Laurier's successor. It was here that the Liberal party pledged itself "in so far as may be practicable," and "having regard for Canada's financial position" to introduce "an adequate system of insurance against unemployment, sickness, dependence in old age, and other disability, which would include old age pensions, widows' pensions, and maternity benefits."[5] King himself had realized that there might appear to be some superficial resemblance between the ideas he was pressing and socialism, and was therefore especially anxious to indicate that both the pedigree and the aspirations of his program were securely in the liberal tradition. He recognized that intervention by the state might necessitate "some interference with individual liberty" but he urged that "where wisely applied and enforced, it is an immediate restriction, that a wider liberty in the end may be secured."[6] In regard to the regulation of industrial concerns, he put the difference between a liberal approach and socialism as follows: "It is the business of the state to play the same part in the supervision of industry as is played by the Umpire in sports to see that the mean man does not profit in virtue of his meanness, and on the other hand that nothing should be done which will destroy individual effort and skill. Some may term this legislation Socialism, but to my mind it is individualism."[7]

As we shall see, this apparent similarity between some of the measures favored by welfare liberalism, and those advocated by socialists and social democrats, added a major degree of flexibility to Canadian party policies. It meant that King could introduce old-age pension legislation in the 1920s in response to the urgings of J.S. Woodsworth and more significantly, that he could persuade the Liberal party to adopt a wide-ranging collection of social welfare measures during 1943 and 1944 when the CCF was posing its most serious electoral threat. It should be clear from the preceding discussion that King was not adopting socialist measures only or even mainly because of supposed political expediency, but instead was responding to a deep strain of humanitarian liberalism. King himself was neither insensitive to the arguments of business liberalism nor unaware of the strength of the business liberal element within his party. But hesitation in the face of conflicting ideological pressures within the party, and concern for the popular reception of proposed policies, does not deny a fundamental ideological concern. Rather, King's obsession with the timing of the introduction of his measures reflected an acute perception of the extent to which the politician's understanding of the implications of an ideological position can be out of step with the electorate's. King's unfolding of the implication of Canadian Liberalism had to await subsequent ideological development in the electorate; King was a Liberal, but he was manifestly not in a hurry. His refusal to be publicly out of harmony with either his party or the voters was rewarded by phenomenal political success.

To show that King's dominance over Canadian Liberalism from 1919 to 1948 was not repudiated by his successors, we can quickly note several subsequent reiterations of what I have identified as the hallmarks of Canadian Liberalism. In 1948, the convention that chose Louis St. Laurent as Liberal leader affirmed that: "Liberal policies are those which protect, sustain and enlarge the freedom of the individual. The Liberal...believes in freedom because he believes the resources of human personality and endeavour to be rich and varied beyond calculation or prediction."[8] And later Lester Pearson wrote in his *Introduction* to Jack Pickersgill's pamphlet on the Liberal party that: "The fundamental principle of Liberalism...is belief in the dignity and worth of the individual...the first purpose of government [is] to legislate for the liberation...of human personality."[9] Not surprisingly we see similar principles advocated by Pierre Trudeau: "The first visible effect of freedom is change. A free man exercises his freedom by altering himself and—inevitably—his surroundings. It follows that no liberal can be other than receptive to change and highly positive and active in his response to it, for change is the very expression of freedom."[10]

Canadian Liberalism has, as we have seen, held to these central understandings and values throughout most of its history. Can we conclude that Canadian Conservatism as manifested in the Progressive Conservative party (and its predecessors under several different names) and Canadian Socialism as manifested in the New Democratic party and prior to that in the Cooperative Commonwealth Federation, were similarly unalloyed? Did these parties present voters with stark and clear alternatives? For the most part they did not. That is no great problem to understand since a certain amount of ideological overlap is not only convenient, but is probably a necessary condition for stable democratic politics. It might be superficially appealing to see political parties contesting for power and presenting voters with striking alternatives, but to the extent that these rival views represent fundamentally incompatible modes of community life, the ever-present danger would be that the party in power might not relinquish office peacefully after an electoral defeat if it anticipated that all its good work would be undone by its rival. Jurisdictions where ideological disputes are deep present a sad panorama for supporters of parliamentary and representative government; Northern Ireland, South Africa, Lebanon, Pakistan, Chile and Argentina are only a few recent examples of many spectacular failures.

Canadian Conservatives and Canadian Socialists have offered up an ideological menu of considerably greater variety than Canadian Liberals. Let us look first at the older of the two, Canadian Conservatism.

CANADIAN CONSERVATISM

There are four elements that we can identify as making major contributions to Canadian Conservatism. These are toryism, nostalgia, hostility to rapid change, and business liberalism. This is obviously a bit of a mixed bag, but each separate element is important. Consider toryism first. George Grant and others have told us that one of the distinguishing features of Canada is that it was founded by men who were committed to an orderly, stable, hierarchical and nondemocratic society. It was not by accident that they held these views, and not merely through contemplation of the society to the south, though the horror with which they reacted to developments there to a large extent sharpened their determination not to make the same mistakes. The British North America Act speaks, so this argument runs, in terms of "Peace, Order and Good Government", not "Life, Liberty and the Pursuit of Happiness." Although in Canada representation by population was introduced for the lower house, this democratic notion did not run to universal or even to manhood suffrage; and, moreover, an undemocratic Senate, with members appointed for life to insulate them from electoral pressure, was created and endowed with powers virtually equal to those of the House of Commons. Significantly, Canada was to remain a constitutional monarchy; it was the British, not Macdonald, who opposed the name, Kingdom of Canada.

This toryism had dual roots in Canada. In Québec the Catholic Church had preserved the feudal inheritance from France against the dangerous liberal ideas of the English-speaking traders and merchants. In English Canada, as we have seen, a number of factors were at work. Immigration to British North America, especially after the American Revolution, was not charged with the same ideological character as was immigration to the United States. The United Empire Loyalists, although not a homogeneous social or ideological group, had known a society in ferment and transition and did not wish to experience it again in their new-found home. The proximity of the United States reinforced their tory tendencies and these gained support from some of the later immigrants. This is not to suggest that English-speaking Canada was ever monolithically tory. Quite the contrary! Nobody doubts that liberalism forms the central core of the Canadian political tradition, but there was at least a strong tory element in Canada from the beginning and this element has not been totally destroyed by subsequent developments.

The second element of the Conservative ideological mix is nostalgia. Clearly this longing for the past is not the exclusive property of any political party, or even of politics itself. It is a universal human emotion, but it does not strike all with the same intensity or frequency. At times, however, it comes to be predominant in certain men and certain situations. Arthur Meighen was certainly subject to it in his views on both social and imperial relations. More recently, John Diefenbaker made nostalgia a potent political weapon, one which had, for a time, a significant electoral appeal.

Nostalgia is closely associated with the third Conservative element, a disposition to be hostile to rapid change. Again, this is a well-nigh universal attitude, though it is more powerful in some than in others. It is my contention that the tory strain in Canadian Conservatism has made this party throughout its history the most attractive choice for those whose character or situation leads them to find nostalgia or caution appealing.

From its inception, however, the Progressive Conservative party, or Liberal-Conservative party as it was known for the greater part of its history, has espoused business liberalism as well. This combination of toryism and business liberalism is not at all strange, though these two doctrines are logically incompatible. Like welfare liberalism and socialism, they can serve as useful allies. The business liberal can concede the maintenance of social hierarchy to toryism, and in return can expect that the tory collectivist view of the national interest will be strongly colored by the needs and interests of the business community. Indeed no political thinker in the middle of the nineteenth century in Canada could have hoped to gain the electoral support of the property-owning electors without adopting liberalism in some guise. It was Macdonald's great insight that tory and business liberals could be brought into alliance around the National Policy, with its program of the acquisition of the West, the building of a trans-continental railway, and the protective tariff, that stands as the greatest tribute to the breadth of his ideological vision.

It was the Liberal, Laurier, more than anyone else, who set the tone for the future ideological development of Canadian Conservatism. His brilliant success in undermining the Conservative party's support in Québec slowly isolated the tory element in English Canada from the collectivism and hierarchism of the *bleu* tradition in French-Canadian society. Combined with Macdonald's fateful decision to allow the execution of Louis Riel, the stamp was increasingly set on the Conservatives as the party of English business liberalism. They were cut off from precisely that segment of Canadian society, the rural Catholics of Québec, for whom toryism was a powerfully compelling ideology. Under Borden and

Meighen the liberal aspect of Canadian Conservatism became increasingly powerful.

Nonetheless there remained within Canadian Conservatism an element that manifested itself in the form of a belief in the primacy of politics over economics, the view that it was the responsibility of the government to ensure that the interests of the nation were considered as paramount, superseding all others, including those of the business community. It was this aspect of Canadian Conservatism to which George Grant drew attention when he wrote that Socialism and Conservatism in Canada both protect "the public good against private freedom."[11] It would be wrong to exaggerate this element in Canadian Conservatism, but it would be even worse to ignore it.

R.B. Bennett's unsuccessful New Deal legislation of 1935 is a case in point, and no one who reads the texts of Bennett's radio addresses can fail to notice the subordination of private interests to the national need in a time of grave crisis. Nevertheless, by 1935 this older tradition had become recessive. In the 1920s, 1930s and early 1950s Canadian Conservatism relied increasingly on business liberalism for its public appeal. The tory element in the party served as a check on the transformation of the party's doctrine into welfare liberalism, while giving it a residual element of ideological flexibility it was loathe either to lose or use. The historian R.H. Wilbur commented very shrewdly on the significance of this strain in his biography of H.H. Stevens, one of Bennett's cabinet ministers who broke with the Conservatives in the 1935 election, and formed the Reconstruction Party which received half a million votes that might otherwise have gone to the Conservatives.

> ...both Harry Stevens and James Woodsworth represented vital, historic, and separate streams of Canadian conservatism. Woodsworth was the red tory in Canadian politics, Stevens the tory democrat or populist... The Conservative party remained out of office from 1935 to 1957 not because Stevens, or Bennett for that matter, had wrecked the party or because of the cleverness of Mackenzie King. It was because the Conservative and CCF leaders failed to see that they represented two continuing forces of Canadian toryism.[12]

It was left to John Diefenbaker to revive and attempt to transform the ailing Conservative party. He brought to the leadership not only a personality and eloquence rarely seen in Canadian political life, but also an understanding of the party that was quite uncongenial to the Montréal and Toronto business interests that had come to dominate it. The liberalism to which he had been exposed in his youth was the welfare liberalism of the Progressive movement. But the potential radicalism that led many other Prairie liberals toward socialism, or at least social democracy, was restrained in Diefenbaker by a nostalgic toryism. Diefenbaker's toryism gave him just the element he needed to reconcile and reassure, at least temporarily, the business liberal element within the party. In his campaigns of 1957 and 1958 he offered the voters a skillful amalgam of policies reflecting business liberalism (fiscal responsibility), welfare liberalism (increased pensions), and toryism (loyalty to Crown and Common-wealth). This combination was especially powerful in the mid-1950s. Canadian Liberalism had substantially narrowed the scope of its ideological vision during the leadership of Louis St. Laurent, especially under the influence of his senior cabinet minister, C.D. Howe, who looked unfavorably on the welfare liberal aspects of his party's ideology. This ideological restriction gave Diefenbaker's Conservatism much room.

Under Diefenbaker, however, Canadian Conservatism was a welter of contradictions that could not withstand close analysis and that disintegrated when called on to guide a government. Diefenbaker's failure demonstrates clearly the need for political leaders to have relatively coherent ideologies. His failure to forge a new alliance between toryism and liberalism allowed Lester Pearson to regain a precarious hold on power by bringing the welfare and business aspects of Liberalism into balance once again.

It was Diefenbaker's successor, Robert Stanfield, who articulated the needs of the new toryism with wisdom, if not eloquence. In a memorandum to caucus dated November 14, 1974, he summarized the principles for which he thought Canadian Conservatism stood. There he acknowledged the role the old toryism had played in the party: "Resistance to changes and the support of privilege has [sic] been a part of the behaviour of Conservatives from time to time, but neither is nor ought to be Conservative principle." He went on to outline what he thought the Conservative party should stand for:

> Conservatism recognized the responsibility of government to restrain or influence individual action where this was in the interests of society. Whether a government should or should not intervene was always a question of judgment, of course, but the Conservative tradition recognized the role of governments as the regulator of individual conduct in the interests of society....
>
> The emphasis on the nation as a whole, on order, in the Conservative tradition that I have described, was surely seldom more relevant than it is today.... This is a period when true Conservative principles of order and stability should be most appealing.... Again I emphasize that these kind of bedrock principles are national in scope and reflect an overriding concern for society at large. Enterprise and initiative are obviously important; but will emphasis upon individual rights solve the great problems of the day; I mean the maintenance of acceptable stability, acceptable employment, and an acceptable distribution of income. Would we achieve these goals today by a simple reliance on the free market, if we could achieve a free market?
>
> It would certainly be appropriate for a Conservative to suggest that we must achieve some kind of order if we are to avoid chaos; an order which is stable, but not static; an order therefore which is reasonably acceptable and which among other things provides a framework in which enterprise can flourish. That would be in the Conservative tradition.[13]

Stanfield's memorandum provoked a lively interchange within the Conservative caucus, itself testimony to the ideological diversity of the party. The most eloquent and insightful of the responses came from Perrin Beatty, then only twenty-four years old. Beatty showed a penetrating insight into the fundamental traditions of the party when he wrote:

> We have to begin by realising that freedom, dignity, pride, compassion, and a sense of industry are not the gift of government—they are the property of the individual. Except insofar as government is needed to create sufficient order for an individual to achieve his own potential, these qualities cannot be legislated. But government can quickly take them away.
>
> In my opinion the primary function of government is to ensure that the individual can live his life in his own way, free from unwarranted intrusion and in a climate of sufficient order essential to freedom within society.[14]

Beatty is here drawing on the business liberal tradition in the Conservative Party, but he sees clearly that that tradition must be melded with the tory heritage, "a climate of sufficient order". In addition, Beatty incorporated elements of tory democracy, or tory populism, into his ideological vision, to broaden and deepen its political appeal.

> I believe that the Progressive Conservative Party should be the voice of the Canadian who does not belong to powerful organized groups—the small businessman, the senior citizen, the family farmer, the housewife, the young, and the unorganized worker. Both in terms of numbers and of their contributions to our country, these people are the mainstay of our society.[15]

Seven years later, Beatty brought these principles together in a powerful attack on the Liberal government's constitutional resolution. In the House of Commons he appealed to the Conservative Party's sense of tradition, its recognition of diversity and its respect for individual rights. As he put it:

> I pray that [Canada] will never become a homogenized society. I come from rural Ontario where diversity is a source of pride and where various groups have maintained their ethnic and traditional cultures. This has helped enrich the whole of our society. They have maintained their right to freedom of religion, and I hope that we will never find ourselves in a situation where those rights are taken away.
>
> Why are we proposing when it comes to the very essence of federalism, and the rights of people to maintain historical legislation, historical traditions, historical ways of life, that these be suddenly swept away by Ottawa and this juggernaut? I say that this is wrong and it is something which this party cannot support.[16]

Not long ago it would have been thought nonsense to talk about Canadian Conservatism in ideological terms; yet by the time of the Conservative leadership convention in 1976 even journalists were attempting an ideological analysis of the positions of the various candidates. The candidates themselves took these matters seriously, and the single most dramatic event of the candidates' speeches occurred when the former Liberal minister, Paul Hellyer, attacked the "red tories" in the party. The convention revealed with brilliant clarity the extent to which the Progressive Conservative party still exists as a coalition of disparate ideological groups. As Jim Gillies put it in a newsletter to delegates: "Red Tory. Blue Tory. Nobody has to tell you about these divisions. They're real. And they've hurt us at the polls. And in part, this leadership contest is a contest for control of the party being waged between different groups."[17]

In the first edition of this book, I wrote, soon after Joe Clark had been elected leader, that it remained to be seen whether he would be successful in welding these disparate groups into a new ideological synthesis. The election of May 1979 brought his government into power, and the election of February 1980 ushered the Progressive Conservatives back into opposition. What sort of vision inspired Joe Clark?

The answer to this question does not give great confidence to those who had hoped for a new vision from Canadian Conservatism. In his first address to Parliament as Prime Minister, Clark spoke of the measures which his government aimed to promote. Then, he talked of open government, a strengthened role for Parliament, Canada as a community of communities, a more flexible spirit in federal-provincial relations and a determination "to place much greater reliance on the private sector, and the private sector broadly defined, whether in terms of business or in terms of volunteer agencies, to achieve our economic and social goals."[18]

In itself, such a program does not amount to an ideology, which I have taken in this chapter to mean a more or less coherent set of principles which serve as a guide to action. James Gillies, Clark's chief policy advisor, suggested that "philosophically, (Joe Clark's) pretty close to neo-conservatism...." This ideology Gillies defined as marked by a belief in the withdrawal of the federal government from some social services, fewer services, fewer laws and fewer trade barriers.[19]

David MacDonald, Secretary of State in the Clark government, did not treat his leader as quite such a doctrinaire. He suggested that Clark was "pink with blue tinges", by which he meant that Clark was a welfare liberal on such matters as human rights, minority groups and cultural issues, but a business liberal when it came to matters of economic policy. As for the inner cabinet as a whole, MacDonald felt that it represented a coalition of diverse ideological groups, running "from bright red through pink to good solid shades of blue."[20]

That Canadian Conservatism represents an ideological compromise, and that this compromise is reflected in opposition and in government cannot be in doubt. As for Joe Clark's own ideological position, it still remains obscure. Perhaps the most perceptive comment on this matter was made by Geoffrey Stevens before the election which brought the Conservatives their temporary victory.

> There are a couple of reasons, I think, for Mr. Clark's aversion to taking positions which are rooted in principle. The first is simple expediency; he does not want to offend any segment of the electorate whose votes he needs.
> The other reason may be Mr. Clark's uncertainty about where he wants to go, what he wants to accomplish...he has not developed much of a personal

body of thought. Mr. Clark wants to be Prime Minister. He thinks he can manage the country better than Pierre Trudeau. But manage it to what end? Where does he want to lead the country?[21]

Those who doubt the significance of ideology for the Liberals and the Conservatives should consider well Stevens' words together with the fate of the Clark Government.

CANADIAN SOCIALISM

If it used to be disputed whether or not there was much of an ideological difference between the Liberals and the Conservatives, at least there was never much disagreement that the Cooperative Commonwealth Federation and the New Democratic Party represented a distinct and radical alternative. Two features stand out in connection with the electoral success of Canadian Socialism. First, and unlike most socialists in the United States, Canadian Socialists have for the most part been flexible rather than dogmatic and doctrinaire. They have looked for inspiration to the British Labour party and to the Social Democrats in Sweden, rather than to German Marxists. Second, and in this they also differ from American socialists, they have usually sought to make an electoral impact in alliance with welfare liberalism, rather than as a pure ideology.

We have seen in the analysis of the political traditions in the United States and Canada, that the former country lacks the presence of a distinct feudal or tory strain from which a socialist response could emerge. In contrast, Canadian toryism made collectivist modes of thought acceptable, and toryism's defense of privilege gave socialists a real ideological target. How much harder it must have been in the United States where the public philosophy held that all men were created equal! These egalitarian protests against privilege could, in Canada, take on a collectivist hue, and hence produce in the combination of collectivism and egalitarianism, an indigenous Socialism. Woodsworth put the case clearly in an attempt to steady the direction of the newly formed CCF:

> Undoubtedly we should profit by the experience of other nations and other times, but personally I believe that we in Canada must work out our own salvation in our own way. Socialism has so many variations that we hesitate to use the class name. Utopian Socialism and Christian Socialism, Marxian Socialism and Fabianism, the Latin type, the German type, the Russian type—why not a Canadian type?[22]

In addition to the indigenous ideological material which existed in Canada, and from which Socialism could be generated, it is appropriate to mention three other sources that made important contributions. First there was the inspiration of the Social Gospel movement. Especially in the West, there were Christian ministers, generally of evangelical inclination, who rejected the notion that they should restrict their attention to the care of the souls in their pastoral charge, and preferred instead to devote their energies to social trans-formation. The first leader of the CCF, J.S. Woodsworth, came from this background. When faced with the problem of the immigrants in Winnipeg, Woodsworth cried out that they posed "a challenge to the church" and demanded that it no longer "merely preach to the people". In future it ought to "educate them and to improve the entire social conditions."[23] Woodsworth's *My Neighbour* indicated even more clearly the change from a concern for eternal, to one for secular, salvation. "Someone is responsible! Every unjustly treated man, every defenceless woman, every neglected child has a neighbour somewhere. Am I that neighbour?"[24]

Second, there was the continuing immigration from the United Kingdom. The ideological structure of Canada had not congealed in the same way as that in the United States, and as a consequence immigrants from Great Britain, who arrived bearing socialist ideas that had developed in their native land in the century and a half since the American Revolution, were not rejected out of hand as strange and alien. Although some brought with them a more extreme kind of socialism, the failure of the One Big Union and the Winnipeg General Strike of 1919 to create a serious revolutionary movement persuaded most Canadian Socialists to stay with the British Labour tradition, with its emphasis on reform through electoral and parliamentary means.

Finally, and this factor was very significant, by about 1900 the Canadian trade union movement had been converted to Gomperism. This doctrine, named after the American trade union leader Samuel Gompers, emphasized the principle of bread-and-butter unionism, stressing that unions should use their strength to obtain better wages and working conditions for their members through direct bargaining with employers rather than through legislation. Politically, the trade union movement was to work within the framework of the established political system, supporting friends of labor within either of the major parties, wherever they were to be found. Indeed, Wilfrid Laurier achieved a notable success in weaning the trade unionists away from the Conservatives, and in establishing the Liberal party as the chief beneficiary of their support. In this he was aided by the young Mackenzie King who in 1909 became Minister of Labor. This victory of Gomperism meant that for the most part the Canadian trade union movement, representing the most politically active and conscious part of the working class, leaned in a Liberal rather than a Socialist direction. The attempt to forge close ties with the trade union movement was perhaps even more significant than the search for electoral success, in imbuing Canadian Socialism with a strong liberal element.

It is impossible here to trace the ebb and flow of the doctrinal compromises that mark the history of both the CCF and the NDP. It is enough to note Walter Young's observation about the CCF, which applies equally well to the NDP: their "liberalism kept them from becoming communists while their socialism prevented them from becoming liberals."[25]

Canadian Socialism had to wait until 1961 to consummate its formal alliance with the trade union movement. A growing number of unions felt that Gomperism was unsatisfactory in a parliamentary system with as strong a tradition of party discipline as Canada's; individual members of parliament, however sympathetic to labor they might be, were unlikely to defy the party whip in order to support labor's cause against the policies of their party. As a consequence it was thought necessary for the labor movement to ally with a political party dedicated to advancing its cause. This alliance involved the infusion of a heady dose of the welfare liberalism favored by the trade union movement into the ideology of the New Democratic Party. This new balance has not lacked critics.

In 1971 the leadership convention that met in Ottawa to choose the successor to T.C. Douglas was faced with an intense and dramatic challenge from a socialist faction with the party; known as the "Waffle", it chose the relatively obscure James Laxer as its candidate. The strength of his showing (he ran second to the heir-apparent David Lewis who enjoyed the confidence and support of the vast majority of trade union delegates), indicated the depth of dissatisfaction with the liberal-socialist ideological mixture within the party. Lewis's success was followed by the isolation and destruction of the Waffle movement as a challenge to the party's ideological compromise, but the NDP convention that met in 1975 to choose David Lewis's successor was also split ideologically.

This time there were two candidates from the parliamentary caucus, Ed Broadbent, the eventual winner, and Lorne Nystrom, as well as three candidates from outside the caucus who presented challenges in various ways to the more moderate parliamentarians. Douglas Campbell, a perennial contender for NDP leaderships at various levels, represented an extreme and almost revolutionary brand of Socialism which the NDP has strongly and consistently combated. His appeal, of which the following is a representative sample, fell on deaf ears and he was quickly eliminated from the race.

> Cuba, Portugal and Vietnam have shown us how to stand up to the last bastion of decaying capitalism—the U.S.A. and its colonies—Canada, Britain, etc. We must unite with our progressive sisters and brothers of this planet and break the chains of capitalism.
> We have nothing to lose but our chains.[26]

John Harney, a former member of the NDP federal caucus, also offered a more distinctive socialist appeal, though he eschewed Campbell's Marxist rhetoric.

> Should I be chosen by you to be leader, I promise you nothing but renewed effort and hard work, a total dedication to the socialist, democratic and egalitarian principles which move and guide us all, and a burning hope that someday this Party, during or after my leadership, will be chosen to shape the destiny of this nation to the kind of greatness we socialists all desire.[27]

Rosemary Brown from British Columbia made the attack on the party's ideological moderation that struck the most responsive chord among the delegates. She offered the following pledge:

> That I will never forget that our party has its roots in the prairie soil, where it grew in spite of the dust and depression, fed by sweat and tears and the passionate hatred of injustice:
>
> that I will never forget that we are the party of the working people, and that our task and our duty is to bring them legal and moral justice in the face of attacks from power and privilege:
>
> that I will be unbending in my stand against every form of oppression which deforms and crushes people and prevents them from the fulfillment of their lives: and that as leader of our New Democratic Party, I will be answerable to the members of this party as we go forward to become the government that will build a truly socialist, truly humane society—here in Canada.[28]

Ed Broadbent couched his eventually successful appeal in much less radical terms, directing it both to moderate socialists and, more important, to welfare liberals within the party.

> Our democratic socialist objectives will be outlined clearly and honestly. We will challenge the supremacy of corporate power and private decision-making....I am confident that, united together, we in the New Democratic Party can accomplish in the days ahead a record of economic change every bit as profound as the great transformation in social legislation that stands as our proud record in the past. We can build a nation with a sense of compassion, a sense of community and above all a sense of equality.[29]

Thus it can be seen that the Liberals, the Progressive Conservatives and the New Democrats have each put forward rival visions of the central values that ought to shape the Canadian nation.

IDEOLOGY IN ACTION

These differences between the parties on matters of ideology work themselves out in policy alternatives. Energy policy is a particularly good area to examine in order to see these differences in action. It was, after all, the energy problem which brought down the Clark government in the House of Commons, and the debate over the future Petro-Canada which contributed subsequently to his party's electoral defeat in 1980.

With respect to Petro-Canada, there was an important difference between the Conservatives on the one hand, and the Liberals and new Democrats on the other. Petro-Canada had originally been established during 1972-73 when the minority Liberal government relied on NDP support to stay in office. Its creation was a measure on which welfare liberals and socialists could agree. The former welcomed it because it appeared to strengthen individual freedom by using the government's power to check the rival power of the multinational oil companies which dominated the Canadian industry. To socialists, it represented government taking control of one of the commanding heights of the economy, and putting itself in a better position to direct the economy as a whole. These latter saw it, although by no means completely satisfactory, as a step in the right direction.

The Progressive Conservative government under pressure from the most radical of business liberals in the cabinet, Sinclair Stevens, was determined that Petro-Canada would be one of the crown corporations that would be "privatized", that is sold by the government to private interests. It would remain a Canadian-owned company.

Petro-Canada was the keystone and symbol of the debate over energy policy, but there were other issues as well, not the least significant of which, especially in Southern Ontario, was the price of gasoline and home heating oil. Here again the ideologies of the parties were significant factors in forming their policies. At the one pole, the Conservatives were determined to diminish the government's role. It was their intention to free the industry as much as possible from government restraint, to encourage private initiative in the discovery of new oil and natural gas sources and in energy conservation measures, and generally, to use the mechanism of the market to balance supply and demand. If, they argued, you let the price of oil rise substantially, to 85% of the world price, the higher price will discourage consumption, and will also encourage production. As the Conservatives saw it, reliance on market forces would bring the situation under control without unnecessary government interference, and Canadians could enjoy energy self-sufficiency by 1990.

The Liberals and the New Democrats did not agree. Both expressed concern about the effect of higher oil prices on the poor who needed oil to heat their houses and to fuel their cars. The Liberals offered, in the 1980 election campaign, a vague, "made in Canada", blended price for oil, which would be, they promised, lower than the price the Conservatives had set in the Crosbie budget. The Liberals, then, were much more willing to see the state take an active role in energy pricing.

The New Democrats went even further. Their dream was to see much greater state activity in the entire oil industry. They proposed a dramatic increase in the role of Petro-Canada, extending to involvement in oil refining and the creation of a coast-to-coast network of service stations, and the sole responsibility for importing of crude oil into Canada.

Such a superficial survey of a complex policy area hardly does justice to the positions of the parties. It must also be remembered that since each of the parties represents an ideological coalition, the policies are often the result either of a compromise, or else of one segment of the party triumphing over its rivals, as was the case with Sinclair Stevens and the business liberals in the Clark cabinet. None the less, the main point is clear. Ideology is an important factor in the decisions parties make. We can scarcely imagine the New Democrats adopting the position of the Conservatives, advocating increased private ownership and freeing market forces. Neither can we imagine the Conservatives advocating a dramatic increase in state activity. To understand the behavior of Canadian politicians, political parties and governments in terms of their ideological commitments and presuppositions, then, makes a major contribution to our understanding of how our country works.

LIMITATIONS AND ADVANTAGES OF THE IDEOLOGICAL APPROACH

There are, naturally enough, limitations to this approach. The ideological approach is not a comprehensive explanation of decision-making, especially in regard to day-to-day decisions. Politicians may misunderstand the nature of the situation they face, and because of this mistake, may respond in a way totally out of harmony with what ideology would suggest. The application of principles to situations is never an easy task, and even two Liberals who understand a particular situation in roughly similar ways may want to respond to it by emphasizing different aspects of their ideology.

Moreover, matters of modern government are often technically difficult, and all governments rely heavily on advice from civil servants. As a consequence, ministers may be subtly guided in unintended directions on complex issues. John Diefenbaker, for example, never trusted the senior civil servants who had been appointed by, and who, Diefenbaker thought, had become unwarrantedly accustomed to associating with, a Liberal government. He suspected them of offering him advice on possible policies that reflected their, rather than his, preferences. This kind of dispute came to the fore in the 1961 conflict with James Coyne, governor of the Bank of Canada, and eventually led to Coyne's resignation.

Finally, all political parties are associated with powerful interest groups whose concerns and perspectives are limited to their own needs and aspirations. To them, national problems or ideological considerations stand in the way of achieving their own goals. Western farmers want their wheat sold at high prices; Maritime fishermen want protection against foreign overfishing; oil companies want what they consider a reasonable return on their investment in exploration and development. Pressure from such groups may induce a government to compromise its ideological principles.

What, then, are the important advantages to be gained from approaching Canadian politics through the study of the ideologies of its political parties? (It should not be forgotten that there are many political parties in Canada, especially at the provincial level, the study of which would repay attention.) Perhaps the chief advantage is that it allows us to understand, better than any other approach, that there are important questions to be decided about the kind of country Canada will become. Although these may be obscured in the details of day-to-day parliamentary debate, or in the drama of a leadership convention, or the excitement of an election campaign, they remain at the heart of civilized political life. Any country that fails to deal with them honestly and directly runs the continual danger of drifting into consequences that a little foresight may have averted.

Almost as important, by understanding that there are differences of principle separating the major political parties, we can compensate for the excessive concentration on images that newspaper and television reporters and editors find so fascinating. Much, of course, does depend on individuals, on their personalities, and even more on their capacities.

It is also valuable to pay attention to the nature of the Canadian ideological conversation so that we do not forget that we are not Americans. It is no doubt important to us what goes on in the United States and we cannot help at times being saturated by the debates that take place there. We may even, at times, listen to them and benefit from them, as we could also profit from greater attention to the discussions in the United Kingdom, France, Germany, Japan, and other nations. But eavesdropping on a conversation should not make us a party to it. We do not want to spend all our time listening to others, lest we ourselves forget how to talk and how to think.

CONCLUSION

Prior to the 1970s the dominant interpretation of the motivation of Canadian politics was to balance the competing claims of rival interests in such a way as to satisfy the greatest possible number of these claimants. The view that I have advocated here suggests that this American-inspired theory does not apply well in Canada.

Canadian political parties, throughout their history, have not consisted solely of individuals seeking power for its own sake. All Canadian political parties, not just the more idealistic CCF and NDP, have been committed to their own visions of what sort of country Canada should be. Sometimes these commitments have led to serious conflict over basic principles between the parties. More often, though, the parties have disagreed, not that liberty and order, or equality and hierarchy, were important, but instead about the relative importance of these values, or on the relative weight each should be given in a particular historical circumstance.

To ignore ideology is a mistake for two reasons. First, if we discount this factor, we can never come to a full understanding of our national political life. We are now well into the second century of Canadian Confederation, and ideology, rather than declining as a factor, is becoming more important than ever. I need only point to the success of the Parti Québécois to prove my case. But, second, there is an even more compelling reason to study Canadian ideologies with intense seriousness. The Fathers of Confederation, particularly Macdonald and Cartier, were committed to an image of Canada as a country and a people who had rejected the route of homogenizing modernity taken by the great republic which fate had given us as our neighbor. We betray the vision of our founders, and violate the spirit upon which Canada was founded, if we do not ask the questions: Why does Canada need to exist as a separate sovereign state? What is good for its citizens? What good can Canada do in the world? These are difficult questions, and the responsibility for answering them lies heavily on our shoulders at this moment in the destiny of the western world; but we cannot escape them.

SUMMARY

1. Because ideology has not been as visible a factor in Canadian politics as it has been in Europe, commentators on Canadian politics have thought that our political life was very similar to that of the United States. This view was mistaken. Although our ideologies are not identical to those in Europe they are similar. They were formed out of the ideas which European immigrants brought with them when they settled in their new home.

2. Liberalism lies at the center of our ideological life. However, each major Canadian political party is a coalition of different ideological groupings.

3. The Liberal Party contains business liberals and welfare liberals. Both are committed to enhancing individual freedom, but the business liberal believes that the main threat to freedom comes from the state, while the welfare liberal believes that it comes from other sources of concentrated power, large corporations and trade unions, and that the state is the instrument for preserving individual freedom against these groups.

4. The Conservative Party contains business liberals and tories. Toryism as an ideology has been mostly assimilated by business liberalism, but it still represents an identifiable strain which values hierarchy and collectivism, the latter in the sense that it sees the nation as a unit of fundamental importance.

5. Canadian Socialism finds its primary expression through the New Democratic Party. Its main ideological tenets are a strong belief in the importance of equality, and in the value of collectivism, though unlike toryism, the collectivism it finds important stresses social class rather than the nation.

6. Studying ideologies cannot answer all questions about Canadian politics, but it can make an important contribution to our understanding of our national life. First, it can show us that our major parties have been guided in their policies by reference to certain important principles. Second, it can open our minds to a contemplation of what sort of country we want Canada to be.

STUDY QUESTIONS

1. What is the basic difference between the Hartz-Horowitz thesis and that of George Grant?

2. Why does socialism flourish much more successfully in Canada than in the US?
3. What is toryism and is it likely to increase or decrease in Canada? Why?
4. To what extent have the major Canadian political parties engaged in brokerage transactions?
5. In what ways, according to the author, has the Canadian Liberal Party "revealed a remarkable consistency"?
6. In the next decades, which strain of liberalism is likely to take precedence, business liberalism or welfare liberalism? Why?
7. The author describes four elements which have made major contributions to Canadian Conservatism: toryism, nostalgia, hostility to rapid change, and business liberalism. Which of these are likely to become more important and which less important? Why?
8. Why has the Liberal Party been dominant in Canada in the twentieth century?
9. Why do many Canadian socialists seem to prefer to be called social democrats?
10. How successful has Gomperism been for the Canadian trade union movement? Will Gomperism likely play an increasing or decreasing role in Canadian politics in the future? Why?

ENDNOTES

1. Louis Hartz, ed., *The Founding of New Societies* (New York: Harcourt Brace, 1964), p. 6.
2. D. Forster, *The Mackenzie King Record* (Toronto: University of Toronto Press, 1970), IV, p. 295.
3. *Ibid.*, p. 235.
4. National Liberal Federation, *The Liberal Party of Canada* (Ottawa: Liberal Party of Canada, 1957), p. 15. Quoted in G. Horowitz, *Canadian Labour in Politics* (Toronto: University of Toronto Press, 1968), p. 34.
5. D.O. Carrigan, ed., *Canadian Party Platforms* (Toronto: Copp Clark, 1968), p. 82.
6. W.L.M. King, *Industry and Humanity* (New York: Houghton Mifflin, 1918), p. 336.
7. Quoted in H.B. Neatby, "The Political Ideas of William Lyon Mackenzie King," in *The Political Ideas of the Prime Minister of Canada*, ed. H.B. Neatby (Ottawa: University of Ottawa Press, 1968), p. 125.
8. "Resolution Adopted by the Third National Liberal Convention," (Ottawa, 1948). Quoted in Carrigan, *op. cit.*, p. 181.
9. Lester Pearson, "Introduction," J.W. Pickersgill, *The Liberal Party* (Toronto: McClelland and Stewart, 1962), p. ix.
10. Pierre Trudeau, *Conversations with Canadians* (Toronto: University of Toronto Press, 1972), p. 86.

11. George Grant, *Lament for a Nation* (Toronto: McClelland and Stewart, 1965), p. 71.

12. R.H. Wilbur, *H.H. Stevens* (Toronto: University of Toronto Press, 1977), pp. 206-7.

13. Robert Stanfield, "Memorandum to Caucus," November 14, 1974, mimeo, pp. 13-14.

14. Perrin Beatty, "Letter to the Hon. Robert Stanfield," November 18, 1974, mimeo, p. 5.

15. *Ibid.*, p. 7.

16. *House of Commons Debates*, April 22, 1981, p. 9410.

17. Jim Gillies, "Letter to Delegates," Progressive Conservative Leadership Convention, February 1976, p. 4.

18. *House of Commons Debates*, October 10, 1979, p. 42.

19. Quoted in the *Globe and Mail*, August 27, 1979, p. 5.

20. Quoted in the *Globe and Mail*, February 7, 1980, p. 9.

21. Geoffrey Stevens, "Where would he lead us?" *Globe and Mail*, May 8, 1979, p. 6.

22. Quoted in Grace MacInnis, *J.S. Woodsworth: A Man to Remember* (Toronto: Macmillan, 1953), p. 274.

23. J.S. Woodsworth, *Strangers within our Gates* (Toronto: Missionary Society of the Methodist Church, 1909. Reprinted 1972 by the University of Toronto Press), p. 311.

24. J.S. Woodsworth, *My Neighbour* (Toronto: Methodist Book Room, 1911. Reprinted 1972 by the University of Toronto Press), p. 20.

25. Walter Young, *Anatomy of a Party* (Toronto: University of Toronto Press, 1969), p. 137.

26. Douglas Campbell, "Nomination Speech of Douglas K. Campbell, NDP Leadership Candidate," Winnipeg, July 6, 1975.

27. John Harney, "Notes for an Address by John Harney," Winnipeg, July 6, 1975.

28. Rosemary Brown, "Rosemary Brown for NDP Leader," Winnipeg, July 6, 1975.

29. Ed Broadbent, "The text of a Speech by Ed Broadbent given at the Eighth Biennial Convention of the New Democratic Party," Winnipeg, July 6, 1975.

SELECTED REFERENCES

Hartz, Louis, ed. *The Founding of New Societies*. New York: Harcourt Brace, 1964. Particularly recommended are the articles by Hartz and McRae.

Horowitz, Gad. *Canadian Labour in Politics*. Toronto: University of Toronto Press, 1968. Horowitz's study of the Canadian intellectual heritage appears as the first chapter of this book; the rest of his work is devoted to a study of the relationship between the Canadian labor movement, and the CCF and the NDP, and would be of interest to anyone concerned with the trade union influence on Canadian socialism.

Christian, William and Colin Campbell. *Political Parties and Ideologies in Canada*. Toronto: McGraw-Hill Ryerson, 1974. Attempts to look at the Hartz-Horowitz thesis in some detail, examines the history of Canadian ideologies and presents a coherent framework for analysis.

Grant, George. *Lament for a Nation.* Toronto: McClelland and Stewart, 1965. A classic analysis of liberalism and its effect on other Canadian ideologies.

_____. *Technology and Empire.* Toronto: House of Anansi, 1969. Those interested in Grant's analysis can follow it up in this collection of essays.

Winn, Conrad and John McMenemy, eds. *Political Parties in Canada.* Toronto: McGraw-Hill Ryerson, 1976. A critique of Grant's general approach can be found in this collection of essays.

DOCUMENTS

Carrigan, D. Owen, ed., *Canadian Party Platforms.* Toronto: Copp Clark, 1968.

Craig, G.M., ed. *Lord Durham's Report.* Toronto: McClelland and Stewart, 1963.

Waite, P.B., ed. *Confederation Debates in the Province of Canada.* Toronto: McClelland and Stewart, 1963.

CANADIAN LIBERALISM

King, W.L. Mackenzie. *Industry and Humanity.* New York: Houghton Mifflin, 1918. A somewhat turgid work, but required reading for students of Canadian Liberalism.

Pickersgill, J. *The Liberal Party.* Toronto: McClelland and Stewart, 1962. A flaccid polemic with which students must eventually come to terms.

Smith, Goldwin. *Canada and the Canadian Question.* Toronto: University of Toronto Press, 1971. A reprint of Smith's nineteenth century tract.

Trudeau, Pierre Elliott. *Federalism and the French Canadians.* Toronto: Macmillan, 1968. Along with Smith, Trudeau is an exciting and controversial liberal.

CANADIAN CONSERVATISM

Creighton, Donald. *Sir John A. Macdonald*, 2 vols. Toronto: Macmillan, 1952, 1955. A classic biography of Sir John A. Macdonald.

Diefenbaker, John George. *One Canada.* Toronto: Macmillan, 1975. An entertaining, though at times tendentious, account of the career and principles of the man who brought the Conservatives back to power after twenty-two years in opposition.

Graham, Roger. *Arthur Meighen*, 3 vols. Toronto: Clarke, Irwin, 1960, 1963, 1965. Biography.

Meighen, Arthur. *Unrevised and Unrepented.* Toronto: Clarke, Irwin, 1949. Meighen's own collection of speeches is a good introduction to one of the most intelligent and articulate Canadians.

Perlin, George. *The Tory Syndrome.* Montreal: McGill-Queen's University Press, 1980. An important study of the Conservative party which points to factors other than ideology to account for the party's obvious internal divisions.

Wilbur, J.R.H., ed. *The Bennett New Deal.* Toronto: Copp Clark, 1968. Wilbur's collection of documents and commentary is a useful introduction to Bennett's controversial attempt to reconstruct Canadian conservatism.

Report of the Round Table on Canadian Policy. Port Hope Conference, 1942. This report was the Conservatives' attempt to recreate a policy alternative to the Liberals in the early 1940s.

CANADIAN SOCIALISM

Avakumovic, Ivan. *Socialism in Canada.* Toronto: McClelland and Stewart, 1978. An interesting study of the CCF and NDP dealing primarily with organization, but containing discussion of principles as well.

CCF. *Regina Manifesto.* Regina: CCF, 1933.

CCF. *Winnipeg Declaration of Principles.* Montreal: CCF, 1956. Both of these works are essential reading and are part of the considerable treasurehouse available concerning socialist thought in Canada, not least because of the Canadian academic community's close ties with the CCF and the NDP.

Horn, Michiel. *The League for Social Reconstruction.* Toronto: University of Toronto Press, 1980. Traces the impact of this group of bright, young intellectuals on the formation of Socialism in Canada, particularly on the CCF.

League for Social Reconstruction. *Social Planning for Canada.* Toronto: Thos. Nelson and Sons, 1935. Also an essential work.

Penner, Norman. *The Canadian Left.* Scarborough: Prentice-Hall, 1977. An important study of Canadian Socialism which deals with Canadian Communism as well. Makes the point that Marxism had more importance than previous historians had credited it with.

Woodsworth, J.S. *My Neighbour.* Toronto: Methodist Book Room 1911. Repr., Toronto: University of Toronto Press, 1972. Shows particularly well the Social Gospel inspiration of the early Canadian socialists.

Young, Walter. *The Anatomy of a Party: The National CCF, 1932-1961.* Toronto: University of Toronto Press, 1969.

There is a longer selected bibliography covering all the forementioned areas in:

Christian, William and Colin Campbell, *Political Parties and Ideologies in Canada.* Toronto: McGraw-Hill Ryerson, 1974.

6

Political Culture: Attitudes and Values as the Determinants of Politics

Michael S. Whittington*

It is a basic assumption of the political culture approach to the study of politics that our feelings, our attitudes towards political phenomena and personalities, and our fundamental values will have an effect on the way we behave in political roles. For instance, when we vote there are factors other than cold reason that determine our choice. Similarly when we identify with a national symbol such as a flag or an anthem, our emotions, our attitudes towards Canada, and our assessment of the worth of the Canadian way of life are more important than the objective characteristics of the symbol itself. The theme of this chapter is that understanding the political values and attitudes of Canadians—the Canadian political culture—is important to us if we are fully to understand political institutions, behavior and processes in Canada. But first, what *is* political culture exactly?

The dominant set of values and attitudes in any social system is referred to as its "culture",[1] and it is the study of culture that has been the dominant concern of anthropologists, sociologists and even social psychologists up to the present. As political scientists, however, we are concerned with explaining the specifically political patterns of human interaction in society. We believe that because there are patterns of behavior we can identify as political, there are also specialized political attitudes and values shared by members of society. Thus, when we focus on the set of political values and attitudes that are dominant in a society we are focusing on what is referred to as the "political culture" of that society.

While the term political culture is of fairly recent coinage, the concept itself dates back at least to Plato who recognized better than many who followed him that certain public attitudes had to be fostered to achieve the ideal political

*Associate Professor of Political Science, Carleton University.

order. This theme has remained current and appears continually in the writings of political philosophers up to the present day.[2] More recently, theories of national character have been developed by anthropologists and psychologists in an attempt to explain the persistent "misbehavior" of certain countries in the international community and the consistent "sweetness" of others. However, it was the development of techniques such as survey research that opened the door to the study of political culture as we know it today in political science. By combining the analytical insights of earlier anthropologists and social psychologists with the methodological tools of behavioral research, it was possible for people such as Gabriel Almond, G. Bingham Powell, Lucien Pye and Sidney Verba to flesh out the concept of political culture and to formulate some empirical generalizations about actual political cultures in the modern world.

Before considering the specific utility of the concept of political culture in the study of Canadian politics, it is necessary to clarify some of the ambiguities which are implicit in the term. In the first place, the "stuff" of political culture is attitudes and values, which are "phenomena of the mind". While the behavior of people in political life may provide us with clues as to what attitudes probably underlie their behavior, and while attitudes are significant to social scientists precisely because of the potential impact they have on behavior, we must always remember that political culture is an attitudinal and not a behavioral category. A second implication of defining political culture in terms of attitudes is that attitudes exist in individual minds. While political scientists try to "add together" all the individual attitudes in a society in order to generalize about the political culture, we must remember that, in the real world, political culture is no more and no less than the sum of the attitudes of many separate individuals.

Our definition of political culture also presumes that it is possible to distinguish between political and nonpolitical attitudes. We assume that all things in the real world can be classified as political or nonpolitical objects, and that attitudes toward or about specifically political objects are the relevant ones to a student of political culture. Thus, the general problem of political science, that of defining the boundary between the political and the nonpolitical, is of specific concern to the student of political culture. All that can be said is that some real world phenomena such as political leaders, governmental institutions and regime-related symbols are clearly in the political category and others such as sun spots, microorganisms and pebbles on the beach are clearly not. There remain a large number of social objects such as labor unions, religious groups and bureaucratic agencies that are hard to categorize.

A factor that further complicates the boundary problem is that political culture is in some ways only a subset of the general culture of a society. In other words, we must recognize that our political attitudes are probably affected by our nonpolitical attitudes. The best example of this is the apparent relationship between how we perceive ourselves generally, as intelligent, adaptable, competent and so on, and how we perceive ourselves in political roles, as able to have an impact on government, competent to make political judgments, or politically aware.[3] Therefore, while we must recognize the difficulty in drawing the line between political and nonpolitical attitudes, having drawn it we must also keep in mind that political and nonpolitical attitudes may well be interrelated.

To this point we have established that political culture is made up of political attitudes, and while we have considered some of the implications of this sort of definition nothing has been said about whose attitudes count. On the one hand, from the perspective of policy analysis, it would be fairly easy to conclude that it is the attitudes of the policy-making elite that are significant; on the other hand, if we are interested in predicting the outcomes of elections, it is perhaps the attitudes of the mass public that are more significant. The political culture approach, however, makes no distinction between mass and elite attitudes and values, but merely states that the political culture of a nation is the overall distribution of attitudes in a society. We must conclude from this, and from the fact that most studies of political culture have in fact focused on mass attitudes, that elite attitudes need not be viewed as anything unique or special in terms of defining political culture. Such a view may be a weakness in the approach and will be examined later.

THE UTILITY OF THE CONCEPT

The original intention in developing the concept of political culture was to foster cross-national comparison of political systems. If we simply look at the formal constitutions and the basic political structures of systems around the world we find that there are misleading similarities. Canada, Nigeria and the Soviet Union for instance all have federal constitutions and are explicitly committed to free elections. "On paper", these three political systems have many similarities, but even a casual observer of world politics will quickly recognize that in practice they are extremely different. A large part of the difference lies in the values and attitudes which underly the formal institutions of the regime. Thus when we use the political culture approach to analyze Canadian politics, we can compare the Canadian system with others in the international community. This approach tells us how we are different from other systems and may help us to identify the political characteristics that make us unique.

At another level of analysis, however, the political culture approach can be used to explain regional and provincial differences in political life within Canada. It has long been recognized that in Canada the style of politics varies from province to province and from region to region even though the basic institutions of government may be virtually identical. For instance, it has been argued that Canada has at least three political cultures if we focus on levels of political development. John Wilson describes the Atlantic Provinces as under-developed, Ontario, Québec, Manitoba and British Columbia as transitional, and Alberta and Saskatchewan as developed, according to the type of party system operating in the provinces. From another perspective, Simeon and Elkins demonstrate the generally high levels of trust and efficacy in Ontario, BC and Manitoba in contrast with the Atlantic Provinces, which are characterized by "a pervasive disaffection from the political process". French-speaking Québecers fall more closely in line with the Atlantic Provinces, while English-speaking Québecers seem to reflect more closely the positive attitude of Ontario.[4] By focusing on regional or provincial cultures we may be better able to understand the underlying divisive forces within our federation.

From a very pragmatic point of view, the political culture approach is useful in the study of Canadian politics because it can be studied from many angles. The most obvious and perhaps the most reliable technique for analyzing basic political attitudes and values is survey research: one simply finds out what attitudes prevail in a society by asking a scientifically selected sample of individuals a set of carefully structured questions which basically answer the question: "What are your values?" However, we may also uncover dimensions of the political culture by simply observing the behavior of individuals in political circumstances. Because we know that people's behavior is affected by what they believe, it is often possible to guess what attitudes underlie certain behavior patterns. For example, if we observe a high voter turnout at elections it is logical to suppose that there is a generally favorable attitude to taking part in elections, although it is not possible to make very sophisticated deductions about what kinds of positive attitudes. At the most macroscopic level, we can discover something about the long-run value preferences of a society by investigating the legal and institutional framework within which politics occurs. For instance, the very existence of parliamentary institutions probably reflects a deep-seated commitment to representative democracy in Canadian society. While this might seem obvious, we have to make the assumption that the values in the political institutions of a society are congruent with the dominant values of the society. Any great discrepancy would probably not last very long, for if the institutions are nondemocratic and societal values are democratic, there would be considerable pressure for change and even for revolutionary change. Thus we can say that the most elementary values of a system will normally be embedded in its political structures and may, in a limited way, reflect the political culture of a society.[5]

There is a substantial and growing literature in Canada which deals with ideology, and with "Canadian political thought". Here the approach is to look at the teachings and writings of Canadian political commentators and historians over time as a way of understanding our basic values. The assumption in the most recent of these studies of ideology is that we can find out more about our political values from the study of history and of the writings of historians than we can through the putatively more rigorous techniques of survey research.[6]

Finally, while there have not been a large number of studies of political culture *per se* in Canada, the attitudes that are the "stuff" of political culture have been studied from two broad perspectives. The most established of the two perspectives looks at attitudes and values as independent variables which have a causal impact on political behavior. In this regard we have studied attitudes such as partisanship or political interest not as entities in themselves but as factors that can help us explain behavior. The more recent of the two perspectives looks at attitudes as dependent variables, which are themselves caused by the process of learning known as political socialization. Again the interest of the researcher is not in the substance of the attitudes and values but rather in how and in what circumstances individuals acquire them. Thus we would look at party identification among children to discover the relative roles of the family, school or peer group in teaching us about politics. In sum, although there is a paucity of data that focus primarily on political culture, there are a great many studies that provide us with information which is secondarily useful in building up a generalized picture of the Canadian political culture.

THE CANADIAN POLITICAL CULTURE

Canadian Political Values

Values are perhaps the most fundamental and complex of all human mental phenomena. They not only provide the ultimate criteria for our behavior, but they also set the mental context within which we develop our attitudes or orientations to specific objects in the real world. In our political values, those values which define for us the appropriate goals for government and the legitimate means to be used to achieve those goals, we have the ultimate foundation of our political culture; all other political attitudes must fall within the boundaries established by our basic political values. The problem with values is that they are often so fundamental that we do not recognize them and consequently may have difficulty articulating them. Accordingly it may be difficult to study values through survey techniques. In the case of political values we may be a bit more fortunate because we can assume that to a large extent, our institutions reflect the values that currently prevail in our society and simply use the institutionalized values as a reflection of our political values. In fact, many studies of Canadian political values have employed precisely this basic technique.

Perhaps the fundamental political value in Canada is popular sovereignty, for it is the principle that goes the farthest toward operationalizing the basic goal of democracy, the common good or the common interest. Athenian democracy, where all citizens participated equally in the policy decisions of the state, represents a sort of ideal of popular sovereignty but because modern societies are too large and complex for everyone to participate directly in the policy process, we have evolved a system whereby citizens choose their policy-makers through periodic elections. A system of representation by popular election presumes a secondary value, that of political equality. This value is institutionalized through the principle of "one man (or woman), one vote" and the guarantee of political freedoms such as freedom of assembly, association, conscience and expression. These political freedoms are necessary to ensure that we have real alternatives from which to choose when we exercise our franchise.

Another value that can often conflict with the value of political equality is majority rule, a principle aimed at ensuring that the many, not the few, are the ones whose interests are served first. The problem here is that majorities can become oppressive *vis-à-vis* minorities, even to the extent of denying them their political freedoms. While Canadians seem to agree that there must be a balance between the rights of the minority and the rights of the majority, their ideas differ considerably on where the balance should be. For instance, while all Canadians would agree with the principle of freedom of expression not all would agree that political movements advocating the overthrow of the regime should be permitted to publish their views freely. Similarly, while all would agree with the principle of freedom of the press, many would like to see censorship of various kinds to ensure that what is published is not greatly at odds with the dominant values and morality of our society. In fact, once we move beyond a discussion of a few of the most fundamental political values it becomes increasingly difficult to generalize about the whole of Canadian society; the best we can hope to do in such a situation is to describe the "value mix" typical of Canada in order to make cross-national comparisons. Where the value mix varies among regions or provinces within Canada, we can use the resultant generalizations to attempt internal comparisons.

The conflict between liberal and non-liberal values is another central aspect of Canadian political life, and in fact our unique mix of these values helps to set us apart from those societies closest to us in political values, the United States and the United Kingdom.[7] While these countries are very similar in their commitment to liberal values such as individual rights, private property and a basically free market economy, the political culture approach helps us to distinguish between them according to a varying presence of socialist, conservative and corporatist values. It is these non-liberal values and the extent to which they encroach upon or 'dilute' their basically liberal political cultures, which comprise the difference between Canada, the US and the UK.

To conclude this section we should emphasize that the evidence concerning our political values is based primarily on impressions. We can be fairly sure about some of our value differences *vis-à-vis* non-Western societies, and we can even feel fairly confident, although only at a high level of generalization, about some of the differences and similarities between our national political culture and that of the United States and United Kingdom. However, what the usual historical and institutional approaches to defining our political values fail to do is to explain adequately the distribution of political values among the subcultural groups that make up our society. Such explanations will only be possible through extensive and systematic research designed specifically to discover the political values of Canadian society.

Canadian Political Attitudes

Whereas political values define the goals of government in Canada as well as the scope of legitimate means for achieving these goals, political attitudes are very specific orientations to things in the real world. The most primitive of our political attitudes involves simple awareness or knowledge of political objects which is usually referred to as "political cognition". These cognitive orientations to political objects, for instance, knowledge of who the prime minister is or about the role of Parliament, form the attitudinal "ground zero" on which all our more sophisticated attitudes are built. In the absence of these cognitive political attitudes there can be no political culture at all. While it is obvious that we have to know something exists before we can have positive or negative attitudes towards it, we must add that such political knowledge is seldom untainted by our values and our emotional preferences. For instance, if we become aware of an actor in the political system called Pierre Trudeau through comments about him from parents or friends, we will soon acquire a general perception of him as somebody we like or do not like. This is an "affective attitude". The sum of our affective attitudes consists of the positive and negative feelings we have about objects in the real world. We tend to acquire political likes and dislikes at the same time as we first become aware of a political object. Similarly, as we become more sophisticated we develop evaluative attitudes which are judgments about the goodness and badness of political things based on how they measure up to our basic political values. For example, we might conclude that wiretap legislation is bad because it contains provisions that compromise the right of privacy, or that televising parliamentary debates is good because it will make MPs more sensitive to public opinion. Obviously there is a spillover effect here for few people can totally separate their emotional preferences from their value judgments, and often we will selectively perceive the real world in such a way that it conforms to our preconceived notions about it. Thus if we believe all Liberals are in favor of bilingualism and we meet a Liberal who speaks out against it, we will try a number of interpretations of his behavior before changing our general perception of Liberals. We can entirely overlook the statement he has made; we can dismiss his statement as a lie designed to fool us; we can simply view him as an exception; or we can argue that he never was a Liberal in the first place! In sum, while it is possible to separate cognitive, affective and evaluative attitudes analytically, in reality they are usually interrelated. In other words, our values and emotions color our perception of the real world; our feelings may depend upon what we perceive and our values themselves may only be rationalizations of what we feel.

One of the first attempts to classify political cultures was made by Gabriel

Almond and Sidney Verba.[8] Their three categories—parochial, subject and participant—have since been used by many political scientists. A parochial political culture exists where there is a low awareness of the political system as a generalized object, where there is virtually no cognitive awareness of specific political structures, and where the individual does not see himself in any way as an actor or participant in the political process. The best examples of parochial cultures are the bushmen of southern Africa, the remote tribes of the Amazon basin and some primitive peoples in New Guinea. The subject political culture exists where there is a high awareness of the system as a generalized object, and a high awareness of the output structures of the system, but a relatively low awareness of input structures. The individual sees himself as affected by the activities and outputs of the system, but does not see himself as a participant in the process. The Spain of Franco or the Portugal of Salazar might be considered examples of subject political cultures, although in neither case are they pure subject societies. The most highly developed type is the participant political culture where the individual is aware of both the input and output structures of the system and perceives himself as an active participant in the political process. The participant accepts the system as something that influences his life, but, unlike the subject, he sees himself as having the potential to influence the system as well. The western liberal democracies are hailed as participant political cultures, with the United States as the paragon of this type. It must be noted here that these three categories are ideal types and that political cultures are all heterogeneous in varying degrees. Societies with predominantly participant attitudes to the political system will always include some individuals who are basically subjects and even some who are parochials. In Canada, for instance, a country that has normally been viewed as having a predominantly participant type of political culture, rural Québec has often been styled a "subject fragment" and some of the native peoples, particularly in the far North, have until very recently been seen as parochials. A further caveat that must be entered here is that the parochial-subject-participant classification is developmental, with the more developed or participant orientations superimposed on the earlier subject and parochial ones. Thus the empirical differences among modern democratic systems, most of which are predominantly participant, can be seen in the way parochial and subject attitudes are blended into the dominant participant culture. For example, it is possible that the greater emphasis on liberal values in the United States and on conservative values in Canada is related to a better integration of subject orientations in Canada. In other words, the often violent and disruptive nature of political dissent in America may be a result of lower levels of subject orientation to political authority. By contrast, Canadians' more ordered and acquiescent attitudes to political authority may be a result of subject orientation modifying the basically participant attitude towards government.

Richard Van Loon has described the Canadian political culture as generally spectator-participant.[9] Because Canada has a very high level of political involvement in comparison with other countries, it is fairly obvious that at the broadest level of generalization our national political culture can be said to be participant. There are wide variations in the levels of participation within Canada, and significant regional, ethnic, class and educational differences do exist. However, if we look at Canada as a whole, compared to other systems, there is no question that we are political participants. We have high voter turnout, high awareness of politics and a high level of interest in political events. However, what is unique to Canada, by comparison with other generally participant political cultures such as the United States, is the apparent psychological motivation for our political activity. While Canadians feel they have a considerable effect on politics, this does not seem to be as significant a motivating factor as their general interest in politics as a sort of game. Thus, as Van Loon has put it, we are interested and involved spectators in the game of politics. We are often very excited about the outcome of an election, but there seems to be a general feeling that little in the way of major policy shifts is likely if our side does not win. This spectator orientation to politics is related to the nonideological nature of our political parties, which is in turn related to the lower (relative to the US) levels of partisan identification in Canada. One interpretation of this phenomenon, which Van Loon has dubbed "apolitical" politics and which Kornberg[10] has called a "generally less politicized" society, is that it is in the interest of Canadian elites to avoid the real gut issues that should concern Canadians. Therefore they foster a politics that is uncreative and conceals the real issues in order to maintain the status quo.[11] Another interpretation might be that the parties reflect a genuine and fairly widespread satisfaction with the status quo among the vast majority of Canadians. Whatever the reasons, Van Loon's description of our political culture as spectator-participant seems fairly apt at the national level of generalization.

In the past few years there has been a new spate of material that emphasizes regionalism as a critical factor in determining political events in Canada. These writers argue convincingly that there are very wide attitudinal differences from one part of Canada to another, and that therefore it is misleading to speak of a Canadian political culture.[12] They argue that we have two, several, or many, political cultures depending on which political community one chooses to study. No one would disagree that there are wide attitudinal variations in Canada, variations that reflect regional as well as cultural, economic and demographic cleavages. Furthermore, who can disagree with the assertion that these attitudinal variations are critical in determining political behavioral differences? However, by accepting this point of view, we need not denigrate attempts to generalize about the political culture at the national level. As we have already pointed out, a political culture, be it national, regional, provincial or even local, is still simply an aggregation of the attitudes of individuals who are members of the relevant social matrix. The larger the aggregation, the more difficult is the task of generalizing, but the task must be carried on at all levels if we are fully to understand the value and attitudinal foundations of Canadian politics. The attitudes we have in common, even if very few, are as important as our attitudinal differences in determining the nature of Canadian political life.

THE POLITICAL CULTURE APPROACH: SCOPE AND LIMITATIONS

The political culture approach is perhaps the most inclusive of the approaches considered in this collection. In fact none of the approaches to Canadian politics described in the other chapters are so incompatible with the concept of political culture that they could not be plugged into the model we have just described. The first four chapters look at aspects of the environment of the Canadian political system. These are some of the most significant independent variables which, through the process of political socialization, come to color the values and attitudes that make up our political culture. In other words, one of the ways in which these variables shape Canadian politics is by shaping our political culture.

The third section of this volume focuses on the structures of the Canadian political system. From the political culture perspective, these are some of the political objects toward which we acquire attitudes. Conversely, however, the political structures must reflect the dominant values of our political culture if they are to be effective. If political structures serve to enshrine political values that are not congruent with the values of Canadian society, then either the people's attitudes must change to conform to the institutionalized values, or the institutions must change to reflect societal values better. One way or the other, the analysis of political structures is an essential and integral companion to the political culture approach.

The section dealing with processes is also completely compatible with the political culture approach. The processes of Canadian politics are to a large extent the product of our political culture and in an immediate sense the motivation for studying political culture has been to gain a better understanding of parties, elections, ethnic conflict, the broad directions of public policy and so on.

In the fifth section of this book, the two chapters focusing on political elites are compatible with the political culture approach in a unique way. We have already pointed out that the political culture of a society is composed of the attitudes of all its members, not only the attitudes of the politically powerful or influential. It may be a limitation of the political culture approach that its proponents are very willing to accept the assumption that mass values and attitudes are significant even in elite-dominated processes such as policy-making. It is clear that the decision-making that produces public policy is influenced by the values and attitudes of the policy-making elites. Therefore, in the short run, it is possible that the policy makers could implement policies that are not in the interest of the mass public and are even incompatible with the general political culture. However, because Canada has a system of representative democracy, the authorities or political elites of our system must periodically face a critical electorate; hence, if the values of our political elites are incompatible with the values of the mass, then the elites will ultimately face electoral defeat.

A second factor to be considered in attempting to integrate elite approaches and the political culture approach, and one that is perhaps more important, concerns the role that the elites play in the socialization process. It seems likely that the political elites in Canada are composed of leaders whose influence helps to stimulate change in the public's political values and attitudes, and thus enable our political culture to develop. In this sense the political elites stimulate the attitudinal change that enables our political culture to develop.

While there is no reason to assume that elite values will necessarily be incongruent with mass values, a Marxist approach to Canadian politics assumes that major incongruities do exist. The basic assumption here is that there is a primal and unresolvable conflict of interest between the ruling class and the working class, and that to a large extent the working class is not conscious of the conflict. In this sense, through the socializing agencies of the system, political culture is manipulated by the elites, or the ruling class, to maintain a set of bourgeois political values that will perpetuate the status quo. The problem of Canadian politics from a Marxist perspective is to alter the political culture so that the working classes become conscious of their economic and psychological enslavement and work together to overthrow the dominant capitalist minority. While many Marxists would dismiss the political culture approach as one that has a status quo bias, it can be argued that, because the attitudinal status quo must be overturned to foster true class consciousness, the political culture approach can help people to understand more precisely what it is they are attacking. Thus, it might well be that the Marxist and political culture approaches are completely compatible and mutually helpful if their proponents will assume a broader intellectual perspective.

The major analytical limitation of the political culture approach, ironically, is a result of the inclusiveness that gives it such a broad analytical scope and utility. In some ways the political culture approach is so inclusive that it is impossible to study it empirically. The *de facto* paucity of comprehensive research focusing on Canadian political culture is a reflection of the difficulty in carrying out conceptually adequate research projects that are also tight enough to be readily fundable. Despite these limitations, and even if we are unable to do the kind of systematic and comprehensive research that would give us a full picture of the Canadian political culture, we should continue to use the approach macroscopically, for it is an analytical tool that gives us the conceptual perspective to integrate all the partial and piecemeal research flowing from the other approaches to Canadian politics. But we must remember that there is no single approach that will magically provide all the answers to all the questions we have about our political system. What is required, in effect, is an eclectic approach to the study of politics—one which takes the most useful insights from many different approaches and then integrates them into an overall picture.

SUMMARY

1. Political culture may be defined as the sum of the political attitudes and values held by the individuals within a society.
2. Elite attitudes need not be viewed as anything unique or special in terms of defining political culture.
3. Political values define appropriate goals for government and the legitimate means to be used to achieve those goals.
4. Popular sovereignty is a fundamental political value in Canada; related values include political equality and majority rule.
5. Political attitudes may be defined as specific orientations to things in the real world; the most primitive political attitudes involve simple awareness or knowledge of political objects.
6. According to Gabriel Almond and Sidney Verba, political cultures may be classified as parochial, subject and participant.
7. Canadian political culture differs from American political culture in several important respects; in Canada we tend to find less expectation of change, lower levels of partisan identification, and more of a spectator mentality.
8. The political culture approach to Canadian politics is very inclusive.
9. If a society's political structures are not congruent with its dominant political values, then either people's attitudes must change to conform to the institutionalized values, or the institutions must change to reflect societal values more closely.
10. Though mass values and attitudes are important even in elite-dominated situations, political elites play a crucial role in that they stimulate attitudinal changes that enable political culture to develop.

STUDY QUESTIONS

1. Is Canada best described as having one dominant political culture with regional variations, or as having several distinct cultures?
2. How valid is it to assume that the values incorporated in Canada's political institutions are congruent with the dominant Canadian political values?
3. What is the difference between studying attitudes and values as independent variables and as dependent variables?

4. What are "effective attitudes" and how do we acquire them?

5. What evidence can be marshalled to demonstrate that Canadian political culture is best described as parochial, subject or participant?

6. What is meant by Richard Van Loon's description of Canadian political culture as spectator-participant?

7. What aspects of Canadian political culture seem to be declining in importance; what aspects seem to be increasing in importance?

8. How has television influenced the development of Canadian political culture?

9. In what specific ways does Canadian political culture influence political decision-making in Canada?

10. In pronouncing their decisions should judges strive to reflect political culture, to change political culture, or to ignore political culture?

ENDNOTES

1. The uses of the term culture in psychology, sociology and anthropology are many and varied. The one used here is the least elaborate as well as the least ambiguous.

2. Rousseau is perhaps the most outspoken advocate of using the educational system to mold public attitudes to foster better government. Dicey analyzes English constitutional government in terms of attitudes that make it possible; more recently Lasswell has written on the personality traits that best contribute to democracy. Finally Louis Hartz and his followers such as Gad Horowitz and Ken McRae have tried to explain differences in political systems in terms of the dominant ideological commitments of their citizenry.

3. See J.H. Pammett and M.S. Whittington, "Political Culture and Political Socialization," in *Foundations of Political Culture*, ed., J.H. Pammett and M.S. Whittington (Toronto: Macmillan, 1976), pp. 5-10.

4. See R. Simeon and D.J. Elkins, "Regional Political Cultures," and John Wilson, "The Canadian Political Cultures," in *Canadian Journal of Political Science* (September, 1974). See also Allen Gregg and M.S. Whittington, "Regional Variation in Children's Political Attitudes," in *The Provincial Political Systems*, eds. D. Bellamy, J.H. Pammett, and D. Rowat (Toronto: Methuen, 1976).

5. See Gabriel Almond and S. Verba, *The Civic Culture* (Toronto: Little Brown, 1965), pp. 20-21.

6. See for instance R. Whitaker, "Images of the State of Canada," in *The Canadian State: Political Economy and Political Power*, ed. L. Panitch (Toronto: University of Toronto Press, 1977), pp. 28-68.

7. Louis Hartz, ed., *The Founding of New Societies* (New York: Harcourt-Brace, 1964), Chs. 4 and 7. See also Gad Horowitz, "Conservatism, Liberalism and Socialism in Canada," *Canadian Journal of Economics and Political Science* (May, 1966), pp. 144-71.

8. Almond and Elkin, *op. cit.*

9. R. Van Loon, "Political Participation in Canada," *Canadian Journal of Political Science* (September, 1970), p. 385.
10. A. Kornberg, I. Smith, and D. Bromley, "Some Differences in the Political Socialization Pattern of Canadian and American Party Officials," *Canadian Journal of Political Science* (March, 1969), p. 73.
11. John Porter, *The Vertical Mosaic* (Toronto: University of Toronto Press, 1965).
12. Simeon and Elkins, and Wilson, *op cit.*

SELECTED REFERENCES

Almond, Gabriel, and Sidney Verba. *The Civic Culture.* Boston: Little, Brown, 1965. This is the classic work on political culture. It defines the basic concepts and provides the basic typologies that are for the most part being used. The book does not deal with Canada so the substance is not as important to us here as is the theoretical material in the first chapter.

Bell, D., and L. Tepperman. *The Roots of Disunity.* Toronto: McClelland and Stewart Ltd., 1979. Perhaps the best comprehensive text book on Canadian political culture. For a briefer piece on the subject see D. Bell, "Political Culture in Canada" in Whittington and Williams, (eds.) *Canadian Politics in the 1980's*, Toronto: Methuen, 1981. p. 108.

Hargrove, Erwin. "Popular Leadership in Anglo-American Democracies." *Popular Leadership in Industrialized Societies*, ed. L. Edinger. New York: Wiley, 1966.

_____. "Note on Canadian and American Political Culture." *Canadian Journal of Economics and Political Science.* (February, 1967). While somewhat outdated, these two pieces give a fairly enlightened overview. Based on historical comparisons of Canadian and American political values.

Horowitz, Gad, "Conservatism, Liberalism and Socialism in Canada." *Canadian Journal of Economics and Political Science*, (May, 1966). In part a criticism of the Hartz-McRae interpretation, this article has been very influential in Canada. It is based on historical analysis and explains the ideological mix of Canadian politics in terms of importation of values in successive waves of immigration.

Lipset, S.M. *The First New Nation.* New York: Basic Books, 1963. While the book focuses on the United States, Lipset contrasts United States political values with those of Canada and offers explanations for the differences through the use of census data.

Manzer, R. *Canada: A Sociopolitical Report.* Toronto: McGraw-Hill Ryerson, 1974. Not strictly speaking a book about political culture but chock full of data relevant to political culture. The framework of this book is also significant because it provides a model of the basic values of Canadian society.

McRae, K.D. "The Structure of Canadian History," *The Founding of New Societies*, ed. L. Hartz. New York: Harcourt Brace, 1964. Must be read in conjunction with Horowitz. It is an interpretation that uses much the same approach but comes to slightly different conclusions.

Pammett, J., and M.S. Whittington, eds. *The Foundations of Political Culture: Political Socialization in Canada.* Toronto: Macmillan, 1976. A collection of original articles focusing on political attitudes as dependent variables.

Presthus, Robert. *Elite Accommodation in Canadian Politics.* Toronto: Macmillan, 1973. The first chapter is a very perceptive overview of the basic political values of Canadians.

Simeon, R., and David Elkins. "Regional Political Cultures in Canada." *Canadian Journal of Political Science,* (September, 1974). Excellent article based on survey data which looks at attitudinal differences across the regions of Canada. Limitation of the article is that it looks only at efficacy, trust and involvement as dependent variables.

Van Loon, R. "Political Participation in Canada." *Canadian Journal of Political Science,* (September, 1970).

_____, and M.S. Whittington. *The Canadian Political System.* Toronto: McGraw-Hill, 1981, Chs. 4-5. This material develops the theory of a spectator-participant political culture at the national level in Canada.

Wilson, J. "The Canadian Political Cultures." *Canadian Journal of Political Science,* (September, 1974). Excellent article based on survey data which rejects the existence of a national political culture because the regions are at different stages of political development.

Zureik, E. and Robert Pike. *Socialization and Values in Canadian Society,* Vol. 1. Toronto: McClelland and Stewart, 1975. A collection of original articles dealing with political socialization. The introductory article is particularly interesting for it is a critique of existing approaches to political socialization from a Marxist perspective.

Part Three

Structures are Central in Canadian Politics

Structures and institutions are probably the most permanent elements of Canadian politics. The first chapter in this section deals with structures in general; the second examines the nature and far-reaching consequences of Canada's federal arrangement.

Institutions can be thought of as agencies and offices arranged in a hierarchy with each agency or office having designated functions and authority. Individuals holding these offices and exercising these functions possess status and carry out roles. A broader definition of institutions refers to stable patterns of group behavior. In either case we can think of institutions as the result of specific kinds of political socialization but also as central agents of such socialization.

As you read the first chapter you will come to understand that political institutions such as Parliament, cabinet, courts or political parties, no matter how important and powerful they may be, reflect human characteristics and thus are not totally rational, efficient, consistent or ideal. Among other things Professor Redekop argues that the institutional approach draws our attention to our political heritage and helps us to understand legitimacy, liberty and responsibility, three important elements in Canadian politics. As you proceed through the second chapter you will see why federal structures have been central in Canadian politics and, quite appropriately, in writings about Canadian politics. Recent Canadian crises involving the Canadian Constitution of 1982, energy policies, control of off-shore resources, language laws, financing of higher education and health care, taxation, ecology, rights of native peoples, and regional disparity all illustrate the point. Professor Meekison has amply demonstrated that almost all important issues in Canadian politics are either directly or indirectly related to federal-provincial relations.

7

Canadian Political Institutions

John H. Redekop*

INTRODUCTION

In recent decades much has been written about new ways of looking at Canadian politics. A tendency to minimize the role of formal structures has won considerable popularity. Analyses that explain how political affairs operate within institutional patterns and according to constitutional arrangements are sometimes rejected as being too formal and too traditional. But surely the important question is not whether a perspective is traditional or formal but whether it helps us to get an accurate picture of political reality and thus to understand the complexities and dynamics of Canadian politics. In this chapter we shall see how important it is that we understand Canada's institutional and constitutional arrangements, both formal and informal, as they function in our parliamentary democracy.

Naturally, no one approach to so large a subject can tell us everything that we should know, and therefore students would do well to familiarize themselves with other interpretations. Writers who draw attention to powerful groups in Canadian society, to elites, to important individuals, to economics, to geography, to the impact of the United States, to French-English interaction, and to much else, help us to broaden our understanding. However, what many writers seem to overlook is the very important fact that whatever the source of political pressures, whatever the reason for political demands, and whatever the vehicles for their expression or satisfaction, Canada's integrating political institutions constitute the arena in which competing assertions and claims are adjudicated.

*Professor of Political Science, Wilfrid Laurier University.

Having a general knowledge of the formal arrangements and actual workings of the Canadian political system will provide us with the overall framework; explanations of various aspects of Canadian politics can then be fitted into place.

Having stressed the importance of focusing our attention on political structures, I must hasten to emphasize that even in a stable parliamentary democracy these are constantly evolving. Pressures for adaptation and reform seem to be unending. At any given time many individuals and groups, as well as political jurisdictions such as cities and provinces, are pressing hard for official changes. That in itself indicates how important the formal and informal political institutions actually are.

This chapter will not concentrate on making a case for the institutional interpretation, although it will do that in part; it will mainly describe and assess that approach. The central hypothesis is straightforward: whether we define political science as the study of the state, the study of government, the study of power, the study of the authoritative allocation of values, the study of political behavior, the measurement of verifiable political facts, or, indeed, almost any other way, we must have a sound knowledge of political institutions if we wish to understand Canadian politics.

At the outset we need to clarify our terms. I define political science as the study of the institutions and processes of government, as well as of the organization, behavior, policies, beliefs and doctrines of individual people and groups of people associated with government, for the purpose of making explanations and generalizations of political phenomena. Government, in turn, is defined as the office holders in certain institutions who, by whatever means, have come to be recognized as the bearers of ultimate power within a polity and whose main role is the authoritative allocation of resources and values in that polity. Politics, then, refers to all activity whose main purpose is one or more of the following: to reshape or influence governmental structures or processes; to influence or replace governmental office holders; to influence the formation of public policies; to influence the implementation of public policies; to generate public awareness of, and response to, governmental institutions, processes, personnel and policies; or to gain a place of influence or power within government. Clearly, institutions are very important in such a view of political reality.

Let me further clarify my perspective. When I speak of the institutions of government I am referring to the recognized and accepted arrangement of ultimate power in a country. Thus government institutions consist of those structures whose incumbents actually or potentially regulate all other power centers or institutions, such as families, businesses, churches, labor unions, professional associations, within that country. Normally this set of government institutions consists of the executive, legislative, judicial, bureaucratic, policing and military branches. Political parties and, to a lesser extent in Canada, educational institutions, organized religion, economic structures, the media and other interest groups overlap somewhat with the institutions of government defined more narrowly. The boundary problem can be a thorny one but if we keep our central focus on those institutions whose members or incumbents claim collectively to be maintaining general control over the whole political jurisdiction and whose authority is generally accepted, though not necessarily respected, then we can probably avoid some of the problems of definition. In any event, our main concern is not to delineate precisely the limits of government but to evaluate the importance of those institutions or structures that lie at the heart of government.

In most countries, formal institutions of government are clearly spelled out in the constitution; however, the actual arrangement rarely conforms to the formal prescription or description. Canada is a prime example of such a situation; the cabinet, for example, is not even mentioned in the British North America Act, yet it ranks as probably the most important of all Canadian political institutions. Similarly, the prime minister remains unrecognized in the 1867 constitutional documents though in actual fact he wields more power than any other individual. These examples, and others that could be cited, tell us that, while written constitutions and official descriptions may provide useful information about government institutions, they tend not to be accurate or adequate. In Canada, and even more so in Britain, New Zealand and certain other countries, an adequate description of government institutions can be gained only by studying the actual power arrangements and structures produced by tradition and convention. Most countries, including all federal countries, have a constitution which is at least partly written.

Sometimes the institutions of government are viewed mainly as arenas of conflict or as "rules of the game of politics"; other times they are seen in terms of people in action. Doern and Aucoin, for example, define structures as "regular patterns of behavior that exist between policy actors and organizational units."[1] Such a view helps us to understand the importance of what political actors do but seems to minimize the legitimizing significance of the continuing power arrangements themselves. Small wonder, then, that many writers look beyond the incumbents and place much emphasis specifically on the institutional units. One such writer, Milliband, identifies the following as the key institutions that, in a functional sense, together comprise the state system: the executive government, the ministerial departments, the public corporations, the central banks and regulatory commissions, the military, the judiciary and the legislative assemblies.[2] Whatever our inclination, we do well to avoid a mechanistic, an organismic or an overly idealistic view of government institutions. As far as Canadian politics is concerned, preoccupation with any one of these emphases probably takes us away from a clear understanding of political reality. Canadian politics, I suggest, consists of a great diversity of sometimes haphazard activity, arising from an amorphous array of ideas and ideologies. This activity is undertaken by thousands of people who constitute the mammoth governmental establishment or are significantly associated with it. The general unity, legitimacy and continuity of their activity derives logically and obviously from the more or less official institutions of which they are a part and through which their activities are expressed.

SPECIFIC INSTITUTIONS

Of all Canadian political institutions Parliament is probably the most consequential. Our whole parliamentary tradition, going back to the establishment of parliamentary supremacy in the British Isles, proceeding to the establishment of a representative assembly in Nova Scotia in 1758 and subsequently in all the other British colonies in North America, through to the winning of responsible government in the colony of Nova Scotia in 1847 and in the Province of Canada in 1849, and the creation of the Dominion of Canada in 1867, all involved verbal and sometimes even physical battles over how various institutions should relate to one another. Should the monarch be subordinate to Parliament? Should the executive be responsible to the elected members of Parliament? Should Parliament be bicameral and, if so, how should the two houses relate to one another? What powers should be exercised by the governor general and the lieutenant-governors? How should the provinces be officially represented in Parliament? To what extent should the Canadian Parliament be subordinate to the British Parliament or to the British judiciary? These and many additional questions obviously focus specifically on institutions and the debates and controversies involving these institutional relations were not inconsequential niceties or formalities undertaken while the real stuff of politics was conducted elsewhere. These problems and their resolution *were* the real stuff of politics! The sometimes heated confrontations at Charlottetown, Québec City, and London were first and foremost debates over institutional accommodations and arrangements.

Institutional powers and relationships continued to be matters of much importance in later years. In 1896 the governor general, Lord Aberdeen, challenged the cabinet's power by refusing to agree to appointments made by a defeated government. The entire King-Byng crisis of 1926 was essentially a battle for institutional supremacy rather than a personality conflict or a partisan ploy. Prime Minister King's response to the Chanak Crisis in 1922 together with the Balfour Declaration of 1926 and the vitally important Statute of Westminster in 1931 expressed and, in the last instance, legitimized the full autonomy of Canada and the institutional supremacy of the Canadian Parliament in external as well as internal affairs. More recently, a 1949 amendment to the British North America Act which gave Parliament the power to amend that Act except for areas involving provincial matters, certain education guarantees, certain language guarantees, and parliamentary sessions and terms, constitutes another important stage in the development of the Canadian Parliament as an institution.

In our own day Parliament, as an institution, still looms large. Politicians can make promises on the hustings or agree to deals in smoke-filled rooms but no statutes can be enacted or amended, no taxes legally imposed and no funds legally appropriated unless formally approved by Parliament. Of course, Parliament may delegate certain powers to others and, on occasion, will allow governments to collect and spend monies before the legislation is finally approved, but as an institution it always has the right to intervene and to call a halt to any executive action. It did exactly that on February 19, 1968 when the House of Commons rejected a tax measure the cabinet had assumed would pass and some of whose provisions the cabinet had already implemented.

Perhaps the most important role of the House of Commons as a formal institution involves the matter of expressing official confidence or nonconfidence in the cabinet. After an election it is the official party representation in the House of Commons and not any behavior of elites, classes, groups or individuals that determines what party will form the government and whether it will have majority or minority status. Whatever the result, any government of the day must resign or call an election as soon as the House of Commons by a majority vote expresses nonconfidence in it. Admittedly, in February 1968 the Liberal government maneuvered the House, more particularly Opposition Leader Robert Stanfield, into a second vote which reversed the original decision but such a reversal does not indicate any kind of weakening of Parliament's power; rather, it illustrates once again that the life of Canada's national government depends on the collective decision of the House of Commons.

It is at times suggested that Parliament does not matter much; that it is merely a rubber stamp and that most members play an inconsequential role in political life. Granted, at times the backbenchers are inconspicuous and seem to lack clout but anybody who followed the national election campaigns of 1979 and 1980, the Ontario campaign of 1980, or, indeed, any other campaign, knows how desperately party leaders want a majority status in the legislature. Structures are obviously very important.

When we look to the Senate we see an institution whose power, while formally substantial, has in fact been largely eroded. However, during the Coyne affair in 1961, and on numerous other occasions when the Senate has amended, criticized or held up government legislation it has shown that governments still do well to reckon with it. The relatively weak position of the Senate illustrates the fact that an institution's actual powers are often quite different from its official powers. It also tells us that institutions are dynamic entities that can gain or lose political power. That the upper chamber, despite its weaknesses, remains an important structure was constantly underscored during the heated constitutional debates of 1980 and 1981.

The institution we know as the cabinet lies at the center of our political system. Its great power derives not from the personal qualities of its members, though these qualities do have some significance, but from the political power that has devolved upon that institution over the centuries. The incumbents decide how that power is to be used, they may even extend or reduce it, but it exists quite apart from who they are because it rests in the institution itself. Individual ministers, even all of them collectively, might wish to see a death sentence commuted, new tariff rates proclaimed, support for the UN terminated, the monarchy abolished, or increased government subsidies given to deep-sea fishermen but their wishes are of little consequence until, as cabinet, via orders-in-council, they transform these wishes into public policy. Not surprisingly, Doern and Wilson assert that "no understanding of the political policy processes in Canada can be fully and intellectually complete until one examines (or attempts to mentally simulate) policy-making from the vantage point of the collective cabinet."[3]

The prime minister, similarly, cannot be seen only as a powerful individual or the epitome of the elite. He must be seen for what he is in our system; the top leader in the country who derives his power from the office he holds in formal institutions: party, cabinet and Parliament. His personal traits—eloquence, intelligence, leadership skills, general charisma or whatever—may be very important in helping him to achieve his office and may greatly influence what he does while in office but they are not the source of his power. As an individual he may wish to appoint a new senator or judge, to establish a royal commission, to invoke the War Measures Act, or to call a general election but his wishes in themselves will achieve nothing until he acts as prime minister in an official capacity. Quite accurately his position has been termed the *Apex of Power*.[4] Though as a person he may not change one iota, he holds that power only so long as he retains his parliamentary seat and he and his cabinet enjoy the support of a majority in the House of Commons. It is this institutional support that gives him his political legitimacy and political clout. Prime Minister Trudeau once stated that when backbenchers leave the parliamentary chambers they are "nobodies." When a prime minister ceases to be prime minister he may still be popular and even influential but in terms of wielding official power he becomes a nobody himself for he has then lost his institutional base. Pierre Trudeau experienced this traumatic loss of power in 1979 as did Joe Clark in 1980. The office made the difference.

Space limitations do not permit us to describe in any detail the importance of all our other national, not to mention provincial or municipal, political institutions and structures. We could discuss at length the institution of the monarch; the office of the governor general; the special, joint and standing committees of the House of Commons; the various committees of the cabinet but especially the Treasury Board; the ministers who head departments; the speaker; the auditor-general; the commissioner of official languages; and the chief electoral officer. In each instance the power exercised arises not from the person as person but from the person as office holder, as bearer of powers of an institution. The Treasury Board, for example, does not consist merely of a half dozen prominent and powerful Canadians who have taken it upon themselves to decide to negotiate with government employees about working conditions or to apportion the country's budget to various governmental departments and agencies; rather, the Treasury Board functions as an official institution charged with official duties. As in the case of the House of Commons and the cabinet, so also here, the whole is more than the sum of its parts and, in the long run, the fact that the official responsibilities of that institution are properly carried out is much more important than who the individuals happen to be who are currently entrusted with doing what needs to be done.

In addition to all the institutions already mentioned we have a large number of regulatory commissions, Crown agencies and corporations, and the whole

gamut of the federal bureaucracy comprising part of our governmental structures. It is one thing to know that a certain prominent Canadian is opposed to
the building of any Mackenzie Valley pipeline, that five big-name Canadians
oppose all wage and price rollbacks, that ten influential Canadians favor
governmental subsidization of Canadian television, that twelve wish to terminate all government grants for medical research done outside Canada, that
fifteen favor the nationalization of the CPR, or that nine concur with Prime
Minister Trudeau's constitutional stance; but it is something quite different to
know that the prominent Canadian is Commissioner Thomas Berger, that the
five big-name Canadians constituted the Anti-Inflation Board, that the ten
comprise the Canadian Radio-television and Telecommunications Commission,
that the twelve make up the Medical Research Council, that the fifteen serve as
the Canadian Transport Commission and that the nine are the Supreme Court
of Canada. By and large, as far as politics is concerned, people's opinions and
wishes have far-reaching and continuing importance only if associated with
some recognized institution or structure. Of course, what we have surveyed at
the national level exists also at provincial and local levels, albeit sometimes in
modified forms.

As we survey the political scene, it quickly becomes evident that institutions
are still proliferating and, on balance, still growing in significance and power.
Nationally, we are witnessing the development of various new agencies, most
notably the very important political institution known as the Federal-Provincial
Conference of First Ministers with its continuing secretariat and its official
location in Ottawa's refurbished Union Station. Provincially, we see increasing
power emanating from workmen's compensation boards, pollution control
agencies and the burgeoning ombudsman offices, to name some obvious instances. Canadian political institutions are still very much alive and thriving. To
attempt to understand Canadian politics without becoming generally familiar
with Canada's constitutional arrangements is like trying to build, or in a major
way repair, the CN Tower without a set of structural drawings.

INSTITUTIONALISM AND OTHER PERSPECTIVES

We have seen that it is impossible to understand Canadian politics without
substantial knowledge about the structural arrangements; now we want to see
how the institutional interpretation fits in with all the other orientations set
forth in this book.

If we attempt to explain Canadian politics from a geographical point of view
it quickly becomes evident that institutions cannot be overlooked. The original
fixing of boundaries—national, provincial or municipal—and the establishment of governments in those jurisdictions illustrate the inseparable connection.
But that is only the beginning. Subsequent jurisdictional disputes and coopera-

tion involving resource ownership and development, transportation and communication policies, pollution control, commodity marketing regulations, industrial development grants, recreational and parks policies, and the establishment of regional governments and district boards of various sorts, all involve continuing institutional decisions. A geographical orientation draws our attention to the physical environment and the people in it, but unless we add the dimention of institutions we cannot really talk of politics other than the "politics" of anarchy.

Turning to the continentalist interpretation we find a similar situation. The overwhelming impact of various American institutions on Canada, from the Federal Reserve System to the Department of Agriculture and from the Pentagon to the Immigration and Naturalization Service, is common knowledge. Then, too, quite apart from the effect of all the specifically American structures we have the very wide range of effects arising from such joint structures as NORAD, the St. Lawrence Seaway Authority, the International Joint Commission, and the dozens of other Canadian-American institutions.

Economics, our next orientation, may well be defined as the science of the production, distribution and consumption of wealth but such activity cannot be carried on without a clearly recognized and relatively stable institutional arrangement. The traditional discipline of political economy reflected well the existing and continuing close interrelationship of economic activity and formal governmental structures. Especially in our day, when governments are becoming very much involved in regulatory, welfare and proprietary activity in the economy, a re-emphasis of that relationship is timely. Virtually every organization of government influences the Canadian economy, is influenced by it, or both. To attempt to explain Canadian politics from an economic vantage point without giving a large place to cabinet decisions, to the Department of National Revenue, to the Treasury Board, to the Canadian Transport Commission, to the Tariff Commission, and the whole host of relevant provincial agencies from marketing boards to tourist bureaus is to attempt the impossible. The 1980 government guarantees of Chrysler loans illustrates the increasingly close relationship between economic activity and political institutions.

The historical approach to Canadian politics, the next on our list, relies particularly on structural relationships and evolution. How can we possibly understand the nature of Crown powers in Canada, the dynamics of responsible government, or the extent of personal rights and liberties if we are not prepared to learn about the evolution of the constitutional monarchy, about cabinet precedents, or about the British court system and common law? Many of the critical points in our history, such as the passage of the Quebec Act of 1774, of the Constitutional Act of 1791, of the Act of Union in 1840, of the British North America Act in 1867, of the Statute of Westminster in 1931 and of the new Canadian constitution, to name only the most obvious ones, either established new institutions or gave greater legitimacy to those already existing. Of course, Canadian history involves leaders and movements and ideologies and resources but it involves institutions in a profound way. Any attempt to explain Canadian politics from a historical perspective must address itself to the development of our institutions.

We turn now to approaches that focus particularly on values and ask ourselves how institutions fit into ideological or value-oriented interpretations of Canadian politics. Not surprisingly, much attention is given to institutions. Discussions about conservative or liberal or socialist or social credit ideologies boil down largely to questions about what should or should not be done by various governmental institutions. The conservatives revere traditional institutions such as the monarchy and the Empire-Commonwealth; they tend to see contemporary institutions as the product of centuries of community experience and they are generally reluctant to change anything very much or very quickly. The liberals are more ready to alter institutions and to work through them to enhance personal liberty and general welfare. The socialists, of course, want to strengthen and expand governmental institutions to further the welfare state and to bring about greater public ownership of the major sectors of production and distribution; while social credit apologists have as their main idea the notion that state institutions should control credit and the whole financial sector much more than they do now. Thus we see that, in explaining Canadian politics, writers who emphasize ideology must deal with institutions to show how the important ideologies have developed and what their supporters advocate.

Next, we consider political culture. Let Michael Whittington state his observation as given elsewhere in this volume:

> ...the political structures must reflect the dominant values of our political
> culture if they are to be effective. If political structures serve to enshrine political
> values that are not congruent with the values of Canadian society, then either
> the people's attitudes must change to conform to the institutionalized values, or
> the institutions must change to reflect social values better.

There we have it, stated unequivocally. Other writers in that area agree with Whittington that institutions are important. That is not surprising, for institutions do have a great impact on our political culture, responses to them are part of our political culture, and if they are to function successfully they must be in fundamental alignment with the central values in our political culture.

Looking at the federalist analysis of Canadian politics we see that here, too, institutional arrangements are basic. Confederation itself can be defined as institutional accommodation and evolution. Such later developments as decisions by the Judicial Committee of the Privy Council, the establishment of shared-cost programs, national disallowance of provincial legislation, the drawing up of taxation agreements, several important amendments to the BNA Act, and the continuing and eventually successful discussions about constitutional "patriation" and an acceptable amendment formula all involve the question of institutional jurisdiction. One of the great studies of Canadian politics, the 1940 Rowell-Sirois Royal Commission report, dealt largely with institutional responsibilities and resources in our federal arrangement. Almost by definition, a federalist interpretation of Canadian politics, obviously relevant and important, makes sense only if we think in terms of constitutions and institutions.

As Richard Simeon has pointed out, "Federalism is not only a response to regionalism, but also ensures that it will continue."[5] It does so in several ways. In the first place, the federal framework leads many politicians, pundits, academics and opinion leaders to assume, even assert, a provincial perspective which, in turn, filters down to the electorate and the general population. Also, it provides "an institutional focus for loyalty and identity" and as "a political cleavage laid over other cleavages in the society... it tends to force other cleavages into the same mold."[6] If we analyze the operations of various kinds of pressure groups, of political parties and of governments themselves, we can see that federalism as an institution tends to highlight "those cleavages which reinforce the territorial division" while other cleavages "will either be defined in such a way that they do conform to the pattern, or they will tend to be ignored."[7] To the extent, which is considerable, that the formal federal structures fragment social forces, blunt social cleavages, and in general inhibit the development of national pressures and sentiments, they not only perpetuate regional and provincial differences but greatly influence Canadian politics as a whole. Noting that when Alberta and Saskatchewan were created in 1905 from a single undifferentiated area, they "rapidly developed into two quite distinct political systems,"[8] Simeon writes as follows:

> This suggests that institutions are not simply the outgrowth or products of the environment and that they are not just dependent variables in the political system. They can also be seen as independent forces, which have some effects of their own: once established they themselves come to shape and influence the environment.... There must be some congruence between institutions and the underlying social system, but it is equally evident that the effect is two-way.[9]

We turn our attention now to political processes and the exercise of power. Let us deal first with processes. Many political scientists today are much attracted to studying the dynamic, integrative, aggregative and redistributive aspects of political processes. Such an emphasis is well taken but processes do not take place in a vacuum. We have earlier noted that government itself can be defined, at least in part, in terms of authoritative allocation of values, but what makes such allocation authoritative? I suggest that it is mainly the institutional setting, that is, the formal offices held and the official powers exercised. Let us assess the validity of such a view as we scan the next four approaches.

To talk about political parties is to talk about organizations whose leaders seek to control state institutions. In a functional sense, of course, the party structures themselves, while technically not part of the governmental machinery, form part of the total complex of political institutions. And when we talk about political elections we are not describing the selection of leaders in the sense that a Rotary Club chooses its executives, but we are describing the selection of leaders for external, or at least overarching, institutional positions.

Many students of Canadian political parties have described the importance of institutions.[10] Even Winn and McMenemy, while striving to move beyond the traditional institutional descriptions, acknowledge that an adequate analysis must give a large place to structures. Quite appropriately, they study "the place of parties in the larger political system and in the ongoing political process."[11] Their input-throughout-output model helps us understand Canadian politics only if we apply it to actual institutions. Where there are no structures, there can be no flow; without governmental institutions, no party platforms or cross-pressure compromises ever become governmental policies. Whatever else political parties may be, they are fundamentally important because they are political institutions that express and accommodate the interests of various regions, classes and groups.

If parties, as institutions, play a major role in politicizing certain societal cleavages, the electoral system, as an important institution in its own right, has a major effect on political behavior and electoral results. As Alan Cairns has demonstrated,[12] Canada's electoral system operates in a way that greatly exaggerates regional differences and that fact, by and large, results in under-representation for those parties whose support is more evenly distributed throughout the country. Consequently, and quite logically, party leaders tend to adopt policies and programs that have the greatest appeal in regions where they are already strong. Thus the Conservatives under Diefenbaker and the Liberals under Trudeau, while vociferously espousing the virtues of unhyphenated Canadianism and national unity, actually adopted policies with specific regional appeals which would, presumably, produce the best possible electoral results.

Moving on to the perspective that stresses dualism, we find that English-French cooperation and conflict in Canada often involves governmental institutions. Constitutional provisions set much of the framework but they did not resolve the problems. The question of "adequate" French-Canadian representation in the military, the regulatory agencies, the bureaucracy, the Crown corporations, the courts and the cabinet remains a matter of contention. The Royal Commission on Bilingualism and Biculturalism, the Canadian Radio-television and Telecommunications Commission, the Public Service Commission, the Commissioner of Official Languages, and other institutional centers have dealt with various aspects of this deep division, but if the 1976 election of a separatist government in Québec, and its re-election in 1981, reflect public opinion even in a limited way, then the division persists. And, of course, separatism itself involves a quarrel over institutional relations. If the institutional dimension were of no great consequence, then the champions of the French-Canadian culture would surely ignore it and attend to the business of protecting and building their "nation". But they know that the institutional situation is not peripheral; they know that it is central and that is why they have made institutional autonomy a first priority. A separatist movement may have a great political program but unless institutions are altered such a program comes to nothing.

Public policy, as suggested earlier, cannot be divorced from governmental structures either. It differs from the policies of private organizations primarily in its scope and in the coercive institutional power that lies behind it. Introducing their important study of public policy, Doern and Aucoin point out that "the emphasis on the plurality of structures is an important feature of the book."[13] Lamenting the fact that the "structuring of those policy roles" has not been studied intensively and asserting that "part of the problem was the dominance of constitutional studies,"[14] their balanced analysis nonetheless gives full recognition to the formal or institutional relationships among the several components of the policy process. The titles of seven of their nine chapters include names of formal government institutions.

Most obviously, the development of public policy involves extensive and complex bargaining among structured pressure groups and distinct units of government. As far as the competing and cooperating governments are concerned, relative institutional autonomy is an ongoing concern and not only in Québec. Accordingly, attempts to deal with poverty in Canada tend to be transformed into problems of regional and provincial disparities; transportation debates focus on such problems as in which province a service facility will be located rather than on meeting social needs; and issues such as medical insurance, funding post-secondary education, and the operation of pension plans are debated in terms of governmental jurisdictions rather than how the public can best be served. Similarly, the language question becomes an Ottawa-Québec problem and oil export policies degenerate into an Alberta-Ottawa controversy or confrontation rather than a discussion of what is, in the long run, in the best interest of Canadians.

The foregoing discussion clearly demonstrates that any attempt to explain Canadian politics from a policy perspective cannot avoid an emphasis on institutions since our statutes from the Criminal Code to the War Measures Act are the products of institutional interaction; they are enacted by governmental institutions and then are applied by governmental institutions of one kind or another.

We have seen how important institutions are for the approaches that emphasize environment, values, structures and processes; now we ask ourselves what significance institutions have for the approaches that focus on political power and behavior. Admittedly, all institutions are made by men but they are the products of many generations and, once established, seem to have a character and momentum of their own, a character that greatly influences the behavior of incumbents. Even mass movements and social classes tend to develop as responses to certain arrangements of authority.

If we consider the role of individual leaders we see a mixed situation. An explanation of Canadian politics emphasizing key people tells us that to a large extent people such as John A. Macdonald, Wilfrid Laurier, J.S. Woodsworth, Mackenzie King, John Diefenbaker, Pierre Trudeau, René Lévesque, William Aberhart or Maurice Duplessis probably shaped political institutions as much as they were shaped by them. But that does not detract from my central thesis, which simply asserts that institutions are important. The issue is not some kind of institutional determinism or even institutional preeminence, it is only a question of institutional significance. I suggest that, by and large, the men and women whose ideas and actions dominated or now dominate Canadian politics operated mainly as office holders in, or shapers of, governmental institutions. The role of Pierre Trudeau during the 1980-82 constitutional issue is a classic example.

The place of institutions in an elitist interpretation of Canadian politics is similar to that described in the previous approach; elites influence governmental institutions but they also work through them. Of course, not all elites, or all members of elite groups, are necessarily political. What, we may ask, transforms certain elites into political elites? The answer is simple; they have either maneuvered themselves into positions of power in governmental institutions or have found ways of influencing other people who fill those positions. C. Wright Mills, perhaps the foremost advocate of the elitist approach, agrees. "No one…can be truly powerful unless he has access to the command of major institutions, for it is over these institutional means of power that the truly powerful are, in the first instance, powerful."[15]

Moving on to the "group theory" view of Canadian politics, we quickly come to realize that a major, if not *the* major, reason for the formation of pressure groups is the goal of putting pressure on office holders in governmental institutions. In our parliamentary system this means focusing mainly on the cabinet rather than on backbenchers. Group leaders and lobbyists tend not to be interested in just any people who happen to be eloquent or charismatic or who possess gifts of leadership. Quite understandably, they give their attention to people who possess institutional power. From 1963 till 1968 pressure group spokesmen took their message to Lester Pearson. Then suddenly they seemed to forget about him altogether and zeroed in on Pierre Trudeau. Why? Pearson had not changed as a person but he had given up his institutional position and the group spokesmen fully realized that that basic fact made all the difference. Not only do Canadian pressure groups strive to influence institutions such as the cabinet, the Canadian Transport Commission, the CRTC, or the House of Commons Standing Committee on Veterans' Affairs, but in our pluralist society they themselves function as important institutions.

Experts in the area agree on the close association between pressure groups and governmental institutions. David Truman states: "The power such groups dispose is involved at every point in the institutions of government, and the efforts of these formations are in various ways aided by, restricted by, and identified with institutionalized government."[16] A. Paul Pross, in commenting on the authors who contributed to his volume, notes that "They have turned their attention to the impact major institutions—particularly Parliament and the civil service—have had on pressure groups, and they have noted the way in which such groups have adapted to the requirements of the constitution."[17]

The last approach in this general category, at least as presented in this book, is the Marxist class analysis of Canadian politics. How important are governmental institutions from a leftist vantage point? Even a brief glance at Resnick's chapter in this volume, or a survey of almost any other Marxist study, indicates that institutions are given a prominent place. Stanley Ryerson has described in detail how the bourgeois class gained control of governmental institutions in the nineteenth century.[18] Resnick echoes similar views. Social classes always play major roles but the really important aspect is that the dominant class exercises its power through governmental structures. The main purpose of politicizing the proletariat, it appears, is to enable it to gain control of government institutions and then reform or maybe abolish them, depending on which Marxists are speaking. Consider some of Resnick's statements: "the analysis of the state should be at the very heart of political science"; "Marxist theory would argue that state intervention becomes necessary as capitalism fails to function"; "the state has been involved in fostering capitalist accumulation for centuries"; "labor relations boards, labor codes and the like can be important carrots in winning labor support"; and, "the capitalist state exercises very effective behind-the-scenes control over such institutions as the CBC." Clearly, a Marxist analysis has much to say about political institutions. Marxist critics are sometimes inclined to reject the so-called institutional approach as sterile but in fact they employ it! Constantly they use the standard institutional categories. Perhaps most of them would, upon reflection, even agree that formal political institutions such as federalism and Parliament have played an important role in inhibiting the development of a national, class-based politics in Canada.

Where does this necesarily brief survey leave us? Well, it leaves me with the distinct impression that consideration of political institutions has an important place in every interpretation of Canadian politics presented in this book. Many approaches, of course, go far beyond institutional considerations but none can, or in fact does, ignore them. But these fifteen approaches do not exhaust all possibilities and presumably some readers might believe that there are other approaches and methodologies in which institutions play no part. Naturally, I cannot deal with all possible ways of looking at Canadian politics but let us touch briefly on three general methodologies that have thus far not been considered specifically: structural-functional analysis, behavioralism and systems theory.

Discussing the first of these three, Oran Young asserts that the "conceptual framework of the structural-functional approach centers around the question, What structures fulfill what basic functions and under what conditions in any given system?"[19] Marion J. Levy, Jr. reminds us that the first basic step in structural-functional analysis involves definition of "the unit to be discussed."[20] The units, it turns out, are mainly political institutions. Philippa Strum and Michael Shmidman add the following observations: "Functionalism concentrates on the political functions performed by people and institutions."[21] "In the final analysis, the functionalist will take the basic, formal structure of government and attempt to discover who within it actually has power, how much, and how it is used."[22] Functionalists, they conclude, "ask what political functions are performed in all societies, and then they are able to move to a consideration of the institutions or structures that perform them."[23] Institutions, clearly, are very important for structural-functional analysts.

Arguing, as they do, that one cannot understand the workings of political institutions without first examining the behavior of the individuals who comprise them, behavioralists have often paid little explicit attention to institutions. However, as Robert Murphy points out, when they talk about voting behavior, political participation, the psychological characteristics of political man, and the rest of their quantifiable or non-quantifiable data and concepts, the institutions of the political system form the integrating framework.[24] Without such an integration, voting statistics, the results of multivariate analysis, or data on leaders remain unrelated if not meaningless facts.

As its name suggests, systems theory, which can be seen either as an area within behavioralism or as a separate methodology in its own right, focuses on the relationship of political institutions to one another and to other phenomena. The conceptual structures that Easton and others have developed bear a striking resemblance to actual institutions.[25] That makes sense since all the systems theory emphasis on demands, supports, transformation, feedback and so on becomes credible only if one postulates an actual set of political institutions. The whole approach correctly assumes that processes are important but that, at least in politics, processes do not exist without institutions.

SOME GENERAL PROPOSITIONS

While the main thrust of the institutionalist perspective is that in any polity, be it Soviet, South African or Canadian, institutions play a major role and deserve serious study, there is also a second, more ideological thrust that contends that certain kinds of institutions are especially important because they play a vital role in the development and functioning of free democracies. The following propositions will serve to illustrate this second thrust.

1. The institutional approach, following in the Enlightenment tradition, gives a large place to continual refurbishing, modification and reform. It rejects the Platonic or Marxist views that political problems can be resolved once and for all. For most institutionalists politics is, or at least should be, open activity and social conflict converted into peaceful, continuing competition. Institutions of government, especially representative assemblies, are seen as arenas in which, over time, proximate solutions are worked out for society's political problems.

2. The institutionalist interpretation of politics acknowledges that power is the basis of politics and asserts that while establishing institutional safeguards is not a sufficient condition for an orderly exercise of power, it is a necessary one. Given the fact that the "great problem of history has been to turn absolute power to democratic uses," the development in Canada of a set of

institutions through which political power is exercised as an efficient, controllable, and largely predictable force is a major achievement.

3. Most institutionalists hold to the view that rationality can be applied to the realm of politics and that it can modify or even replace continuity and traditional practices as the basis of authority. In Canada, political changes involving, for example, Crown powers and the head of state incorporate this phenomenon. Political institutions are thus important inasmuch as they exemplify the highest achievement of the enlightened, rational mind.

4. By and large, institutionalists agree that those institutions that check authority, balance power and generally promote limited government are most important. In Canada the federal arrangement, the electoral system, cabinet accountability, the independent judiciary, the functioning of official opposition parties, parliamentary supremacy and the whole body of British common law serve to protect a substantial sphere of private life and to reinforce freedoms.

5. Institutionalists generally have great respect for a society's political constitution, whether it is formally spelled out as the American was intended to be, whether it is largely unwritten as the British is, or whether it is a blend of a formal document, of largely inherited conventions and of formal legislative enactment as the Canadian constitution has come to be. Any country's basic law is important because it establishes both the organizational framework and a fundamental philosophical orientation. In addition, it assigns responsibilities, describes basic processes, sets forth the conditions and terms of office holding, and usually spells out formal amending procedures.

6. Competition, as an operating principle, is a central notion for most institutionalists. The basic argument is that individual as well as collective competition produces substantial freedom and progress, and that institutions of government play a vital, conducive role in achieving those ends. The problem, as institutionalists see it, is to prevent competition from degenerating into oppression by any single segment of society. The way to prevent such oppression, it is argued, is to establish constitutional limits on governments and to have periodic and uncoerced elections. In such an arrangement, individual and group competition operates to produce collective benefits. Those institutionalists with a socialist inclination do not object to a relatively great concentration of power, provided it is held by the government, but they, too, believe that such a concentration of power, indeed, the whole question of socialism itself, should be decided by a free electoral vote.

CONCLUSION

In light of all that has been said so far we can say that, all things considered, an emphasis on governmental institutions is an important perspective on Canadian politics in its own right and that institutions cannot be ignored by any of the fourteen not explicitly institutional orientations presented in this book. Accordingly, we should perhaps see the institutional approach as a common denominator for all approaches, for surely, despite all the protestations to the contrary, its terms are the common language of the discipline and the standard reference points. Admittedly, in a sense the institutional approach may be elementary but that makes it no less important. Only a thorough knowledge of the basics enables us to probe more deeply.

There are additional limitations inherent in the institutional approach. In itself it tends to see politics as too static; arrangements are sometimes presented as too fixed. That is why we do well to consider other perspectives. As in the study of the human body, so also in political science, a thorough knowledge of anatomy is essential, though not sufficient, for an understanding of the processes of the body politic.

This approach also tends to neglect foreign affairs and international politics. Perhaps this shortcoming arises from the fact that, as there were no really important world institutions for a long time and even now there is no form of world government, there seems to be nothing of substance in this area to talk about. Let us not overlook international institutions that may be less than governmental in authority.

Similarly, a narrow conception of the institutional approach may lead us to overlook the importance of the individual, be he prime minister, lobbyist, newspaper columnist or voter. There is a danger that we separate institutions from people and thus lose touch with reality.

Finally, a narrowly delineated institutional approach may well underestimate the significance of violence in politics, even in Canadian politics. Without doubt, violence, the threat of violence, and the whole phenomenon of unanticipated disruption of normal affairs is becoming more important. Preparation for defense, planning for the possibility of insurrection, and the fear of war are very real preoccupations of Canadians and Canadian governments. A straightforward institutional emphasis on agencies and offices often overlooks such matters but that inadequacy can surely be corrected.

The importance of structures and institutions is attested to by the degree of attention devoted to them by major authors writing textbooks about Canadian politics. Here are the numbers of institution-oriented chapters in some common texts: Van Loon and Whittington, nine out of seventeen;[26] Ward's revision of the abbreviated text by Dawson and Dawson, fourteen out of fifteen;[28] Fox's fourth edition of collected articles, ten out of nineteen;[29] Khan, McNiven and MacKown, seven out of sixteen;[30] Kruhlak, Schultz, and Pobihushchy, twelve out of twenty-three;[31] Vaughan, Kyba, and Dwivedi, twenty out of twenty-five;[32] Mallory, ten out of ten;[33] and White, Wagenberg, and Nelson, seven out of eleven.[34]

It may currently be popular in some circles to reject any institutional emphasis but such rejection, as we have seen, is not warranted. Moreover, some of it seems to rest on a false assumption, namely, that some of us believe that once we have described all our institutions, nothing more remains to be said.

But those of us who give institutional studies a significant place make no such claim. What we emphasize, unabashedly, is that political institutions, simultaneously the reservoir and culmination of our collective experience, are of considerable importance. We believe that a good case can be made for the view that they constitute an integrating framework, both theoretically and actually, and that any interpretation that ignores institutions is incomplete.

SUMMARY

1. Political institutions provide the essential framework for political activity; the two phenomena are inseparable.
2. In a free country such as Canada, power derives more from offices and institutions than from the personal qualities of office holders.
3. Institutions play a major role in all the usual explanations of politics.
4. The institutional perspective is sometimes associated with the development and functioning of free societies.
5. Despite its limitations, the institutional approach remains a prerequisite for more specialized analysis.

STUDY QUESTIONS

1. Why has the traditional emphasis on political institutions been largely neglected, or even rejected, in the last several decades?
2. Why do federal countries have written constitutions?
3. What makes governmental institutions unique?
4. Why is institutional autonomy the dominant concern of Québec separatists? Should they not place primary emphasis on cultural matters?
5. Can you think of any significant approach to Canadian politics which ignores institutions?
6. Are informal institutions generally less significant than formal institutions?
7. Will extensive television coverage of political activity tend to enhance the importance of personality and weaken the importance of institutions?
8. In which of the approaches to Canadian politics described in this book is the institutional emphasis, in your estimation, least significant?
9. How are institutional change and institutional legitimacy related?
10. Which Canadian political institutions seem to be losing power and which seem to be gaining power? Why?

ENDNOTES

1. G. Bruce Doern and Peter Aucoin, *The Structure of Policy-Making in Canada* (Toronto: Macmillan, 1971), p. 4.

2. Ralph Milliband, *The State in Capitalist Society* (London: Wiedenfeld and Nicholson, 1969), pp. 53-4.

3. G. Bruce Doern and V. Seymour Wilson, eds., *Issues in Canadian Public Policy* (Toronto: Macmillan, 1974), p. 1.

4. Thomas A. Hockin, ed., *Apex of Power* (Scarborough, Ont.: Prentice-Hall, 1971).

5. Richard Simeon, "Regionalism and Canadian Political Institutions," *Queen's Quarterly*, 82, (Winter, 1975), p. 508.

6. Simeon, *Ibid.*, p. 508.

7. *Ibid.*

8. *Ibid.*, p. 504.

9. *Ibid.*

10. See, for example, Frederick Engelmann and Mildred Schwartz, *Canadian Political Parties: Origin, Character, Impact* (Scarborough, Ont.: Prentice-Hall, 1975).

11. Conrad Winn and John McMenemy, eds., *Political Parties in Canada* (Toronto: McGraw-Hill Ryerson, 1976), p. 1.

12. Alan C. Cairns, "The Electoral System and the Party System in Canada, 1921-1965," *Canadian Journal of Political Science*, 1, No. 1 (March, 1968), pp. 55-80.

13. Doern and Aucoin, *op. cit.*, p. 1.

14. *Ibid.*, p. 7.

15. C. Wright Mills, *The Power Elite* (New York: Oxford University Press, 1956), pp. 3-4.

16. David B. Truman, *The Governmental Process* (New York: Alfred A. Knopf, 1960), p. 7.

17. A. Paul Pross, *Pressure Group Behaviour in Canadian Politics* (Toronto: McGraw-Hill Ryerson, 1975), pp. 1-2.

18. Stanley Ryerson, *Unequal Union; Confederation and the Roots of Conflict in the Canadas, 1815-1873* (Toronto: Progress Books, 1968).

19. Oran R. Young, *Systems of Political Science* (Englewood Cliffs, NJ: Prentice-Hall, 1968), p. 28.

20. Marion J. Levy, Jr., "Some Aspects of 'Structural-Functional' Analysis and Political Science," *Approaches to the Study of Politics*, ed. Roland Young (Evanston, Ill.: Northwestern University Press, 1958), p. 53.

21. Philippa Strum and Michael Shmidman, *On Studying Political Science* (Pacific Palisades, California: Goodyear, 1969), p. 58.

22. *Ibid.*, p. 59.

23. *Ibid.*, p. 60.

24. Robert Murphy, *The Style and Study of Political Science* (Glenview, Ill.: Scott, Foresman, 1970), pp. 26-8.

25. See, for example, David Easton, *A Systems Analysis of Political Life* (New York: John Wiley & Sons, 1965), especially Part One.

26. Richard J. Van Loon and Michael S. Whittington, *The Canadian Political System: Environment, Structure and Process*, 2nd ed. (Toronto: McGraw-Hill Ryerson, 1976).

27. R. MacGregor Dawson, *The Government of Canada*, 5th ed. rev. by Norman Ward (Toronto: University of Toronto Press, 1970).

28. R. MacGregor Dawson and W.F. Dawson, *Democratic Government in Canada*, 4th ed. rev. by Norman Ward (Toronto: University of Toronto Press, 1971).

29. Paul W. Fox, ed., *Politics: Canada*, 4th ed. (Toronto: McGraw-Hill, 1977).

30. Rais A. Khan, James D. McNiven and Stuart A. MacKown, *An Introduction to Political Science*, rev. ed. (Georgetown, Ont.: Irwin-Dorsey, 1977).

31. Orest M. Kruhlak, Richard Schultz, and Sidney I. Pobihushchy, eds., *The Canadian Political Process*, rev. ed. (Toronto: Holt, Rinehart and Winston, 1973).

32. Frederick Vaughan, Patrick Kyba, and O.P. Dwivedi, eds., *Contemporary Issues in Canadian Politics* (Scarborough, Ont.: Prentice-Hall, 1970).

33. J.R. Mallory, *The Structure of Canadian Government* (Toronto: Macmillan, 1971).

34. W.L. White, R.H. Wagenberg, and R.C. Nelson, *Introduction to Canadian Politics and Government*, 2nd ed. (Toronto: Holt, Rinehart and Winston, 1977).

SELECTED REFERENCES

Despite the widespread reliance on the institutional approach, political science literature contains very little explicit analysis, on the topic. However, the following works should be useful, especially for the beginning student.

Apter, David E. *Introduction to Political Analysis.* Cambridge, Mass.: Winthrop, 1977. Chapters 6 and 7 provide a useful description of the role of institutions, especially in Western democracies.

Charlesworth, James C., ed. *A Design for Political Science: Scope, Objectives, and Methods.* Philadelphia: The American Academy of Political and Social Science, 1966. Three major essays, together with responses, dealing with the aspects mentioned in the title.

——————. *The Limits of Behavioralism in Political Science.* Philadelphia: The American Academy of Political and Social Science, 1962. The best treatment of the topic in a concise form.

Dahl, Robert A. *Modern Political Analysis*, 2nd ed. Englewood Cliffs, NJ: Prentice-Hall, 1970. A good discussion of major concepts and issues with some references to approaches.

Hyneman, Charles S. *The Study of Politics: The Present State of American Political Science.* Urbana, Ill.: University of Illinois Press, 1959. A useful analysis of the major questions and conflicts in American political science.

Irish, Marian D., ed. *Political Science: Advance of the Discipline.* Englewood Cliffs, NJ: Prentice-Hall, 1968. Six original essays dealing with basic concepts in political science traditions, methodologies and emphases.

Murphy, Robert. *The Style and Study of Political Science.* Glenview, Ill.: Scott, Foresman, 1970. An elementary introduction to the fields of political science and a cursory survey of the major approaches set mainly in an American framework.

Simeon, Richard. "Regionalism and Canadian Political Institutions." *Queen's Quarterly* 82 (Winter, 1975), pp. 499-511. A first-rate analysis that challenges some traditional assumptions about Canadian regionalism.

Somit, Albert, and Joseph Tanenhaus. *The Development of American Political Science: From Burgess to Behavioralism.* Boston: Allyn and Bacon, 1967. A very informative account of the development of American political science; contains a major section on behavioralism and its limitations.

Strum, Philippa and Michael Shmidman. *On Studying Political Science.* Pacific Palisades, Cal.: Goodyear, 1969. A primer about political science; major concepts, major divisions and major approaches are described briefly; very elementary.

Van Dyke, Vernon. *Political Science: A Philosophical Analysis.* Stanford, Cal.: Stanford University Press, 1960. This wide-ranging and very useful introduction to the study of politics has an excellent, but brief, section on approaches.

Young, Oran R. *Systems of Political Science.* Englewood Cliffs, NJ: Prentice-Hall, 1968. A very useful, short introduction to some of the major approaches; several chapters deal with the nature and utilization of approaches.

Young, Roland, ed. *Approaches to the Study of Politics.* Evanston, Ill.: Northwestern University Press, 1958. Twenty-two essays dealing with various approaches but not specifically with institutions except for one chapter on "structural-functional" analysis; assumes considerable knowledge of basic concepts.

8

Federal-Provincial Relations

J. Peter Meekison*

There is an oft-told anecdote which describes very perceptively one of the most significant features of Canadian politics. The story, which has a number of renditions, is as follows. Once upon a time an international committee was established to study the elephant. After agreeing on the terms of reference each delegate was asked to propose a tentative title for the final report. The delegates made the following suggestions:

Great Britain: The Elephant and the Commonwealth
United States: The Elephant and Free Enterprise
France: The Love Life of the Elephant
USSR: The Elephant and Marxism
West Germany: An Introduction to the Study of the Elephant
Canada: The Elephant: A Federal or Provincial Problem?

Today more than ever Canadian politics is the politics of federalism. No other single factor has had such a profound and significant impact on Canada's political system. Energy, medicare, hospitals, post-secondary education, RCMP, drought relief, offshore resources, fisheries, income tax and pay TV have one thing in common. They are all influenced by the federal system. Few, if any, issues which are discussed in Canada today do not in some way impinge on federal-provincial relations.

The anecdote says more about the realities of Canadian politics than one might realize.

The literature on federalism today is extensive, ranging from broad theoretical works to specific studies of individual states, including Canada. In these

*Deputy Minister, Department of Federal and Intergovernmental Affairs, Alberta; Professor of Political Science (on leave) the University of Alberta.

writings federalism has been characterized as a network of legal relationships, as a process, as a sociological phenomenon and as a bargain.[1] Given the number of federal states and the emergence and collapse of many new federations, such studies deserve careful scrutiny for the insights they give into the problems and pitfalls of governing under this complex system.

In approaching a study of Canadian politics from the perspective of federalism one encounters terms such as classical federalism, quasi-federalism, decentralized federalism, economic federalism, executive federalism, dual federalism, emergency federalism, flexible federalism and co-operative federalism. While the qualitative differences among these particular terms are often hard to isolate, their usage suggests that Canadian federalism means different things to different people or that only a particular characteristic or phenomenon of the federal system is being analyzed. While each commentary is describing an aspect of Canadian politics and certain common characteristics may emerge, the qualification attached to the word federalism suggests that each author has a different perspective on the problem.

Instead of attempting to develop an ideal prototype, it is more useful to begin with the widely recognized structural approach of K.C. Wheare. Wheare defined a government as federal when there exists "a division of power between general and regional authorities, each of which, in its own sphere is co-ordinate with the others and independent of them."[2] The federal principle according to Wheare's analysis has three main components: the division of powers, two orders of government and a statement of the relationships between them.

Although the cornerstone of a federal constitution may be the division of powers, these divisions are usually not sufficiently clear to prevent disputes from occurring over their precise meaning. These disputes arise as governments endeavor to fulfill their obligations and either trespass or are perceived to have trespassed on another's territory. Conflicts over the interpretation of the British North America Act provide an excellent example. The number of instances that the courts in Canada have had to determine whether a question is a matter relating to "peace, order and good government" (national) or "property and civil rights" (provincial) are too frequent to mention. Regardless of the outcome of such cases, their existence serves to confirm the fact that perceptions of the division of powers change over time. Whether the changes in the division of powers occur as a result of judicial interpretation, amendment, convention, attrition, delegation or something else, significant changes do take place in the relationship between the two orders of government. The initial equilibrium within the federation, usually achieved after painstaking negotiation, is soon disturbed.

The factors contributing to change are reasonably well documented and need not be dealt with extensively. Cataclysms such as war, depression or inflation have had a profound influence on Canadian federalism. Canada's transformation from an agricultural and rural society and economy to an industrial and urban one has greatly affected the system. Other forces such as advances in technology, improvements in communications and the increased mobility of the population have also contributed to changes in Canadian federalism. Nor can one ignore the existence and development of cultural awareness in Québec. Another factor that has created many problems and led to piecemeal adjustments is the disparity between the fiscal means and the fiscal needs of provincial governments. A more recent phenomenon is the debate over energy policy and natural resources and the revenue distribution from these resources. Each of these factors has contributed to adjustments in, or strains upon, the division of powers.

Adjustments within the Canadian federal system have been made as the need for them has arisen. What has been the principal effect of these changes? At first glance one might conclude that governments are simply doing more and as a result clash more as they attempt to redefine the boundaries of their respective areas of jurisdiction. A more careful analysis indicates that decision-making in many areas of public policy once believed to be within the exclusive jurisdiction of either government is now shared. Interdependence more than independence is one of the chief characteristics of Canadian federalism; consequently we need to be concerned not only with the division of powers but also with the processes by which the adjustments or, if one prefers, accommodations are reached.

At this juncture it is necessary to emphasize the difference between the legal and political dimensions of Canadian federalism. Under the British North America Act (1867) (to be called the Constitution Act, 1867) the federal and provincial governments were assigned particular responsibilities. The distribution of legislative powers is contained in Sections 91-95 of the BNA Act. Other provisions of the constitution establish or confer certain powers, rights or privileges on either the federal or provincial governments. For example, Section 101 authorizes Parliament to establish a general court of appeal—the Supreme Court of Canada. Under Section 109 provincial proprietary rights over lands, mines, minerals and royalties were established. Section 125 provides that "no lands or property belonging to Canada or any province shall be liable to taxation." In analyzing the federal system, therefore, one must be conscious of what the constitution, either as amended or interpreted, means. In this respect the constitution serves as a reference point. Only if we understand the importance of the legal basis of the federal system can we comprehend the political aspects of Canadian federalism.

Having established the nature of each government's powers we can then examine intergovernmental relations and the interdependence that has become more and more apparent. Presenting the legal basis for developing and expanding a policy represents only part of the story. For example, Alberta's ownership of its oil and natural gas does not mean that provincial policies can be developed independently from the policies of the federal government. The federal government controls oil and natural gas exports through the National Energy Board; it has maintained a uniform national price for crude oil; and it regulates interprovincial marketing of oil and natural gas. Another example is health and hospital services where the federal government established national goals and

standards. To have these translated into services, however, provincial governments had to develop and maintain the necessary administrative machinery,
train health personnel, and plan and develop related services. The list of areas
where policies of one government affect or influence the policies of the other is
endless. The consequence of these influences has been to change dramatically
both the character and functioning of Canadian politics. Initially governments
were concerned about invasions of their exclusive jurisdictions, invasions that,
to a great extent, came about as both the federal and provincial governments
developed the basic legislation necessary to fulfill their constitutional obligations.
While governments still jealously guard their jurisdictions they are also conscious
of the effects of policy interdependence. A careful assessment of the communiqués
from the two First Ministers' Conferences on the Economy held in 1978
dramatically illustrates this point. The federal government and the provinces
made a number of collective policy commitments.

In summary, while Canadian federalism has a firm legal foundation, it is also
a complex and dynamic system continuously being subjected to pressures or
change. That the Canadian political system has been able to adapt to meet new
challenges and conditions represents a significant achievement. Change in any
political system is inevitable and federal systems are no exception as the debates
over Canada's constitution illustrate. While formal amendments to the constitution are infrequent and usually difficult, incremental changes do take place
through a variety of techniques.

Before discussing the main focus of this chapter, which is the extent to which
federalism is the central phenomenon of Canadian politics, some attention
should be given to the effects federalism has had on a number of Canadian
political institutions. The composition of both the Senate and the House of
Commons reflects the federal system. Though the Canadian Senate, unlike its
United States counterpart, was not based on equal provincial representation, it
was based on equal regional representation. With the addition of the Province
of Newfoundland in 1949 the principle of regional equality was partially
modified. Representation in the House of Commons is also influenced by the
federal system. Constituency boundaries are limited by provincial boundaries.
The unit for redistribution of seats within the House of Commons is the
province. Provinces are guaranteed that their representation in the House of
Commons will not fall below their representation in the Senate. As a result of
this policy Prince Edward Island has four Members of Parliament, a membership greater than its entitlement under representation by population.

Perhaps the most federalized of Canadian political institutions is the federal
cabinet. One of the chief tasks of any prime minister in putting together a
cabinet is ensuring that each province has representation. This practice began
with Sir John A. Macdonald and has continued to the present. The cabinet
ministers for each province act as spokespersons for that province in the cabinet,
act as spokespersons for the government in the province, and act as conduits for
patronage for the governing party. In instances where a province has not
elected any members from the governing party, such as in British Columbia,

Saskatchewan and Alberta after the 1980 election, senators may be appointed to the cabinet to reflect the provincial perspective.

The composition of the Supreme Court of Canada is also affected by the federal system. Under the Supreme Court Act three judges are to be appointed to that court from the bar of Québec. By convention, the remaining six are appointed as follows: three from Ontario, two from the west and one from Atlantic Canada. This convention was modified in 1979 when a vacancy, which occurred when a justice from Ontario retired, was filled by one from British Columbia, increasing western members on the Supreme Court from two to three.

The Canadian party system is also influenced by the federal system. In some provinces one finds separate federal and provincial party organizations with different constitutions, finances and, sometimes, supporters. For example, the Liberal party in Québec split into two different organizations in the early sixties. Some of the great federal-provincial disputes have been between individuals of the same party, such as the Hepburn-King debate over the war effort and the Lesage-Pearson debate over the Canada Pension Plan. Various theories have developed over time to relate the party system to the federal system. Some of these have attempted to explain the reasons for voters supporting different parties federally and provincially. In the span of about one year Québec voters gave overwhelming support to the federal Liberals, electing 74 out of 75 seats; defeated the referendum on sovereignty association; and returned the Parti Québécois government of René Lévesque to a second term with a comfortable majority. Some authors have tried to illustrate how the opposition's function in Canada is performed by provincial governments. For example, in January 1980 no province had a Liberal government in office. The success of third parties, such as the Union Nationale, the Parti Québécois, the CCF/NDP and Social Credit at the provincial level, has also been the subject of several studies. Finally, some observers suggest that opposition parties in Ottawa are far more sensitive than the government to provincial rights and claims.

In short, the structure and operation of Canadian political institutions have been greatly influenced by the existence of the federal system. Indeed, to a great extent politics in Canada is determined by the restraints imposed by the federal arrangement. In considering federal-provincial relations one should not overlook the broader aspects of the political system and the profound effects that federalism has had on their development.

THE FEDERAL SYSTEM:
THE DEVELOPMENTAL STAGE—1867-1940

At the time of Confederation the constitutional draftsmen did not approach the division of powers with any degree of scientific precision. The criterion that was employed was a relatively simple one: important subjects were given to the central government while those relating to local matters were assigned to the provinces. It is no secret that Sir John A. Macdonald cherished the idea of a unitary state but had to settle for something else—a system that Wheare describes as quasi-federal. Describing the division of powers, Macdonald said:

> We have given the General Legislature all the great subjects of Legislation.... [W]e have expressly declared that all subjects of general interest not distinctly and exclusively conferred upon the local governments and legislatures, shall be conferred upon the General Governments and Legislature.... We have avoided all conflict of jurisdiction and authority.[3]

In addition to the broad grant of legislative power, the federal government exercised partial, but still significant, control over the provinces through its powers of disallowance and appointments of lieutenant-governors. Although the provinces were given taxing powers, their revenue position was fairly weak and a complex system of federal subsidies and grants was written into the constitution. There is little doubt that Canada, at its formation, had a highly centralized form of federalism with the provinces being subordinate to the federal government. That it has changed from the highly centralized quasi-federal system of 1867 to one where central and provincial governments are roughly equal is not really questioned today. Whether the change has been for good or bad is another matter entirely.

Those who cherish the notions of 1867 have one view of the Canadian federal system while others harbor other attitudes. Professor Cairns, in his usual perceptive style, expressed this concern as follows:

> With the passage of time the intentions of the Fathers unavoidably became an increasingly artificial concept with an ever attenuated contact with reality. Their visions were responses to the problems they faced in the light of prevalent conceptions of the role of government. Many of the conditions to which they addressed themselves faded away, to be replaced by conditions they could not predict. In such circumstances deference to their intentions became impossible, for they had none.[4]

While one cannot ignore the roots or foundations of any federal system, to base all current decisions only on a strict historical interpretation is to invite disaster.

The mechanisms of change have been fully discussed elsewhere and do not require too much elaboration. From 1867 to 1940 judicial interpretation by the courts would appear to have been the single most important device for refining the division of powers. The 1896 decision in the *Local Prohibition Case* was the first in a series of cases which reduced the scope and importance of the peace, order and good government clause.[5] In 1925, in *Toronto Electric Commissioners* v. *Snider*, the general grant of power was reduced to an emergency power only.[6] This trend favoring the provincial governments continued through to the Depression, with the rejection by the Judicial Committee of most of the Bennett New Deal legislation.

At the same time that the scope of federal legislative power was reduced, the privy council also gave recognition to the status of provincial governments. They were more than local governments. In *Liquidators of the Maritime Bank* v. *Receiver General of New Brunswick* their lordships stated:

> The object of the Act was neither to weld the provinces into one nor to subordinate provincial governments to a central authority, but to create a federal government.... each province retaining its independence and autonomy.[7]

A detailed examination of both the development of Canadian society and the evolution of the federal system up to 1940 yields certain observations about its operation. In the first place, provincial powers had taken on a new significance —a prominence which they did not have in 1867. These governments had started to develop and expand their education and social assistance programs. Highway systems were being built. The migration from farm to city had increased the responsibilities of municipal governments. If anything, the transformation in Canadian society had required the provinces to assert themselves more than ever. This transformation had been reinforced by judicial interpretations which confirmed their responsibility for labor legislation, unemployment assistance and a wide range of controls over commercial transactions. Macdonald's belief in the importance of federal powers failed to meet the test of time. As the urban industrialized social welfare state emerged, the provincial governments assumed or were given the major responsibilities for meeting the needs of the citizens. This assessment does not suggest that the federal powers were insignificant. It is just that over time the relative relationship between the two governments shifted with the junior partners becoming full partners.

A second observation was that by 1940 there had been no corresponding shift in fiscal responsibilities between the two governments. By the late 1930s it was evident that the fiscal responsibilities of the provincial governments exceeded their fiscal capacities. The constitutional grants and subsidies, which were a condition of Confederation and which had represented a significant portion of provincial budgets in the period immediately after 1867, were inadequate to meet the needs of the provinces. To fill the gap the provinces had developed their own systems of taxation, but their capacities were limited.

A third observation is that intergovernmental cooperation, although in its formative stages, had already emerged as a fact of life. Conditional grants or shared-cost programs were initiated in 1912. Federal-provincial and interprovincial conferences had been held. Because delegation of powers was not possible, the practice of parallel legislation developed. In reviewing the emergence of federal-provincial interaction, the Rowell-Sirois Commission stated somewhat critically that:

> The evolution of political policies within the framework of the constitution is leading to joint activity between the Dominion and the provinces. This contrasts sharply with the original conception of federalism as a clear-cut division of powers to be exercised separately, and experience indicates that it is injurious both to sound public finance and efficient administration.[8]

The Commission argued further that: "The experience with conditional grants leads us to doubt whether joint administration by the Dominion and a province is ever a satisfactory way of surmounting constitutional difficulties."[9]

The Commission recommended that provincial responsibilities in areas such as unemployment insurance and contributory old age pensions be transferred to the federal government. While the sweeping reforms proposed by the Commission were not implemented, an amendment to the British North America Act in 1940 transferred the responsibility for unemployment insurance to the federal government and in 1951 the federal government assumed the principal responsibility for old age pensions.

In summary, during its first seventy years the federal system had been dramatically altered. The ascendancy of the provinces could neither be denied nor reversed. Nonetheless, the realignment of the division of powers combined with the fiscal needs of the provinces created the need for an assessment of the federal system and its future direction.

THE FEDERAL SYSTEM:
CHANGE AND ACCOMMODATION — 1940-1981

From the Depression to the present there have been several issues which have shaped the federal system. Perhaps the most continuous and persistent of these has been the debate over the constitution. Knowledge about this area gives one a reasonable understanding of change, accommodation and conflict within the federal system and tells us much about the workings of Canadian politics in general. Discussions on patriation and an amending formula have given way to negotiations on constitutional reform. Closely intertwined with this debate has been Québec's concern about its role in Confederation. Central to this theme is the question of provincial autonomy—whether it be fiscal, constitutional or cultural. That these should be recurring concerns indicates that the federal system is continuing to adapt and adjust to new circumstances.

Before analyzing constitutional change a brief overview of the period in question may be useful. In 1957 Professor Corry, in "Constitutional Trends and Canadian Federalism", described the centralizing trend within the federal system.[10] Corry commented on the nationalistic sentiments among business and labor elites and the integrative effects of the transportation and communications infrastructure. Along with a powerful federal government, nationally-oriented institutions or organizations influenced the centralization of Canadian federalism. Preponderant federal influence flowed from the powers and resulting policies acquired and developed by the federal government during the Second World War. To this had been added program responsibilities resulting from the spiraling number of shared-cost programs and the economic centralization resulting from the tax agreements.

Around 1960 the forces of centralization peaked and a process of decentralization began. The pendulum of power gradually swung back towards the provinces, gathering momentum as it moved. The election of John Diefenbaker, the Quiet Revolution, a series of minority governments in Ottawa, and the power of well-entrenched provincial governments were factors influencing this transformation. In 1964 Smiley characterized this metamorphosis as a change from joint to consultative federalism, in which administrative relationships were replaced by principles of diplomacy.[11] In 1966 Black and Cairns discussed the emerging confidence of provincial governments and suggested that while Canada as a nation had evolved, so had the provinces.[12] Collectively they rivaled the federal government in the development and initiation of new directions in public policy. Writing in 1968, John Saywell stated: "In 1965, when the extension of provincial autonomy threatened to destroy legitimate federal power, he [P.E. Trudeau] entered federal politics as a defender of constitutionalism and Canadian federalism."[13] Over the last few years the decentralizing tendencies of the early sixties have been halted, with the federal government regaining much of its influence.

Throughout the latter part of the seventies and into the eighties the federal government has attempted to restore its influence. It has consistently asserted that Canada is the most decentralized federation in the world.[14] The main justification for this argument is that collectively provincial and municipal governments spend more money than the federal government. While the observation is correct, the conclusion drawn from it does not necessarily follow. Levels of government expenditure are neither indices of decentralization nor of the state of Canadian federalism. On balance it is probably correct to say that at present the pendulum appears to have come to rest, at least momentarily, at dead center.

The Courts and the Constitution

Central to the theme of constitutional change are judicial interpretations of the constitution, the search for an amending formula and, more recently, the wide-ranging reviews of the constitution. If, during the first seventy years of Canada's federal experiment, the courts were active in shaping the federal system, it would appear that in the past forty this process has been less significant. Many observers, including Chief Justice Laskin, have noted the tendency on the part of governments to avoid referring matters to the courts for resolution. While much of the present day constitution is a direct result of judicial interpretation, solutions to today's problems are developed through what Professor Simeon has called federal-provincial diplomacy. (This particular question will be discussed later when intergovernmental relations are considered.)

Though the role of the courts has been modified, they still play an important role in shaping the constitution. With the abolition of appeals to the Judicial Committee of the Privy Council in 1949, the Supreme Court of Canada has become the umpire of Canadian federalism. While the number of constitutional cases heard by the court over the past few years is relatively small in relation to the total case load, some very significant decisions have been made. For example, in 1967 the court decided in the *Off-Shore Mineral Reference* that Canada, not British Columbia, owned the off-shore mineral resources.[15] In 1974 the court upheld the constitutionality of the Official Languages Act, 1969, in *Jones* v. *A.G. Canada.* [16] In July 1976 the court confirmed the constitutionality of the federal government's Anti-Inflation Act. [17] This case may be described as one of the most important constitutional law cases heard by the Supreme Court since it became the final court of appeal in 1949. Why? The court's task was to assess the current relevance of the Judicial Committee's previous interpretation of peace, order and good government which had evolved since 1896. The court had three basic choices to make. It could declare the Act unconstitutional or it could declare the Act constitutional on one of two grounds—that inflation was a matter of serious national concern or that inflation could be considered an emergency. A majority of the court decided that the Act was constitutional on the grounds that inflation in Canada in the fall of 1975 constituted an emergency. Had the majority of judges accepted the argument of serious national concern, the existing equilibrium within the federal system would have been considerably altered. Provincial governments which presented their views on the Act's constitutionality argued that the law could be upheld only on the grounds of an emergency.

Two other Supreme Court cases of considerable importance to resource-producing provinces were the CIGOL and Central Canadian Potash decisions. [18] Both cases arose in Saskatchewan and in both instances provincial legislation was declared unconstitutional. The first case dealt with tax legislation while the second was concerned with provincial controls over resource production. The significance of these decisions is that they immediately generated a proposal to amend the constitution.

Perhaps the most crucial constitutional law case in Canadian history was adjudicated by the court in the spring of 1981. The court was asked to determine whether the federal government could submit a request to the United Kingdom Government to "patriate" the British North America Act without the consent of the provinces. They were also asked whether the Joint Resolution discussed by Parliament would limit provincial powers. During the course of the hearing the federal government conceded that the proposed Charter of Rights would in fact limit provincial powers under Section 92. The basis of the decision hinged on whether the constitutional conventions which had emerged with respect to the constitutional amendment were binding. The federal government, Ontario and New Brunswick said they were not while the other eight provinces said they were.

The consequences of the "patriation" case are enormous because it is a one-time decision. Either patriation could be pursued by the federal government unilaterally or it could not. While the federal government had originally argued that the issue was political as distinct from legal, the federal government made it clear that it would observe the court's ruling.

Reforming Canadian Federalism

For the past fifty years Canadians have been searching for a means to amend the Canadian constitution—the British North America Act. When the BNA Act was enacted by the United Kingdom Parliament in 1867 it did not contain an amending formula. Acts of the United Kingdom Parliament could be amended by that Parliament. While this state of affairs may have been satisfactory in 1867 it could not last forever. By 1927, 60 years after Confederation, it had become clear that an amending formula was necessary.

At first glance developing a formula appears relatively easy. But is it? Since the subject of an amending formula has been debated for more than fifty years the immediate answer is "it is not easy." Part of the dilemma is writing a formula after the fact—after the country has evolved from four to ten provinces and has expanded from coast to coast. Answers are needed to questions such as: Should the formula be rigid or flexible? Is unanimity essential? Should Québec's special concerns be protected? Should provinces be accorded equal status? Should representation by population be observed? Should regional interests be reflected? As soon as one starts to explore these questions a myriad of problems unfolds and the enormous challenge becomes readily apparent.

Before examining the most prominent constitutional proposals, some background is essential if these are to be placed in the proper context. From 1927 to 1965 successive governments in Canada were primarily concerned with patriation of the constitution and developing an amending formula. Patriation means eliminating the last legal responsibilities which the Parliament of the United Kingdom retained for amending the Canadian constitution, and transferring that responsibility to Canada. Before that transfer could take place a means of amending the constitution in Canada was required. Patriation, *per se*, was not the problem. The obstacle was securing agreement on an amending formula and on what other—if any—amendments to the constitution should be included.

Generally speaking, from 1927 to 1971 each proposal for an amending formula that was seriously considered by governments had two basic components or procedures. One could be described as the general formula while the other was the unanimity rule. The unanimity rule was designed to protect those parts of the constitution which were of critical importance to the provinces. One can appreciate the fact that there were widely divergent views over what parts of the constitution should be subject to the unanimity rule. In addition to the two basic components it was thought that a few sections of the constitution should be amendable by either Parliament or a provincial legislature acting alone. Consequently one could not identify a single amending formula but rather a number of different formulae which could be used to amend different sections of the constitution. The dilemma was agreeing which sections of the Act should be subject to which formula.

Before considering some of the proposals for an amending formula it is necessary to examine how the constitution was amended before patriation. From the outset, when amendments to the BNA Act were required, the actual amendment was enacted by the Parliament of the United Kingdom. The Canadian government made the request for the amendment after securing approval by resolution of both Houses of the Canadian Parliament. After the 1907 amendment revising the scale of constitutional subsidies, the practice of consulting the provinces emerged. The 1940 amendment transferring jurisdiction over unemployment insurance to the federal government was not enacted until all provinces had given their consent. In 1949 Parliament secured an amendment that gives it authority to amend "the Constitution of Canada". The section reads as follows:

> Section 91(1).   The amendment from time to time of the Constitution of Canada, except as regards matters coming within the classes of subjects by this Act assigned exclusively to the Legislatures of the provinces, or as regards rights or privileges by this or any other Constitutional Act granted or secured to the Legislature or the Government of a province, or to any class of persons with respect to schools or as regards the use of the English or the French language or as regards the requirements that there shall be a session of the Parliament of Canada at least once each year, and that no House of Commons shall continue for more than five years from the day of the return of the Writs for choosing the House: provided, however, that a House of Commons may in time of real or apprehended war, invasion or insurrection be continued by the Parliament of Canada if such continuation is not opposed by the votes of more than one-third of the members of such House.

At the time this amendment was being discussed in Parliament some provincial governments expressed the view that they should have had a say in the matter. The federal government argued that it was seeking no more power than what the provinces had over their constitutions, as provided for in Section 92(1) of the BNA Act.

Three amendments affecting those matters that, according to the 1949 amendment, still had to be enacted by the Parliament of the United Kingdom have been enacted since that date. The issues involved were old-age pensions in 1951, retirement of judges in 1960 and the 1964 amendment to the old-age pensions section. All three amendments were enacted only after the unanimous consent of the provinces had been secured. Other amendments have been made to the constitution by Parliament acting alone. Recent examples are the 1975 amendments granting Senate representation for the Yukon and Northwest Territories and increasing the size of the House of Commons.

While it should be clear that the constitution can be and has been amended, the fact remains that parts of it could be amended only by legislative action of another country. For many Canadians this situation was one that needed rectifying. Successful resolution of this matter was intended not only to assuage feelings of Canadian nationalism but also to provide a measure of flexibility to the constitution.

Between 1960 and 1964, under the auspices of both the Diefenbaker and Pearson governments, an amending formula, which became known as the Fulton-Favreau formula, was developed. This formula provided for two general amending procedures: Parliament in conjunction with two thirds of the provinces representing 50% of the population; and Parliament in conjunction with all the provinces. Those areas where unanimous provincial consent was required included provincial powers, rights, privileges and language rights.

Although all eleven governments agreed to the formula in 1964, the Government of Québec later changed its position, thereby bringing that episode to a halt. The cause-and-effect relationship between the Quiet Revolution and the decision by the Québec government is an important one. Of more importance to the Québec government was the whole question of the future direction and operation of the federal system. In effect Québec made her support for patriation and an amending formula contingent upon the other governments in Canada addressing themselves to a more far-reaching review of the constitution. What had started as a very limited exercise became far more comprehensive.

The Quiet Revolution and the concerns expressed in the *Preliminary Report* of the Royal Commission on Bilingualism and Biculturalism made it clear that severe problems existed within the political system. The increasing isolation of Québec, the dissatisfaction of provincial governments with their fiscal position in the mid-sixties, and the rapid development of federal-provincial shared-cost programs precipitated a review of the Canadian constitution during the period 1967-1971. This review was not restricted to finding an amending formula but encompassed a total review of the constitution.

1967-1971

The proceedings of the 1967 Confederation of Tomorrow Conference, an interprovincial meeting, and of the first Constitutional Conference in 1968 highlighted the crisis atmosphere which existed at that time. At the 1968 conference the eleven governments agreed to undertake a comprehensive review of the constitution including such matters as a bill of rights, language rights, the division of powers, institutions related to federalism (such as the Senate and Supreme Court), regional disparities, an amending formula and mechanisms of federal-provincial relations.[19] While it was agreed that seven broad areas were to be discussed, there was no clear statement about how that task would be approached. At the second meeting of the conference in February 1969 the priorities of the review were more clearly defined but the issue of "review" versus "reform" was not resolved. The culmination of all the study, negotiation and soul-searching over the constitution and its adequacy as Canada entered its second century was the Victoria Charter of 1971.

Much of the Charter dealt with structural matters such as an annual conference of First Ministers, provincial participation in the appointment of Supreme Court of Canada judges and an amending formula. A few substantive issues were contained in the Charter such as entrenchment of fundamental freedoms, political rights and language rights. A special concern of Atlantic Canada was partially met through a section outlining the responsibilities of governments to reduce regional disparities. Many of the issues discussed by governments during the three-and-one-half-year review did not find their way into the Charter. Matters such as limits to the federal spending power, modifications to provincial taxing powers, Senate reform and recognition of a provincial role in international affairs were discussed but not resolved. The only change in the division of powers was described as "revised Section 94A." At the urging of Québec the provisions of Section 94A were extended to include "family, youth, and occupational training allowances." Apart from this change no agreement was reached on the most sensitive issue, a redistribution of government powers.

The general amending formula proposed in the Victoria Charter was as follows:

> Amendments to the Constitution of Canada may from time to time be made by Proclamation issued by the Governor General under the Great Seal of Canada when so authorized by resolution of the Senate and House of Commons and of the Legislative Assemblies of at least a majority of the Provinces that includes:
> (1) every Province that at any time before the issue of such Proclamation had, according to any previous general census, a population of at least twenty-five per cent of the population of Canada;
> (2) at least two of the Atlantic Provinces;
> (3) at least two of the Western Provinces that have, according to the then latest general census, combined populations of at least fifty per cent of the population of all the Western Provinces.

This formula represented a significant departure from previous proposals in a number of ways. Of perhaps greatest importance was the deletion of a unanimity rule for certain kinds of amendments. Up to this time all formulae that had been considered had had a unanimity requirement, the most recent example being the Fulton-Favreau formula of 1964. A second change was that the provincial majority was structured on the basis of region as opposed to a straight majority of provinces. Clause (1) ensured both Ontario and Québec a perpetual veto over amendments.

No other country has approached the reform of its political institutions in the manner Canada did during the period 1968-71. Most countries discuss these fundamental issues at the time that they are founded; no other federation has undertaken a constitutional review one hundred years after the fact. The assessment was conducted at a leisurely pace and without any clearly defined objectives or timetable. In this sense the review in Canada is unique.

With the Government of Québec's rejection of that Charter in late June 1971 the subject of constitutional reform quietly faded. It was raised once again by Prime Minister Trudeau in 1974, although then he restricted his concerns to patriation and the amending formula.

1976-1977

The amending formula favored by the federal government was the one developed in 1971, the Victoria Charter. This formula was presented once again to the provinces for their consideration by the Prime Minister. Significantly, his letter of March 31, 1976 left the door open for some substantive changes to the constitution, including entrenchment of French language rights, provincial participation in the appointment of Supreme Court judges, a non-constitutional obligation to reduce regional disparities, and certain safeguards designed to protect Québec's cultural sovereignty. With the exception of the cultural guarantees to Québec the other provisions are to be found in the Victoria Charter.

The provincial governments reviewed the federal proposals during the summer and fall of 1976. Their discussions extended far beyond the limited goal of patriation and an amending formula. They discussed and reached unanimous agreement on a number of changes to the constitution including entrenchment of language rights, an expansion of the provincial role in immigration, increased taxing powers over resources and limits to the federal government's declaratory powers under Section 92(10)c.

On the topic of the amending formula, the provinces were divided with the majority favoring the Victoria formula. Alberta took the view that a constitutional amending formula should not permit an amendment that would take away existing rights, proprietary interests or jurisdiction of any province without the consent of that province. British Columbia advocated a five-region Canada which would have the effect of giving that province a veto along with Québec and Ontario.

In January 1977, two months after the election of the Parti Québécois in Québec, the federal government responded to the proposal from the provinces. In his commentary on the provincial suggestions Prime Minister Trudeau stated that these were either too little or too much. They were too little in that they did not address the total range of constitutional problems facing Canada. They were too much in that the proposals went far beyond the limited goal of patriation and adoption of an amending formula. The Prime Minister gave the provinces two alternatives—constitutional review by stages or the undertaking of a global review similar to and building on that which had taken place from 1968 to 1971.[20]

The first option—constitutional review by stages—would be a continuation of the discussions which had taken place on an ad hoc basis since 1975. This stage would include: patriation, an amending formula and limited changes to the constitution. The option of a comprehensive review would, of course, subject all aspects of the constitution to scrutiny. The latter alternative was probably proposed as a result of the November 15, 1976, Québec election.

As Prime Minister Trudeau told the nation on November 24, 1976, the debate on the future relationships between French-and English-speaking Canadians could not be postponed any longer.[21] This debate transcended the question of language rights and of necessity had to encompass an analysis and assessment of the federal system. The Parti Québécois had stated that federalism was not working. An attempt to answer this charge, at least in the minds of the Québec electorate, was essential. The situation in Québec was not the only reason for a resumption of constitutional discussions; Western Provinces were also becoming increasingly concerned about the federal system.

1978-1979

The next phase of constitutional discussions built on the work that had been done previously. Unlike earlier discussions there was a sense of urgency, in part because of the pending referendum in Québec and in part because the Trudeau government was well into its mandate. In the late spring of 1978 the federal government published a White Paper on constitutional reform, *A Time for Action.* This paper signalled that this time discussions would be global in nature. There could be no mistaking the desire on the part of the federal government to meet the challenge of the separatist threat through constitutional reform. Speaking in Parliament the Prime Minister placed two conditions on the proposed constitutional discussions. The conditions were: "(i) that Canada continue to be a real federation...and (ii) that basic human rights and freedoms be entrenched in the Constitution."[22]

The White Paper was followed by the tabling in Parliament of the Constitutional Amendment Bill. Bill C-60, as it was known, was a combination of the British North America Act and a significant number of amendments.

One of the most prominent features of Bill C-60 was a detailed Charter of Rights, not the limited one contained in the 1971 Victoria Charter. The Charter was to be binding on the federal government while provinces could "opt in". Once a province had opted in, the federal government's powers of disallowance and reservation would no longer apply to that province. Other proposals included: entrenching the Supreme Court, establishing a House of the Federation to replace the Senate, and detailing several of the existing conventions of cabinet government. The Bill did not contain a proposed amending formula, made no changes to the existing division of powers, and had no mention of natural resources, an omission which prompted some close questioning by the Western Provinces.

The provinces responded to the federal constitutional proposals at the 1978 Premiers' Conference. The communiqué released on this subject stated "that the division of powers is the key issue in constitutional reform." While indicating their willingness to discuss Bill C-60 the Premiers made it clear that this was not the only proposal to be discussed. Others included the 1976 provincial proposals, which the Parti Québécois government generally endorsed, and the then potential report of the Pepin-Robarts Task Force. The provinces also made it clear that discussions could not be successful "if arbitrary deadlines are imposed." Finally the provinces expressed some concern over certain provisions of Bill C-60. They described the House of the Federation as "unworkable" and opposed "constitutional changes that substitute for the Queen as ultimate authority, a Governor General whose appointment and dismissal would be solely at the pleasure of the federal cabinet."[23]

A Constitutional Conference was convened in October 1978. To expedite progress the federal government tabled an "Agenda for Change" which contained a priority list of items for immediate resolution. The list included the following items related to the division of powers: federal spending power, indirect taxation, natural resources and interprovincial trade, family law and communications. In addition to the seven specific items the federal government included Bill C-60 and stressed in particular the provisions on the Charter of Rights and the Supreme Court. The final item contained in the federal government's proposal was the amending formula. The provinces agreed to the federal proposals and added Senate reform, fisheries, offshore resources and the monarchy. First Ministers also agreed to have their Ministers review each of these items and to report back to them in February 1979.

Consequently these thirteen items were the subject of detailed discussion and negotiation among the First Ministers for the next three months. Other matters were for a second stage, a phase which would take place after agreement had been reached on the first package of amendments. Some subjects such as the Charter, Supreme Court, equalization and the amending formula had been thoroughly discussed during the 1968-71 discussions. Others such as natural resources and communications were currently the subject of federal-provincial policy disputes. Still others such as fisheries and the Senate were of concern to specific provinces.

The Ministers reported to First Ministers in February 1979. While progress had been made on some of the items, on others there was no consensus or agreement. For example, the majority of provinces did not agree with entrenching a Charter of Rights, which had been a federal pre-condition to the discussions. There was no agreement on offshore resources, communications and fisheries. On the other matters there was a varying degree of federal and provincial support for what was known as "best efforts" drafts. These drafts served as the basis for the continuing negotiation which took place amongst First Ministers.

Discussions on the amending formula initially focused on the Victoria formula. An alternative proposal, which became known as the Toronto formula, was floated in December 1978. This formula provided for amendments to the constitution which had the support of two thirds of the provinces representing 85% of the population. In an effort to bring Western Provinces on-side, amendments relating to natural resources would be subject to unanimity. Under the population provisions both Québec and Ontario would have to support an amendment before it would take effect. The basic difference between the Victoria and Toronto formulae was that the former was based on a regional consensus while the latter was not. Both required support from Ontario and Québec before an amendment could be adopted. Neither formula was acceptable to Alberta which proposed its own formula at the February 1979 First Ministers' Conference.

The Alberta proposal provided for a general formula whereby amendments to the constitution could be adopted by two thirds of the provinces representing 50% of the population. In addition the proposal provided that a province dissenting to any amendment that took away *existing* provincial rights, proprietary interests or jurisdiction could opt out of the amendment. In other words, a dissenting province could not veto an amendment but could state that the amendment did not apply to it. No agreement was reached on this proposal or on any other.

Discussion on the Charter focused on two key aspects: should rights be entrenched in the constitution and if the answer was yes, should they be as comprehensive as the ones included in Bill C-60. The general consensus of the First Ministers was that a limited Charter consisting of fundamental freedoms and democratic rights could be incorporated into the constitution paralleling the 1971 Victoria agreement.

Despite the time and effort which had been expended in preparing for the February conference, agreement on "Agenda for Change" was not forthcoming. There was insufficient time to forge a consensus and the conference adjourned without any provision for a further meeting.

Immediately before the February 1979 conference the Pepin-Robarts Task Force on National Unity released its recommendations and Report. Because discussion and negotiations were so far advanced on the specific items agreed to the previous October, the Report had little impact on the Conference.[24]

Time ran out for the Trudeau government which was well into the fifth year of its mandate. A general election was called in March. The majority Liberal government was defeated and replaced by a minority Conservative government. With the dissolution of Parliament Bill C-60 died on the order paper.

The Conservatives were in office for nine months and did not have an opportunity to devote much attention to constitutional reform. During the 1979 election campaign the Conservatives promised to transfer ownership of offshore resources to the provinces. One ministerial meeting on the constitution was held in the fall of 1979 which attempted to pick up where the February 1979 Conference had left off. The defeat of the Conservative government in Parliament in December 1979 and their subsequent defeat at the polls in February 1980 paved the way for Prime Minister Trudeau to have one last chance at constitutional reform.

1980-1981

Immediately after being returned to office the Trudeau government focused on the Québec referendum which had been scheduled for May 1980. The Prime Minister and many of his cabinet colleagues were active participants in the referendum debate. They urged the Québec people to reject sovereignty association and, in return, made a strong commitment to Québecers to undertake constitutional renewal and reform. The Western Premiers at their 1980 Conference urged Québecers to defeat the referendum and become active participants in constitutional reform. Other provinces also underlined the importance of Canadian unity and argued the need to discuss constitutional reform once more. Three weeks after the defeat of the referendum the First

Ministers met in Ottawa to agree on an agenda for constitutional change and establish a timetable for the resumption of discussions.

The agenda for reform was virtually identical to the one which had been agreed to in the earlier discussions. One new topic was added: "Powers affecting the Economy". Governments devoted the summer of 1980 to review of the constitution and preparation of a report to a Constitutional Conference of First Ministers scheduled for September 1980. During the 1980 Premiers' Conference held in Winnipeg in August, the ten Premiers were briefed on the progress of the discussions which had taken place up to that time. In their communiqué they once again stressed, as they had in 1978, the importance of the division of powers as the key to constitutional reform. They also recognized the commitments made to Québec during the referendum debate.

The September 1980 Constitutional Conference lasted a week and ended without agreement. In part the atmosphere was greatly influenced by the leak of a secret cabinet memo which reviewed the summer's activities and outlined various federal strategies including the possibility of unilateral federal action should the conference fail. Another factor influencing the outcome was the sharp difference of opinion between the federal and provincial governments over entrenching a Charter of Rights. The majority of provinces opposed entrenching a Charter and argued that rights were best protected by vigilant legislatures. The federal government interpreted the provincial position as an attempt to trade-off the entrenchment of rights for concessions on the division of powers. It should be recognized that the Prime Minister had recently won a majority and was no longer confronted with a pending election. In addition the bargaining position of the Québec government was weakened because of the defeat of the referendum. All these factors were at work throughout the week and influenced the outcome of the meeting.

During the conference each of the issues was explored in far greater detail than it had been in February 1979, but still a consensus was not forthcoming. The amending formula of the Alberta proposal had now been accepted by the other nine provinces, and the federal government, according to the leaked cabinet memo, was prepared to consider it. The Victoria formula had not been given serious consideration during the summer's meetings.

During the negotiations it became evident that the position of the federal government on the subject of natural resources had changed significantly since 1979. The two main differences were: the removal of the proposal agreed to in 1979 to limit the federal government's declaratory power under Section 92(10)c of the BNA Act as that power affected natural resources, and confining the extension of provincial legislative power to interprovincial trade only through the elimination of any reference to international trade. It should be emphasized that the extension of provincial legislative jurisdiction remained subject to federal supremacy, a situation similar to federal legislative authority over agriculture and immigration.

One of the principal reasons for the failure of the conference was the widely divergent view of federalism held by the federal and the provincial governments.

Generally speaking, the two views focused on the relative strengths, roles and responsibilities of the two orders of government. If there is a clash between national and regional interests which view should prevail? The answer to that question is not easy because it depends upon one's understanding of the term "national interest". Who defined that interest? The two views identified by the Prime Minister were: that national interest is equivalent to the sum total of the views of the ten provinces, such as might be reflected in the communiqués of the Annual Premiers' Conferences; or that it is equivalent to a national majority as reflected by a majority vote in Parliament. A third interpretation would be to mix or blend the preceding two approaches, or as Premier Blakeney suggested, a double majority. These widely divergent views are not new to Canadian federalism and have surfaced throughout our political development. The contradictory interpretations could not be reconciled in September 1980 and a compromise solution on constitutional reform could not be reached.

As the conference ended the Prime Minister informed the Premiers that he would reflect on matters and meet with his caucus and cabinet to discuss what action the federal government should pursue. Three alternatives were possible: do nothing—as had been done in the period after Québec had rejected the Victoria Charter in 1971; defer discussions for a few months—a proposal suggested by a number of Premiers during their closing remarks; unilateral action—an alternative outlined in the leaked cabinet memorandum. If it was to be effective, unilateral action would have to be swift and decisive.

Three weeks after the conference adjourned the federal government announced its decision. The Prime Minister addressed the nation on October 2, 1980. He stated that the federal government would proceed unilaterally with patriation, an amending formula and a Charter of Rights. Provincial consent would not be requested and, he argued, was not required. The suggested amending formula was a slightly modified Victoria formula. He proposed this formula because it had previously been accepted by all governments in 1971. By advancing this argument the Prime Minister ignored completely the negotia-tions which had taken place during the summer. In addition there were promises for referenda as a deadlock-breaking mechanism between the federal and provincial governments. A referendum could only be initiated by the federal government and not the provinces. The Charter of Rights was virtually the same as the one discussed during recent constitutional conferences. This time there was no provision for opting-in by provinces as there had been in Bill C-60. The Charter was binding on the provincial governments.

Two arguments were advanced by the Prime Minister to justify the unilateral course of action. The first was a rejection of the principle of unanimity. Prime Minister Trudeau stated:

> [W]e took that ideal of unanimity and made it a tyrant. Unanimity gave each
> First Minister a veto: and that veto was increasingly used to seek the particular
> goal of a particular region or province... We were led by the dictates of unanimity
> to bargain freedom against fish, fundamental rights against oil, the independence
> of our country against long distance telephone rates.

But we were led further still, towards a radically new concept of Canada, one in which the national good was merely the sum total of provincial demands....[25]

By his first argument the Prime Minister rejected the conventions which had evolved over the years with respect to constitutional amendment. He also came down squarely in opposition to provincial arguments that the division of powers was the key to constitutional reform. In stating the federal position he did not remind the public that it had been the federal government which had earlier established a pre-condition to the discussions — inclusion of a Charter of Rights.

The second argument advanced by the Prime Minister was a restatement of the commitment to constitutional renewal made by all Canadians during the Québec referendum debate. "It was more than a commitment to Québecers, even though the Québec referendum was the immediate reason for it. The commitment was from each Canadian to every other Canadian to change our country for the better."

It was clear from the beginning that the federal government wished the matter to be dealt with expeditiously by Parliament. The Resolution was to be examined by a parliamentary committee which was asked to report on the matter in approximately two months. The federal government's timetable was neither acceptable to the Official Opposition nor to various groups which intended to make submissions. Eventually the deadline was extended to February 1981. This extension gave the provinces additional time to mount a counter-offensive.

After the Resolution had been tabled in Parliament the ten Premiers met to determine what position the provinces should take. Initially, Alberta, British Columbia, Manitoba, Québec, Prince Edward Island and Newfoundland decided to challenge the federal government's actions. They were soon joined by Nova Scotia. A few months later Saskatchewan, which for a variety of reasons had pursued bilateral discussions with the federal government, joined the other seven. Ontario and New Brunswick threw their support behind the federal government.

Generally speaking, the eight opposing provinces, which became known as the 'gang of eight' criticized the federal action on both the unilateral process and various aspects of the content of the Resolution. The provincial counter-offensive had a number of components. One key activity was the initiation of a series of court challenges. A second was to propose an alternative resolution. A third was to make the Canadian public aware of the position of the provinces and the fact that the federal government was breaking with constitutional convention. A fourth was to make United Kingdom parliamentarians aware of and sensitive to the provincial position. Over the course of the year following the introduction of the Resolution in the Canadian Parliament the eight provinces met constantly to discuss their tactics and strategies.

Legal challenges were initiated by the provinces in Manitoba, Québec and Newfoundland. The provinces lost in Manitoba and Québec but won in Newfoundland. The Manitoba decision was appealed to the Supreme Court of Canada which agreed to hear the case at the end of April 1981. In effect the court reviewed the judgments from all three provincial Courts of Appeal. Primarily as a result of a successful filibuster by the Official Opposition, Prime Minister Trudeau in March 1981 agreed to delay the final vote on the Resolution until the Supreme Court had delivered its decision. Again time worked in favor of the opposing provinces.

The opposing provinces also developed an alternative proposal. On April 16, 1981 (three days after the Québec election) the eight provinces met in Ottawa and signed an agreement which called for patriation of the constitution. In addition they proposed an amending formula based on the one developed by Alberta in February 1979 and which had been generally agreed to at the September 1980 conference. The provinces also agreed to an extensive series of constitutional discussions after patriation had been achieved. It is important to note that the eight provinces did not include any reference to the division of powers in their patriation proposal. The element of bargaining which the Prime Minister had found so objectionable was gone. In signing the Accord, Québec altered one of its fundamental positions making patriation conditional on resolution of long standing constitutional concerns. While the federal government, Ontario and New Brunswick were invited to sign the Accord, all three declined.

On September 28, 1981, the Supreme Court gave its decision.[26] The court unanimously agreed that the federal proposal would limit existing provincial powers. On the more important question of the conventions surrounding constitutional amendment, the court divided its judgment into two opinions. A majority of the court (7-2) determined that there was no legal impediment to the Parliament of Canada passing a resolution requesting the United Kingdom to amend the constitution. Put another way, the court determined that there was nothing in the existing constitution which prevented the Canadian Parliament from passing a resolution on any matter, including one amending the constitution.

With respect to the question of constitutional convention, a different majority (6-3) stated that a convention had emerged which required provincial participation and consent to any constitutional amendment affecting provincial legislative powers. In this opinion, the judges reviewed the history of constitutional amendments in Canada and concluded that there were no exceptions to the rule that provinces were both consulted and had agreed to amendments affecting their responsiblities. The constitution of a country was the sum of the written parts plus constitutional conventions. By this statement the court gave recognition to the significance of conventions in the Canadian constitution.

While the court did not prescribe an amending formula, they did cast doubt on the unanimity rule which had been part of conventional wisdom to that date. While unanimity may not have been required, the court also stated that an amendment supported by the federal government, Ontario and New Brunswick "would not pass muster". The courts concluded by saying:

> We have reached the conclusion that the agreement of the provinces of Canada, no views being expressed as to its quantification, is constitutionally required for

the passing of the "Proposed Resolution for a joint Address to Her Majesty respecting the Constitution of Canada" and that the passing of this Resolution without such agreement would be unconstitutional in the conventional sense.

In summary, the court stated that while legal in a technical sense the federal government's proposed course of action was unconstitutional.

The fall-out as a result of the judgment was soon apparent. The court had said the process the federal government proposed to follow was unconstitutional in the conventional sense without expressly prohibiting the federal government from doing it. Through its judgment the court left the way open for further political discussions among the federal and provincial governments.

November 1981

Immediately following the Supreme Court decision the eight provinces called for a federal-provincial conference to resolve the constitutional matter. The Prime Minister agreed to a meeting but warned the Premiers that it would be their final opportunity to resolve the constitutional question in Canada. The conference convened on November 1, 1981, and lasted four days. At several points throughout the meeting it appeared as if the conference would break up without reaching an agreement.

What was discussed? Essentially two documents were on the table. One was the Resolution before Parliament while the second was the April 16 Accord of the eight opposing provinces. The Resolution had undergone a number of significant changes both as a result of the parliamentary committee hearings and through amendments made by the House of Commons to the draft proposed by the parliamentary committee. The basic structure of the Resolution was: a comprehensive Charter of Rights, the Victoria amending formula, recognition of equalization, a section on natural resources, plus a few other provisions.

When the meeting opened Premier Davis of Ontario stated that he was prepared to give up Ontario's veto. By doing so the future of the Victoria formula became doubtful. Premier Lévesque agreed with a federal proposal to hold a referendum on the Charter of Rights following two years of further negotiation. A similar provision for the amending formula was already contained in the Resolution before Parliament. This proposal was rejected by the other provinces who wished to see the issue resolved more quickly. By giving his agreement Premier Lévesque broke the common front established by the eight provinces. This development was a key factor in leading to the final consensus.

On November 5, 1981, a constitutional agreement was reached between the federal government and nine provinces. Québec did not agree with the Constitutional Accord and refused to join the consensus. What was agreed to? In effect it was a blending of the two positions which were on the table: the federal Resolution which had had the support of Ontario and New Brunswick, and the provincial amending formula. To arrive at a consensus it was necessary for a variety of compromises to be made. In the case of the federal government it was acceptance of a "notwithstanding clause" covering sections of the Charter and the provincial amending formula. In the case of the provinces it was acceptance of the Charter and modification of their amending formula by dropping a section on financial compensation for provinces which chose to opt out of amendments.

The Canadian Constitution, 1981

The Charter of Rights, as it is now written, is unique. It is both comprehensive and detailed. It covers fundamental freedoms such as free speech, and democratic rights such as the right to vote; recognition of English and French as the offical languages of Canada; establishment of mobility rights, equality rights and affirmative action programs, and legal rights such as the right to be secure against unreasonable search and seizure. The opening section of the Charter "guarantees the rights and freedoms set out in it subject only to such reasonable limits prescribed by law as can be demonstrably justified in a free and democratic society." It is clear that rights are not absolute but relative, being subject to reasonable limits.

Critics of an entrenched Charter argued that the courts would substitute their opinions of "reasonable" for that of elected legislatures. To meet this criticism a "notwithstanding" clause, Section 33, was included. The "notwithstanding" clause applies to the sections on fundamental freedoms, legal and equal rights. By this section, either Parliament or a provincial legislature may pass a law saying that notwithstanding the Charter a particular law shall apply. The maximum period for such a law to operate is five years, after which it either lapses or must be re-enacted.

While there is no doubt that the courts will be called upon to interpret the Charter of Rights, legislatures will also continue to have an important role in safeguarding rights. The five-year sunset clause, a period which coincides with the maximum life of a Parliament or a legislature, also means that the exercise of the "notwithstanding" clause very early or very late in the life of a legislative session means that the issues could very well become part of an election campaign. The net consequence in the future of both legislative and court action is that the public should become far more sensitive to the question of rights and the importance of protecting them.

The new Canadian amending formula was designed to overcome the rigidity of unanimity and still provide provinces with an equivalent degree of protection. The technique agreed to was "opting-out". Amendments to the constitution are to be made by resolutions passed by Parliament and two thirds of the provinces (currently seven) representing 50% of the population. The two thirds-50% rule is derived from the Fulton-Favreau formula. The 50% rule means that either Ontario or Québec must agree to an amendment; The two thirds rule means that at least one Western Province or one Atlantic Province must favor an amendment before it can be passed. Thus the passage of any amendment needs a reasonable degree of support throughout the country.

If an amendment is one which takes away existing legislative powers, the proprietary rights or any other rights or privileges of a legislature or a province, then a province not agreeing to the amendment can "opt out" of that amendment if its legislature adopts a resolution of dissent. It should be stressed that "opting-out" can only take place when amendments limit or curtail what provinces now do. It could not take place if there were an amendment transferring responsibilities to provinces. Generally speaking, the "opting-out" provision applies to Sections 92, 93, 94A, 95 and 109 of the British North America Act. At most, only three provinces may opt out—any more and the amendment would fail because it would not meet the two-thirds test.

The principal criticism of this formula was that it would lead to a checkerboard effect. In assessing this criticism it must be remembered that any formula developed would have to provide some measure of protection to Québec. If a unanimity requirement would place the constitution in a straitjacket then the only plausible alternative would be opting-out. The advantage of this principle is that change to the constitution is possible—but individual provinces remain protected.

The prototype of possible future amendments as found in the existing constitution is Section 94A which authorizes Parliament to legislate in the area of pensions provided no such law affects any existing or future law of a province. This section made possible the co-existence of the Canada and Québec pension plans. If one examines the terms by which individual provinces were admitted to Canada one finds different provisions, be it natural resources for Alberta, Saskatchewan and Manitoba or denominational schools in Newfoundland. Section 133 of the BNA Act places an obligation on Québec—and through the Manitoba Act on that province—to provide services in French and English. A similar obligation was not placed on the other provinces. Thus from the very beginning of the country to the present, there has been a recognition that individual provinces may be treated differently in certain circumstances. Constitutional amendment is such a circumstance and the formula provides for it but does not require it. It should be expected that future governments will seek a consensus to avoid opting-out.

There were other constitutional changes found in the 1981 agreement. One is recognition of equalization and that both orders of government have an obligation to overcome this problem. Another is a recognition of existing aboriginal rights and a requirement to hold a constitutional conference to define these rights. Finally, there was a provision on natural resources. This section is the first amendment to Section 92 of the constitution and is a direct result of the CIGOL and Potash cases. By this new section provinces are given limited authority to legislate in the area of interprovincial trade and commerce and to levy indirect taxes on resources. The importance of the resource section is that it does indicate that change to the division of powers is possible.

In tracing the evolution of the Canadian Constitution, 1981, one must look as far back as 1968 for the Charter of Rights and to the Victoria Charter for the section on equalization. The amending formula and the section on resources are a result of the discussions in late 1979. There is no doubt that these amendments will shape the future of the Canadian political system.

Areas for Further Study

The above presentation represents a generally traditional analysis of Canadian federalism; for one who wishes to probe deeper there are many fascinating questions still to be considered. For example, one might wish to study more fully general public awareness of the federal system. Are people familiar with the complexities and dynamic nature of the system? Do they care which government administers a program so long as services are provided? Do they know the extent to which federalism shapes Canadian politics? Our knowledge of public attitudes toward the federal system is surprisingly weak. Much more behavioral research is necessary if a more complete understanding of this complex subject is to be developed.

Another problem that should be considered is the meaning of the term "the provinces". On any given policy question one can expect to find a number of provincial viewpoints. Consider the problem of oil pricing. Alberta and Saskatchewan (producing provinces) have different views on oil pricing than do Ontario (a consumer of domestic oil) and Nova Scotia (a consumer of imported oil). Sometimes the interprovincial differences are so great that they cannot be reconciled; other times compromises can be achieved. One should not forget that while, under the constitution, legislative powers of the provinces are identical, their social, economic and political climates vary considerably. When analyzing the federal system one should assess not only the similarities among provincial positions but also the differences. Indeed on a given matter there is often a greater congruence between the federal position and that of some provinces than among the ten provinces themselves.

While federal-provincial relations represent one facet of the federal system, interprovincial relations represent another. One cannot assume that all problems within the federal system are confined to the federal-provincial dimension. Interprovincial relations are becoming increasingly important. For example, since 1960 the Premiers of the ten provinces have met annually to discuss problems of mutual concern. The matters discussed range from the economy, to resource taxation, to education. One consequence of the 1976 Premiers' Conference was the negotiation of a common provincial position on the renewal of fiscal agreements. If this process continues, both the content and dynamics of federal-provincial discussions will change considerably.

Another aspect of the federal system that warrants careful scrutiny is increasing regional cooperation among both the Western and Maritime provinces. Since 1973, with the Western Economic Opportunities Conference, the four Western provinces have worked together closely to develop common positions toward the federal government on a number of matters such as transportation, economic development and international trade. In addition, matters of a regional nature are explored and, where possible, common solutions developed.

The Council of Maritime Premiers represents a significant achievement in the area of interprovincial cooperation. The three Maritime provinces have institutionalized their arrangement through joint legislative action. While still far short of Maritime union, the Council has a budget and employees and administers for the three provinces certain programs such as the Maritime Provinces' Higher Education Commission, the Maritime Municipal Training and Development Board, and the Land Registration and Information Service. The effects of this policy harmonization in the East and West cannot help but have consequences for the federal system as a whole, either by presenting a common front to the federal government or by solving problems through interprovincial, as distinct from federal-provincial, mechanisms. Whether these regional groupings have resulted from feelings of alienation from the federal government or from a regional desire to cooperate, or some combination of both, is a matter for further study.

Another matter of continuing great importance in Canadian federalism is the question of Québec. Concerns over English-French relations and the status of Québec within Confederation are of long-standing duration. Indeed they are as old as Confederation itself. National unity, while always a fundamental dilemma confronting successive governments in Canada, is of immediate concern today because of the 1976 electoral victory of the Parti Québécois in Québec. Although the referendum on sovereignty association was defeated in May 1980, the Parti Québécois was re-elected in April 1981. Although the Parti Québécois pledged to the electorate that a second referendum would not be held during their next term in office, the resolutions adopted at their party convention in the fall of 1981 demonstrate that the issue of separatism is by no means forgotten by party members. Premier Lévesque threatened to resign over the changes in party policy and held a referendum among party members to modify the resolutions of the convention. Nevertheless the question of Québec's role and future in Canada is one which will continue to be debated both inside and outside the province.

One area which has not been discussed is that of federal-provincial financial relations. A key problem in any federal country is balancing the division of powers with the assignment of revenue sources between the federal and provincial governments. Put another way, the fiscal capacities of governments should be sufficient to allow them to meet their fiscal needs. From the very beginning of Confederation there was a fiscal imbalance between provincial needs and means. It is for this reason that fiscal relations have so often been the subject of federal-provincial negotiations. In part to overcome this imbalance and in part to develop a uniform income tax system, governments in Canada have developed a complex system of fiscal arrangements. These arrangements can be traced back to 1941. An important component of the agreements is the equalization program where provincial revenues of the so-called "have-not" provinces are supplemented by unconditional transfer payments. Over the past few years equalization payments have increased considerably and the federal government has sought ways of reducing its expenditures. How and why the program has been modified provides a fascinating insight into the area of fiscal federalism. The importance which all governments attach to equalization is reflected in the principle being enshrined in the new constitution.

Closely intertwined with the discussions on fiscal arrangements has been an ongoing debate over shared-cost programs. Shared-cost programs are those which are jointly financed by both governments. Policy matters such as health care, hospital care, social assistance, the construction of the TransCanada Highway and post-secondary education are examples of issues where costs have been shared between governments.

Another subject that furthers one's understanding of the working of Canadian federalism is the negotiations on energy policy and natural resources. This topic dominated federal-provincial relations throughout most of the seventies. The subject of energy and natural resources has a significant impact on western economic development and the influence of Western Canada in federal-provincial relations. The 1980 National Energy Program placed a severe strain on Canada-Alberta relations and was a principal factor in fostering a small but vocal western separatist movement. The five-year energy agreement on pricing and revenue-sharing reached between Alberta and Canada in September 1981 greatly alleviated the tensions between these two governments. That agreement was soon followed by one between Canada and Saskatchewan and British Columbia. Disputes over natural resources are not confined to Western Canada. Negotiations over offshore resources are being actively pursued by Newfoundland and Nova Scotia. Federal economic development priorities for the 1980s have focused on the development of natural resources. Since most natural resources are both owned and regulated by the provinces their development is of crucial importance to each provincial government. One can expect that this subject will continue to be a key factor of intergovernmental affairs.

Provincial criticisms of the shared-cost principle have been constant and have rested on the premise that these programs are primarily in areas of provincial jurisdiction. The provinces have also argued that the federal government has used its spending power to circumvent the division of powers. In addition, the provinces have argued that these federally-inspired programs distort provincial priorities. If provinces wish to participate in federally-sponsored programs they must adjust provincial priorities accordingly. Another provincial concern is the possibility that the federal government may either terminate a program or reduce levels of funding leaving the provincial government the option of reducing services or filling the void, thereby possibly affecting the levels of funding of other programs. The provinces currently find themselves in this situation with the announcement by the federal Finance Minister in his November 1981 Budget that federal transfers for health care and post-secondary education would be reduced.

The federal government has strongly defended its policies by arguing that the exercise of the spending power is fully within the competence of Parliament under the constitution. It has justified these programs on the grounds that society has become increasingly interdependent and that there are "national consequences of inaction" if provinces permitted their standards to fall below a certain level. The federal government argues that in certain policy areas there exists a national interest. Two other justifications advanced for federal policy initiatives are the interdependence of government policies and the sense of community which exists in Canada. In various endeavors, the federal govern- ment has sought to establish national standards of service.

CONTEMPORARY TRENDS IN CANADIAN FEDERALISM

Two characteristics appear to dominate the current federal scene: the inter- dependence of governments, and the existence of a federal system in which one finds a strong central government and strong provincial governments more or less in equilibrium. These two phenomena are to some extent contradictory and lead to clashes between the federal and provincial governments.

If the events of the past few years illustrate anything it is that the federal system is in a constant state of transition. Mechanisms to assist in accommodating change were developed. One approach was to implement corrective action through adoption of an amending formula and, later, through constitutional reform. A second technique was the emergence of the federal-provincial conference.

The locus of conflict shifted from the courtroom to the conference—be it a constitutional conference or one on the economy. With the advent of confer- ences, came the establishment of federal-provincial committees, forging institu- tionalized links between the two orders of government. If anything has transformed the dynamics of the federal system in the past few years and greatly influenced Canadian politics in general, it is the emergence of the conference technique for resolving federal-provincial disputes. At first glance the notion of a high level of conference activity conjures up visions of harmony and coopera- tion. While this image is partially correct it overlooks the fact that increased contact may also produce discord between the federal and provincial govern- ments arising from intergovernmental competition. To a considerable extent the debate on energy policy has been a result of competition over control and development of natural resources. The dispute over cablevision between Québec/Saskatchewan and Ottawa is another example. While these disputes have a jurisdictional dimension, they transcend the simple legal question of defining jurisdictional boundaries. The issues are more complex than that and relate directly to the relative power and responsibilities of the federal and provincial governments within Confederation.

During the fifties and sixties, one frequently encountered criticism that the principle of cooperative federalism extended only to subject matters within provincial jurisdiction such as education and health and social assistance. During the seventies there has been a phenomenal explosion in the range of issues which have been subject to federal-provincial scrutiny. It is not just that governments are meeting more often but there are now no limits to the subjects they consider. For example, in the past few years consultations, discussions and/or negotiations have taken place on oil pricing, energy supply, international trade, health care, taxation, pensions, demography, transportation, immigration, manpower, communications, municipal planning, banking, wage and price controls, scientific research and consumer protection. In effect, no area of public policy can be placed outside the framework of federal-provincial relations.

The purposes of these interactions are many and varied. Sometimes an agreement is sought such as was the case for the 1975 anti-inflation program. Occasionally the federal government seeks provincial input, as with the revisions to the Bank Act. In some instances the provinces wish to modify existing federal policies dealing with, for example, transportation or foreign investment. If the purposes behind intergovernmental discussions vary, so do the results. In some instances, such as the energy negotiations, a specific result may be achieved. In other instances, such as the two First Ministers' Conferences on the Economy in 1978, broad policy guidelines or principles were endorsed by the eleven governments. At other times no immediate or tangible conclusion may be achieved, often leading to mixed reactions from the participants. Why was the conference held? What was behind the meeting? Was one government seeking political advantage? These are questions frequently asked in such instances.

Despite the apparent success of this means of accommodation, certain criticisms of it have been expressed. Perhaps the most fundamental of these is the possible effect such meetings may have on parliamentary government. To what extent does prior agreement between the executives of the federal and provincial governments erode parliamentary supremacy? Can either Parliament or a legislature undo what has been agreed on in the give and take of negotiation? Another concern is that most meetings or parts of them are conducted behind closed doors. Critics are of the opinion that these meetings should be open to the public, although they often overlook the reality that certain portions of any negotiations will be carried on in private among the parties concerned. The conference of first ministers has been compared to a super-cabinet; however, unlike a cabinet, it is responsible not to one but to eleven legislatures. Finally one must assess the effect of so many meetings and conferences on the climate of federal-provincial relations. Do they enhance or inhibit the decision-making capabilities of governments? Do they create or destroy the chance of reaching agreement within the federal system?

CONCLUSION

In summary, certain points merit careful consideration. While intergovernmental conflict may appear to be on the increase in Canada, it should also be recognized that governments consult on a much broader scale than ever before. Naturally, some conflict is inevitable, especially if new initiatives are involved.

Finally, the stresses within the federal system appear to be a result of increased competition between the federal and provincial governments in achieving their respective policy goals. Sometimes these objectives can be harmonized; at other times, differences are irreconcilable. But if conflict appears endemic, so too is the desire to solve mutual problems. The constitutional and energy agreements are examples of instances where unilateral federal action provoked a confrontation with all the provinces. Only after the federal government realized that unilateral action would not succeed was a negotiated settlement possible.

The capacity for adjustment within the Canadian federal system is considerable, as the 1981 constitutional agreement illustrates. Federalism as a form of government is premised on diversity and the Canadian federal system is no exception. Problems and issues will continue to arise in Canada, given our social, cultural and economic diversity. As new challenges confront governments, as new crises arise in Canadian politics, they must be met, reconciled and resolved within the framework of our federal system.

Canadian politics has been and will continue to be greatly influenced, if not even dominated, by the federal system. There is no reason to believe that this situation will change in the near future. This is true whether it is a matter of settling the Crowsnest Pass freight rates, negotiating the GATT, developing natural resources or training skilled labor. Indeed, with the development of an amending formula it is possible that governments will resort to this device far more frequently as a means of resolving disputes. The constitutional agreement has by no means settled all the outstanding federal-provincial disputes. For example, there remains the important question of reform of central political institutions such as the Senate. Should provinces have a direct say in decision-making at the federal level? A change of this magnitude will have a profound effect on the future course of Canadian politics.

By focusing on federalism we will not come to understand everything we should know about Canadian politics, but to neglect the federal dimension is to overlook probably the most enduring and critical facets of the Canadian political scene. Canadian political parties, pressure groups, political institutions and public policies are influenced by federalism. From 1867 to 1982, and beyond, many of the mundane—as well as the vitally important—aspects of Canadian politics can best be described and understood as the politics of a fascinating federal experiment.

SUMMARY

1. The structure of every major political institution—the House of Commons, the Cabinet, the Senate and the Supreme Court—has been influenced by federalism.

2. Controversies involving federal arrangements have been at the heart of most Canadian political problems since 1867.

3. Changes in federal arrangements have been brought about through judicial interpretation, convention, constitutional amendment and federal-provincial negotiation.

4. The British North America Act, 1867, did not contain an amending formula. For 60 years this situation seemed to be acceptable, but since 1927 governments in Canada have sought to develop an amending formula.

5. Since the Quiet Revolution in Québec there has been increasing pressure on the federal government to reform the Canadian constitution.

6. Beginning in 1968 and continuing to 1981 governments in Canada displayed great urgency in trying to "patriate" the British North America Act and develop an amending formula. Extensive negotiations led to a constitutional agreement on patriation, on an amending formula and on a Charter of Rights in the fall of 1981.

7. Over the years an increasing number of issues have been subject to federal-provincial dialogue and negotiation. These have included medicare, energy, trade, acid rain, communications, transportation and taxation.

8. Federal-provincial conference activity has become more pronounced in recent years.

9. Federalism in Canada has proven to be remarkable flexible and adaptable.

10. Canadian politics is largely the politics of federalism.

STUDY QUESTIONS

1. What are likely to be the long-term consequences of Canada's new amending formula?

2. To what extent was the long delay in achieving constitutional "patriation" attributable to partisan squabbles, regionalism, personal ambitions, ideological differences or other factors?

3. Is Canadian federalism mainly the result of social-political diversity, the cause of social-political diversity, or both?

4. Is Canada likely to become a more centralized or a more decentralized federation?

5. What are the major arguments for the proposition that the federal government should, or should not, continue to fund medicare and post-secondary education programs?

6. Has Québec separatism passed its high point? Were the commitments made by the federal government in 1980 fulfilled by the 1981 constitutional agreement?

7. What are likely to be some new areas of federal-provincial controversy?

8. In your view, to what extent does the Canadian experience with federalism support the view that "federalism is an inherently unstable and probably a transitional arrangement"?

9. What areas or aspects of Canadian politics are unaffected by federalism?

10. What, in your estimation, are the weaknesses in a federalist interpretation of Canadian politics?

ENDNOTES

1. See A.H. Birch, "Approaches to the Study of Federalism," *Political Studies*, Vol. XIV, No. 1 (1966), pp. 15-33, and W.H. Riker, "Six Books in Search of a Subject or Does Federalism Exist and Does it Matter," *Comparative Politics*, Vol. 2, No. 1 (October, 1969), pp. 135-46.

2. K.C. Wheare, *Federal Government*, 4th ed. (London: Oxford University Press, 1964), p. 33.

3. *Confederation Debates*, 1865, p. 40.

4. Alan Cairns, "The Living Canadian Constitution," *Queen's Quarterly*, Vol. LXXVII, No. 4 (Winter, 1970), reprinted in J. Peter Meekison (ed.), *Canadian Federalism: Myth or Reality*, 2nd ed. (Toronto: Methuen Publications, 1971), p. 144.

5. *Attorney General of Ontario* v. *Attorney General of Canada*, [1896], A.C. 348 at p. 361.

6. [1925], A.C. 396.

7. [1982], A.C. 437 at p. 422.

8. *Report of the Royal Commission on Dominion-Provincial Relations*, reprinted (Ottawa: Queen's Printer, 1954), Book I, p. 255.

9. *Ibid.*, p. 259.

10. J.A. Corry, "Constitutional Trends and Canadian Federalism," in A.R.M. Lower, F.R. Scott et al., *Evolving Canadian Federalism* (Durham, N.C.: Duke University Press, 1958), pp. 92-125.

11. E.R. Black and A. Cairns, "A Different Perspective on Canadian Federalism," *Canadian Public Administration*, Vol. IX (March, 1966), pp. 27-45.

12. D.V. Smiley, "Public Administration and Canadian Federalism," *Canadian Public Administration*, Vol. VII (September, 1964), pp.

13.8.From the "Introduction" in P.E. Trudeau, *Federalism and the French Canadians* (Toronto: Macmillan Company, 1968), p. xii.

14. Government of Canada, *Federalism and decentralization: where do we stand?* (Hull: Supply and Services Canada, 1981).

15. *Reference re Ownership of Off-Shore Mineral Rights*, 65 D.L.R.

16. *Jones* v. *Attorney General, New Brunswick*, [1974], 16 C.C.C. (2nd) 297.

17. *Re Anti-Inflation Act*, [1976], 2 S.C.R. 373.

18. *Canadian Industrial Gas and Oil Ltd.* v. *Government of Saskatchewan et al.*, [1978], 2 S.C.R. 545 and *Central Canada Potash Company Ltd. et al.* v. *Government of Saskatchewan*, [1979], 1 S.C.R. 42.

19. For a comprehensive report and discussion on this subject see *The Constitutional Review, 1968-1971*, Secretary's Report, *Canadian Intergovernmental Conference Secretariat* (Ottawa: Information Canada, 1974).

20. For copies of the correspondence between the Prime Minister and the provinces

see Alberta Department of Federal and Intergovernmental Affairs *Fourth Annual Report To March 31, 1977* (Edmonton: April 1978), pp. 55-8.

21. For the text of the Prime Minister's speech see Toronto *Globe and Mail*, November 25, 1976.

22. *Commons Debates*, June 12, 1978, p. 6278.

23. See Communiqués from the Annual Premiers' Conference, August 9-12, 1978, Regina. Reprinted in Alberta Department of Federal and Intergovernmental Affairs *Sixth Annual Report To March 31, 1979* (Edmonton: October 1979), pp. 42-6.

24. Task Force on Canadian Unity, *A Future Together: Observations and Recommendations* (Hull: Supply and Services Canada, 1979).

25. "Statement by the Prime Minister," Ottawa, October 2, 1980, Office of the Prime Minister.

26. *Reference re Amendment of the Constitution of Canada (Nos. 1, 2 and 3)* (1981), 125 D.L.R. (3rd) 1.

SELECTED REFERENCES

Black, E.R. *Divided Loyalties: Canadian Concepts of Federalism.* Montreal: McGill-Queen's University Press, 1975. An important work which analyzes a number of theories of Canadian federalism.

Cairns, Alan C. "the Judicial Committee and its Critics." *Canadian Journal of Political Science*, Vol. IV (1971), pp. 301-45. An assessment of the quality of Canada's jurisprudence through an examination and review of the Judicial Committee of the Privy Council's role as final authority for constitutional interpretation.

Careless, Anthony. *Initiative and Response.* Montreal: McGill-Queen's University Press, 1977. A study focusing on Canadian federalism and regional economic development.

Dupré, J.S. et al. *Federalism and Policy Development: The Case of Adult Occupational Training in Ontario.* Toronto: University of Toronto Press, 1973. An excellent case study examining the process of policy development in Canada's federal system.

Gérin-Lajoie, Paul. *Constitutional Amendment in Canada.* Toronto: University of Toronto Press, 1950. A history of amendments to the constitution to the time of writing, and the problems surrounding the "amending formula" debate.

Hogg, Peter W. *Constitutional Law of Canada.* Toronto: The Carswell Co. Ltd., 1977. A Canadian constitutional law text which gives one an excellent grasp of this important subject.

Lederman, W.R. *Continuing Canadian Constitutional Dilemmas.* Toronto: Butterworths, 1981. A collection of essays on Canadian constitutional law by one of Canada's most distinguished constitutional scholars.

Lévesque, René. *An Option for Quebec.* Toronto: McClelland and Stewart, 1968. The book presents Mr. Lévesque's case for a sovereign Québec associated with the rest of Canada in an economic union.

Meekison, J.P., ed. *Canadian Federalism: Myth or Reality*, 3rd ed. Toronto: Methuen, 1977. A collection of articles and documents which gives the reader a feel for the dynamics—both theoretical and practical—of the Canadian federal system.

Morin, Claude. *Quebec versus Ottawa.* Toronto: University of Toronto Press, 1976. A presentation of the Québec case for its consistent provincial autonomist stand in negotiations with the federal government.

Parliamentary Task Force on Federal-Provincial Fiscal Arrangements. *Fiscal Federalism in Canada.* Ottawa: House of Commons, 1981. A report from a committee of the House of Commons established to examine fiscal arrangements.

Rowell-Sirois Report. *Report of the Royal Commission on Dominion-Provincial Relations.* Ottawa: King's Printer, 1940. An important work which examines in detail the economic and financial basis of Confederation and the development of the distribution of powers and responsibilities from 1867-1940. It remains one of the most important analyses of federal-provincial relations.

Simeon, Richard. *Federal-Provincial Diplomacy: The Making of Recent Policy in Canada.* Toronto: University of Toronto Press, 1972. Through an examination of the negotiations involving three important issues, the process of bargaining between the federal and provincial governments is examined.

Simeon, Richard, ed. *Must Canada Fail?* Montreal: McGill-Queen's University Press, 1977. A collection of essays analyzing the issue of Québec separatism.

Smiley, D.V. *Canada in Question: Federalism in the Eighties,* 3rd ed. Toronto: McGraw-Hill Ryerson, 1980. Provides an overview of a number of aspects of the federal system of Canada, including the constitution and federalism, the evolution of the system, mechanisms for federal-provincial relations, fiscal and economic federalism, cultural duality, and the author's observations on national unity. *See also his bibliography.*

Stevenson, Garth. *Unfulfilled Union.* Toronto: Macmillan Co. of Canada, 1979. An assessment which examines some of the economic forces underlying Canadian federalism.

Task Force on Canadian Unity. *Coming to Terms: The Words of the Debate.* Hull: Supply and Services Canada, 1979. A useful document explaining political terms and parts of the constitution.

Task Force on Canadian Unity *A Future Together: Observations and Recommendations.* Hull: Supply and Services Canada, 1979. The Task Force Report which explains in detail their recommendations for constitutional change.

Wheare, K.C. *Federal Government,* 4th ed. London: Oxford University Press, 1964. A book which examines what a federal system is and how it works, by examining the workings of the federal systems of the US, Canada, Switzerland and Australia—in theory and practice.

Part Four

Processes:
The Essence
of Canadian Politics

In studying Canadian politics we are very much interested in actual events, in the dynamics of political activity. The first chapter in this section describes the extent to which the democratic Canadian political system is based on the operation of political parties and electoral activity; activity which might well be termed the life-blood of the Canadian political system. The analysis may well substantiate the hypothesis that without a free and viable party system with its periodic and uncoerced elections, there can be no continuing democratic system. This approach, as Professor Engelmann points out, does not explain everything about Canadian politics but it does tell us a great deal.

In the second chapter, Professor Cameron identifies, describes and assesses a continuing and now critical dimension of Canadian politics—English-French conflict and cooperation. This process of interaction has never been more important than it is today for, with separatists having formed the government in Québec, the very existence of the country is at stake. Surely no one understands Canada until he understands the processes by which the two largest segments of our society formed a country, worked together to develop it, and must now reconcile some basic differences if the country is to survive. Whether one takes the sociological or the institutional approach, the dualist controversy is central.

The third chapter in this section draws our attention to the complicated and Byzantine process of how public policy is shaped and administered, and makes a strong case for multidisciplinary analysis. As Professor Wilson demonstrates, the conventional dictum that "politics determines policies" is largely valid but equally valid is the opposite notion that "policies determine politics". He argues convincingly that since the public policy process involves virtually every institution of government and its results impinge in countless ways on all of us, we cannot comprehend the reality of Canadian politics without studying public policy. As governments grow and as their policies become more pervasive, the public policy approach must move into centre stage. For the approximately 1.5 million Canadians who are employed by our national, provincial and municipal governments, the topic will naturally have special significance.

9

Canadian Political Parties and Elections

Frederick C. Engelmann*

INTRODUCTION

"Party" is one of the few household words in the political vocabulary of Canadian students. All are likely to know about Liberals, Progressive Conservatives and New Democrats, and that they are political parties. Those who know only a little about parties tend to identify them, as Edmund Burke did two hundred years ago, as groups tied together by similar ideas. In fact, modern political parties have come to be both less and more than this definition: less, in that supporters of a party may disagree among themselves, and to some degree even with their leaders; more in that parties are in fact concerned with people more than with policies. Parties mobilize voters at election time, hire party bureaucrats and workers, recruit potential leaders, nominate candidates for elective office and for top leadership posts, and attempt to elect these candidates so they can, as a final goal, organize the governments and thus furnish the political leaders of the nation and its provinces.

In any country in which parties compete, the election is the arena of competition. Here, the ruled select their rulers. Each voter may simply vote for the representative from the constituency he or she lives in, as in Canada, or voters may have candidates for all kinds of offices to vote for, as in the United States. In any case, elections make it possible for people to vote for representatives and thus have representative government. If, as in Canada, their vote for a member of Parliament helps determine which party governs the country, there is responsible government.

The earlier definition of party should make clear that not all political groups are parties. Many political groups raise demands for public policies; these

*Professor of Political Science, University of Alberta.

groups represent particular interests, and they are therefore called interest groups. Such groups will be discussed in Chapter 14.

Several functions of parties were mentioned in the initial definition. The principal ones are recruiting and selecting leaders, mobilizing voters and providing policy decisions. Of these, the first two, selecting leaders in part and mobilizing voters entirely, are connected with elections. Parties recruit potential leaders all the time, but they normally nominate candidates just prior to an election. Insofar as parties deal with policy decisions, they do so in an overall, general way when they prepare the election platform. The party needs to win the election or become part of a governing coalition (a highly unlikely event in Canada) in order to put into effect policies contained in its platform. In this fast-moving age with its fast-changing environment, governments may enact a number of policies which have never been before the people in an election, but which nonetheless can be identified as policies of the governing party.

Where parties compete—we usually designate such countries as democracies—the competing parties make up the party system. The number of parties with at least a realistic hope of gaining legislative seats determines the system's designation. Thus, there is a two-party system in the United States and a multiparty system in France and Italy. Canada had a pure two-party system until the First World War. Since then, our party system has become difficult to classify. A later section of this chapter will show why this is so.

IMPORTANCE OF POLITICAL PARTIES AND ELECTIONS IN CANADA

As a general proposition one can safely assert that Canadian politics consists to a large degree of the structures, values, processes and personnel associated with political parties and elections. Remove parties and elections, and the Canadian political system as we have come to know it does not exist. From Confederation in 1867 to the constitutional crisis of 1981, political parties and elections have served as both cause and effect in much of Canadian political life.

Post-Confederation Canada has always been governed by a political party. With a brief exception in 1925, the leader of the strongest party in the House of Commons has always been the prime minister of Canada. As elections in Canada have become more and more a plebiscite between leaders, the importance of parties, whose leaders compete for the political leadership of the nation, has been maintained throughout.

The united colony of Canada, based on representative government, achieved responsible government in 1849. Responsible government means that the ministers of the Crown are in office only so long as they enjoy the support of the majority of the House of Commons. It also means that these ministers actively try to maintain such support. Not surprisingly, the Liberal Conservative party (now the Progressive Conservatives) was formed in the legislature to support a ministry as early as 1854. After Confederation, the task became one of governing the young Dominion of Canada, and the organization of a second party became necessary to provide alternate leaders. By 1878, those who had successfully opposed John A. Macdonald over the Pacific Scandal and had come to govern under Alexander Mackenzie were permanently organized into the Liberal party.

The result of a party's leadership selection process may be to give the country a new prime minister. The prime minister may come to dominate his party but, as events in the 1890s showed, no prime minister has attempted to stay in office without his party's support. Parties have provided not only prime ministers and provincial premiers, but also leaders of the opposition and usually all the ministers in federal and provincial governments. Generally, these positions are unavailable without partisan election. Executive positions require appointment by the party leader, whether prime minister or premier.

Beyond and including these visible leaders, Canadian political parties recruit virtually anybody who can be called a professional politician, whether this person sits in a legislative body or works for a political party. In addition, most people who aspire to candidacy for elective office work through political parties. Wherever political appointments are made—to the Senate, to the judiciary or to some, usually provincial, administrative posts—these come about through political parties.

Canadian parties have had considerable impact on the style of Canadian politics. Both Tories (Conservatives) and Grits (Liberals) have done their share in defining leadership roles. Conservatives have usually been led by a *primus inter pares*—a parliamentary colleague who became first among equals—or by a successful provincial premier who was seconded to the Ottawa scene. For most of the time since Confederation, the Liberals have been led by men who have not come up through party ranks but have been recruited and selected by the party after becoming well-known as administrators, lawyers or writers. This difference in recruitment has produced a more independent and less controlled style on the part of Liberal leaders. Since 1887, when Laurier was selected, all Liberal leaders—King, St. Laurent, Pearson, Trudeau—have become prime minister. In this century, the leaders of all major parties died in office or resigned voluntarily, except John Diefenbaker, who was removed as leader by the Progressive Conservative party in 1967. In the CCF/NDP, leaders have to rely more on formal consultation with councils representing party members and with party bureaucrats. Wherever the CCF/NDP has been important, its leaders have been in real or potential conflict with the organized party faithful, but the leaders have tended to win such conflicts. In other important parties— Social Credit or the Union Nationale—such conflicts hardly, if ever, existed. The Parti Québécois has been shaped by its founder and leader, René Lévesque, who has been premier during nearly half of the party's existence. As of early 1982, Lévesque and his party are in the midst of exactly such a conflict.

Until the end of the nineteenth century, it appeared that Grits and Tories would continue to be the parties of all Canadians, sharing a generally common electoral base. Since the 1890s, however, the parties' sources of support have differed. The Liberals have been French Canada's principal representative in Ottawa. Though this seems strange in the present era, the Liberals were for decades essentially the party of the Canadian farmer, a position occupied by the Conservatives since the late fifties. Both parties have continued to compete for the support of the Canadian worker. Since the Great Depression they have had to compete with the CCF/NDP which, at least nationally and to a large extent also provincially, has not so far been able to realize its objective of becoming the party of Canadian labor.

Readers who expect the Canadian party system to generate much policy conflict will be disappointed. Liberals and Conservatives (and Social Credit in British Columbia) all support the prevailing economic system, though the captains of free enterprise are not happy with their taxing and regulating efforts. The NDP, while critical of the distribution of ownership and the management of the economy, has not attacked the prevailing economic dogma frontally when and where it has been in a position to do so. As I will show later, the federal anti-inflation program of 1975 was a nearly perfect example of the limited, or at least unreliable, impact of party on policy, even though public policies ostensibly are associated with party preferences and are enacted by parties in parliament.

The parties' interaction with Canada's federal system is complex. The federal system gives Canadian parties eleven arenas in which to compete, not just one as in the United Kingdom or France. Third parties have been able to score successes regionally, and have had strong-to-moderate success in all but the four Atlantic provinces. Provincial success of third parties is a major reason why Canada does not revert to its original two-party system. In this way, third parties provide more variety in Canadian politics, but they often prevent the formation of majorities in Ottawa and have therefore sometimes been accused of weakening not only our system of parliamentary government, but also Canadian unity.

The strong current emphasis on Canadian federalism, however, is not the creation of political parties. According to Richard Simeon,[1] party differences have made little difference in federal-provincial conflicts. Yet the powerful emphasis on Prime Minister and premiers, which has given Canada what Donald Smiley calls executive federalism,[2] has tended to make federal elections and, with the possible exception of the three Maritime provinces, provincial elections, plebiscites between Ottawa and the province(s). Confrontation and antagonism are common. Many a provincial campaign has included a significant anti-Ottawa emphasis. Thus, there is a strong tendency for provincial governing parties to win elections, and an equally strong tendency for provincial Liberals to lose provincial elections while Pierre Elliott Trudeau, the living symbol of centralism, governs in Ottawa. We find this tendency particularly evident in Newfoundland and west of Québec. The weakness of provincial Liberals facing William Davis in Ontario and Peter Lougheed in Alberta is of long standing. It exists in Québec also, where the provincial party called

Liberal is totally independent of, and often in conflict with, the federal Liberal party.

Elections in Canada are now waged, with minor provincial exceptions, in single-member constituencies in which the candidate with the largest number of votes wins. Not only does the electoral system distort party strength in favor of the party getting the largest vote, it also gives undue representation to parties having regional strength in a country as regionally varied as Canada. Because of this factor, in six of the ten elections since 1957, no party has had a majority of seats in Parliament. Equally important is the almost complete shutting out of Liberals from the West and Conservatives from Québec in recent federal elections. This development obviously has important long-term consequences, as no party can claim to represent Canada as a whole.

It is clear then, that if we want to gain an understanding of the evolution of Canada, of the direction it has taken, of the ways in which leaders have shaped and continue to shape our society, indeed, much of our way of life, we need to focus on the political parties which produce those leaders. We need to know what, if anything, they stand for, how they function—especially in our federal system, how they seek to win elections, how they develop and implement policies and, in general, how they integrate and energize Canadian political life. It has been hinted already that producing leaders, fighting elections and organizing governments may be more effective party functions than providing ideology and policies, national unity and the harmonious operation of our federal system. A brief examination of these aspects will enable us to arrive at a reasonably balanced evaluation of the significance of parties to the development of Canadian politics.

PARTIES AND ELECTIONS IN CANADA

Origins and their Consequences

Even in the early years political parties played major roles in consolidating diverse groups and views, and generally giving shape and form to the Canadian political system. During the first fifty years of Confederation, party functions in Canada, federally and provincially, were performed by the Conservative and Liberal parties. The former had existed since 1854, the latter organized in the early years of Confederation. The party names are British; their sources however, are a British-Québécois-American mixture. The Conservatives represented Macdonald's and Cartier's successful amalgamation of conservative interests in Québec, Montréal and Toronto, of the Tories of Canada West (now Ontario)— often descendants of Loyalist refugees from the American Revolution—and of the *bleu* faction of French Canadians with close ties to the Roman Catholic Church. The Liberals represented the farm proprietors of Canada West— known as the Clear Grits—and the smaller *rouge* element in Québec, the liberals opposed to church leadership. To some degree, the parties reflected the split between the main body of *habitants* and the few followers of the French Revolution; they did not reflect the British split between Conservative land-owners and Liberal merchants. There was a reflection among the Tories of the nation-building impulses of the early American Federalists, and among the Grits of the small-landowner base of the American Jeffersonians. Twenty years after Confederation, the Liberals under Wilfrid Laurier made peace with the Catholic Church in Québec; from then on, the Liberals have been successful in representing French Canada.

The two original parties, as mentioned before, developed within the structure of government and for decades the major function of the parties was to support or oppose the government. After Manitoba and British Columbia came into Confederation, delayed voting in the West swung votes to the "Ministerialists", members of Parliament who would support the government in return for favors for their region. Only from the 1890s on, with some development of constituency organization on both sides, did the two parties compete on more equal terms. At the beginning of this century, they were firmly established as government, opposition and contestants in elections at federal and provincial levels.

Western agriculture was the first social segment to create, outside of Parliament, organizations that were more than pressure groups. These organizations went about persuading large groups of voters to elect people who were neither Conservatives nor Liberals. Western farmers were alienated by Canada's rejection of free grain trade with the United States just before the First World War. As the War ended and an agricultural depression set in, more farmers became disenchanted. The United Farmers movement spread east, where it had its first flash success in the Ontario election of 1919. Nationally, the movement joined with fragments of the Liberal caucus to form the Progressive Party which came out second strongest in Parliament in the 1921 election but refused to accept the responsibility of becoming the official opposition. Partly as a consequence of this, the party declined during the twenties. The most lasting effect of the United Farmers movement was in Alberta, where it formed the government from 1921 to 1935.

The drive of western farmers to form parties had consequences during the Great Depression. In 1932, it was the main force, with some workers and a few intellectuals, behind the formation of the Cooperative Commonwealth Federation (CCF). A generation later, in 1961, this party, by now supported by an important segment of the labor movement, reformed as the New Democratic Party (NDP). It is significant, however, that the NDP still has its steadiest support in comparatively rural Saskatchewan.

A second depression offshoot of western agriculture was the Social Credit movement which, led by the messianic evangelist William Aberhart, swept Alberta in 1935 and governed that province till 1971. Though much of the later Social Credit in Alberta, and Social Credit in British Columbia, had little to do with the western farmers' movement, that movement was the original vehicle for Social Credit.

French Canada had developed a nationalist movement around 1900, but only during the Great Depression did it result in the formation of a party, the Union Nationale of Duplessis. It had no real impact on federal politics, but governed Québec for two decades. The Bloc Populaire went federal in the forties, but was not important. The Parti Québécois, being separatist, has not seen itself as a competitor on the federal party scene thus far but there are indications that this situation may change.

The developments described above indicate the extent to which regional protest movements of various kinds were expressed through party structures. In general we can say that many, perhaps most, of the important regional and social cleavages in the Canadian body politic have either been accommodated by the two major parties or have been reflected in the development of new parties. Regional, economic and social protest, thus, have been closely related to party activity.

Everywhere else in the democratic world, except in the United States, industrial labor—some would say the working class—has launched important parties. In Canada, this effort has been restricted to the CCF/NDP, which has never drawn overwhelming labor support; to the only worker-based Social Credit party in Canada, the one in Québec; and to the perennial but infinitesimal Communist party.

What difference has it made to Canadian politics that two parties originally within Parliament existed from the beginning, and that parties developing outside Parliament did not emerge until at least fifty years later? As I will show later, Liberals and Conservatives have organizations dominated by their parliamentary leaders, much of the time they have received the support of all social groups in Canada, and their appeal to voters has, in most instances, been pragmatic; that is, they have claimed to have the leaders most likely to succeed in governing Canada. None of the other parties has had the same breadth and flexibility. One may disagree about the virtues of such qualities, but one cannot deny their success. Liberals and Conservatives have been government or opposition in Ottawa throughout, and in the provinces most of the time. They have persisted and at present most Canadians would probably agree that they will continue to compete for the prize of federal office for some time to come.

Support and its Relevance

While splinter parties existed in various parts of the country, an average of 98% of Canadian voters supported Conservative and Liberal candidates until the First World War. The period showed variations of support between the two parties. From the time both parties had a firm identity, 1878, through the election of 1891, the Conservatives under Macdonald had a majority of the vote, not only overall but also in each region of the country. In 1896, Laurier's Liberals won the election by winning in Québec, but in the three subsequent elections they had majority support everywhere except in Ontario. In terms of the popular vote all victories since 1878 had been fairly close; it took only minor vote changes, mostly in Ontario and British Columbia, for Borden's Conservatives to emerge victorious in 1911.

If we had had public opinion surveys during the first fifty years of Confederation, we would probably find that the vote of both parties was spread fairly evenly not only over Canada's regions and provinces, which we do know, but also over the country's major social groups. Before the Empire went to war in 1914, there was every reason to believe that Canada would have the kind of stable two-party system for which the United States has been known for more than a century.

The First World War and the struggle it occasioned in Canada, the Conscription Crisis, changed all that. The Conservative Borden government formed a coalition with war-supporting Liberals and passed the Wartime Elections Act, which dropped Québec's share of the Canadian vote from the normal 25% to a bit above 15%; this was partly done by enfranchising females related to men fighting the War. In that election, 73% of Québec voters supported Laurier's Liberal opposition, while 64% of voters in the rest of Canada supported the government. This polarization of the vote between Québec and the other provinces was unprecedented and has never recurred to the same extent. Whatever else it did, this crisis put an end to the established pattern of competition in which the two parties had social support spread broadly over society. Significantly, this coincided with the rise of electorally important third parties, especially in Western Canada.

After 1921, peremptory two-party competition seemed to regenerate, with only Alberta voting Progressive. But the founding of the CCF and the Social Credit party has kept support of the major parties down. Since 1935 in the West and 1962 in Québec major party support has been below 85% and usually significantly lower. Exceptions were the "Diefomania" election of 1958, and the "Trudeaumania" election of 1968.

Of the major parties, the Conservatives have lacked adequate support in French Canada since 1917, 1958 being the sole exception. Conservatives also did poorly in the West between the Depression and Diefenbaker; since 1957 the Liberals have lacked adequate western support. In federal elections, Liberals do well mobilizing voters in Québec and usually in Ontario, and Conservatives do well mobilizing voters in the West. What is more, Liberal dominance of the Québec federal vote and Conservative dominance of the western federal vote have been fairly stable phenomena throughout the sixties and seventies: a far cry from the all-Canada competitive elections before 1917.

Surveys of the postwar years have given us a picture of the support social groups give to parties. Professional and white-collar people tended to support Conservatives until Diefenbaker; since then they have favored the Liberals. Workers have tended to support Liberals a bit more than Conservatives; despite its ties to organized labor, the NDP ranks third in ability to mobilize workers. Conservatives have consistently done the best job of mobilizing farmers.

Mobilization of the highly educated goes with mobilization of those in nonmanual occupations: before Diefenbaker, the Conservatives did best with that group; since then, the Liberals do. Until the last decade, the NDP had among its supporters the highest proportion of those without a high school degree. With regard to religion, the Conservative and NDP voters strongly tend to be Protestant, while Liberals show a small Catholic majority. That franco-phones vote heavily Liberal is not surprising; nor is the fact that postwar immigrants to Canada also support the Liberal party.

The relevance of the party support pattern to political competition will be discussed in a later section. I want to emphasize at this point that the parties are different in their social composition, but more along religious and ethnic than along social class or occupational lines. Both Conservatives and New Democrats are strongly English-speaking, Protestant parties; the supporters of the Liberals, however, especially in recent decades, have come from both of the two major faiths and both of the two founding races, complemented by the bulk of recent immigrants.

Although (as will be shown later) the two major parties are both strongly pragmatic and even the minor parties have a distinctly pragmatic aura about them especially when they are in office, many Canadian voters retain a firm party loyalty. The party name and tradition loom large for many Canadians; indeed, it can well be argued that for millions of Canadians politics consists either of following cues from their traditional party or merely of party leaders, party policies, party electoral success or failure, party promises (admittedly often broken), and party performance in Parliament.

Leadership

Political parties do many things: they mobilize the electorate; they help develop programs to deal with the demands of interest groups; they help produce policies if called upon to govern; and they perform a number of tasks aimed at organizing the political government and providing effective government for society. The one thing any party does, even in countries where there is only one party, is to recruit people for political leadership. Where, as in Canada, there is more than one party, each party nominates candidates for public election to office.

In Canada, of course, the parliamentary system channels the nomination of party candidates and their election to Parliament. Since party leaders are selected by leadership conventions and not, as in the United Kingdom, by their parliamentary party (caucus in Canada), they need not be, although they usually are, members of Parliament to begin with. The system of responsible government gives great power to the leaders of the parties in Parliament, certainly to those with any chance of forming the government. The leader of the strongest party remains prime minister only so long as support of the party is retained in the House of Commons. This need for support is less of a check than it is a weapon. It enables the leader of the governing party to direct the party with the near-assurance that all followers will lend support on every issue that comes to a vote in Parliament. The caucus discipline is almost as strong in the principal opposition party and in other parties represented in the House of Commons as it is in the governing party.

While the selection of leaders and the conduct of electoral campaigns will receive brief discussion later in this chapter, I want to point here to the role of the party leader *vis-à-vis* the electorate. The leader of the opposition, the prime minister and other national party leaders, most likely in that order, are engaged in an ongoing mobilization of the electorate, even when there is no likelihood of an early election. This is one leadership role that has been magnified by television. Clearly, the interests of the media and the leaders are served equally when a network representative interviews one of the leaders: the leader of the opposition to tell us what would or would not have been done had the opposition been in office, the prime minister to justify the governing party's actions, and other party leaders to give us the whys and wherefores of their views on various matters. On television, a party leader's status is greatly reinforced. The unprecedented treatment of Joe Clark, since 1979, will be discussed in a later section.

Canada's constitution—the term as used here goes well beyond the provisions and conventions of the British North America Act even as altered in 1981—gives power to the prime minister and to the leaders of the other parties, but it also detracts from these powers. It does so through the operation of Canada's highly decentralized federal system. Each party considers itself one unit, but the national leader, even when the prime minister, may have to allow those of the party's provincial leaders who hold office more influence than anyone else. At this time in Canadian history, prime ministers are expected to deal diplomatically not only with premiers from other parties, but also from their own, and leaders of other parties have to use language considerate of their provincial leader in office. In the federal election of 1980, all this intra-party consideration was a problem for the leaders of the Conservatives and the NDP only. Prime Minister Trudeau had no Liberal premier to be considerate of. The impact of the federal system on party competition is the subject of a later section; however, one fact is clear: in Canada, at present, an understanding of the country's complex federal system is impossible without some knowledge of the influence of party competition, party stance and party leaders.

Within each level of government, however, there is a nearly uniform opportunity for the governing party and its leader. The parliamentary system empowers leader and party to organize the government, especially its personnel. This is done by appointments of partisans to governing positions and by maintaining strict party discipline in the legislature, using not so much the stick of dissolution as the carrot of advancement to and through cabinet positions. As of early 1982, it is no exaggeration to say that the Liberal party *governs* Canada, or the Conservative party *governs* Ontario or Alberta, or the NDP *governs* Saskatchewan.

Structure

Political parties are organizations, and their organizational structure is relevant to the functions they perform. These functions, especially leadership selection and voter mobilization, can be undertaken in Canada only by adapting to our federal and electoral systems. If parties are to compete successfully on a nation-wide basis, and if they are to compete in several of or all the provinces, they need organization at the provincial as well as the national level. By offering leaders for provincial government, the provincial structure of Canadian parties gains and maintains its importance. This importance leads Smiley[3] to assert that Canadian parties are to a large degree confederal; that is, their provincial structures have a great deal of autonomy.

Party structure also has to face up to Canada's parliamentary system, but here the story is less uniform. In the early parliamentary parties, and Liberals and Conservatives certainly are among the world's early parliamentary parties, the parliamentary leaders enjoyed a historical priority: the party's parliamentary structure was in place first, and the electoral (also called associational or extragovernmental) structure of the party was created to serve this parliamentary party by nominating candidates and mobilizing voters to elect them. With the exception of short-lived fragment parties, all parties arriving on the scene after the development of the Tories and Grits formed outside Parliament and worked their way in. Their electoral structure, therefore, was established prior to their parliamentary structure. But election to office enhances the standing of legislators within any party structure; gaining official opposition status and especially forming the government—and in some provinces some third parties have done either or both—does so even more. These parties thus have tended to join Liberals and Conservatives in becoming "cadre" parties, where the electoral structure serves as a cadre, or a group of helpers, for the parliamentary party.

Only a strong commitment to the rights and significance of individual party members has been able to halt the trend toward this cadre development, and of important parties in Canada only the CCF/NDP has shown such a commitment. No matter how small the number of individual NDP members, each is given rights to participation by the party's constitution. The emphasis on members' rights and influence makes the NDP's structure that of a mass party. Electoral success generally, and election to office in three western provinces, has, however, obliterated much of the structural difference between the NDP and the other parties. It is important to remember, nonetheless, that Saskatchewan, where the party has attained most importance, has a special tradition of lay participation in politics, which helps to keep the entire NDP structurally distinct.

The actual structure of parties having parliamentary representation on the federal or the provincial level is anchored in the parliamentary, or legislative, caucus. Whether participation of lay members is important or not, there is a federal, or provincial, convention, with appropriate executive bodies, which oversees the electoral operations of the party. Only the NDP seriously adds the overseeing of broad policy to the task of its conventions. The federal, or provincial, office, a headquarters employing at least a skeleton professional bureaucracy, is formally responsible to conventions or the executive, actually to the leader or caucus. In constituencies held or seriously contested by a party, there may be a permanent constituency executive. Only in the NDP do party members in a constituency meet to try to influence party policy; in other parties, members who may have bought a single-shot party membership meet mainly to nominate candidates.

The use of the terms "federal" or "provincial" in this discussion should remind the reader that there tends to be provincial autonomy in political parties, which means that the federal-provincial links are generally weak. In all democratic federal systems, provincial parties have a certain amount of autonomy. It should not surprise us that this is very much the case in present-day Canada, where the importance of provincial government is so great that a provincial career is sufficient for many ambitious and able political leaders.

Appeal and Ideology

Initially I pointed out that Edmund Burke described political parties as groups tied together by common ideas, but that they were in fact doing a number of things not necessarily on the basis of common ideas. I know, however, that most students, and much of the general public, continue to believe that Burke was correct. There is an element of truth in his definition as applied to Canadian parties (see Chapter 5), but it applies least to Liberals and Conservatives. For these parties, a certain style connected with their past is much more important than a definite set of ideas. But largely because of their long-standing success in competing for office, their appeal to the voters, especially at election time, is primarily one of trying to demonstrate that they will do better in office than their opponents.

Liberals and Conservatives, then, appeal to voters largely in terms of the alleged quality of their candidates for office, and of the way in which they do, or would, handle the issues of the day. This kind of appeal is termed "pragmatic". As Pierre Elliott Trudeau demonstrated between 1974 and 1975, it is quite possible to retain office promising that Canada would be kept free from the wage and price controls proposed by the Conservatives, and then to impose those same controls, with cosmetic changes, one year later. Whether one considers such action flexible genius or electoral perfidy, it is a glorious example of pragmatic politics.

The opposite of a pragmatic appeal is one based on ideology, on a coherent set of party principles. In its pure form, such an appeal exists in Canada only in the various Communist parties, each of which selects issues and presents them in terms of its dogma. These parties, however, run few candidates and get only a few votes. The only Canadian party competing nationally and electing members that displays anything approaching ideological appeal is the NDP. Its predecessor, the CCF, adopted a socialist program in 1933. Some of its appeal to the voters was based on this program; to other aspects of its appeal, for instance the support of the North Atlantic military alliance, the program was irrelevant. In 1956 the party gave up doctrinaire socialism. If the appeal of the NDP has been ideological, this ideology has been confined to trying to create a general atmosphere favoring the wage earner and people on fixed incomes rather than those enjoying the fruits of the profit sector.

Does this mean that federal elections have been tweedledum-tweedledee games? Not quite, despite the limited impact of parties on policies, which I will discuss in the next section. The nearly century-old identification of French Canada with the Liberal party has, on balance, given the Liberals more electoral credibility in Québec, even when French language rights are not an issue. What we have here is more a difference of style than of policy. There are other style differences of more recent vintage. The West used to be a Liberal preserve, but since Diefenbaker, that region has responded to Conservative and not to Liberal cues. Attitudes toward federalism also make a difference in major-party appeal based on style rather than substance. Of all provinces, Québec, strongly Liberal in federal elections, raises the most demands. Outside Québec however, those jealous of provincial rights are being appealed to more by Conservatives than by Liberals, often regardless of the issue.

In the absence of important ideological appeals to Canadian voters, policy differences between parties have been products of situation rather than dogma. Most of the parties' appeals to Canadians have been based on differences in style or simply on seeking office. What is important in our context is that, whatever the nature of the electoral appeal, it does come from political parties, and Canadians expect it to come from there.

Programs — Federal and Provincial

I have just said that dogmatic differences in party policies have been unimportant in Canada. On the federal level, there appears to be one important difference: external relations. It is true that from the Boer War of 1900 until the Statute of Westminster in 1931, the Conservative party had been more colonial, imperial and pro-British, and the Liberal party more autonomous and thus nationalist. It is equally true that, certainly from the reciprocity crisis of 1911 till the missile crisis of 1962, the Liberal party has been the more pro-American of the two. That this is not clearly an ideological matter is shown by the Trudeau era, in which the Liberals have been more insistent on an independent Canadian foreign policy, and at times more worried about US domination in general, than the Conservatives.

The Liberals have placed more emphasis on bilingualism than the Conservatives, but their major support base in Québec has encouraged this emphasis. Multiculturalism finds as much encouragement under Trudeau as it did under Diefenbaker.

In the area of economic redistribution, massive programs have been in effect for the past two decades, regardless of the governing party. If there has been dogma, it has been the belief that programs should be undertaken within the framework of the free-enterprise system and it has been shared by both major parties. A Conservative-appointed royal commission suggested taxation of nonworking income at a rate as high as that of wages and salaries. The proposal was turned down by the Liberal government at that time, but there is no certainty that the Conservatives would have adopted it. A universal prepaid health-care program was adopted by the Liberals after the recommendation of a Conservative-appointed royal commission and a pioneering effort of the CCF government of Saskatchewan.

The CCF/NDP has formed the government in three western provinces, but most of its policies have been similar to those of other provincial governments. Saskatchewan's Medicare policy of 1962, and public automobile insurance in Saskatchewan, Manitoba and British Columbia are exceptions. Saskatchewan is appropriating some of its resource industries, while Alberta coinvests in its resources with some of the proceeds going into public royalties and public profits. The provinces, one governed by the NDP, the other by right-wing-liberal Progressive Conservatives, are protecting their provincial resource rights with similar vigor.

The emphasis in this brief section should perhaps be more on Liberal-Conservative similarity than on their similarity with the NDP, which has not held federal power, and is not expected to be the chief competition in the foreseeable future. The absence of effective federal competition by a leftist party will be taken up briefly later.

The fact that party programs tend not to differ greatly does not mean that they are unimportant. Much of our present way of life has been shaped by policies that were once part of a party program. The growth of the welfare state and the increasing government intervention in the economy involving oil prices, aid to the Chrysler Corporation, and a host of other matters, all illustrate the importance of party, particularly government party, programs.

Electoral System, Elections and Participation

The House of Commons and the provincial legislatures are subject to quin-quennial acts, which means statutes ending them after five years unless they are dissolved earlier. These days, executives at both levels are expected to dissolve the legislative body no later than four years after its election. Dissolution is timed by prime ministers and premiers with the strategic aim of winning the next election, and favorable circumstances may not arise close to the five-year limit. Coming so close to this limit contributed to Trudeau's defeat in 1979. Canadians thus can expect to be called upon to vote in a general election, provincial or national, on the average, every two years or less. Effective timing of dissolution is one of the chief weapons in the arsenal of the leader of the governing party.

Since 1966, all members of the House of Commons are elected from single-member constituencies; the candidate with the most votes is declared elected. After each census, seats are distributed among provinces and territories according to a complicated formula, with population having the most important influence on how the seats are distributed. Constituency boundaries are drawn by provincial commissions of essentially nonpartisan composition. In establishing the provincially agreed-upon constituencies, the House of Commons has but little leeway to differ.

Canadian citizens of both sexes, aged eighteen years or more, have the right to vote. They are placed on voters' lists by enumerators nominated by the parties that have polled the highest and second-highest vote in the constituency.

Canada's electoral system favors the party strongest in electoral strength over the second party. It favors both of these parties even more over all other parties. Only the geographically unequal distribution of party strength gives third, and sometimes fourth or even fifth, parties a chance to gain seats. Alan Cairns[4] rightly points out that the realities of geographic distribution of party strength among constituencies affects the balance of parties, and of parties within regions, in the House of Commons. In the Parliament elected in 1980, a 20% vote in the West gave the Liberals two seats out of 77, and a 13% vote in Québec gave the Conservatives one seat out of 75. Such results are doubtless related to regional sentiments of alienation and neglect.

It is up to the parties contesting an election to mobilize the voters. This they do by various means: they canvass promising voters, help individuals to vote by transporting them to the polls and/or baby-sitting, randomly distribute literature, conduct campaign meetings, and spread propaganda over radio and television. The latter, because of its range, is usually done by federal or provincial headquarters; the other activities center on the constituency. Central headquarters is in charge of the campaign schedule and itinerary of the party leader, and possibly of other party luminaries.

Campaigns, being a competition for votes, deal only to some extent with attempts to convert the opposition. Stronger efforts are made to persuade the undecided and, even more important, to make sure that as many as possible known supporters go to the polls.

Who does go to the polls? On the average, about 75% of those eligible to vote in federal elections, 70% in provincial elections. Data from the 1965 federal election survey show that those with higher socioeconomic status and those with more education tend to vote more regularly. Interestingly, strong participation among the highly educated is found in federal but not in provincial elections.

Whatever the actual significance of elections, the fact remains that for vast numbers of Canadians the excitement of election night constitutes the high point of their political experience. On election day the voter, at least in the aggregate, is supreme. As he watches the returns roll in and is bombarded with computer projections, with concession speeches and victory speeches and celebrations, he may bask in the satisfaction that in a small way he has helped make it all happen; or he may feel that the parties are presenting him with a contest as exciting as the final game for the Grey or Stanley Cups.

Leadership Selection: Nominations and Recruitment

Since 1961, all federal parties have selected their leader in a federal leadership convention. Originally, they all selected them in a more traditional mode, in the parliamentary caucus. The Liberals, with an almost all-Québec caucus, decided to hold the first leadership convention in 1919. The Conservatives followed in 1927. The CCF had all along used their convention to confirm their caucus-selected leader; in 1961 the NDP also chose the convention as the way to select their leader.

Conventions of all parties have complex rules of representation. Invariably, all members of the parliamentary caucus are seated. The other delegates represent the party from all over the country. Voting is by individuals and by secret ballot. In all conventions a majority of delegates' votes is needed to select the leader. On each ballot, the lowest candidate is dropped, though additional ones may withdraw.

Smiley[5] finds that leadership conventions help to make Canadian parties more national. Unlike their famous American model, they are not bargaining places for the provinces. However, the person selected as leader will spend most of his time, if appointed prime minister, bargaining with the provinces. In any case, leadership conventions usually end in a show of unity. The presence of the candidates and their staffs on the floor of the convention sometimes makes such shows more credible than the American model, where some of the principals may prefer to stay in their hotel rooms.

Who gets to be federal leader of a major party? By and large, leaders are closer to the American pattern of inexperienced politicians than to the British pattern of experienced ones. Liberal conventions have always chosen a man with little experience in federal or, for that matter, any politics, though King and certainly Pearson had considerable experience in the federal bureaucracy. Trudeau especially was an outsider, whose Liberal experience was restricted to a brief stint as Minister of Justice. Conservative conventions have selected men with varying experience in the House of Commons, and provincial premiers. Joe Clark was not known to the public when he became Conservative leader in 1976, but he had played a role in the federal organization of his party for fifteen years.

Virtually all the candidates for party leadership, federal and provincial (where the convention process is like the federal one), have been successful nominees of their party for at least one legislative body. In order to gain a party nomination to the House of Commons or a provincial legislative assembly or parliament, a person needs to be selected by a constituency nomination meeting. This may be open to all members or to elected delegates. The former is the usual mode employed in the Liberal and Conservative parties, and it is here that these parties acquire many of their formal members who simply buy a membership in order to vote for one of the candidates vying for the nomination.

Most of the candidates for constituency nominations have something in common: they have been recruited for an active political life by a political party. Some who do not make it try again, but the political system allows each party only one nomination in a constituency, and only one victor among those getting a party nomination. Parties have few bureaucrats, and there are few places indeed for those who choose, as Max Weber[6] called it, "politics as a vocation". But for those who make it to "the top", to the top echelons of leadership, there is the satisfaction of knowing that they vie for real power. Those in the winning party find themselves at the epitome of power, at the helm of their country's destiny.

Party Competition and Party System

As long as there were only two parties in Canada and the provinces, party competition was simple. Conservatives and Liberals were sufficiently evenly matched in all the political arenas so that power changed at least occasionally in every jurisdiction. In addition, both parties were pragmatic, using office-seeking appeals.

The federal election of 1917, the United Farmers' victory in Ontario in 1919, and the federal success of the Progressives in 1921 seemed to have changed all that. But this change did not last; the UFO disappeared, the Progressives lost their importance, and by 1926 the old competitive pattern appeared to have been restored everywhere except in Alberta and Manitoba. What did change, however, was the loss of the Conservatives' competitive position in Québec.

Until the Great Depression the two major parties were at least assured of dividing the lion's share of the vote between them. But after the creation of the CCF and Social Credit they were not able to do that any more, least of all in the West. Only the unique success of John Diefenbaker, the charismatic western Conservative in 1958, gave the two parties more than 85% of the vote; the rest of the time they had to be satisfied with 5 to 20% less than that.

The increased number of parties denied the governing party a parliamentary majority seven times between 1925 and 1980. But in all these situations except one, there were enough members of loosely organized caucuses generally supportive of the government to keep it in office, though four of the seven minority governments were eventually defeated in the House of Commons. From 1972 to 1974, when Trudeau's Liberals needed the support of the NDP under David Lewis's leadership to stay in office, the fate of the government depended on the disciplined caucus of a strong third party. Neither Liberals nor NDP wanted a coalition; in fact, federal coalitions seem to have fallen into disrepute after Borden's coalition during the First World War. The NDP really held the balance of power between Grits and Tories and brought down the Trudeau government over the 1974-75 budget.

In the wake of Diefenbaker's triumph in 1958, many observers assumed that the CCF/NDP would go away, and that the two-party system, desired by many supporters of a traditional parliamentary system, would reappear. This did not happen. Despite the ups and downs of the NDP, that party probably is here to stay. At the same time, it is difficult to imagine how it could, in the foreseeable future, push either of the major parties into a position as weak as the one it now holds.

In these days of change between majority and minority government, Canada has adopted a qualitative party competition which, though unique in the parliamentary world and different from that of the United States, will probably be around for a while. Everywhere else, one of the two competitive parties is, in terms of support at least, what we usually call "left of center". By this phrase political scientists mean that the party draws most of its support from wage and salary earners, and that about two thirds or more of the wage and salary earners support it. Canada does not have such a party competing effectively for federal office. Everywhere else wage earners could have punished the Trudeau government at the polls for the full-wage, partial-profit control program of 1975. In Canada alone, such action is politically impossible; the NDP, the sole appropriate vehicle for such action, shows no signs of mustering the strength to serve as a left-of-center alternative. Canadians owe such welfare innovation as they have received, Medicare being a prime example, to well-meaning Liberals and "red" Tories, not to demands organized from the left or from below, at least as far as federal implementation is concerned.

Now, if this is the state of party competition in Canada, what kind of party system do we have? We do not have a two-party system like the Americans, who really have no third party. Since 1980, with fourth parties deprived of representation, we again have a two-major-party system with one reliably placed third party.

Our party system is not best described by numbers. It has two main characteristics. The first is that there is only one third party with organizational stability, the NDP. Any party needing the NDP to support a minority government can pretty well predict what it is getting. And second, while the major parties hardly differ in appeal, especially in economic matters, they do differ ethnically and regionally. Party competition based on these two factors, in which by definition there can be little rational persuasion, is incapable of providing real contests over innovative policies. If it brings on redistributive policies, it does so largely by accident rather than by design. Canada, despite the underlying significance of political parties and elections, cannot be said to be well served by party competition in which ethnic, religious and regional support outweigh policy demands.

Recently, executive federalism has had a deleterious effect on party competition. Provinces with "anti-Ottawa" governments are not new. As Garth Stevenson[7] shows, Ontario and Québec had them before 1900. But from 1920 to 1970, Alberta and, to a lesser extent, Québec were the only provinces who would fit this "anti-Ottawa" description over a long time span. In the present age of confrontation between Prime Minister and premiers, it is no accident that Trudeau's party forms no provincial government. It competes with some hope in Nova Scotia, New Brunswick, Prince Edward Island and Québec, though we must remember that Trudeau's federal and Ryan's provincial parties do not share much more than a label. Until there is a change in Ottawa, non-Liberal governing parties are favorites in provincial elections, especially when the premier wages a credible campaign against Ottawa.

In the coming years, we may well find that the federal Liberals have an advantage beyond the one that they are the only bilingual party. They have come to be identified with central politics, and central politics is popular with central Canadians from Ontario and Québec, especially when resource owner-ship and demands for offshore resource ownership magnify the centrifugal position of a number of provinces. It is thus possible that Liberals will continue to have the edge in federal elections as incumbents, as habitual masters of the bureaucracy, as the party of French and English, of Catholic and Protestant and, foremost, as the "federal" (meaning central) party. Such an advantage, with the resultant likelihood of electoral success, is awesome, for it may mean that the foreseeable future of Canada lies largely in the hands of the Liberal party, unrepresented in the West and with heavy overrepresentation from Québec, and opposed by parties almost totally devoid of a relationship to federal power.

LIMITATIONS OF THE USEFULNESS OF POLITICAL PARTIES IN EXPLAINING THE CANADIAN POLITY

It is exactly because "political party" is a household phrase in Canada that it is easy to exaggerate the obviously major role of parties in the Canadian polity. This exaggeration has brought on a backlash, and only recently John Meisel,[8] the father of Canadian election studies, added force to this backlash. Meisel's criticism will be used in this attempt to evaluate to what extent the study of political parties does not, or indeed does, explain Canadian political life adequately.

The limited role of parties in policy-making, used by Meisel as the chief indicator of party decline, has been asserted earlier in this chapter. Among the long-range reasons for this decline mentioned by Meisel, I am especially impressed by the rise of the bureaucratic state, the rise of interest group politics and the rise of the electronic media and investigative journalism. Along with this limited role of parties in policy-making goes a limited policy effect on elections. It is doubtful that Canada has had a truly policy-oriented election campaign since 1911, when Grits stood for reciprocity with the United States and Tories for support of the imperial navy.

I find it more difficult to side with Meisel when he ascribes party decline to the Liberal style under Trudeau. While I agree with all the symptoms Meisel cites—disdain of parliament, public confusion over wage and price controls, decline in ministerial responsibility, plebiscitarian tendencies—I see these rather as excesses of a party doing the dirty work for an autocratic leader than a decline of the party role. In this interpretation, I have the benefit of hindsight of the masterful coup of December 1979 that threw Clark out and the already resigned Trudeau back in.

Does the parties approach tell us very much about governing Canadian society? In regard to Western alienation, one can no longer say, as I did in 1978, that Liberal support in British Columbia (1974) shows the irrelevance of party—that support is no longer there. But party continues to tell us little when it comes to the behavior of the Western provinces: the western stance of the leftists, Blakeney and Barrett, is similar to that of the rightists, Lougheed and Bennett, and the latter two do not even belong to the same party. Obviously political parties still carry out major functions, they still form governments, and they still dominate the polity but party differences appear not to be very consequential.

Regarding Québec, even after the referendum of 1980, the parties approach does not tell us very much. The governing Parti Québécois, defeated in the referendum, maintained power in the provincial election of 1981. Later in 1981, the PQ and many provincial Liberals opposed Trudeau's constitutional resolution, but the federal Liberals gave it overwhelming support in Parliament.

One of Meisel's factors in the decline of party may not turn out to be one—the electronic media. The long campaign from late 1978 to early 1980 makes one wonder just which one is the active political force, the parties or the media. Media manipulation was very much in evidence, but both source and effect need to be investigated. There is some substance to Clark's belief that the media did him in, but such an assertion raises questions, and not just about Clark's genes. Is there a direct line from the ill-fated suitcase trip of early 1979 to the electoral defeat one year later? Who in the electronic media was it who be-angeled Trudeau and Broadbent and bedeviled Clark? Was it owners, managers, editors, reporters, cameramen? Was this strange taking of sides planned or accidental? We can only hope that election studies and memoirs of media people will provide some of the answers. Meanwhile, in early 1982, Clark's manipulation by television continues to fuel attacks on his leadership, regardless of his performance or stand on issues.

But no matter how interesting the role of the media in these two elections, we must look to the parties for some of the answers. The elections of 1979 and 1980 were both won in Southern Ontario. Did the Tories manipulate the media in 1979 and did the Grits do so in 1980? Or were the respective winning campaigns of the two parties in Southern Ontario so successful that the media did not play that much of a role?

The reason I have dwelt on these points is that here we deal with central party functions: leadership selection and voter mobilization. The more that questions about the relevance of the parties approach are directed at these areas, the closer we can come to a definitive evaluation of the approach.

One area in which the parties approach is patently barren because of almost universal nonperformance is that of government and elections below the provincial level. In most Canadian cities elections to council are nonpartisan. Sometimes, but not too often, municipal elections are fought by one or more ad hoc tickets.

Lack of parties in municipal government need not, however, stop the party-oriented analyst. He can point out that party labels, if introduced, could split the propertied or property-brokerage interests that tend to have an above-average interest and influence in our cities. Where there are demands for, or attempts at, partisan activity in municipal politics, they are likely to come from the NDP, the party most often opposed to urban landed interests. Yet such efforts are exceptional. There is a semblance of democracy in our cities: to hold office, one needs to be elected. But the master broker between the governors and the governed, the political party, normally is not on the scene. Our approach, then, cannot tell us what goes on in city politics, and it cannot tell us, with indisputable evidence, exactly how and why the chief actors came to occupy their leading positions. The party approach remains a major approach, but its limitations must be acknowledged.

SCOPE OF THE APPROACH USED IN THIS CHAPTER

This chapter has given a general introduction to the subject of Canadian parties and elections. It has discussed the subject in its various aspects in some detail, and examined briefly the limits on party functions themselves, the desirability of parties, and their potency in explaining Canadian politics. In this final section, I shall attempt an overall evaluation of the performance of Canadian political parties and, incidentally, of Canada's electoral system. This evaluation will lead to an assessment of the importance of studying parties and elections.

An outsider might think that parties perform *too* well in Canada. Though there are occasional oddballs and occasional intentional absentees on opposition benches, why do Canadian legislators almost always vote with their party? Do government members always think the government is right, and do opposition members almost always think the government is wrong? I do not believe so; but I also do not believe that, in Canada at least, a vote on a bill is an exercise in the search for truth. Rather, it is an exercise in following one's leader, after having had a chance at attempting to exercise influence on those few issues that really matter to the individual member. The reasons we tolerate this nearly perfectly predictable performance are the following: first, only by voting for the leader can a member of Parliament carry out the leadership mandate of the governing party; and second, deviations, as they accumulate, would destroy either governmental stability or responsible government itself.

Another outsider, coming from a country where the principal parties provide clearer policy alternatives, might think that our parties perform very poorly. This criticism has been leveled by many political scientists and other informed Canadians. Yet, in fairness, it must be admitted that Liberals and Conservatives do not have a constitutional or statutory duopoly on political competition. After all, at the time of writing, all provinces west of New Brunswick have at least one third party as chief competitor on the provincial level, making for more meaningful competition than we have in Ottawa. However, it may be exceedingly difficult for the NDP, or another different party, to become number two in federal politics, and thus one of the chief competitors. It is also improbable that the Liberals will emulate the US Democrats and become the left-of-center party of the employed, of economically dependent Canadians, thus making major-party competition more meaningful. Meanwhile, Canadians have the kind of political competition they evidently want and therefore deserve, and we cannot fault political parties as such for failing to present more in the way of policy alternatives.

Critics of an institution should be prepared to develop a scheme without it. I am not a critic of political parties; but those who are critics, here and elsewhere in democracies, fail to provide serious schemes without parties. Let me therefore try briefly to develop one. There would be little difficulty in having specific policies worked out by interest groups and bureaucrats, and in having them enacted by legislators elected in nonpartisan elections. There is, likewise, no need to have parties mobilize voters; we could have elections in which only those who felt inclined voted, and these people would presumably find ways of informing themselves. For me the unanswerable questions are: How would we find political leaders; how would we remove them; and, should we find answers to these questions, how would we as voters make sure that there is any kind of long-term influence on our governors, the kind of influence that is sanctioned by what we call "responsibility"? Until someone can persuade me how to accomplish all this without political parties, I insist on considering them a good thing for democracy.

How well does our electoral system work? Looking at the federal scene in the eighties, it looks as though in most of Québec only Liberal votes count, in Alberta only Conservative votes, and that the election is decided by one or two million voters in southern Ontario. This means, looking at it cynically, that Alberta does not count while the Grits are in office, and that the only reason why Québec might count while the Tories are in office is that Québec has so many seats. But let us consider the alternative, some form of proportional representation where, technicalities aside, a party gets about as high a percentage of seats as its percentage of the vote. This may be satisfactory on the input side: each Liberal vote, for instance, would be equally significant, whether cast in Alberta or in New Brunswick. Yet such a system fails us on the output side: in the past fifty years we would have had majority governments only twice, having come close another three times.

But do we need majority governments? Lester B. Pearson's minority governments gave this country many constructive policies, including Medicare, the Canada pension and the flag, but they could do so only because with their silent partners, the Créditistes, they had a majority. The cabinet system, to have any stability at all, needs reliable majorities. Joe Clark's fate in 1979 shows what happens to a government when a non-existent stability is taken for granted. Yet the case for majority governments should not be made in too facile a fashion. In 1980 and 1981, Trudeau's disciplined majority almost managed to impose on Canada, over the formal opposition of eight provinces and contrary to the sentiment of two thirds of Canadians, the most fundamental of policies, a constitution. The Conservative opposition fought its unilateral imposition, but it probably would have faltered without the support of the Supreme Court of Canada.

Yet, what is the alternative? The American or Swiss system of separated legislatures and executives is possible for Canada, but each would require a massive reorientation for everyone actively and passively engaged in the political process. Intellectually, there may be a lot wrong with the cabinet system, especially the phenomena of the disciplined government caucus and the disciplined opposition. Yet, to take the American alternative, there would be two prices to pay: first, prolonged trust in an essentially sole-ruling chief executive; and second, giving up most of what little remains of a connection between party and policy.

Barring a structural alternative, we must be prepared to live with our party system. It may not present Canadians, with their regions and powerful provinces, with reliably rational alternatives. It looks as though only the parties themselves can make the system more rational. In turn, this requires efforts in that direction by intelligent, concerned Canadians within the parties. Let us hope that they will try to light candles before they curse the darkness.

CONCLUSION

I hope I have demonstrated that parties and elections are important to the functioning of the Canadian polity. But then, so are buildings in which government is housed and the paper flow of government communications. Political scientists do not make a special effort to study such matters, but they do study and analyze political parties and elections. Let me now present the argument that the student of Canadian politics needs to study parties and elections to get to know and understand his subject.

Canada is a representative democracy. With the monarchy serving only as a symbol and to maintain the rules of the game, the government is entrusted to elected representatives, their executive leaders and their administrative appointees. Representation in Canada implies, as it does in all democracies, the public election of representatives. Beyond this, it implies the competitive election of representatives. As I have shown throughout this chapter, in Canada, and in other democracies, parties are the active agents in this competition. It is, in sum, the election that gives us our governors, and the parties that compete in the elections.

The structure of Canadian government, its policy processes, even its policies, can be studied without using the parties and elections approach. However, the roles of *people* who form part of a system of representative government such as Canada has, whether elected members, candidates, managers, election workers and, last but not least, voters, can be understood only through the study of parties and elections.

SUMMARY

1. Political parties are probably the most visible and most familiar part of our Canadian political system. Their familiarity probably derives from their

principal functions: recruiting and selecting leaders, mobilizing voters and providing policy decisions.

2. Ever since Confederation, Canadian political parties have had considerable impact on the style of Canadian politics. They have defined leadership roles, aggregated a diversity of demands, and provided voters with options, if not always of clear-cut policies then at least of different groups of leaders.

3. "Third" parties have developed mainly in Western Canada and Québec where they have generally fared well. Nationally the Liberals and Conservatives have always been in control.

4. Though political parties play important roles, they have generated relatively little policy conflict. Even the NDP, while critical of the distribution of ownership and the management of the economy, has not attacked the prevailing economic dogma frontally when and where it has been in a position to do so.

5. Canada's single-member constituency electoral system distorts party strength in favor of the party getting the largest vote. It gives undue representation to parties having regional strength. It also deprives each party of a nation-wide group of representatives. At present, the Conservatives are rewarded disproportionately in the West and the Liberals in Québec.

6. The media are playing an increasingly important role in Canadian politics, especially in the presentation of party leaders and the activities of those leaders.

7. Given the dominance of pragmatic parties in Canada, elections are generally not fought over clear-cut policy issues and commitments. However, the fact that parties are pragmatic does not prevent them from initiating many new policies and generally increasing their intervention in the economy and society generally.

8. Leaders are important. Leadership conventions probably help to make Canadian parties more national. If the resulting leadership makes parties more national in scope, putting them in a position to play a broker role, it can help unify the country.

9. Canada's national party system has two main characteristics: first, there is only one third party, the NDP, with organizational stability; second, while the Liberals and Conservatives hardly differ in appeal, especially in economic matters, they do differ ethnically and regionally.

10. In some respects, particularly in policy-making, party influence may be in decline. But though the party influence may be declining in some ways, and though the party approach provides only a partial explanation of Canadian politics, it remains important in explaining the selection and role of leaders, and the role of voters.

STUDY QUESTIONS

1. What can be done to strengthen Conservative support in Québec and Liberal support in Western Canada?

2. Should national parties be more doctrinaire? Should elections be fought on clear-cut policy options and ideological commitments? Justify your responses.

3. Is too much emphasis placed on party leaders? Explain your answer. To what extent does Canada's parliamentary system depend on personally strong leadership of each party?

4. Explain how Canada's party system, on balance, has served to strengthen or weaken national unity.

5. If a party's major functions are the selection of leaders, the mobilization of voters and the provision of policy options, what are some additional minor functions?

6. Why is "party" one of the few household words in the vocabulary of Canadian students?

7. What, if anything, can be done to counterbalance the apparent dominance of the Liberal Party in Canada?

8. What, if any, controls should be placed on how the media present political parties and party leaders?

9. In what ways can political parties work to reduce provincial-national antagonisms and confrontation?

10. Would a different electoral system, for example one including some proportional representation, be desirable for Canada? If so, why?

ENDNOTES

1. Richard Simeon, *Federal-Provincial Diplomacy* (Toronto: University of Toronto Press, 1972).

2. Donald Smiley, *Canada in Question: Federalism in the Eighties* (Toronto: McGraw-Hill Ryerson, 1980), Ch. 3.

3. *Ibid.*, Ch. 4.

4. A.C. Cairns, "The Electoral System and the Party System in Canada," *Canadian Journal of Political Science*, I, No. 1 (March, 1968).

5. Donald Smiley, "The National Party Leadership Convention in Canada," *Canadian Journal of Political Science*, I, No. 4 (December, 1968).

6. Reprinted in H.H. Gerth and C.W. Mills, *From Max Weber* (London: Oxford University Press, 1958), pp. 77-128.

7. Garth Stevenson, *Unfulfilled Union: Canadian Federalism and National Unity* (Toronto: Macmillan, 1979).

8. John Meisel, "The Decline of Party in Canada," in H.G. Thorburn, ed., *Party Politics in Canada* (Scarborough: Prentice-Hall, 1979), pp. 119-35).

SELECTED REFERENCES

After the pioneering efforts of John Meisel, C.B. Macpherson, S.M. Lipset and a few others, there was a lull in writing on Canadian parties until the mid-sixties. Since then, there has been a veritable explosion. Extensive and not completely overlapping bibliographies can be found in the following volumes:

Englemann, Frederick C., and Mildred Schwartz. *Canadian Political Parties: Origin, Character, Impact.* Scarborough: Prentice-Hall, 1975.

Van Loon, Richard J., and Michael S. Whittington. *The Canadian Political System: Environment, Structure and Process.* Toronto: McGraw-Hill Ryerson, 1976.

In using these bibliographies, I want to call attention especially to the periodical literature, much of it in the *Canadian Journal of Political Science*, where a good deal of original research has been published. There are three standard books on Canadian political parties in general. One important differentiation is that the first title listed is co-authored, the second a mixture of co-authorship and co-editorship, and the third a collection of readings. All three expand on, and illustrate, materials discussed in this chapter. These books are:

Engelmann, Frederick C., and Mildred Schwartz. *Canadian Political Parties: Origin, Character, Impact.* Scarborough: Prentice-Hall, 1975.

Winn, Conrad, and John McMenemy. *Political Parties in Canada.* Toronto: McGraw-Hill Ryerson, 1976.

Thorburn, H.G., ed. *Party Politics in Canada*, 4th ed. Scarborough: Prentice-Hall, 1979.

The most helpful books on the three principal parties are:

Perlin, George. *The Tory Syndrome: Leadership Politics in the Progressive Conservative Party.* Montreal: McGill-Queen's University Press, 1980.

Wearing, Joseph. *The L-shaped Party: The Liberal Party of Canada, 1958-1980.* Toronto: McGraw-Hill Ryerson, 1981.

Young, Walter. *The Anatomy of a Party: The National CCF 1932-1961.* Toronto: University of Toronto Press, 1969.

The present leaders of the two major parties are best described in:

Gwyn, Richard. *The Northern Magus* (Trudeau). Toronto: McClelland and Stewart, 1980.

Simpson, Jeffrey. *Discipline of Power* (Clark). Toronto: Personal Library, 1980.

10

Dualism and the Concept of National Unity

David R. Cameron*

INTRODUCTION

How does one understand one's country? This question confronts citizens of many lands from time to time; it is never a simple question to cope with and, in times of domestic strife or crisis, the search for an answer can be an acute and pressing business. The way people understand their country will guide the way they act as citizens. For example, during Alexander Dubcek's period as premier of Czechoslovakia, many of the country's citizens were struggling to realize in political activity their understanding of Czechoslovakia as a free, socialist country; others, however, viewed Czechoslovakia as a member of the Soviet bloc of countries and thus as subordinate to the will of the USSR. As we all know, the issue was authoritatively resolved in favor of the latter view, with the help of Russian military force. Poland today finds itself in rather similar circumstances, although the ultimate outcome remains unclear. A survey of the international scene will reveal the extent to which many countries of the world face painful questions about their character and future. Canada's is but one case among many and, in global terms, is far from being the most critical.

Canada has been experiencing a period of profound disagreement among its citizens about the nature of the country, disagreement not just between French- and English-speaking Canadians, but between various regions, groups and governments. Until recently, the most salient line of conflict concerned the role and place of the country's French-speaking society within (or outside of) the framework of Canada as a whole. In the period following the Québec referendum of May 1980, French-English relations receded from their position of

*Assistant Secretary to the Cabinet, Strategic and Constitutional Planning, Federal/Provincial Relations Office, Government of Canada.

prominence, to be replaced or supplemented by a more complex architecture of discord involving a broad range of social and political forces.

However, the energy agreements between the federal government and the three Western-most provinces reached in the autumn of 1981, together with the outcome of the First Ministers' Conference on the Constitution of November 2-5, 1981 (which isolated the Parti Québécois Government of Québec), served at once to diminish the aggressive expression of Western alienation and to isolate Québec, thus putting the spotlight back on questions of duality.

Central to the tensions which Canada is currently experiencing is the debate about the nature and future development of federalism. Behind that debate lies the jockeying of governments for power and position; and behind that, again, are the shifting economic fortunes of the main regions of this country.

If the country's political leaders are in any way faithful representatives of the cross-cutting concerns of Canadians, the discord involves to a significant extent alternative and competing conceptions of Canada and what it stands for. At the fateful September 1980 First Ministers' conference on the Constitution, the Prime Minister and several provincial premiers attached some importance to "the two views of Canada" competing with one another. This theme recurred from time to time in the course of the winter of 1980-81 as the Government of Canada's Constitutional Resolution made its way through Parliament. It was also employed frequently by both the Government of Alberta and the Government of Canada in the course of the energy negotiations.

One of the reasons it is so difficult to arrive at a general consensus about the nature and purposes of Confederation and, more specifically, about the position of French- and English-speaking persons within it, is the sheer variety and complexity of our country. In this respect, Canada is by no means unique. Practically speaking, it is impossible to create an image or provide a summary account of the country which will be easily understood by others but which, at the same time, will not simplify or neglect the diversity of the land and its people.

If a foreigner asks you what kind of a place Canada is, what do you say? If you are like most of us, you attempt to list several of the features or qualities you deem to be most important, leave an enormous amount unsaid, and in the end feel very unsatisfied with your reply. In fact this is about all any of us can do. We work out a simplified account, a caricature, that will help us to come to terms with our country, to communicate our understanding of it to others. We develop theories that highlight those features we think are most important at the expense of those features we believe are less significant. The selection of an approach is as necessary for the ordinary citizen as it is for the political scientist or historian. For example, many Canadians, especially French Canadians, see Canada as a country composed of two nations; many others see it as a single nation. That this confusion is more than simply linguistic will become apparent in the balance of this chapter.

This volume contains not simply approaches to Canadian politics but approaches to an understanding of Canada itself. Theories of regionalism, continentalism and class advance our understanding of the nature of our country while at the same time helping us to comprehend its politics. Given the intimate connections that abound, this is only to be expected. The function of this chapter is to identify, describe and assess one of the major avenues of understanding Canadian politics, namely, the theory of cultural dualism.

The reality of English-French relations, and the theories of cultural dualism which have been developed to represent that reality, have resided at the center of Canadian public affairs as long as the country has existed. Indeed, they were probably the main reason for establishing Confederation in 1967 as it was established, and were vitally important factors in the 1980 Québec referendum on sovereignty association and the constitutional crisis which followed in 1980-81. Whether we speak of constitutional reform, the functioning of the federal party system, major public policy issues, the attitudes of citizens or national unity, we cannot escape the pervasive effects of dualism in Canada.

I should like to begin this discussion by examining the concept of national unity, for it provides us with the broad intellectual framework within which the theory of dualism may be best understood.

THE CONCEPT OF NATIONAL UNITY

I suspect that the phrase "national unity" is the most frequently used expression in the Canadian political vocabulary. That this is a plausible contention at once tells us a good deal about the country and the character of its politics. National unity identifies what is most problematic about Canadian life, at least as it is perceived by the country's citizens, and delineates the major factor that politics in this country must take into account. But there are two points that need to be made at this stage.

First of all, as a phrase, "national unity" lacks substantive content. It indicates that a major problem Canadians face is keeping the country together, but it does not show why this is a problem, what the primary disintegrative forces are, what the constellation of public opinion on the subject is, how unity is to be achieved, or even why it should be achieved. Opinion on any of these subjects is likely to diverge considerably.

The second point arises out of the first. We have suggested that there is a recurrent preoccupation with national unity, but not necessarily any agreement about the substantive issues that should engage our attention under this rubric. What this implies in terms of our earlier discussion, is that we Canadians have not so far been successful in establishing an authoritative answer to the question of what kind of a country this is. There are many competing responses or conceptions of what Canada is, or should be, some of them clearly incompatible with the continued existence of any kind of country at all; but none has succeeded in establishing itself generally and gaining broad acceptance throughout the land.

Indeed, to the extent that there is any nationally accepted vision of the country these days, it appears to be found in the residual and formally paradoxical idea that there *is no* nationally accepted vision and that this absence is a defining characteristic of the society. Canadians have traditionally found it easier to celebrate their diversity than their union. For some people, this fact is to be applauded and supported; for others, it is to restate in the form of a solution what had formerly been articulated as the problem.

Canada is undeniably a diverse country, and it is one which has sustained, perhaps in some ways even increased, the range of diversity over the period of its national existence. For a variety of reasons, it has run counter to the historic trend toward increasingly centralized and homogeneous forms of political community and society. The federal system of government was established in the nineteenth century in response to the brute fact of politically significant diversity, and this political structure has itself helped to maintain and advance diversity.

Even a cursory examination of the British North America Act,[1] Canada's major constitutional document, makes it clear that there were several different lines of cleavage that the Fathers of Confederation deemed sufficiently significant to warrant attention in the proposed federal system. This is not to say that they necessarily liked having to take account of them—indeed, Macdonald and others would have preferred a legislative union, could they have had it—but rather that they recognized the inability to avoid these cleavages. Thus they were moved to support the principle of a federal rather than a unitary system of government, but bent their efforts to ensuring that the balance of power lay decisively with the central government. The American Civil War was, in this context, a critical event in the minds of most of those who framed Confederation.

One major cleavage was, of course, the regional and political differentiation expressed by the British colonies of Nova Scotia, New Brunswick and Canada (composed of Canada East and Canada West, subsequently Québec and Ontario), the original members of the new confederation. The necessary recognition of these claims to regional autonomy provided the context in which the federal system grew, eventually extending from coast to coast and including ten provinces and two territories in its political framework. The acute problem of communications in the mid-nineteenth century constituted a further incentive to recognize the principle of decentralization in a large territory with a very small population.

Another cleavage of great significance at the time was that of religious belief, entangled with language questions. There appears to have been a belief, which proved wrong in the event, that if religious rights, particularly in the area of education, were protected, then linguistic rights would follow. Constitutionally, the major provision protected the existing separate school rights of Protestants and Catholics. Section 93 of the BNA Act, dealing with education, became a major clause around which French-English conflict was to revolve in subsequent years. The Manitoba schools question at the end of the last century was perhaps the most dramatic demonstration of the extent to which the interlocking considerations of religion, language and culture lay at the very center of Canadian political life.[2]

The overlapping but distinguishable linguistic cleavage between French and English was recognized as a fact of Canadian life by the 1860s. It was by then evident that a policy of assimilating French Canadians to the English-speaking world of North America would not work without intolerable costs, and it was therefore understood that at least minimal formal protection of language was necessary. This fact was reflected in Section 133 of the BNA Act which provided for the use of the English and French languages in Parliament and the courts of Canada and the legislature and courts of Québec.

A final division that received some modest attention in the British North America Act was that which separated the native population of British North America from the European settlers. The lines of coexistence between the aboriginal and European cultures were not developed in any detail; it was thought constitutionally sufficient to vest authority for the care of aboriginal peoples in the federal government.

No mention was made of other cultures. The theory of multiculturalism as a significant aspect of Canadian life had to await the waves of immigration, primarily European, that began in the late nineteenth century and have continued to the present.

The point to be made here bears on our discussion of dualism for it suggests the broader social, economic and cultural context within which dualism must be considered. A variety of politically significant cleavages were recognized in the nineteenth century, cleavages that any political structure would have to take into account. The French-English question, although the most important, was only one of a number that confronted the colonial politicians in the 1860s.

If anything, the range of cleavages and their significance has increased since then. We have today the increasingly acute question of the country's Inuit and Indian peoples, and their relationship to the rest of society. We have theories of multiculturalism, arising out of the persistence of distinctive subcultures, vying for attention and public support with theories of biculturalism. We have a number of energetic and thriving regional economic and social systems, in many instances led by highly sophisticated provincial governments. And we have a more acute sensitivity to what has been described as the "two nations" of the rich and poor, whether the dividing line is drawn in regional terms or horizontally in class terms. One might say that Canada is not so much a mosaic as a collage in which qualitatively different elements and objects are distributed rather haphazardly within a single frame.

So the question remains: In view of this diversity, what image of Canada do people have in mind when they speak of the need to foster national unity? They cannot mean that we should become a unified country in the juridical sense, that is to say, a state, for assuredly we are that already. There is no gainsaying the existence and authority of our constitutional structure as stated primarily in the British North America Act, nor is there any doubt about the actuality of our federal and parliamentary system of government, the general efficacy of our legislative, judicial and administrative systems, nor about our standing and reputation internationally.

But neither can people, when they speak of promoting national unity, mean that in Canada we should try to make ourselves a single people, a nation with one national culture and a single dominant mode of life. If that is what people mean, they are surely pursuing a chimera. The United States of America has been neatly described as "the American people organized", a state which is "co-extensive with a particular culture whose interest it is its primary responsibility to serve and protect."[3] It would be folly to claim the same for Canada, whose political system is a framework within which the various people and communities can seek their respective goals.

René Lévesque has made the derisive comment that "Le Canada, c'est un soufflé qui n'a pas pris." The comment conveys Lévesque's main point clearly enough, namely, that in his judgment the Canadian "experiment" has been a flop, but the analogy he employs is at once malapropos and highly revealing. To think of Canada as a soufflé that did not rise is to intimate that the historic task which faced the country was to create out of the constituent elements of the population a new compound, a Canadian people in which all the elements would be transformed and homogenized. It is, in other words, a Gallic (and a gastronomic) rendering of the American melting-pot idea, and, while it may speak in some way to the political experience of a French Canadian who is a member of the only fully articulated cultural nation in the country, it misses the point as far as Canada as a whole is concerned. With the exception of a few abortive attempts, which proved the inadvisability of the effort, the Canadian experience has never involved the wholehearted pursuit of a national mission or ideology, and to impose upon Canada a standard drawn from cultural nationalism is to misrepresent and distort its character. Canada is a country and a state; it is not a nation-state.

One might suggest with pardonable exaggeration that the reason there is a crisis in Canadian federalism today is that Canadian federalism has been so successful. We *are* a diverse country, and we have, and have sustained, a political system that reflects and protects much of that diversity. National unity will be problematic so long as federalism is vital.

Before the Canadian federal system was created, George Etienne Cartier stated in a few words the continuing challenge that was to face the country in the century that followed. He claimed that, should British North Americans achieve a union, they "would form a political nationality with which neither national origin, nor the religion of any individual would interfere." It is that form of national unity which is suggested by the evocative phrase, political nationality, which Canadians have been attempting to fashion for themselves for more than a century.

In the opening chapter of their 1979 report, *A Future Together*, the Commissioners of the Pepin-Robarts Task Force on Canadian Unity discussed the matter in the following terms: "For some people, unity seems to imply the submersion of diversity into one homogeneous mass. For others, it conveys an image of artificial, government-induced flag-waving, and "patriotic" celebrations which do not spring from any natural emotional source. For the members of the Task Force, however, Canadian unity is neither of these things: it is the sum of conditions upon which the various communities and governments of Canada agree to support and sustain the Canadian state. As such, it endows each of the parts with something it would not have if it stood alone. Is it, then, a just union of constituent elements, or is it a harmonious combination of parts?[4]

But Canadians understandably seek some greater clarity and detail than this as an aid to understanding their country. There are a number of different ways in which the country can be conceived: for example, as an urban, industrialized society with a developed capitalist economy and a population divided along class lines; as a hinterland of the American empire; as a conservative, traditionalist community that defines itself in contradistinction to the democratic republicanism of the United States and claims continuity with the parliamentary and monarchical principles of Great Britain and British society; as a multicultural society; as a country founded upon the principle of dualism.

Our object in this chapter is to explain the last.

DUALISM IN CANADA

Dualism in Canada may be generally described as the view which holds that the most significant cleavage in Canadian society is the line dividing English from French, and which identifies as the major challenge to domestic statecraft the establishment of harmonious and just relations between the English and French-speaking communities of Canada. It is an understanding of the Canadian situation that has its origins in the British defeat of the French forces at Québec in 1759; since that time, the reconciliation of French and English has been a continuing preoccupation of Canadians and their political leaders.

Those who would assert the importance of the dualist approach to an understanding of Canadian politics need to do little more than point to several of the major events of Canada's history. Again and again, one finds either that the explicit issue is one which involves French-English relations, or, if it begins as something else, it is soon transmitted into that kind of conflict. Quite apart from the years of accommodation and adjustment that followed the British assumption of civil authority in the eighteenth century, there have been a series of significant occurrences which have extended to the present: the 1837 Rebellion and Lord Durham's *Report* which was a response to it; the controversy between Upper and Lower Canada and the increasingly obvious unworkability of the united-province system; the recognition of the two communities in the Confederation debates and in the new federal system; the Riel Rebellions; the Manitoba schools question; the controversy over French-language schools in Ontario during the First World War; and conscription in the two world wars. Since 1960, Canada has experienced the cultural awakening of the Québécois people, an awakening that has gathered force and momentum until we now have a government in Québec City which has held an unsuccessful referendum on its platform of sovereignty association, but which remains committed to achieve sovereign independence for its people. It is events such as these that provide empirical support for the contention that questions of dualism lie at the center of Canadian public life.

Dualism, however, is a slippery concept to catch hold of. It obviously implies two things, French and English, in some kind of relationship with one another. But what are the two things? Do we mean French Canada, or the francophone community, or the province of Québec on the one hand? Do we mean English Canada, or the anglophone community, or the other nine provinces, or the other nine plus the federal government on the other? The way in which one defines these two entities is of signal importance in determining the type of dualist theory which is advanced.

Dualism is by no means a straightforward, self-explanatory view of Canada. It involves, first of all, choosing an angle of vision that will bring into prominence one set of characteristics of the country and neglect others; then it requires that one specify the meaning of the various critical elements and what that viewpoint can be expected to show.

TWO VIEWS OF DUALISM

For purposes of illustration, one might identify two broad strains of dualist thought in Canada. Each overlaps the other extensively, but they are character- ized by a distinct focus or orientation and they lead to distinguishable policy alternatives. We might call them the "sociological" and "institutional" approaches to dualism.

The sociological approach defines the two communities in non-institutional terms. All those whose native tongue is French or all those who are French Canadian by origin are part of one community; those who speak English or whose origin is not French Canadian are part of the other community. In recent times, and partly, perhaps, because of the unacceptable implications of any attempt to understand an ethnically diverse population in terms of just two ethnic categories, the sociological approach has tended to define the two communities in terms of language rather than ethnicity. For example, while the terms of reference of the Royal Commission on Bilingualism and Biculturalism, established in 1963, spoke of two founding *races,* the Commissioners in fact concentrated their attention primarily on the two communities defined as francophone and anglophone, i.e., as French- and English-speaking.

It is this sociological approach to dualism that has been adhered to consist- ently by the federal government and by Prime Minister Trudeau. It takes seriously the demographic data showing extensive interpenetration and geo- graphic dispersion of the two linguistic communities, and the consequent fact that no single political jurisdiction can be considered solely responsible for one of the linguistic communities or for policies relating to dualism. Thus there is an assumption that in provinces where both communities are strongly represented the respective provincial governments must assume partial responsibility for making appropriate arrangements. The protection of English-language minority rights in Québec, and the protection of Franco-Ontarian and Acadian minority rights in Ontario and New Brunswick are perfectly consistent with this sociological approach to dualism. To the extent that responsibility is distributed, at least in principle, among all the provincial governments, there is a corresponding reduction, relatively speaking, in the importance of any single provincial government's role.

There is, of course, a practical recognition of the special tasks facing Québec in nurturing the well-being of the francophone community, but always on the understanding that there are reciprocal obligations on the part of all governments in Canada to provide for the needs of both language groups. Thus, embedded in this approach, there is a bias against recognizing any one provincial government as having a special standing or responsibility that might properly receive constitutional recognition. Québec, as a matter of constitutional principle, is a province like the others, and any arrangements or liberties extended to her must in principle be applicable to the others as well.

A practical implication of the sociological approach to dualism is the strengthening of the federal government's role in the area of bilingualism and biculturalism, since it is the only government in the country with obligations to all Canadian citizens. It is the federal government that has comprehensive responsibility for the population as a whole, and it is therefore reasonable for citizens and provincial governments to look to the federal government for leadership in developing and implementing policies relating to dualism. Broadly speaking, this is what has happened during the past decade and a half, at least so far as English Canada and the provinces other than Québec are concerned. The central government has been looked to for leadership in these areas and has helped to define broad policy directions that both levels of government might pursue.

Within its own area of jurisdiction, virtually all the steps taken by the federal government have been consistent with the sociological approach to dualism. Many of the specific policies have their origin in the recommendations of the Royal Commission on Bilingualism and Biculturalism, although that body itself did not in fact adopt the sociological approach to dualism unequivocally. One of the reasons for a high degree of consistency in federal cultural policy is that it is the expression of the firm convictions of a prime minister who has enjoyed a virtual monopoly on federal policy formation in matters of dualism for almost a decade. The Official Languages Act of 1969, the principle of establishing bilingual districts where the size of the francophone or anglophone minority group warrants it, the bilingualization of the federal civil service, the effort to provide service to the citizens of the country in whichever official language they customarily use, the general encouragement of bilingualism throughout the country and the linguistic provisions of the federal government's 1980-81 Constitutional Resolution—these are all emanations of the sociological approach to dualism.

What of the approach to dualism which we have called institutional? This interpretation of dualism starts from the same premise; that is to say, from a belief that the two communities compose the basic elements of Canadian society, but its development from that point on is significantly different from that of the sociological approach. While recognizing the demographic facts of interpenetration and dispersion, the institutional approach makes a hardheaded judgment, namely, that a minority culture that does not enjoy concrete expression in a set of political institutions is unlikely to endure in the long run.

The institutionalists are inclined to view the sociological approach with suspicion because in their view it neglects the issue of political power in working out accommodations between the two cultures. Where everyone is said to be responsible, no one is responsible; where the federal government and perhaps half the provincial governments are deemed to have responsibility, no government has genuine responsibility, at least not in the direct, painful sense in which a political regime accountable to its people will find it difficult to avoid vigorous action on behalf of the citizenry.

Who is responsible for the welfare and advancement of Canada's French Canadians? The federal government asserts this responsibility, but its sense of obligation must inevitably be blunted by the demands and claims of the myriad other interests and groups to which it has to attend, not least of which are those of the majority English Canadian community. It cannot push the claims of French Canada, but must balance them against others. For the provinces other than Québec, the French-Canadian question is necessarily—however warm their sympathies may be—a relatively peripheral issue (New Brunswickers, I presume, would not accept this assertion for a minute). What political jurisdiction other than the province of Québec, where the overwhelming majority of residents are French-speaking, can wholeheartedly take on the primary responsibility for the protection and well-being of French Canada?

So those who adopt this view are inclined to see the historical continuance of French-Canadian culture in North America as being in very great measure the product of a set of arrangements that gave room in the political organization of Canadian society to the existence and the claims of French Canada. During the past century, this has taken the form of a federal system that, at least informally, vested in one government, that of the province of Québec, direct obligations with respect to French Canada. This arrangement has ensured the expression and protection of French Canada's interests in part, no doubt, because there is a definable government that can be held accountable by the electorate for its actions. The particular role of Québec has also been a factor in combating the forces of centralization and in maintaining a genuinely federal system of government.

There are some close connections between this institutional approach to dualism and many theories of nationalism. Most important is the fact that both take seriously the question of political power, assuming that cultural vitality depends on a suitable distribution of power and must, for its continued health, enjoy political expression. A minority culture cannot depend on the goodwill of the majority for its support; it must be in a position to command fair treatment. It must, in all likelihood, find a way of turning itself into a majority.

The logic of federalism in this respect is that a minority can be given political power, can be turned into a majority, in those culturally sensitive areas that require it, but can be treated as a portion of the population as a whole in those matters which are deemed to be common throughout the system and not intimately related to culture. Understandably, there is great difficulty in distinguishing clearly between those matters which are common and federal and those which are local and provincial, and there is traditionally controversy between the two spheres of government over whose judgment is to prevail. Where there is persistent conflict between the minority and the majority about matters of significance, it is frequently the case that a theory of institutional dualism held by the minority culture will be transformed into a theory of nationalism and national independence; certainly, the institutional approach lends itself more easily than the sociological to this type of change.

Another important connection between institutional dualism and nationalism is the collective dimension. Both assume that the vitality and welfare of the individual depends heavily upon his active membership in the cultural group or the nation. The sociological approach to dualism, in contrast to both, tends to be more concerned with the protection of the individual's linguistic and cultural rights rather than with the well-being of the collectivity as a whole.

There are, at this point, several important implications to be drawn from the institutional approach. First, the adoption of this way of understanding dualism leads one to downplay the significance of those minorities that do not constitute a political regime of some sort. In the Canadian context this means that there is less concern for the well-being of francophone or French-Canadian minorities outside the province of Québec, or, perhaps more precisely, a fatalism about the chances of survival of such politically unprotected minorities. Institutional dualists believe that the issue is not so much how well the various governments in Canada cope with the requirements of individuals who speak one or another of the two official languages, but rather how well two relatively coherent collectivities can live together "within the bosom of a single state."

Secondly, neither the federal government nor any of the other nine provinces is deemed to have nearly so important a responsibility for the direct working out of arrangements for French Canadians as is the case in the sociological approach. The important actions in this sphere belong to the government of Québec so far as French Canadians are concerned, and to the other governments of Canada so far as English Canada is concerned. The relationships between Québec and the rest of Canada become quasi-diplomatic in character, with the provincial government at Québec City speaking for French Canada and seeking to represent and protect its interests.

I would hazard a guess that the English-speaking citizens of the country and the francophone minorities outside Québec find the sociological approach to dualism congenial, whereas the French-speaking Québécois, the French Canadians within the province of Québec, approach the question of dualism much more in institutional and political terms and with a much more acute sensitivity to the connection between cultural well-being and political power.

DUALISM, ENGLISH-SPEAKING CANADA AND MULTICULTURALISM

Let us complicate the picture further by examining one assumption that supports both these conceptions of dualism. Whatever version of dualism is held, two entities are related to each other — two nations, two nationalities, two cultural or linguistic groups, or whatever. It is assumed that there are two collectivities, and that they each possess an identity of some kind, a set of specifiable characteristics and orientations.

This assumption appears to work reasonably well in the case of French Canada or the francophone community, but what of English Canada? Indeed, what is English Canada? We seem to be able to talk intelligibly about English Canada so long as we do not examine too carefully what we are referring to. But when we do undertake such an examination, what we discover is diversity which reaches so far and so deep that it forces us to call into question the very concept that we have been happily employing. English-speaking Canadians are distributed throughout all the ten provinces; vast numbers of them are not Anglo-Saxon in ethnic origin; many speak English as a second language. Diverse religions, cultural practices and languages teem beneath the placid surface of English Canada. What is more, the economic, occupational and social composition of this collectivity varies not only in class terms but also by region, and increasingly strong loyalties are developing which attach segments of the Canadian population to provincial governments and sub-system political cultures.

How are these phenomena to be fitted into a theory of dualism?

When the Royal Commission on Bilingualism and Biculturalism was established in 1963, its terms of reference were recorded in privy council minutes as follows: "To inquire into and report upon the existing state of bilingualism and biculturalism in Canada and to recommend what steps should be taken to develop the Canadian Confederation on the basis of an equal partnership between the two founding races, taking into account the contribution made by the other ethnic groups to the cultural enrichment of Canada and the measures that should be taken to safeguard that contribution."

The first part of the terms of reference postulates a theory of dualism or biculturalism, while the second, dealing with "other ethnic groups", implies some theory of cultural pluralism or multiculturalism. These distinct conceptions of Canadian society existed in uneasy relationship with one another throughout the life of the B and B Commission. They were reflected in the composition of the Commission itself; that is to say, in the cultural and linguistic background of the Commissioners, in the Commission's research activities, in its hearings and in its reports.

It is, I think, fair to say that the questions which plagued the B and B Commissioners in the 1960s remain unanswered today. How is the contribution of the other ethnic groups to be taken seriously if the country is to be developed on the basis of an equal partnership between the two founding races? How, more generally, might we reconcile cultural pluralism with dualism? These have proven to be awkward questions, not only for the country as a whole, but for specific provinces and regional communities as well. The Government of Québec, for example, has not found it easy to settle on a satisfactory approach to the brute sociological fact of cultural pluralism in the midst of Québec society, and it is not always clear whether "Québécois" indicates French Canadians in Québec, French-speaking Quebeckers, or *all* the people of Québec—French, English, Italian, Greek and the rest.

While it is probably true to say that the existence of a large French-Canadian community in British North America created the conditions within which both the form and the theory of cultural pluralism could take root in Canada, and while it is most certainly true that the other ethnic groups share many of the concerns of the French-Canadian community, it is nevertheless the case that, as theories and as social patterns, pluralism and dualism tug in quite different directions, and each poses a problem for the other.[4]

If bilingualism and biculturalism are to be the defining concepts for Canadian life, then the possibility of extensive institutional recognition and support of pluralism is markedly diminished. If one is preoccupied with French-English relations, it is difficult to bring into bold relief those social facts and relationships which are neither French nor English. Where do the native people fit into such a scheme? Where might the Italians of Toronto be placed? The Greeks of Montréal? The Ukrainians on the Prairies or the Asians of British Columbia? If dualism is the explanatory model that is employed, then concern for and sensitivity to multiculturalism in Canada will necessarily be reduced. Politically, the choice of a model can have serious ramifications; for example, the two-nations theory opens up, at least in principle, the possibility of a set of relationships and political structures that reflect the two dominant cultural entities. How does that fit with a federal system of ten provinces and a central government?

If, to take the opposite position, multiculturalism is accepted as the dominant norm, with English as the *de facto lingua franca*, then the French-Canadian fact will tend to be assimilated to that theory of pluralism, and French Canadians will tend to be regarded simply as members of one of the several minority cultures that together compose the Canadian mosaic. Such a frame of mind has had considerable appeal in Western Canada, where the demographic facts encourage and support it. The divergent principles of dualism and multiculturalism lie at the center of a good deal of misunderstanding in Canada; it is in many ways difficult for Westerners to understand and appreciate the way in which central Canadians define the cultural composition of Canada, but the citizens of Ontario and Québec find it equally difficult to comprehend and respect the point of view that Westerners employ to understand their community and its culture.

CONCLUSION

The principle of multiculturalism, then, is a useful aid, in that it helps us to appreciate the limitations of dualism as an approach to Canadian politics, limitations that will, in fact, be duplicated in some form by any coherent theory or explanatory principle. Each, if it is any good, is like a searchlight which brings some things of significance into bold relief and which helps us to explore unfamiliar territory. But like any bright light on a dark night, it blinds us to other things and may, if we are not careful, lead us to overlook things that should not be neglected. So it is with the theory of dualism. It is most appropriately treated as a tool to help us understand, and as a guide and reference point for some of our activities as citizens and political actors.

As an approach to Canadian politics, dualism has the signal virtue of directing our attention toward what is undeniably a major and continuing issue in Canadian social and political life. As we have indicated, there is massive evidence throughout our history to support the view that English-French relations cannot be ignored in any serious attempt to understand the Canadian people and the country's political institutions. It will remain an indispensable guide to Canadian politics, because of the salience of French-English relations in Canadian life.

On the other hand, the theory does have its limitations. It is ambiguous in that it covers at least two distinguishable orientations, the institutional and the sociological, which lead in quite different directions and toward distinctly different conclusions. The particular version which one is employing needs to be specified and handled with care. More significant is the fact that, while the dualist approach encourages sensitivity to some aspects of Canadian life which are profoundly important, it has the effect of obscuring other aspects which are by no means inconsequential. We have attempted to illustrate this fact by contrasting the dualist view with the theory of cultural pluralism.

There is even a geographical bias in the theory to which many Westerners in particular have taken exception; they argue, not without some justice, that to concentrate on French-English relations is to concentrate on central Canada, particularly Ontario and Québec, at the expense of the Atlantic region, the Prairies and British Columbia. They claim that the idea of national unity should not be exhausted by the notion of achieving harmony between the two cultures, but should involve granting a square deal to the various regions and provinces of Canada. Freight rates, tariffs, agricultural and natural resource policies—these are the stuff of which national unity is made, or not made.

This last point suggests a broader limitation to which we might refer in closing. It applies to both the theory of dualism and the theory of multiculturalism. Each is concerned with culture and with the relationships between culture and political life. Accordingly, each approaches the social world with a particular concern for such cultural artifacts as language, religion, ethnicity, and, broadly speaking, the constellation of attitudes and sentiments which cluster around these artifacts.

But there are many other avenues by which we may seek to understand the world in which we live. Several are explored in this volume, and they may depend little or not at all upon the cultural factors that have loomed so large in this chapter. It is, I think, unwise to deal with this variety of explanations by asserting that one approach is right and the others are wrong. Instead, one ought to think of these theories as tools in a box, indispensable aids in accomplishing certain things, but radically dependent upon the craftsman's intelligence and sensitivity. The effectiveness of a theory, or of a tool, will depend upon the user's sophistication, upon his skill in manipulating the instrument, his familiarity with the material with which he is working, the clarity of his objectives, and a sense of limitation. These, I think, are some of the important qualities that the student of politics should possess. Certainly, it is in this spirit that one might properly employ the theory of cultural dualism as an approach to Canadian politics.

That having been said, however, we must underscore this basic fact; the reality of French-English relations has been an enduring preoccupation of Canadians for as long as the country has existed. It is inconceivable that this state of affairs will cease to exist in the future.

SUMMARY

1. Most countries, Canada included, are extraordinarily complex entities that can be understood in a variety of different ways and approached from a variety of different perspectives.

2. In Canada, the concept of national unity is used to accommodate and explain the diversity of the country and provides the framework within which we can understand a variety of possible approaches.

3. Dualism, the theme of French-English relations, is an approach which addresses a fundamental reality of Canada.

4. Dualism has been important in Canadian affairs since before Confederation.

5. Though the French-English division is the most important, it is only one of several basic cleavages in Canadian society.

6. There are two broad forms which the dualist approach may take: the

sociological, which focuses on the spread of French- and English-speaking Canadians across the country and the responsibility of all governments to attend to their needs; and the *institutional*, which focuses on the concentration of French-speaking Canadians in the province of Québec and the special responsibility of the Québec Government to protect the needs and interests of the "Québécois".

7. The actions of the government of Canada have generally been consistent with the sociological approach to Canada.

8. The institutional approach to dualism has much in common with many theories of nationalism.

9. The "English" side of the dualist equation raises complications since it is a culturally plural, highly regionalized community in which theories of multiculturalism have considerable appeal.

10. While it is true that dualism is only one of many possible approaches to Canadian society and politics, it remains an indispensable tool because of the salience of French-English relations in Canadian life.

STUDY QUESTIONS

1. Why is Canada currently experiencing a period of profound disagreement among its citizens about what the nature of the country should be?

2. To what extent is dualism evident in Canada's political parties?

3. Can the sociological and institutional views of dualism be advanced, or implemented, simultaneously, or are they mutually exclusive?

4. Is the dualist division in Canada weakened or reinforced by the Canadian federal structure?

5. On balance, does a multicultural emphasis weaken or reinforce the dualist cleavage?

6. To what extent do you agree with the view that French Canada is "the only fully articulated cultural nation in the country"?

7. If the majority in Québec should vote to separate from the rest of Canada, should Québec be allowed to secede? Give reasons for your response.

8. Why is it, or is it not, proper to deal with dualism by simply guaranteeing all concessions granted to French Canadians in 1867 and rejecting all additional requests or demands?

9. To what extent is Canada's dualist crisis simply the result of political power shifting from the national government to provincial governments?

10. How can the country survive perpetual dualist squabbles and crises? Does dualism, in the final analysis, involve an insoluble problem?

ENDNOTES

1. The text of the British North America Act may be conveniently consulted in an appendix to R.M. Dawson, *The Government of Canada*, 4th ed., revised by Norman Ward (Toronto: University of Toronto Press, 1963). Part I of that volume provides a brief historical sketch of constitutional development in Canada while Part II examines the framework of the Constitution itself.

2. Lovell Clark, ed., *The Manitoba School Question: Majority Rule or Minority Rights?* (Toronto: Copp Clark, 1968). This book provides a useful collection of contemporary and critical material on this issue.

3. Allan Smith, "Metaphor and Nationality in North America," *Canadian Historical Review* (September, 1970), p. 274.

4. The relationship between pluralism and dualism is discussed in D.R. Cameron, *Nationalism, Self-Determination and the Quebec Question* (Toronto: Macmillan, 1974). Ch. 7, esp. pp. 110-2.

SELECTED REFERENCES

There is extensive literature on Canadian dualism, particularly focusing on Québec's position in Canada.

The volumes listed below are examples of those a student will find most useful. Many contain excellent bibliographical information. The list should be regarded as illustrative rather than systematic.

Burns, R.M., ed. *One Country or Two?* Montreal: McGill-Queen's University Press, 1971. A balanced and thoughtful collection of essays by a group of English-speaking Canadians reflecting on the question of Québec separation and its consequences for Canada.

Cameron, David. *Nationalism, Self-Determination and the Quebec Question*. Toronto: Macmillan, 1974. Concentrates on nationalist theory and the principle of self-determination of peoples, and the way in which they bear on Québec.

Commissioner of Official Languages. *Annual Reports*, 1970-71 and onward. Ottawa: Information Canada. An annual review of the development of institutional bilingualism in Canada. Written in a lively and readable style.

The Constitutional Committee of the Quebec Liberal Party. *A New Canadian Federation*. 1980. A major statement of constitutional policy published prior to the Québec referendum.

Cook, Ramsay. *Canada and the French-Canadian Question*. Toronto: Macmillan, 1967. This book and the one below are important collections of essays on nationalism and history in Québec and Canada by one of the country's most distinguished English-Canadian students of Québec.

_____. *The Maple Leaf Forever*. Toronto: Macmillan, 1971.

_____., ed. *French-Canadian Nationalism*. Toronto: Macmillan, 1969. A useful anthology of work by French Canadians writing about themselves and their community.

Dion, Léon. *Quebec: The Unfinished Revolution.* Montreal and London: McGill-Queen's University Press, 1976. A collection of essays on Québec by a prominent French-Canadian political scientist.

Government of Canada. *The Canadian Constitution.* 1981.

The Government of Québec. *Québec-Canada: A New Deal.* 1979. The outline of the Parti Québécois' proposal for sovereignty association.

Granatstein, J.L., gen. ed. *Issues in Canadian History Series.* Toronto: Copp Clark. This series contains a substantial number of thin volumes which make such topics as the Manitoba school question, Louis Riel, Henri Bourassa, Québec, and Duplessis readily accessible to the student interested in the history of Canadian dualism.

McRoberts, Kenneth, and Dale Postgate. *Québec: Social Change and Political Crisis,* Toronto: McClelland and Stewart, 1976. An examination of Québec politics and social life from the point of view of modernization and political development.

Royal Commission on Bilingualism and Biculturalism. *Reports.* Ottawa: Queen's Printer.
Preliminary Report, 1965.
Book I, *The Official Languages,* 1967.
Book II, *Education,* 1968.
Book III, *The Work World,* 1969.
Book IV, *The Cultural Contributions of other Ethnic Groups,* 1969.
The B and B reports, published in the latter half of the 1960s, are perhaps still the main empirical study for those who would explore further the themes of this chapter. See also the studies of the Commission, recording research done on a variety of more specific topics.

Smiley, Donald V. *The Canadian Political Nationality.* Toronto: Methuen, 1967. This book and the one which follows are thoughtful, penetrating studies of contemporary Canadian federalism in the light of the challenge from Québec.

_____. *Canada in Question: Federalism in the 1980s.* 3rd ed. Toronto: McGraw-Hill Ryerson, 1980.

Simeon, Richard. *Must Canada Fail?* Montreal-London: McGill-Queen's University Press, 1977.

The Task Force on Canadian Unity. *Reports.* Ottawa: Minister of Supply and Services, 1979.
Volume I. *A Future Together: Observations and Recommendations.*
Volume II. *Coming to Terms: The Words of the Debate.*
Volume III. *A Time to Speak: The Views of the Public.*

Trudeau, P.E. *Federalism and the French Canadians.* Toronto: Macmillan, 1968. This is an indispensable source, for the obvious reason that Trudeau has been a central figure in recent Canadian public affairs, and for the less obvious reason that it is provocatively argued and explicitly related to an important intellectual tradition.

11

One Perspective on the Study of Public Policy

V. Seymour Wilson*

INTRODUCTION

My task in this chapter is to explain what public policy is and how focusing on it can help to understand the reality of Canadian politics. At first glance this should be an easy task for one who calls himself a serious student of public policy, but unfortunately the task is much more formidable than it appears. I am caught in the same situation as the American scholar Martin Landau: "I have gone through some 50 pieces of research on policy questions in the last few years and every instance is marked by the absence of any attempt to define the term...on subjects of this kind everything one writes tends to meander into hazy speculation. The meandering and the haze occur because we have yet to clearly conceptualize policy".[1]

This book is premised on the fact that there are various perspectives to the study of political activity, and public policy is designated as one of them. But I or anyone else would be courting the charge of intellectual dishonesty by not admitting from the very beginning the problems clearly indicated by the above remarks of Landau: there is no such thing as *one* public policy perspective to embrace all policy. Indeed, there are several perspectives to public policy all readily demonstrated in the literature of the social sciences.

Perhaps a clue to this lack of a quintessential definition of policy can be derived from the following observation. To the best of my knowledge the English language is the *only* Western European language with a separate word for policy, and certainly this is worth noting and thinking about, alerting us to the possibility that when we make such distinctions we may be open to the charge of confusing issues rather than clarifying them. For example, both the

*Associate Professor, School of Public Administration, Carleton University.

French and the Germans believe no such distinction is meaningful. In French, the word *politique* (politics) is the same as *politique* (policy) and in German the word *Politik* is likewise both politics and policy. The use of a single term in these languages suggests that there is no politics apart from policy and no policy apart from politics. Many students of public policy take note of this fact and argue that the differentiation made in the English language is done so for analytical purposes only and does not refer to something concrete.

The admission that the English distinction between politics and policy is useful strictly for analytical purposes opens the door for me to demonstrate what is meant by this. Many conceive of public policy as a subset of the concept political (usually dubbed *policy studies*). For example, the editor of this book conceives the study of public policy as coextensive with the notion of *political process*. Students of policy studies contend that they are primarily interested in the origins, underlying assumptions, limitations and potentialities of policy. They seek not only to describe policy behavior but in addressing the "how" questions of public policy, they attempt to explain why behavior manifests itself finally as goals and policy outputs.

Others conceive of policy as a means of mounting an integrated attack on social problems confronting society (pollution, urban blight, racism, etc.). This conception of public policy is biased towards bringing knowledge of various social sciences to bear on the analysis of discrete policy issues, (variably known as *policy content*). Still others treat policy as a matter of value (*policy advocacy*): to state one's policy is to give a pronouncement of fundamental principle on a particular issue, (for example Canada's policy regarding the defence of Western Europe). Then there are those who restrict the term to strategy, design or program (this meaning is generally referred to as *policy resource management* or *policy science*). The present debate and outlined strategy in both the newspapers and academic journals concerning the National Energy Policy (NEP) of the federal government, which was announced late in 1980, is a good example of this conception. Finally there are those students who comprehend the term in a broad way to mean a compendium of *societal values*, *goals* and the *means* to achieve such over an extended period of time (*policy analysis*). This, to be sure, is a rather amorphous conceptualization, but for the purposes of analysis in this essay I shall put myself in this latter category. This last analytical category has the advantage of being catholic in that one can incorporate many, although not all, of the nuances of meaning involved in the other analytical distinctions made above. (For example, some of *policy content* is omitted in this perspective.)

Following Jenkins, I define public policy as:

> A set of interrelated decisions taken by a political actor or group of actors concerning the selection of goals and the means of achieving them within a specified situation where these decisions should, in principle, be within the power of these actors to achieve.[2]

This definition highlights several important considerations about public policy. It certainly says nothing about politics or policy in a partisan manner: political parties, pressure groups, lobbying, public opinion and the power struggle for preferment, dominance, influence and position. Politics is also deciding the substance of policy in a broad way: the promotion of values, and the choosing among alternatives in an attempt to solve problems and improve human life. This latter aspect of politics corresponds closely to the notion of policy as policy advocacy. Our definition further indicates that decision-making is crucial to public policy-making but normally the decision *per se* is only one aspect of public policy-making. In the vast number of instances, *a series of decisions extending over time* is the crucial distinction between policy-making and decision-making. As Eulau and Prewitt point out: "What the observer sees when he identifies policy at any one point in time is at most a stage or phase in a sequence of events that constitute policy development."[3] The definition also strongly implies the need to attain a thorough knowledge not only of the technical and social considerations, but also of the *institutional setting* (or loosely put, the environment) within which a given policy or policies are to occur. Finally, the latter part of the definition puts an emphasis on *policy process*. As stated earlier policy process is concerned with the "how" questions. How does the system work? How do the problems get to government, how are they defined and how are they acted upon?

VALUES AND POLICY-MAKING

By emphasizing decisions and the premises behind them we are inevitably placing some measure of emphasis on the role our values play in arriving at decisions for the good of the polity. Practical philosophy, public policy and politics (in the sense in which it is defined above), are intimately related to one another. Because politics is largely concerned with helping to shape policies, and policies in turn necessitate choices between contesting value systems, the ethical dimension of policy-making is always a consideration with which we must deal. This ethical dimension is so pervasive that in our own society we are prone to assume it as self-evident.

Let me give you an example of this. Some months ago a prominent CBC announcer in Ottawa, and a friend of my family, conducted a radio interview in which he expressed his absolute boredom with the "political hot air" in Canada concerning the constitution, the Québec referendum, French-English relations, Alberta-Ottawa confrontations on energy and so on. Frankly he was sick of these recurring themes in Canadian political discourse. When next I saw him I gently reminded my friend of his introductory course in politics—that his so-called "hot air" was necessary political discourse couched in the rhetoric of democratic values and that our politicians, thank goodness, were talking to each other! I stressed that if that rhetoric stopped we would be in big trouble. I reminded him of Kenneth Boulding's comment that "The thing that is most fatal to the political process is conclusions: when once the train of thought has reached a terminus, everybody might just as well get off it." I illustrated my arguments by pointing to a few unfortunate countries, in both East and West, where political discourse among politicians is non-existent, and my friend finally got the drift of my argument.

His initial problem was that he took democratic discourse as self-evident. To a certain extent we all do if we live in a country such as Canada. Democratic discourse on which public policy depends, noted the philosopher George H. Sabine, can be reduced to:

> ....the moral problem of human beings obliged to meet and conduct their transactions in situations such that simple coercion is beyond the reach of either party, and in relationships for which the customary institutions of their tradition provide no procedures to regularize the transactions. In a limited sense it is a problem of creating or inventing viable institutions, but in a larger sense it is the problem of finding in the meantime a reserve of good will and good faith that will permit the institutions to establish themselves as the customary media of peaceful and orderly methods of political, economic and social intercourse. ... The belief that some such attitude is humanly possible, and that as an attitude it must underlie the effective operation of any set of political institutions, was ingrained in the long tradition of Western humanism.[4]

Thus, democratic societies have profound views on such broad traditional ethical questions as righteousness, justice, obligation and legitimacy. Even though in the formulation of a particular policy we may assume much without question, a full discourse on such matters would inevitably lay bare our normative assumptions. One example in Canadian public policy would serve here to sharpen my point. The regulatory function of government has been identified as one of the most crucial functions of democratic governance in the 70s and 80s.[5] Much of what Canadians read about the nature of regulation and regulatory activity is written by Americans for Americans in a country with quite different fundamental assumptions about the role of the regulatory function. For Americans, the regulatory activity of government is essentially a *policing role,* that is, ensuring that economic activity closely approximates competitive market conditions. Thus the criteria for judging the utility of regulation in America lay essentially in its perceived value as a tool of economic efficiency.

This is definitely not the case in Canada. Professor Alexander Brady gives us a clue as to why there is such a fundamental difference in assumptions about the respective roles of government in Canada and the United States: "the role of the state in the economic life of Canada is really the modern history of Canada. ..." Furthermore, he contends, the positive, pragmatic state was an absolute necessity because of "the pioneer nature of the country, the physical structure of the half continent, the imperial sweep of settlement after 1867, the influence of the interacting ideas and institutions of Britain and the United States, and the quick response of the whole society to the advance of western industrialism".[6]

This pragmatic view of government intervention can therefore be explained in terms of fundamental political assumptions crucial to nation-building. Regulation is more than a tool of economic efficiency here. In Canada, national unity and regional income redistribution have been explicitly a part of freight rate and air fare setting, and the establishment of agricultural marketing boards has been a deliberate political attempt to transfer income from consumers to producers.[7]

These differences in fundamental political values which lead to differing policies explain why Prime Minister Trudeau reminded US President Ronald Reagan during his official visit to Canada that the role of government in this country has largely been perceived by Canadians as a constructive nation-building necessity. Mr. Reagan may have appreciated this fact about Canada, but he certainly made it clear in his speech to the joint session of Parliament that his Republican administration perceived the present level of government intervention in social and economic matters in the United States as a menace to democratic freedom: "individual responsibility has given way to regimentation by central government." This is an example of different value assumptions about the nature of government leading to two different ways in which policy as a whole is perceived. It stands as a stark reminder that politics and policy are very closely linked.

GOALS AND MEANS

In an oversimplified approach to policy-making and implementation, a step-by-step model is always put forward: the problem is identified, a program is developed and implemented and the problem or problems are finally solved. This is called the rational approach to policy-making. What is striking about this approach is that it seldom exists in practice. The best writers in policy studies warn us that policy-making is a constant process of discovering or "appreciating" reality. We are constantly searching to discover what we ought to value in our societies. The rational model of policy-making disregards this search because it already assumes that we know what to value.[8]

Public problems are never comprehensively or finally "solved". Instead they are "resolved" which means that they have been reduced to a simpler form. Politicians talk about projects, achieving goals and building for the future. But the simple fact is that not one of us can see six feet into the future. The future is always a work of imagination, a mental construct built on the images of our historical past. The future represents constant change, so the problem and its environment can never be held constant. Here are some reasons for this:

1. Events interfere to alter people's perceptions of their needs.
2. Other problems emerge for some people that have a higher priority than those for which a program has been developed.
3. Over periods of time pressures from some sources are reduced or dispersed.
4. Private actions relieve needs, often influencing how people define problems and react to programs.

5. Programs themselves have unanticipated outcomes which may influence how people define problems.[9]

Primarily because of these factors many students of public policy contend that all policy belongs to the class of unverified propositions, that is, *policy is always hypothetical and constantly subject to error*.[10] As Martin Landau puts it: "...whether a policy proposal is engineered, or the outcome of a bargain, or the result of conflict, or the product of historical forces, or whatever—its epistemological status is not altered. It remains hypothetical."[11] Landau goes on to argue that policy formulation engages the future tense, for the object of all policy proposals is to control and direct future courses of action. Thus policies inadvertently carry with them some probability of error and cannot be accepted as correct *a priori*.[12]

This constant flux, this change of relating and searching out values in a changing environment, is a difficult concept to grasp, particularly if one is accustomed to thinking of reality in terms of absolutes: there is a concrete reality out there on which we can constantly depend. The fact of the matter is that we constantly seek changes in our relations. Our goals therefore cannot be held constant because these goals are really means of achieving future goals and so on. Sir Geoffrey Vickers explains this rather well:

> The objects of our desires and aversions are not objects but relations. No one "wants an apple". He may want to eat it, sell it, paint it, admire it, conceivably even merely to possess it—a common type of continuing relation—in any case to establish or change some relation with it. The goals we seek are changes in our relations or in our opportunities for relating; but the bulk of our activities consists in the "relating" itself.[13]

Therefore, because of this constant relating, program goals are almost always drastically revised in the process of administering a program. The most pressing implementation problems exist when one is attempting to move from *a policy decision* to *operations* in such a way that what is put into place bears a reasonable resemblance to the decision and is functioning well in its institutional environment. As Walter Williams puts it: "The past contains few clearer messages than that of the difficulty of bridging the gap between policy decisions and workable field operations".[14]

Studying public policy processes is perhaps the most important contribution which political scientists make to the study of public policy. Process questions help us to understand how problems get to government, how they are defined within government circles, how they are acted upon and so on. While this is not the be-all and end-all of public policy this is a perfectly legitimate conceptualization for study because the nature of problems themselves largely determines how various policy processes will develop and work. Problems influence the processes designed to solve them, the processes in their turn help to explain programs and policies, and policies affect what problems emerge in society and get to the agenda put forward by government.[15]

Let me illustrate what I mean by this. In an earlier part of this chapter, I maintained that politics does affect the nature of policies shaped by various governments. In a word, politics determines policies. Recently students of public policy analysis have been made aware of the fact that the exact opposite is also true: namely, that sometimes policies determine the politics to be followed. The political scientist, Theodore Lowi, the most important exponent of this point of view, argues that "a political relationship is determined by the type of policy at stake, so that for every type of policy there is likely to be a distinctive type of political relationship."[16]

Lowi essentially argues that we should discover the structural characteristics or stable patterns of politics common to different types of policy in order to pinpoint the normal patterns associated with various expected outcomes. In other words, policy is a cause of politics. Lowi therefore argues that to understand fully the reality of the policy-politics equation we should encompass both aspects of it (politics = policy, and policy = politics).[17]

A little earlier I emphasized that a process perspective on policy can lead to both an examination of values and other questions related to policy goals and how they are acted upon and put into effect. Students of policy analysis therefore contend that in designing and advocating policies we must be able to anticipate the actual performance of the government in adopting and implementing the proposed policies. This orientation therefore calls for an outline of the main features of the political and bureaucratic settings within which specific policy proposals will be considered. This orientation is usually referred to as "the politics of implementation".

Recent studies of the politics of implementation have made several significant observations about the implementation process which tend to be overlooked by other students generally concerned with the overall political process. Over the last four or five decades we have increasingly recognized the active role which the bureaucracy plays in both the formulation and implementation processes of policy.[18] Professor Carl J. Friedrich of Harvard University has argued that the bureaucracy was first among the political institutions, indeed it is conceived of as "the core of modern government".[19] While this insight may not be thought extraordinary, seldom do political scholars acknowledge it in organizing their work. As I have argued elsewhere, institutional analyses usually begin with the executive, the courts and the legislatures; sometimes the bureaucracy as a neutral automaton and indispensable converter of public policy into desired political ends is considered superficially.[20] For example, in our recent constitutional debates we have had *ad nauseam* proposals to change the institutions of Canadian federalism—the Senate, the House of Commons, the Supreme Court and so on. Yet for one of the most important institutions in this rostrum, namely the bureaucracy, we have had not a single set of original ideas concerning the role it has played in the evolution of the administrative state, and what a new constitutional order would and should mean for its viability. In the midst of considering the most fundamental changes in our constitutional order, one of its most indispensable and powerful institutions was completely ignored. Why is this the case?

The image of bureaucracy as a neutral instrument of the public purpose is extremely difficult to change, primarily because it is partly true—the bureaucracy in a democracy does exist ostensibly to implement the goals of a democratic government. But bureaucracy is much more than a mere instrument of societal purposes, and this fact is fully appreciated when the literature on the politics of implementation is carefully studied. For bureaucracy has a dynamism of its own which is clearly manifested by its active role in making and otherwise influencing policy formulation; its struggles for survival and self preservation; and its legitimate role in "deciding what has been decided after basic decisions have been made by political authorities; by deciding what further needs to be decided; by defining and weighing alternatives; and by making further decisions."[21]

For purposes of this study we can briefly examine two central aspects of this literature. First, bureaucracy is viewed as a political institution which must monitor the intentions of its political masters and the demands of its clientele. And this perspective supports the generalization made earlier that bureaucrats are inevitably drawn into activities beyond the simple application of rules or standards to public problems and conflicts. Second, this view of bureaucracy as a political institution stresses its need for support. It is not enough to promise efficiency, for agencies need to cultivate their political constituencies every bit as much as do legislators and interest groups.

The other functional activities of bureaucracy besides implementation include fostering and encouraging interest groups important to the policy process. This encouragement has taken a variety of structural forms: from outright financial support of selected interest groups (the Canadian Indian Brotherhood and the Consumers' Association of Canada are two examples); generous help in the creation and funding of many functional and central advisory councils (e.g. the Economic Council of Canada, the Advisory Council on the Status of Women); and the spawning of policy structures for collecting and transmitting knowledge for policy purposes (royal commissions, task forces, etc.).[22] This "political activity" of bureaucrats means that bureaucracies cultivate political constituencies by such devices as the publication of white papers on policy areas; drafting legislation and its presentation in Parliament *without prior group consultation* (thus encouraging group pressures to be fully felt *both* at the political and bureaucratic levels of government); letting it be known that the bureaucracy will be open to "consultation" in drafting regulations once policy legislation has been passed by Parliament; and the use of the judicial system both as an independent and complementary adjunct in decision-making and as final arbiter in group disputes when other attempts at "consensus-making" have failed.[23] Two of the most central points made by this literature are:

1. Many people other than bureaucrats are involved in the formulation and implementation of public policy and this is encouraged by the bureaucracy for very good reasons.
2. Bureaucrats themselves are actively involved in functional activities other than the mere implementation of public policy.

CONCLUSION

A perspective which emphasizes process leaves out some important considerations in the study of public policy. Political process is biased towards understanding the "how" of public policy. As the leading student of policy science once put it: "The science of politics states conditions; the philosophy of politics justifies preferences. [My enquiry which is] restricted to political analysis, declares no preferences. It states conditions."[22] Stating conditions is definitely not the whole corpus of knowledge in public policy. The study of public policy is also concerned with the ethical questions of preferences. Social relations in our community are irreducibly moral relations. Our decision-making then unavoidably will be concerned with ethical questions, since ethics is the art of making wise choices.

Studying public policy can also mean a concentration on the *content* of public policy—an understanding of the sociological, psychological, legal and economic dimensions of policy content. Clearly most political scientists are not professionally competent to give advice in these areas of public policy concerns. Policy formulators must therefore seek this advice elsewhere. Also, public policy process as defined in this essay largely leaves out such political components as debates among politicians in Parliament, the rather amorphous preferences of party platforms, and other determinants of politics not directly related to interaction between the political world and the bureaucratic environment. Perhaps this emphasis might have to be re-examined in the future for serious omissions, but so far the inclination has been to omit this aspect of politics in the process studies of public policy in North America.

Finally, a process orientation to public policy tends to favor process-type solutions. Rather than emphasize this or that substantive proposal, students of public policy as process tend to stress certain methods of decision-making and then live with the results of this emphasis. *In a word, process will take care of content.* As one student of public policy process candidly admits: "I rely wholly on democratic criteria for determining what is the best decision-making—i.e., a high degree of access for those who care to be involved, provision for bargaining and compromise, public accountability of leaders, free elections, etc. This also suggests that my remedies for the social system tend to be of the process variety—more access for more interests, providing for criticism and opposition, publicizing decisions and how they are made."[23]

Understanding what public policy is all about has many facets. As I have tried to indicate, to a large extent the answers sought in studying public policy depend on what the investigator is seeking. However, overriding all these various perspectives is a moral one: the student of public policy cannot escape the facts dealing with the morality of choice in a democratic system. As E.E, Schattschneider puts it: "Democracy is based on a profound insight into human nature, the realization that all men are sinful, all are imperfect, all are prejudiced, and none knows the whole truth."[24] All those involved in the formulation and implementation of public policy should never forget this basic insight.

SUMMARY

1. A policy proposes intervention to alter some existing circumstance or mode of conduct: "*If* such and such happens *then* we must do such and such."

2. There is no one perspective on public policy. What public policy is and how focusing on it can help us to understand the reality of Canadian politics can lead to answers stressing *policy content, policy studies, policy advocacy*, to name a few perspectives.

3. Although policy analysis can be more broadly defined as the "how" of public policy, many students of policy contend that "how" questions cannot really neglect the question of policy preferences (or policy advocacy). Some commentators therefore incorporate the role of values in the study of policy.

4. Values, expressed through general political activity, shape policy in many distinct ways. These values are so deep-rooted in our culture that we tend to overlook them. Some of the ways in which Canadian values have deeply affected the political process (and therefore the way in which we formulate policy) are given.

5. We tend to view policy as the constant setting of fixed goals, objectives or ends. Undoubtedly we do have short term goals. These "goals" are, however, always related to achieving "other goals" and so on. In other words much policy-making is the continuous setting of governing relations or norms and not fixed goals.

6. In this chapter we stress the perspective of policy analysis. Students of this perspective are usually political scientists, a discipline dominated by social scientists more interested in the "how of policy"—how problems get to government, how they are defined there and how they are acted upon.

7. All policies carry with them a great probability of error because two things can happen: a) our hypothesis "if—then" may not occur at all; and b) our appreciation of what is involved in the "if" usually is widened in time. In most cases we come to "appreciate" more and more the reality of "if".

   As an example of this fact let us use the policy area of energy. Decades ago in a few regions of Canada provincial policy-makers leased water reserves (vital in the production of hydroelectric power) either to the United States or neighboring provinces for sometimes eighty years or more. No policy-maker or policy analyst in his right mind today would advocate what was done then: sell the sources of hydroelectric power for the next eighty or ninety years (say until the year 2070 or 2080) under the terms of a lease setting fixed prices from today's market. Second, ten years ago our policy analysts and policy-makers "knew" the extent of our gas and oil reserves. Our government planned or had an oil policy for Canada as we saw the situation then. In the last seven or eight years events have forced upon us a further "appreciation" of the energy problem—energy policy in Canada is changing almost every month. Furthermore, technological advances have allowed us to "know more" about our real energy reserves. We are now able to seriously consider retrieving oil from such previously "inaccessible sources" as the Athabasca Tar Sands or possibly from Hibernia, off Newfoundland, or the Beaufort Sea and other places in the high Arctic. The variables of our "if" are therefore subject to some changes as we appreciate our potential reserves. Policy has therefore changed, in many instances rather drastically, to accommodate the reality of these new factors.

8. Political philosopher David Braybrooke and economist Charles Lindblom sum up what I have been attempting to say about policy in the following manner:

   It is decision making through small or incremental moves on particular problems rather than through a comprehensive reform program. It is also endless; it takes the form of an indefinite sequence of policy moves. Moreover, it is exploratory in that the goals of policy making continue to change as new experience with policy throws new light on what is possible and desirable. In this sense, it is also better described as moving *away* from known social ills rather than as moving *toward* a known as relatively stable goal.[25]

9. Policy process leads to an appreciation of what is involved in policy formulation and implementation. For example, implementation studies certainly pinpoint the bureaucracy as a key actor in policy formulation, but such studies also indicate that the bureaucracy is not the only player in the field. Bureaucracy seeks to "appreciate" what is involved in both policy formulation and implementation. This fact leads bureaucrats into various kinds of relationships with interest groups, politicians and other actors in the political system.

10. Decision-making for democratic societies becomes a complex matter involving inputs from the courts, politicians, interests groups and so on. This essay, however, argues that many of these insights, although well-known, are ignored and not taken into consideration in most studies by present-day students of policy analysis in Canadian universities.

STUDY QUESTIONS

1. What are the major, continuing values underlying the making of public policy in Canada?
2. Do you agree with the insight that all policies are hypotheses? If not, why not?
3. Are regulatory policies in Canada and the United States likely to become more similar or dissimilar? Why?
4. In the formulation of public policy we have assumed that it is *better* for "the many" to be consulted than the "few". What does this say about policy-

making in Canada? Is consultation of the many absolutely necessary in public policy formulation and implementation in Western democracies?

5. To what extent should policy values or aspirations be constant in a country such as Canada? To what extent should they be entrenched in a country's constitution?

6. Is it likely that the Canadian bureaucracy will become more, or less, influential in the development of public policy? What is the basis of your conclusion?

7. To what extent should the development of public policy be seen as the search for final solutions or ultimate answers?

8. To what extent are our parliamentary institutions suited for the development of general public policy goals?

9. To what extent is policy content synonymous with party, or government party, ideology?

10. Are there any significant segments of the Canadian political apparatus which are not associated in an important way with the development of public policy?

ENDNOTES

1. Martin Landau, "On the Concept of a Self-Correcting Organization," *Public Administration Review*, No. 6, Vol. 33 (November/December 1973), pp. 533-42 at p. 537.

2. W.I. Jenkins, *Policy Analysis: A Political and Organisational Perspective* (London: Martin Robertson and Co. Ltd., 1978), p. 15.

3. Heinz Eulau and Kenneth Prewitt, *Labyrinths of Democracy*, (Indianapolis: Bobbs-Merrill, 1973), p. 481.

4. George H. Sabine, *A History of Political Theory* (Third Edition) (New York: Holt, Rinehart and Winston, 1961) pp. 928-9.

5. Barry M. Mitnick, The Political Economy of Regulation: Creating, Designing and Removing Regulatory Forms (New York: Columbia University Press, 1980).

6. Alexander Brady, "The State and Economic Life" in George W. Brown (ed.), *Canada* (Berkeley: University of California Press, 1950), p. 353.

7. G.B. Reschenthaler, "Direct Regulation in Canada: Some Policies and Problems" in W.T. Stanbury (ed.) *Studies on Regulation in Canada* (Montreal: IRPP, 1978) pp. 37-112.

8. For a much more thorough discussion of this aspect of policy-making see Sir Geoffrey Vickers, *Value Systems and Social Process* (New York: Basic Books, Inc., 1968) and his *The Art of Judgment: Making Institutions Work.* (London: Associated Business Programmes Ltd., 1973).

9. Charles O. Jones, *An Introduction to the Study of Public Policy* (2nd edition) (North Scituate, Mass.: Duxbury Press, 1977) p. 212.

10. Martin Landau, "On the Concept of a Self-Correcting Organization," *Public Administration Review*, Vol. 33, No. 6 (November/December 1973), pp. 533-42.

11. Martin Landau, "The Proper Domain of Policy Analysis" (21) *American Journal of Political Science* (May, 1977) pp. 423-7 at p. 425. This piece is one of five under the title: "The Place of Policy Analysis in Political Science: Five Perspectives."

12. *Ibid.*, p. 425-6.

13. Sir Geoffrey Vickers, *The Art of Judgment*, p. 33.

14. Walter Williams, "Special Issue on Implementation: Editor's Comments," *Policy Analysis*, Vol. 1 (Summer 1975), p. 451.

15. Charles O. Jones, *op. cit.*

16. T.J. Lowi, "American Business, Public Policy, Case Studies and Political Theory," *World Politics*, XVL, No. 4 (July, 1964), p. 688. For a more critical evaluation of the utility of Lowi's insights in the study of Canadian public policy see G. Bruce Doern and V. Seymour Wilson (eds.), *Issues in Canadian Public Policy* (Toronto: Macmillan, 1974), especially Chapters 1 and 6.

17. Lowi first conceptualizes policies in "terms of their impact or expected impact on the society" (Lowi, *op. cit.*, p. 689). Later, in discussing redistributive policy he argues that expectations about what it can be "...are determinative" (Lowi, *op. cit.*, p. 691).

18. Brian R. Fry and Mark E. Tompkins, "Some Notes on the Domain of Public Policy Studies," *Policy Studies Journal*, Vol. 6 (1978) pp. 305-13.

19. Carl J. Friedrich, *Constitutional Government and Politics* (New York: Harper and Row, 1937) Chapter 2.

20. V. Seymour Wilson, *Canadian Public Policy and Administration: Theory and Environment* (Scarborough: McGraw-Hill Ryerson, 1981) pp. 423-7.

21. Dwight Waldo, *The Enterprise of Public Administration* (California: Chandler and Sharp Publishers, 1980) p. 180.

22. Harold Lasswell, *Politics: Who Gets What, When, How* (New York: The World Publishing Company, 1971) p. 13.

23. Charles O. Jones, *An Introduction to the Study of Public Policy*, p. 6.

24. E.E. Schattschneider, *Two Hundred Million Americans in Search of a Government* (New York: Holt Rinehart and Winston, 1969) p. 53.

25. David Braybrooke and Charles E. Lindblom, *A Strategy of Decision* (New York: Free Press, 1963) p. 71.

SELECTED REFERENCES

The literature on public policy is generally not geared to the reading of first year students in political science. Perhaps more of it should be, but at the present time introductory public policy courses are set mainly for third and fourth year students in political science. The reasons for this are several, but some of it is merited: an understanding of moral and ethical issues involved in *Policy advocacy* means that the student should have mastered some knowledge in political philosophy, and *policy content analysis* usually calls for some knowledge of the empirical and methodological tools introduced in second year empirical courses in political science. I recommend two pieces in the literature suited to the reading of first year students. They represent the best of a very slim collection.

Anderson, James E. *Public Policy Making.* New York: Praeger, 1975. This book outlines the various ways public policy is viewed by social scientists. For a review of these perceptions see especially pp. 9-25.

Doern, G. Bruce and Peter Aucoin, eds. *The Structures of Policy Making in Canada.* Toronto: Macmillan, 1971. Concentrates on such aspects as instruments of policy-making (white papers, task forces), techniques and structures (budgetary tools, advisory councils), and evolutionary changes in structure and philosophy in cabinet structures. An excellent reference.

Doern, G. Bruce and V. Seymour Wilson, eds. *Issues in Canadian Public Policy.* Toronto: Macmillan, 1974. This book concentrates on the political dimensions of public policy analysis. It examines policy-making from the vantage point of both values and governing instruments and analyses several policy areas concurrently. An excellent reference but for more advanced students.

Eulau, Heinz and Kenneth Prewitt, *Labyrinths of Democracy.* Indianapolis: Bobbs-Merrill, 1973. On pp. 464-88, this book provides an excellent discussion on the various perspectives of public policy.

Hockin, Thomas, ed. *Apex of Power*, 2nd ed. Scarborough: Prentice-Hall, 1977. Focuses on the relationship of the prime minister of Canada to the Canadian political and governmental system. Balanced collection of readings on prime ministerial restraints, assets and policy influence. Highly recommended.

Ranney, Austin, ed. *Political Science and Public Policy.* Chicago: Markham, 1968. This book starts with the question: What professional expertise and obligations, if any, do political scientists have to study, evaluate, and make recommendations about the contents of public policies? The volume covers a broad array of problems from concepts and issues to substantive case studies of US domestic and foreign policy. Highly recommended, in particular Parts I and IV. Somewhat advanced for the beginning students, but suitable for many who are keenly interested in the subject.

Part Five

Canadian Politics: The Exercise of Power

The philosopher Hobbes once stated, "I put for a general inclination of mankind, a perpetual and restless desire of power after power, that ceaseth only in death." Whether or not we agree completely with Hobbes, the most elementary observation of Canadian society tells us that some people exercise political power and that others strive to displace them.

Numerous writers have commented on this fact. Some years ago Frederick Watkins asserted that, "The proper scope of political science is not the study of the state or of any other specific institutional complex, but the investigation of all associations insofar as they can be shown to exemplify the problem of power."[1] More recently William Robson declared, "It is with power in society that political science is primarily concerned—its nature, basis, processes, scope and results... The 'focus of interest' of the political scientist is clear and unambiguous; it centres on the struggle to gain or retain power, to exercise power or influence over others, or to resist that exercise."[2] The four chapters in this section define and assess four explanations of who holds political power.

The first chapter draws our attention to the individual wielders of power; the leaders who have championed causes, dominated political parties, headed governments and sometimes personified the nation. As Professor Young explains, these political leaders, partly because of television exposure, have become the focal points of our political system. "We may be forever unable scientifically to measure and explore the psyche of our political leaders, yet we ought to be properly aware of the impact of human behavior on the political system, especially in the office that is the vital center." He concludes: "Politics is, after all, about control of the levers of power, or the allocation of scarce resources authoritatively, if you must, and that, surely, is what leadership is all about."

In the second chapter we encounter the concept of elites, a notion some observers have explained as describing nothing more than the insight that any social form of action involves division of labor and influence. The idea that societies are dominated and manipulated by elites has been around for centuries. In our day, with the lengthening arm of government reaching ever wider afield, and with obvious connections existing between the political and economic elites, that notion is held with firm conviction by many people. Are such impressions rooted in fact? Professor Forcese assesses that orientation and suggests that, while the study of elites is an important approach to politics, we should always seek to study elites in terms of their interaction with non-elites. Moreover, we should always keep in mind that it is almost impossible to undertake any major political inquiry without somehow dealing with the question of elites or a ruling class.

The third chapter focuses on groups, specifically political interest groups. As pointed out by Professor Schwartz, group activity is widespread and involves both cooperation and conflict. We are reminded that "politics is inherently a group process" and that group analysis can tell us much about Canadian politics. It serves us well as an integrating concept, it is certainly important, but, as the author explains, if we try to make it all-inclusive we will probably find it inadequate.

Our last chapter challenges many of the key arguments advanced by other contributors. A Marxist analysis, we are told, "transcends the parochialism into which so much of the discussion of Canadian politics and economics descends." Only by asking the basic questions about Canadian society can we really come to grips with what Canadian politics involves. Marx has written: "The ultimate causes of all social changes and political revolutions are to be sought, not in the minds of men,... but in changes in the mode of production and exchange." And again, "The mode of production of the material means of existence conditions the whole process of social, political, and intellectual life." Given space limitations, Professor Resnick is not able to explain all the subtleties of a Marxist analysis but he states clearly why he believes that "Marxism poses an integrated social, political and economic theory" that best explains Canadian politics. At least implicitly he suggests that in analysing politics, theory, in this case Marxist theory, must be the vitally important starting point as well as the end point. Is he right?

ENDNOTES

1. Frederick M. Watkins, *The State as a Concept of Political Science* (New York: Harper, 1934), p. 83.

2. William A. Robson, *The University Teaching of Social Sciences: Political Science* (Paris: UNESCO, 1954), pp. 17-18.

12

Leadership and Canadian Politics

Walter D. Young*

No matter what the form of government the universal fact is the rule of the many by the few.
        Gaetano Mosca
        The Ruling Class

INTRODUCTION

As an approach to the study of Canadian politics, there is much to be said for an analysis of political leadership—not because our leaders have been men of heroic proportions and not because they and they alone have been the movers of events, but because the nature of our political institutions in both the broad and narrow sense places leaders at the center of our political consciousness. Although they are as much shaped by events as they shape them, political leaders are nevertheless the focal point of our political system. And however much the level of political awareness and sophistication increases, the importance of leadership moves in advance of it. Television may make the people more aware of what is happening, but it also makes them more aware of who appears to be making it happen. Leaders are more effective—and more powerful—because they have access to a highly effective and extremely malleable means of communication.

On the other hand the very complexity of modern politics places heavy demands on political leaders. Not only must they deal with the problems of government and politics at the executive level, they must also make government intelligible to the people governed, a people more conscious of national and

*Professor and Chairman, Department of Political Science, University of Victoria.

international concerns than ever before. Before the days of radio and television, the job of the leader was a good deal easier and the problems, in some respects, a good deal simpler. Not only were people less knowledgeable about national issues, but they expected less from their leaders, in large measure because they read and heard less about politics from both sides, apart, of course, from election campaigns. Today, the mass media provide an endless stream of political information, much of it presented in the context of the behavior of political leaders. By focusing almost exclusively on leaders, the mass media enhance their power. Constitutional battles become contests between leaders, just as the complexities of Canada's energy policy are reduced to a boxing match between the Prime Minister and the Premier of Alberta. The citizens of the modern state rely on their leaders to establish some kind of order from the welter of information with which they are constantly bombarded.

It is customary to think of a democratic system as one in which people are free to govern themselves, and in which popular participation precludes the rise of dictators. We are, it is true, some distance from the wicked days of absolute monarchy; but we are no less enthralled by our leaders, however much we limit their terms of office and their behavior by the elaborate trappings of constitutional government. Modern democracy has not lessened either the need or the demand for leadership; but it has increased both the demand and the need for information, much of it about leaders.

Our history is written very largely in terms of the people who led parties or a nation. Eras are defined by the leaders who dominated them: the reign of Henry VIII, the Mackenzie King era, the Diefenbaker period, the Eisenhower administration. This does not mean that these people made all the decisions; it does mean that they were the focus of government and of public attention. By virtue of the office they held, they were at the center of events and exerted a major influence. It is natural to view a particular period as characterized by the most prominent leader. There are equally valid arguments to support the view that leadership is as much a reflection of the historical circumstances as it is of the particular system. In fact, of course, one cannot disentangle one from the other; the system and the times conspire to provide us with one leader instead of another. It was once a popular view that history is really the biography of great men and it is still true that popular writers tend to reduce historical events to personal triumph or tragedy. Some of the most readable books about Canadian politics are heavily biographical and focused on one or another of our leaders: Richard Gwyn, *The Northern Magus* (Trudeau); Peter Newman, *Renegade in Power* (Diefenbaker); Geoffrey Simpson, *Discipline of Power* (Clark). Such a focus makes an era manageable and understandable.

Some scholars have argued that the kind or quality of leadership a state enjoys at any particular time is indicative of the quality of the political system itself.[1] While it is obvious that no leaders function in isolation from the political system in which they operate, it is also clear that democratic leaders have a great deal of power and that this power is a reflection not only of the constitutional framework within which they operate, but also of the innate need of people in modern society for leadership. The need tends to vary directly with a number of factors, the most obvious of which is political tension: war, insurrection, severe economic or social disorder, and so on. At the height of the FLQ crisis in 1970, there was an almost universal sense of relief when Prime Minister Trudeau appeared on television expressing his determination to deal with the situation by invoking the War Measures Act. The wide popular support for that decision was less a reflection of public disregard for civil liberties than an expression of support for Trudeau's leadership. Trudeau's timing was superb: he waited until public anxiety was evident, thereby ensuring wide support.[2] It was an interesting example of the effective exercise of the art of leadership.

The need for leadership is not reduced by increasing the availability of structures for participation; indeed higher levels of participation tend to heighten the need for leadership.[3] Different circumstances demand different kinds of leaders, but leadership is always an essential ingredient of politics. There is no evidence to suggest that higher levels of political awareness and literacy diminish either the need for or the reliance upon leadership. Indeed, the more complex and sophisticated life becomes, the more people seem to need someone or some group to provide direction and coherence.

LEADERSHIP DEFINED

A great deal has been written about leadership in general and about the different kinds of leadership.[4] Basically the relationship which we define as leadership is one in which one person or group of persons exercises influence, and another person or group submits willingly to that influence.[5] Coercion is not leadership although political leaders stand at the apex of government, that agency which has a monopoly on coercive power within the state.

There is both more and less to leadership than this definition implies. In Canada, as in most political systems, leadership does not consist of simply getting large numbers of people to do what the leaders want them to do. It is more a matter of getting large numbers of people to accept what the leaders have done or seem to have done, and to accept it not merely as legitimate but also as appropriate. The tacit acceptance of our political system as legitimate is what gives law its effectiveness; in other words, our obedience is not a function of our being led by the current prime minister. After all, many people disliked Mackenzie King intensely and disparaged his kind of leadership, but still obeyed the law. Within the modern constitutional framework, however, leadership lends comprehensibility and legitimacy to the political system. Instead of the vast and faceless bureaucracy, there is a prime minister who speaks for and to the nation. At a time when the engine of the state at both the federal and provincial levels is large and complicated, the existence of a single individual as the functioning head of the apparatus provides credibility and a much needed focus. The need for such a figure increases with the growth of the machine, and the power of such a figure increases accordingly.

When the Liberal government decided to invoke the War Measures Act during the FLQ crisis in 1970, the decision was not taken by the Prime Minister alone, although his views were undoubtedly the most influential. In our cabinet system of government, prime ministers do not enjoy the solitary decisiveness of the American president, for example. But for the nation the identification of one person with a crucial decision is an important part of the willingness to accept the decision as legitimate. As the nation's leader, Mr. Trudeau was not getting the people of Canada to do anything; he was exercising his influence in having them accept and support what his government was doing.

It is important to keep in mind that in most contemporary leader-follower relationships in government, outside of the prime minister-cabinet relationship, followers are passive and are led to accept what leaders do or what they represent. In other words, being a follower does not mean doing what the leader asks as much as it means accepting what the leader is doing or has done. And what the leader or the government is doing can be done to someone else—e.g. the FLQ members and the many others who were arrested under the War Measures Act—or it can be done to the followers themselves; for example, the citizens whose incomes were restricted by wage and price controls. For the most part then, the follower is merely a passive observer or recipient. This is perhaps less so in the case of a party leader and party members when leadership may galvanise members into doing more canvassing, giving more money, etc. The difference is that in this instance the followers have a choice.

LEADERS AND FOLLOWERS

The willingness of well-educated and sophisticated people to accept the leadership of a single individual can be explained, at least partially, as a normal response of creatures whose earliest experience was the authoritarian hierarchy of parent and child. A willingness to be led and, in times of crisis, an eagerness to be led, is as much a trait of people in civilised society as in primitive society. In both circumstances the individual's first conscious experience of organised society is within the family hierarchy. The relationship between the child and the parent through the most influential years establishes an authority pattern which is carried into adulthood. Adults not only behave deferentially toward those in a leadership role, but actively seek individuals to fill that role, especially in times of crisis. There is no evidence to indicate that levels of sophistication and maturity bear an inverse relationship to the need for leadership.

Equally important, of course, is the question of legitimacy. The popularity of leaders lends legitimacy to their actions and enhances the authority derived from whatever office they hold. Unpopular leaders may exercise the power bestowed on them by the constitution, but they thereby rely more on coercion than acceptance. Lech Walesa, leader of the illegal Solidarity trade union in Poland in 1980-81, was, by virtue of his popularity and that of his cause, accorded more legitimacy by the Poles than they accorded their constitutional rulers at the time. And for that reason Solidarity had some major successes.

The relationship of leaders and followers in modern society is complex. It was popular at one time to view leaders as people who "bore the stamp of greatness" and were in some way or other of heroic proportion and therefore born to lead or "born to be great". This concentration on the personality of the leader formed the basis of the "great man" thesis of history and led to the perception of leadership as a reflection of the singular personal traits of the leader.

It is important to understand the personality of any given leader because, obviously, a leader is not simply the person who happened to be closest to the phone when the cry "Who will save the country?" went up. But it is equally important to understand that circumstance is a major part of the equation. It has been aptly said that "leadership is a function of personality and of the social situation and of these two in interaction."[6] Winston Churchill's ability to lead the British people during World War II was as much due to the political and social circumstances of the time as to his own peculiar qualities. Once circumstances changed, as he so eloquently put it himself, he was "immediately dismissed by the British electorate from all further conduct of their affairs."[7]

At this point it is necessary to inject a cautionary note. It is almost too easy to discuss leadership with reference to such colossi as Churchill—to those figures who bestride human history as signal examples of leadership: Stalin, Roosevelt, Hitler, Mao Tse-tung, Gandhi, Kennedy. In each case the interaction of personality and circumstance is not difficult to discern. But there are other leaders and other circumstances. Mackenzie King was hardly a colossus but was nevertheless the leader of his party and his nation for longer than anyone before or since. The exercise of such leadership is perhaps more difficult to discern but it is still leadership. The lesser lights do lead but in a less obvious fashion.

KINDS OF LEADERSHIP

There is little that can be said about the personalities of leaders that would survive any rigorous analysis by a psychologist. Mackenzie King left a voluminous diary that is proving a veritable mother lode for psycho-historians and psycho-biographers determined to explore the mental processes of a man who was so significant a figure in his country's history.[8] For most leaders, however, the data for such analysis are inadequate. They may, however, be characterised by the kind of leadership they provide. Max Weber's categories of charismatic, patriarchal and bureaucratic leadership, are still the most useful.[9] The three are not mutually exclusive. Charismatic leaders are those who lead by virtue of some special personal quality or gift; patriarchal leaders lead because of their status based on experience, traditions, achievements and seniority; and bureaucratic leaders lead by virtue of the legal and purely rational situation in which they find themselves. John Diefenbaker was a charismatic leader in Canada during the period 1956-1969; after his deposition as leader he remained a patriarchal leader for many in the Conservative party and was therefore somewhat of a nuisance for his successor, Robert Stanfield, who was the formal and bureaucratic leader of the party, although never of the nation.

CHARISMATIC LEADERSHIP

The charismatic leader is the most interesting, largely because the great leaders have all been, in one way or another, charismatic. Charismatic leadership is the least stable kind of leadership but the most spectacular. Charismatic leaders are those who have special gifts; who are able to embody the goals or desires of the group they lead; who are, in some significant respects, larger than life and inspirational in their appeal. As Irving Schiffer points out, charismatic leaders are not perfect, but they exemplify the most desired characteristics of their nation at the time of their leadership.[10] The success of John Diefenbaker and the subsequent phenomenon of Trudeaumania are useful demonstrations of charismatic leadership in a modern society. While the enthusiasm generated by Diefenbaker and Trudeau cannot be compared with that produced by the Rolling Stones or Elvis Presley, for example, both phenomena show that the advance of civilisation, and the increased levels of sophistication that such progress brings, does not reduce either the need for or the reliance upon leadership and the continued need for idols.

Because charismatic leaders seem to answer a need, or to personify the goals of the bulk of the people, they are able to exercise authority that bureaucratic leaders would lack. This authority is the product of a marriage of exceptional personal traits and propitious circumstances that is usually fortuitous. The aura that surrounds these leaders generates deference and obedience, and enhances their power. Normally party leaders have certain prerogatives by virtue of their offices themselves. Charismatic leaders have these powers plus those generated by their charisma. And if their charisma is successful nationally (or provincially) and they bring the party they lead to power, then as prime minister they are in a commanding position since victory will be perceived as a result of their appeal, not that of the party *per se*. Until their governments' fortunes begin to slide, they will remain in a position of considerable authority.

It is possible to overdo the notion of charisma and to attempt to find this elusive characteristic in every successful leader. It may be the case, indeed probably is more often than not, that a successful leader happens to be someone who has a good mind, quick wit, a flair for oratory and larger than average ambition. These characteristics may or may not be part of a mixture that spells charisma, but they can often be just as useful as Weber's concept in explaining a leader's success. What the student of Canadian politics must keep in mind is that the personalities of leaders are consequential and may be a major source of their authority within the party or within the nation. Loyalty helps perpetuate leadership, and loyalty may be a response to more homely virtues than to the more flamboyant features of charismatic figures. Robert Stanfield and, to some extent, Lester Pearson, were men who inspired loyalty more than they radiated charisma.

BUREAUCRATIC LEADERSHIP

The bureaucratic leader is the individual who holds an office that confers on its occupant the highest level of authority within the particular organization. While the election or appointment of the individual to that office can be taken as evidence of some superior qualities, it is often the case that seniority alone will ensure an individual reaching the top. In the case of political parties, longevity may serve as the ladder for internal party officials—one becomes national president of the New Democratic Party in some measure because of yeoman service—but it does not offer much assistance to the person who would be leader. Yet all political parties in Canada have at one time or another been led by men who were bureaucratic leaders in that their authority came more from the office than from some particular qualities they possessed.

For the Conservative party John Bracken is perhaps the outstanding example. Recruited directly by the party's patriarch, Arthur Meighen, he left the comfort of the premier's office in Manitoba to become one of the more uninspiring leaders of that party.[12] Louis St. Laurent succeeded Mackenzie King as leader of the Liberal party; although elected over other contestants in a leadership convention, he was the hand-picked successor and until he assumed the avuncular image that characterized his final years in office, a kind of patriarchal charisma, he was a bureaucratic leader—his authority stemmed more from the office he held than from any outstanding personal trait. He was, after all, Prime Minister, and that does do something for a person's influence.[13]

LEADERSHIP AND COMMUNICATION

Successful leaders constantly watch themselves being watched. Few people study the behavior of leaders more carefully than do the leaders themselves. They must be constantly aware of how well or badly they are doing in their various constituencies: cabinet, caucus, party, nation. There is always a danger that they may be getting wrong information; some leaders make the fatal error of surrounding themselves with people who will bring only good news. But since leadership is a process of interaction between leader and led, leaders must be sensitive to the effect they are having on the people around them.

Never before has the apparatus of communication been so beneficial to the successful leader. The assistance lent by television to the dramaturgy of leadership is quite remarkable. The elaborate attention to costume and behavior that was such a large part of Trudeaumania was successful very largely because television enabled several million Canadians to see the Prime Minister at the Grey Cup game in a wide-brimmed black impresario's hat with flowing scarf and cape or emerging from Parliament in an open-necked shirt and sandals. All the devices designed to declare to the public that here is someone special are heavily dependent on the news media, principally television. When Parliament is in session, and especially since the televising of sittings began, the prime minister has a daily opportunity to impress himself on the nation and, it follows, on his party. But reaching those commanding heights is difficult, and staying there no simple task, television and a hungry audience notwithstanding.

The mass media can also undermine a leader. The unfortunate history of Joe Clark underlines this point. The coverage of his ill-planned world tour in 1979 served to establish an image of him as awkward, clumsy and indecisive. In striving to overcome this perception he only exacerbated the problem. His initial refusal to back down from hastily made campaign promises in 1979 helped defeat his party and government in 1980. Once cast, a leader's image is difficult to remould, especially since the mass media themselves tend to follow the lead of their principal commentators. In Clark's case, Allan Fotheringham, columnist for *Maclean's* and the *Vancouver Sun*, was his undoing.

Leaders often appoint to their personal staff men and women with experience in communications, usually former newspaper or television journalists, or people from the advertising trade, to advise them and ensure that their personality and behavior are consistent with public expectation. As Dion has put it, "The successes of great political leaders in the past have been closely related to their ability to understand and express the sentiments of the followers."[14] If leaders are elected because they are perceived as models or ideal figures, they must work to ensure that the voters will retain that perception. The elaborate public relations apparatus that exists in the prime minister's office or within the staff of a provincial premier is best understood in this context. The influence of people like Keith Davey in the Liberal party and Dalton Camp in the Conservative party attests to the importance placed on advice from experts in the arcane techniques of public relations.

The personalities of leaders and their ability to choose men and women to work with them serve to further enhance their authority. A loyal bank of "right-hand men" will serve to reinforce their position. The growth of the Prime Minister's Office (PMO) under Pierre Trudeau provides a useful example of a leader bolstering his position in the several constituencies within which he must work: cabinet, caucus, party, nation. By providing him with the administrative apparatus to keep him abreast of developments within each of these constituencies, and with expert advice as well as the public relations services discussed above, the PMO is a crucial adjunct to the role of the leader.[15] The prime minister must be careful, however, to ensure that the PMO does not restrict supporters' access or usurp those positions usually filled by cabinet members or cabinet committees.[16]

The PMO may help the prime minister with the constituencies he must serve but the ordinary party leader doesn't have such an apparatus and even prime ministers must from time to time substitute their own judgment for that of their professional advisors. Their first constituency must be their party; that constituency has two dimensions: the party itself in its federal riding-by-riding manifestation; and the party in Parliament, the caucus.

CHOOSING LEADERS

The party leader is chosen by the party membership through delegates to national leadership conventions after a vigorous and usually costly campaign.[17] The stakes are high for, in the case of the two major parties, the victor is either leader of the opposition or prime minister. The convention is also an important publicity occasion, for both the party and its future leader. The campaign and the final balloting have assumed much of the drama of American presidential elections. The campaign for leadership provides the candidates with an opportunity to demonstrate their capacity to attract support and, most important, elicit a favorable response from the media. This is not always achieved by an elaborate and expensive campaign. The experience of Brian Mulroney in the Tory leadership race that chose Joe Clark is a good example of this. Equally, it was a relatively low key, almost last minute campaign, that preceded the Liberal choice of Pierre Trudeau as Lester Pearson's successor in 1968. Despite the magicians in public relations, it remains the case that sow's ears cannot be made invisible.

The convention itself is a demonstration of the significance of the national party, and the successful leader is the one who does not ignore the party rank and file. But the leader's contact with the party at the local riding level is inevitably sporadic and, from the point of view of the leader as party decision-maker, of little value. The parliamentary party or caucus is the most important party body. Within this body a leader must demonstrate political skill at close range in order to maintain stature and authority.

The caucus will usually include most of the leader's rivals for office and, possibly, the previous incumbent. It will also reflect the ideological divisions within the party as well as the regional antagonisms that are so typically Canadian. Caucus-leader relations are more difficult for a leader of the opposition than for a prime minister for the latter carries both the aura of the office and the potential for making ministers of back-benchers and senators of the weary — a not inconsiderable asset in the process of encouraging loyalty and support.

THE LEADER AS PARTY CHIEFTAIN

By being chosen leader of the party, the individual is placed in an institutional situation which provides a degree of authority that the ordinary party member does not possess. Rank and file members will, as a rule, defer to the leader. The loyalty of party members to their leader is perhaps only surpassed by a fan's loyalty to the local hockey team. The leader's role in policy-making is pre-eminent and through the media of the press and television that individual becomes the party's most visible electoral commodity. If the party is not in power, the leader is number two in any debate as leader of the opposition, and to the present, in any event, number three if leader of the NDP.

Parties will usually cast off the leader who fails since success in party leadership is measured by electoral victory. In some circumstances this does not hold: M.J. Coldwell continued to lead the CCF despite successive electoral failures. Victory was not anticipated and, in any case, Coldwell's role as moral leader of his party ensured his continuing in office. The same was true for his successors as leaders of the NDP, T.C. Douglas and David Lewis. Unlike the Liberal and Conservative parties, the NDP looks to its leaders as exemplars as much as political strategists.

Not only does the office of party leader confer upon its holder a major portion of authority within the party structure, but that authority is further enhanced by the externalities of the office. To the outside world the leader *is* the party, and as such is expected to make definitive statements on matters of national and international concern in Canada. Leaders will be criticised both within their party and nationally by press and party members alike if they consistently fail to do this effectively.

An interesting and useful example of this particular phenomenon is the career of Joe Clark. In the space of eighteen months he passed from anonymity to national prominence. By any objective standard it would be difficult to deduce from an examination of the early career of Joe Clark that he was destined to be leader of the Conservative party, Prime Minister, and leader of Her Majesty's opposition, or wield the power that those offices confer on their holder. Apart, perhaps, from his mother, few would have discerned anything that might have been taken for a mark of greatness. His meteoric career provides a useful example of the marriage of ambition with circumstance.

Clark was helped by a contest in which there did not appear to be any obvious winner, by his finely tuned organization, and by the added bonus derived from the fact that his most serious opponent represented Québec — not in itself a difficult thing for the Conservative party to digest, but Claude Wagner had been a Liberal as well. As victor, Clark had the customary period of grace in which he enjoyed a kind of immunity from both internal and external criticism. The last phase of this period coincided with a series of political misfortunes for the Liberal government of Prime Minister Trudeau, which served to catapult the fortunes of the Conservative party and its new leader into a commanding lead in the Gallup poll.

The point, of course, is that circumstance served not only to cement his position as party leader after a somewhat divisive leadership campaign but to enhance his authority within the party despite the fact that he did relatively little as leader during his first year in office. The fact remained that he was the only leader the party had, the stock in trade of every new leader, and a new leader, by virtue of that fact alone, is able to command the allegiance of the rank and file of the party and of the party caucus itself. The Liberals' difficulties were a bonus.

But the fickle nature of Dame Fortune was revealed when the Parti Québécois came to power in Québec in November 1976 and the electorate veered back to a position that had contributed in a major way to Robert Stanfield's discomfiture: Pierre Trudeau appeared to be the best person to deal with a difficult Québec. The low profile Joe Clark had adopted and that had served him well as long as the Liberal Government seemed bent on self-destruction, became a liability. Pundits and editorial writers took him to task in the winter and spring of 1977 for his failure to enunciate the policy of the official opposition. His tactic was largely designed to give the party time to heal the wounds from the leadership campaign but it served instead to make him a target. The rapid decline in his party's position in the opinion polls as reported in March 1977 considerably weakened his position as leader. The loss of Jack Horner, MP, who had contested the leadership against Clark and had sat as a Tory from Alberta for 19 years, was another blow. Horner crossed the floor in April 1977, and became a Liberal cabinet minister. In the same way that circumstance may work to catapult politicians into the highest office in their party, it may also undermine their position. The test of effective leadership is, then, longevity and the ability to take advantage of good winds and be close to a snug harbour in the storms.

Clark's predecessor, Robert Stanfield, had mixed results as party leader. He led the party through three general elections and was unsuccessful in each. The intriguing feature of his career was not his inability to win elections for his party—there were Conservatives in the past who also excelled in that respect; rather, it lay in the universal affection and respect in which he was held amongst his intimates, his caucus and the press.[18] Unable to project his undeniably sterling qualities to the multitude of Canadian voters and faced with a Liberal government that was, at that juncture, relatively free from those peculiarly Liberal signs of age, arrogance and bad management, he failed.

He had as well a particularly awkward burden for a party leader, namely, the presence in the party caucus of his predecessor, John Diefenbaker. Diefenbaker was propelled out of the leadership by a cabal within the party apparatus and actually contested the leadership against Stanfield, and others. He remained in the caucus emitting all the baleful radiance of a whore at a family wedding. Clark was not spared this numbing presence, but the eight intervening years served to dim the Diefenbaker effulgence. Moreover, Clark was not associated with the anti-Diefenbaker coup that had begun in the final years of the Diefenbaker administration.

The brief career of Joe Clark as prime minister illustrates the fragility of political success. Beset by an image of indecisiveness and ineptitude, his determination to be decisive only served to make him appear more inept. He effectively denied himself the flexibility a leader must have. Elected in 1979 largely as the result of a decline in support for Trudeau's leadership, Clark accomplished the impossible by losing less than a year later to the same man, after Trudeau had declared he was retiring as leader and his party was about to choose a successor. After the 1980 election the Conservative party convention voted narrowly against a leadership review and Clark's hold on the leadership remained tenuous. [19]

This serves to show the extent to which the interweaving of man, circumstance and followers serves both to create and to undermine leadership. The authority leaders exercise over their immediate followers and over the rank and file of their party in the nation is a product of their capacity to turn events to their advantage; of their capacity to maintain their authority in the party caucus by the skillful management of people and the effective utilisation of events; and of their popularity in the nation itself as demonstrated by opinion polls, press coverage and the response to their public appearances. There is much that is under the control of leaders themselves, but equally there is much that is beyond their personal control.

THE LEADER AS PRIME MINISTER

For party leaders who also become prime minister the process is both easier and more difficult, with the edge going to the former. They have the formal power of their office which places them at the apex of the apparatus of government. [20] In an Order-in-Council to his cabinet, Mackenzie King outlined the prerogatives of the prime minister which included the appointment of all cabinet ministers, dissolution and convocation of parliament, and a number of other appointments including Treasury Board, senators and deputy ministers. According to John Diefenbaker, "More important in many ways was the convention that gave the Prime Minister total control of cabinet discussion." [21] Both aspects of the prime minister's authority are important to the effective performance of prime ministerial duties; they also serve to enhance his effectiveness as party leader.

The interests of the party and the government frequently intersect. The prime minister, by virtue of the prerogative of appointments, is in a position to reward the faithful party servant or the tired parliamentarian with appointments to the bench, the senate or the diplomatic service. As the key figure in the administration of this kind of patronage the prime minister as party leader is able to keep fences mended and troops loyal. The national president of the Liberal Federation of Canada, on assuming that office, is virtually assured a seat in the Senate if he is not already there. The Conservative party functions in the same manner although it has enjoyed fewer years in office and hence has not been able to make the most effective use of that particular device. In summary, the prime minister uses the powers of the office to serve his purposes as leader of the party.

THE PARTY AND ITS LEADER: THE NDP

The parliamentary system dictates that before one can be a leader of the nation, i.e. Prime Minister, one must first be the leader of the party. There are two types of party in Canada, roughly speaking: those which exercise fairly strict control over the party leader, and those which elect a leader and are prepared to follow, always assuming that victory lies in the direction he leads. There is really only one party in the first category, and that is the NDP, successor to the CCF. Describing itself as a democratic party, the NDP not only elects its leader democratically, as the other parties do, it does so at every biennial convention. It is most unusual, however, for the leader to be challenged during what must be described as a ritual expression of democratic intent. It has happened, however, at the provincial level where the party leader is subjected to the decision of the delegates at annual conventions. In British Columbia in 1967 and in Ontario in 1968 the incumbent was challenged. In both cases the challenge was beaten back but the message was clear, and in both cases the incumbent resigned within two years and a new leader was chosen. The challenge produced a deep rift in the party as a whole, a rift that was slow to heal.

What seems important about the party that provides for the regular review of its leadership, whether that opportunity is regularly used to challenge the leader or not, is that this constitutional provision reflects a spirit or ethos in the party that makes demands on a leader that other parties do not make and poses unique problems for that party's leader when in power. The democratic norms that such procedures reflect are themselves an indication of the party's commitment to a specific ideology and of the membership's commitment to an individualist ethic in the interpretation and expression of the party ideology. The kind of person attracted to such a political organization and the kind of behavior these norms elicit — active, vocal, anti-authoritarian — demand a kind of leadership that is managerial, conciliatory and consensus-oriented. The leadership typified by M.J. Coldwell in the era of the CCF and by Ed Schreyer of Manitoba and Alan Blakeney of Saskatchewan in the case of the NDP, reflects this feature of the CCF/NDP.

In this instance leadership is a useful indicator of the character of the party. To the extent that a party has more on its agenda than winning elections, the party's leader will necessarily reflect these interests. The selection of a leader will be influenced by factors that are a product of the party's internal needs. No party is going to ignore the need to choose a leader who will be able to increase the party's support among the electorate at large but in a party such as the NDP the order of priorities is different and the kind of leader chosen will reflect this difference.

In the case of the NDP these priorities include the expression of a socialist philosophy, the provision of a political agency through which the members may express their own interpretation of that philosophy and, as important as the preceding two, the provision of a vehicle which provides its membership with well-defined roles for participation in the policy-making and organizational aspects of the party. People do not, as a rule, join the NDP in order to advance their status in Canadian society. They do not join in order to ensure either advancement or the ear of the government—unless, of course, the party has been in office for a reasonable period of time; for the most part people join parties like the NDP in order to share in the business of politics. It follows that the kind of leader they select would be one who facilitates this kind of membership, whose style of leadership does not pose a threat to the democratic norms of the party and does not interfere with the established rights of the membership to participate in policy-making. Where the NDP has formed the government and the leader has not behaved in a manner consistent with the party norms, the party reaction has been hostile, especially among the most active members—as was the case in British Columbia during the second year of the NDP term of office under the leadership of David Barrett.

THE PARTY AND ITS LEADER: THE LIBERALS AND THE TORIES

With the Liberal and Conservative parties, a different game is played. The objectives of these two parties are more clearly understood and in some ways more basic: winning power and keeping power. Membership is less important and the norms of democracy are less rigidly adhered to; both Liberal and Conservative parties accord defeated candidates the right to be delegates to conventions which the NDP does not do. This may be more a reflection of the relative numbers involved than of inherent differences, although it is not likely. Moreover, the kind of people who do join the Liberal or Conservative party are less likely to be anxious to play so active a part as many who join the NDP. They will tend, by and large, to be more subservient to authority and therefore more readily led. Membership in the Liberal and Conservative parties is more a statement of interest than a declaration of intent.

Accordingly, the leaders of these two parties have a somewhat easier time of it, especially if they are successful. Success is measured by two criteria. One, which is obvious, is the number of elections won; the other, which is more important to the leader who is in opposition, is the track record in the opinion polls. These are not the only means whereby party members judge their leaders; other less obvious measures range from the ability of the leader to accommodate the conflicting interests within the party's ruling cliques to the ability to control the cabinet or caucus.

The selection of party leader by a convention of party delegates alters the traditional assumptions about the source of a prime minister's power. As the choice of the party at large, that is, the party outside Parliament, the prime minister has an additional authority base. As a leader moves from success at the convention to success at the polls, as Pierre Trudeau did in 1968, it is not difficult for both leader and followers to view the leader's authority as stemming from these two electoral contests rather than from his position in Parliament. Accordingly, the leader would pay less attention to Parliament, and have less respect for the institution.[22]

The leaders of the Liberal and Conservative parties need only their mastery of the arts of management within three arenas whereas the leader of the NDP has four. The Liberal or Conservative leader who is also prime minister needs to lead in both cabinet and party caucus. Neither is a particularly difficult task although the standard view would seem to indicate that these two forums are most seriously restrictive. The evidence, for the most part, would seem to indicate the opposite. It is one of the more interesting features of cabinet government that ministers are often prepared to accept quite appalling behavior on the part of their leader presumably because he has control of their political futures, and they are unwilling to jeopardise their careers to further some principle or other which the voters are not likely to appreciate in any case.

Perhaps one of the most classic instances was Mackenzie King's sacrifice of his Defence Minister, J.L. Ralston, in 1944.[23] Ralston had submitted his resignation to King in 1942 on a point of principle, the principle being that the national referendum on conscription indicated the government should take immediate action to reinforce the overseas contingents when the exigencies of battle demanded it, without recourse to Parliament. King, no lover of immediate action on any question, disagreed with this point of view but refused to accept Ralston's resignation, although he kept Ralston's letter. Two years later, when it suited King's purposes to replace Ralston with General A.G.L. MacNaughton, he resurrected the letter, flourished it before a stunned cabinet, and Ralston was out. None of Ralston's colleagues made a move to protest.

Maurice Duplessis was unquestionably the most dictatorial of our provincial premiers. His control over his cabinet colleagues was absolute, even to the point of gross and unrelenting interference with their portfolios and, in some cases, with their personal lives. Antonio Barrette, who later succeeded Paul Sauvé as premier and leader of the Union Nationale, was barred from cabinet meetings, although he kept his portfolio as Minister of Labour, for over a year because Duplessis was annoyed with his behavior in connection with a construction contract. Duplessis even issued orders that the Château Frontenac not serve Barrette any meals so that Barrette, who lived in the hotel, had to go out to eat.[24] Duplessis made all major decisions, expected and received abject declarations of fealty from his ministers, all of whom were clearly unwilling to make even the slightest move to resurrect their own dignity in the face of possible dismissal from a cabinet in which, undoubtedly, access to the pork-barrel was a function of total obedience.[25]

In both cases the authority of the party leader was absolute. No one within the caucus or the cabinet was willing to challenge such authority. Such concentration of power may be explained by the personality of the leader; by the personalities of those who serve under him (after all, a leader would not knowingly name to the cabinet all his chief rivals unless convinced that they were less harmful inside than out); or by the circumstances prevailing at the time. Without more evidence than that presently available, an explanation based on the analysis of personalities and motives is likely to be inconclusive. What is clear, however, is that the nature of the party and parliamentary systems in Canada serves to enhance the position of the prime minister, especially if the political circumstances are propitious.

The prime minister, who is seen by cabinet colleagues and by the House or legislative assembly as being both the architect of victory and the talisman for continued success, is in a virtually impregnable position. There are few checks on his authority for as long as the cabinet is prepared to accept his direction. The House of Commons cannot limit the power of the prime minister with a solid cabinet and a loyal caucus, and these latter two are virtually synonymous. Unlike the American president, who must reckon with Congress as well as with a precise and limited term of office, premiers and prime ministers who are the undoubted masters of their parties have an almost medieval power. No other explanation seems reasonable for the kind of power exercised by Mackenzie King, W.A.C. Bennett, E.C. Manning, Maurice Duplessis, Pierre Trudeau, or John Diefenbaker in the early months of his first ministry.

THE ART OF LEADERSHIP

Joseph Wearing has suggested that such circumstances as the dismissal of Ralston and other examples of prime ministerial autocracy, including R.B. Bennett's New Deal addresses and Pearson's secret meetings with Québec officials on the pension plan, are best seen as indications of a "pathological condition in the Canadian political system."[26] These and other examples displayed a leader working desperately to stave off collapse, collapse that was itself a product of his failure to generate consensus among his colleagues by the arts of persuasion and firm leadership. Undeniably these specific acts were taken during difficult times for the governments concerned. The fact remains, however, that the power to take action unilaterally was not challenged in most cases. Indeed, in the case of Pearson and King, and even Bennett, the moves referred to demonstrate the kind of decisiveness that the government and nation yearned for. Having set the machine in motion, the party and nation expect it to be driven. It is in the absence of decisive leadership that the pathological condition develops and with its exercise that the condition is ameliorated.

By focusing attention on the center or at the apex of the pyramid, it becomes clear that the political system in Canada generates a demand for leadership. There seems to be little doubt that the politicians who have remained longest in office have demonstrated early in their careers as premier or prime minister a capacity for fairly authoritarian leadership within the structure of government itself, particularly at the provincial level where the ability to lead is enhanced by the relatively higher incidence of amateurism in politics.

Equally important, however, is the extent to which the premiers and prime minister use their authority to delegate power to their cabinet colleagues. Duplessis and W.A.C. Bennett did little or no delegation. In the case of the former, virtually all major decisions, regardless of the department, were made by *le Chef.* Mackenzie King, on the other hand, gave to colleagues like C.D. Howe and J.G. Gardiner almost a free hand within their areas of responsibility. Gardiner was the prime minister for the prairies. It was small wonder then that ministers would be loath to give up their fiefdoms in support of colleagues who were foolish enough to place theirs in jeopardy. The art of skillful delegation and management of the barons so created is the art of leadership and when well handled undoubtedly enhances the authority of the person in charge.

When the prime minister begins to lose his grip, when he no longer has those tokens that denote power, when his mistakes begin to outnumber triumphs, his power begins to disintegrate rapidly. It was only four years from Diefenbaker's triumphant and overwhelming victory in 1958 to the ignominy of 1962 which saw the largest parliamentary majority in Canadian history reduced to a minority government of 119 seats. Within the party and the cabinet itself there was growing dissatisfaction with the ledership of John Diefenbaker, a man whose electoral charisma far exceeded his capacity to manage a government. By 1962 he had succeeded in alienating the business community, antagonizing the United States, and annoying the British government. In his cabinet, ministers were moving uneasily on the balls of their feet, waiting for the first sign of collapse and ready to jump with the majority.[27]

The most common explanation for Diefenbaker's failure is that he suffered from a lack of decisiveness and an overabundance of ambition. Unlike Mackenzie King, he was unable to delegate effectively, a weakness that was multiplied by his almost pathological suspicion of many of his colleagues, notably those who displayed anything remotely approaching an independence of mind. A touch of paranoia may indeed be a salutary defect in a leader; an excess, however, can make a wreckage of a ministry in short order.[28] In Diefenbaker's case, the collapse of his government in 1962, following the resignation of Douglas Harkness from the cabinet, set the stage for his subsequent removal from the leadership itself some five years later. This was the direct result of the party's national president, Dalton Camp, actively campaigning against him.

Diefenbaker's experience, however painful it may have been to him, is nevertheless instructive for students of Canadian politics. By 1962 he had failed to establish a Conservative foothold in Québec; he had lost a large portion of his party's power base in Ontario by alienating the business establishment which had previously supported the Conservatives; and he had weakened the party's hold on the West Coast. Only in the Prairie Provinces was the Tory party's hold firm. Once his party was defeated in 1963, Diefenbaker was vulnerable in the extreme. His failure to recoup his losses in 1965 against the remarkably lacklustre Pearson government sealed his fate. He could no longer lead the party because he had nothing to offer it.

His record as Prime Minister was not distinguished beyond the fact that he had brought the party from the wilderness to power. But then he successfully led it back into the wilderness in less than five years as well. His inability to satisfy the power brokers in central Canada gave him only very limited leverage on the party machinery. Party leaders in the Canadian system, indeed in most political systems, must have some currency in their pockets, so to speak. A bankrupt leader cannot lead. Diefenbaker had the party's highest office but it was of no use to him. He became the first party leader and former prime minister to be defeated in convention by his own party as a candidate for the office of which he was the most recent incumbent. His defeat was prefigured by the successful re-election of Dalton Camp as party president in 1966 on a clear and specific commitment to an early leadership convention.[29] Soon after his fall from power in 1980, Joe Clark heard Robert Coates, national president of the Progressive Conservative party, call for a review of his leadership and express criticism of his stewardship of the party's fortunes.

The Canadian political system does not deal kindly with defeated leaders. What, after all, is a better measure of an individual's capacity for leadership than his record of defeats? This is not the case with the minor parties for there the scale of victory is much smaller: an increase in the number of seats, an upward shift in the Gallup poll or the steady growth in the popular vote. These and other lesser advances are the stuff of success for the individual who leads the NDP or Créditiste parties.

The Conservative party has had to cultivate a taste for defeat and this has induced a degree of brittleness in the party so that it cannot abide leaders who do not succeed and therefore chooses its leaders with what some would describe as an almost desperate anxiety to find individuals with the talisman of victory about them. This helps explain the Conservative tendency to reach down into provincial politics to recruit a successful provincial politician in the hope that the same trick can be turned at the federal level. Typical Conservative leaders do not have the same parliamentary background as do their Liberal counterparts. With the exception of Borden, Manion, Meighen and Diefenbaker, the remaining four Conservative leaders since the turn of the century had most of their experience in provincial politics. Bracken, Drew and Stanfield had no federal experience. Joe Clark was virtually an unknown junior backbencher when he became leader. Stanfield's principal opponent for the leadership, Duff Roblin, was, like Stanfield, a successful provincial premier with no federal experience. Clark's opponent at the last ballot, Claude Wagner, had made his reputation in Québec provincial politics as a Liberal.[30]

Unlike the Conservatives, the Liberals are the party of power in Canada, and have the resilience that constant exercise of power brings. Moreover, by virtue of their long tenure, they have built up a back-log of experienced politicians and administrators at the federal level. Persistence of power breeds cohesion in the same way that it blurs principle. Parties that are unable to win power, although they are in the position of the alternative government, are constantly looking both for scapegoats and panaceas. Parties accustomed to power know that retaining power requires unity, and unity becomes very important. A party out of office will find itself badly divided over a policy issue and its leader weakened by supporting one side or another because the issue is seen by both sides as crucial to success. The Conservative party's adoption of wage and price controls as a plank in the 1974 election divided the party. The Liberal rejection of the policy in the campaign and its later implementation of the policy was accepted by Liberals with equanimity. Those in power live in the world of expediency and thereby, it would seem, stay in power. Those out of power sample every potion available in the hope that one will prove to be the elixir of victory and they readily fall to quarreling over which holds the most promise.

The task then of the leader of the opposition party is the more difficult and more fraught with danger. So much does the system emphasise the office of the leader of the party in power, that it is only an extraordinary leader of an opposition party who is able to appear to be innovative, devastating, or in any way a strikingly attractive alternative. For one thing the leader of the opposition does not have the aura of a prime minister in the eyes of the viewing public; for another, it is difficult for him to avoid giving the appearance of desperation from time to time as he struggles to get a flash of the limelight. His counterpart in the American system emerges only during the election year when conventions and primaries generate the atmosphere of elemental battle in which all bets are open. Not for the presidential candidate the role of the weary challenger about to make one more attempt at the title. Few candidates have made two runs at the presidency and succeeded. Robert Stanfield, in contrast, became leader in 1968, and led his party through three campaigns before calling it a day after the 1974 election.

Leaders of opposition parties have a difficult task. Their stock in trade consists of the mandate their party has given them by electing them leaders; the possibility that they may become prime minister or premier and therefore have portfolios at their disposal; and the abilities and internal support that brought them the leadership in the first place.

One of the arts of leadership that is falling into desuetude is the art of using the authority of leadership to educate and guide the public. Today's political leaders are too much the captives of the image makers and advertising experts and, as a consequence, avoid setting out directions which their advisors tell them the public do not accept. In these circumstances leaders tend to prefer to stay with the prevailing view in order to retain power. As a consequence the opportunity to use the focal power of the office to shift the public gaze is often neglected. It is too easy to identify the public interest with the popular or majority interest. Perhaps the true test of effective leadership is the capacity to make the unpopular acceptable. With the vast reach of the mass media at their disposal, contemporary political leaders can effectively educate their followers, if they are prepared to put their capacity as leaders to the test.

CONCLUSION

As an approach to the understanding of Canadian politics, the study of leadership has much to recommend it, particularly in that it will illuminate much of the reality behind the traditional facade of parliamentary government. Much that a study of the institutions of parliamentary government in Canada will necessarily leave out can be provided by an examination of the role and power of the party leader and the prime minister as party and national leader. In the same way that one cannot really understand our politics without some understanding of the party system, so too an understanding of the party system is dependent in considerable measure on an understanding of the role of the leader. And in the areas of administration and communications in politics, once again the position of the leader is of much significance. Premiers and prime ministers alike must be aware of the tendency of their advisors and senior bureaucrats to sift and shape information before passing it up.[31]

How is it possible for us to understand how decisions are made in government without understanding the impact of the presence of a single figure at the apex of the mechanism? If everything in government is political, then the over-arching concern must reflect the awareness of the demands, real or imagined, of the leader. The advisors who surround the modern leader are not insulated from the leader's aura. They will tend to shape their advice to suit their perception of the leader's needs. These advisors serve both to keep the leader informed and insulated. Some of the criticism of the leadership of Pierre Trudeau centered on the role of the Prime Minister's Office (which grew tenfold in size under his direction) in filtering information. The importance of this element in our political system is not diminishing; it is growing. The complexity of government taxes leaders, making leadership more important, which at the same time increases the distance between the leader and the led.

It is nevertheless wise to keep in mind the need to understand the relationship between the leader and led, between the leader and his support mechanisms; between the leader and his cabinet colleagues, party caucus, party members, and the public at large; as well as between the leader and the party elite who are not necessarily in cabinet or caucus. Those who finance parties and, of greater importance, those who finance and run large and powerful corporations that dominate major industries, have an important relationship with party leaders that may be either symbiotic or antagonistic. For the Liberal and Conservative parties the economic elite wield a significant influence on the leader; for the New Democratic party the leaders of the major trade unions cannot be ignored. The relationship between these elites and the purely political elite, especially the party leaders, is an important element in Canadian politics.

There is as well a further advantage in the approach to Canadian politics through leadership, and that is that it ensures an awareness of the practical, earthy, intensely human reality of politics. The precision and clarity of a well-modeled systems analysis, or the charm of institutional description derived from historical precedent, tend to conceal the impact of greed, envy, ambition and deference. Because a good deal of emotion swirls around the office of leader, this approach does retain some of that quality of what is, after all, an intensely human endeavor. We may be forever unable to measure and explore scientifically the psyche of our political leaders, but we ought to be properly aware of the impact of human behavior on the political system, especially on the office that is the vital center.

The danger in the approach is a function of the fascination for the great individual serving to cloud judgment and mask the significance of the other elements of government. The exercise of leadership is a multi-dimensional enterprise that involves both action and reaction to the forces that are the results of decisions made by other levels of government, and in other centers of power in society. No leader acts in isolation. So it is of major importance for students of Canadian politics to have some understanding of the other parts of the system over which the political leader towers. Approaching Canadian politics through the examination of leadership alone would result in a somewhat one-sided view of the system; approaching it without looking at leadership would produce an unrealistic view of Canadian government. Politics is, after all, about control of the levers of power, or the allocation of scarce resources authoritatively if you must, and that, surely, is what leadership is about.

SUMMARY

1. Leaders are the keystone of every political structure, democratic no less than totalitarian.
2. Modern political leaders face heavy demands both in managing complex modern governments and in making those governments intelligible to the governed.
3. Leaders cannot function in isolation from either the political system or the political circumstances; the relationship is interactive: each affects the other.
4. Generally speaking, leadership consists in having people do what the leader wants them to do.
5. The need for leadership is common to all people, the wise and foolish, good and wicked alike.
6. Leaders may be loosely categorized as either charismatic or bureaucratic.
7. Successful leadership depends upon effective communication.
8. In Canada leaders are chosen at party conventions and usually remain leaders for as long as the party believes they can bring victory.

9. The kind of leader and the kind of leadership helps explain the character of the party that is led.

10. Canadian leaders in power must manage their parties as well as the government.

11. Some leaders have exercised extraordinary power over their parties and governments at both the federal and provincial levels.

12. A leader's fall from power is often as rapid as his rise, although perhaps more easily explained.

STUDY QUESTIONS

1. How would you classify the leadership of the premier of your province, of the leader of the opposition, of the present prime minister? (bureaucratic, charismatic, or a combination). Explain the reasons for your classification.

2. Within your own circle of friends, identify the leader or leaders. Is there one commanding figure or different individuals for different purposes? Account for the authority of the leader(s)

3. Provide five examples of the mass media focusing attention on leaders to the exclusion of policy discussion.

4. List the leaders of the political parties in your province. Indicate why, in your view, each was chosen, and which you consider to be the best leader and why.

5. Successful leadership is often dependent on the circumstances. Explain the circumstances that led to John Diefenbaker's rise to power.

6. Using one of the recent political leadership campaigns as an example, do you think delegates are able to make a wise choice?

7. How important do you think the following are in maintaining a leader's authority over his party: patronage, dissolution, cabinet appointment, control of information, access to the mass media, oratorical ability?

8. What dangers are there in the practice of using professional public relations experts to advise leaders on their public image?

9. How important are public appearances for maintaining a leader's authority?

10. How useful is the psychological analysis of leadership?

ENDNOTES

1. Karl Deutsch, *Politics and Government: How People Decide Their Fate* (Boston: Houghton-Mifflin, 1970), p. 204.

2. See John Saywell, *Quebec 70* (Toronto: University of Toronto Press, 1971), pp. 90 ff.

3. See Robert Michels, *Political Parties* (New York: Dover, 1959), especially Ch. 5.

4. See the bibliography at the end of this chapter.

5. Léon Dion, "The Concept of Political Leadership," *Canadian Journal of Political Science* (March, 1968), p. 3.

6. Cecil Gibb, "Leadership," *The Handbook of Social Psychology*, eds. Lindzey and Aronson (Don Mills: Addison Wesley, 1969), 2nd ed., Vol. IV, p. 268.

7. Winston Churchill, *The Second World War, Vol. 1, The Gathering Storm* (Boston: Houghton-Mifflin, 1948), p. 526.

8. See, for example, J.E Esberey, "Personality and Politics," *CJPS* (March, 1973); John Courtney, "Prime Ministerial Character: An Examination of Mackenzie King's Character," and J.E. Esberey, "Prime Ministerial Character: An Alternative View," *CJPS* (March, 1976). See also J.E. Esberey, *Knight of the Holy Spirit: A Study of Mackenzie King* (Toronto: University of Toronto Press, 1980).

9. Max Weber, *The Theory of Social and Economic Organization*, trans. Henderson and Parsons (New York: Collier-Macmillan, 1947).

10. Irvine Schiffer, *Charisma* (Toronto: University of Toronto Press, 1973), pp. 29-34; ch. 2.

11. Donald Peacock, *Journey to Power* (Toronto: Ryerson, 1968); and J.T. Saywell, ed., *The Canadian Annual Review* (Toronto: University of Toronto Press, 1969).

12. See Jack Granatstein, *The Politics of Survival: The Conservative Party of Canada, 1939-1945* (Toronto: University of Toronto Press, 1967), pp. 138 ff.

13. See J.W. Pickersgill, *My Years with St. Laurent* (Toronto: University of Toronto Press, 1963); and Dale Thomson, *Louis St. Laurent, Canadian* (Toronto: Macmillan, 1967), *passim*.

14. Dion, *op. cit.*, p. 6.

15. See Joseph Wearing, "President or Prime Minister," *Apex of Power: The Prime Minister and Political Leadership in Canada*, ed. Thomas Hockin (Scarborough: Prentice-Hall, 1971), esp. pp. 256-7.

16. See D. Shackleton, *Power Town* (Toronto: McClelland and Stewart, 1977), Ch. 2 for a journalistic account.

17. See John C. Courtney, *The Selection of National Party Leaders in Canada* (Toronto: Macmillan, 1973); and Peacock, *op. cit.*

18. See Geoffrey Stevens, *Stanfield* (Toronto: McClelland and Stewart, 1976), pp. 5-11.

19. See Jeffrey Simpson, *Discipline of Power* (Toronto: Personal Library, 1980), pp. 72 ff.

20. See Hockin, *op. cit.*, especially the articles by Hockin, Schindeler, Smith and Wright.

21. John Diefenbaker, *One Canada, Vol. II* (Toronto: Macmillan, 1976), p. 50.

22. See D.V. Smiley, "The National Party Leadership Convention in Canada: A Preliminary Analysis," in Hockin, *op. cit.*, pp. 52 ff.

23. See D.G. Creighton, *The Forked Road* (Toronto: McClelland and Stewart, 1976), pp. 93-5; and Bruce Hutchison, *The Incredible Canadian: A Portrait of Mackenzie King* (Toronto: Longmans, 1953), Ch. 35.

24. Conrad Black, *Duplessis* (Toronto: McClelland and Stewart, 1976), p. 315.

25. See Pierre Laporte, *True Face of Duplessis* (Montreal: Harvest House, 1960); and Black, *op. cit.*, pp. 299 ff.

26. Wearing, in Hockin, *op. cit.*, p. 249.

27. See Peter Newman, *Renegade in Power* (Toronto: McClelland and Stewart, 1963) and *The Distemper of Our Times: Canadian Politics in Transition, 1963-1968* (Toronto: McClelland and Stewart, 1968); Peter Stursberg, *Diefenbaker: Leadership Lost, 1962-67* (Toronto: University of Toronto: University of Toronto Press, 1976); and Donald C. Creighton, *Canada's First Century* (Toronto: Macmillan, 1970).

28. See John Diefenbaker, *One Canada: The Years of Achievement, 1956-1962* (Toronto: Macmillan, 1976), pp. 3-4, 42-4, for example.

29. See Courtney, *op. cit.*, p. 102; Stursberg, *op. cit.*, pp. 163 ff.

30. Courtney, *op. cit.*, p. 151.

31. Interview with T.C. Douglas, March, 1977.

SELECTED REFERENCES

GENERAL

Dion, Léon. "The concept of political leadership: an analysis." *Canadian Journal of Political Science*, (March, 1968). A clear and helpful discussion of the process and character of leadership.

Edinger, Lewis J., ed. *Political Leadership in Industrialized Societies.* New York: Wiley, 1967. A useful collection of essays for the more advanced students.

Gouldner, Alvin W., ed. *Studies in Leadership.* New York: Harper, 1950. In some ways a minor classic in the field; some of the essays are dated, but worth careful reading.

Michels, Robert. *Political Parties.* New York: Dover, 1959. The analysis of leadership in democratic parties and the elaboration of the "iron law of oligarchy" make this required reading.

Schiffer, Irvine. *Charisma: a psychoanalytic look at mass society.* Toronto: University of Toronto Press, 1973. An intriguing examination of leaders and led from a Freudian perspective.

Tucker, Robert. "The theory of charismatic leadership," *Daedalus* (Summer, 1968). The best discussion of Weber's influential thesis.

CANADA

While a great deal has been written about the process of choosing and disposing of leaders in Canada, relatively little has been written about leadership *per se* in a Canadian context. Perhaps the best studies in this latter category are:

Courtney, John C. *The Selection of National Party Leaders in Canada.* Toronto: Macmillan, 1963. This monograph is broader than the title implies and has a particularly good bibliography.

—————. "Prime Ministerial Character: An Examination of Mackenzie King's Political Leadership." *Canadian Journal of Political Science*, (March, 1976).

Esberey, J.E. "Prime Ministerial Character: An Alternative View." *Canadian Journal of Political Science*, (March, 1976).

Hockin, Thomas, ed. *Apex of Power: The Prime Minister and Political Leadership in Canada.* Scarborough: Prentice-Hall, 1971. This is a good collection of essays, a number of which were written especially for this volume. The essays by Hockin, Smiley, Wright, Smith and Wearing in particular are worthwhile.

BIOGRAPHICAL STUDIES

Esberey, Joy. *Knight of the Holy Spirit: A Study of Mackenzie King* Toronto: University of Toronto Press, 1980.

Ferns, Harry and Bernard Ostry. *The Age of Mackenzie King: The Rise of the Leader.* Toronto: Lorimer, 1976.

Gwyn, Richard. *The Northern Magus.* Toronto: McClelland and Stewart, 1980.

Neatby, Blair. *William Lyon Mackenzie King, 1924-1932: The Lonely Heights.* Toronto: University of Toronto Press, 1963.

——————. *William Lyon Mackenzie King, 1932-1939: The Prism of Unity.* Toronto: University of Toronto Press, 1976.

Newman, Peter C. *Renegade in Power: The Diefenbaker Years.* Toronto: McClelland and Stewart, 1963.

Peacock, Donald. *Journey to Power.* Toronto: Ryerson, 1968.

Pearson, Lester B. *Memoirs, Vol. III.* Toronto: University of Toronto Press, 1975.

Pickersgill, J.W. *My Years with St. Laurent.* Toronto: University of Toronto Press, 1975.

Sherman, Paddy. *Bennett.* Toronto: McClelland and Stewart, 1966.

Simpson, Jeffrey. *Discipline of Power.* Toronto: Personal Library, 1980.

Stursberg, Peter. *Diefenbaker: Leadership Gained, 1956-62.* Toronto: University of Toronto Press, 1976.

——————. *Diefenbaker: Leadership Lost, 1962-67.* Toronto: University of Toronto Press, 1976.

13

Elitists and Pluralists: Power in Canada

Dennis Forcese*

INTRODUCTION

Revelations of the machinations of wealthy and powerful minorities have historically tended to attract the interest and allegiance of persons seeking to understand the distribution of benefits and social control in society. Exposés of the real or presumed actions of the powerful titillate audiences predisposed to attribute conspiratorial intervention to a mysterious and shadowy elite.

Illustrative is the publishing success of Peter Newman's *The Canadian Establishment*, an instant Canadian "best-seller", subsequently presented in a television series. Newman's work is not analytical or critical; in fact, it is generally adulatory, intended as an entertaining look at Canada's wealthy entrepreneurs and their families, a glimpse at their remote and intriguing world of luxury and power.[1] Social scientists as well as journalists have pondered such elite minorities, and the extent to which they effectively control a society. In the social sciences the treatment has usually been less lurid or romantic, and generally has focused upon an intent to understand the ways in which elites affect the limits and operations of so-called democratic societies. In other words, the main concern has been the extent to which political power is concentrated or diffused.

Reduced to its most fundamental sense, power can be understood as the ability to get what one wants, regardless of what other people want. It means making the decisions that affect one's life, and the lives of others. At the societal level, power means governing, whether through formal and legitimated political institutions or through the control of resources and organizations that are not nominally or strictly political. It is no new thing to suggest that in Canadian

*Associate Professor and Chairman, Department of Sociology and Anthropology, Carleton University.

society, as in all other societies, there is a small and enduring group of people who exercise such control or government. In some literature such groups are called oligarchies; more often today they are called elites. At issue is the extent to which the study of such elites offers a comprehensive understanding of political institutions and behavior.

ELITISTS AND PLURALISTS

The theoretical basis of the elitist model of society has usually been understood to consist of the works of writers whom James Burnham called "the Machiavellians".[2] Vilfredo Pareto, Georges Sorel, Gaetano Mosca and Robert Michels, although their works differ in important respects,[3] were so labeled by Burnham because each in his own way stressed the contest for and consolidation of power by cohesive minority groups. Of these theorists, Robert Michels is perhaps most often read today.[4]

In 1911, Michels first published his now famous work in which he offered his "iron law of oligarchy". Michels sought to demonstrate the "autocratic tendencies of leaders", and the generalization that, once in power, men will seek to maintain themselves in power and do so successfully. Thus, in modern voluntary associations and organizations, whether political parties, trade unions, government or society itself, a small minority will establish itself the decision-making group. In contrast to the rank and file, the leadership group develops the information, the expertise, and the inclination to persist in decision-making. It also comes to command the rewards and the material resources. For Michels, such an oligarchy was inevitable, a function of modern organization. Some such orientation remains the basis of all present elitist analyses.

The *bête noire* of the elitists has been the pluralist model of society. A pure elite theorist takes the view that at all times, in all societies, and in all subgroups of society, decision-making power is in the hands of a cohesive and persisting minority group. Such a view obviously contradicts any simple model of democracy as idealized in the notion of full and equal participation, or opportunity to participate, in the functioning of society and its political system. Elite theorists, in effect, argue that such a liberal democratic view of the diffusion and plurality of power is naive, and that where it appears to be true it is an artful illusion, an aspect of "symbolic politics".[5] It is, they assert, an ideological deception, created and manipulated by those in power.

In point of fact, it is difficult to find representatives of a simple liberal pluralist view. Rather, one finds in the social science literature, writers who do not insist on the reality of a truly open and egalitarian politics but on a plurality of elites. Such theorists insist that there are many groups exercising power in modern democratic society, and that the basis of effective democracy is to be found in the rivalries, the competition and the countervailing influences of these several elites. There is conflict and a balance of power among contending elites, or what Riesman called "veto groups",[6] with each elite having an expertise and a socioeconomic power base. For the liberal pluralists, therefore, politics is a matter of contending interests and of the groups, or elites, that act for them. While the elitists contend that a unitary group dominates and that the idea of countervailing interests and groups is fictional, the pluralists find the concept of ruling elite no less a fiction or, in Meisel's view, a myth.[7]

In the pages to follow we shall examine North American examples of elite theory and research, both of the ruling elite and the pluralist elite varieties. We shall then analyze the research findings as they pertain to Canadian society and politics, and consider whether there is any resolution to be found in the elitist-pluralist dispute. We shall assess the general significance and utility of the elitist perspective, focusing on strengths as well as limitations, all the while acknowledging that although the concept is ubiquitous in political science, its meaning varies considerably.

ELITE AS CONCEPT

The concept of elite is used in a variety of ways, modified by numerous adjectives connoting functional specialization. Examples include those of ruling elite, political elite, state elite, economic elite, corporate elite, military elite, bureaucratic elite, judicial elite, labor elite, and many others. The first two connote a sense of an integrated oligarchy or cohesive ruling group; the latter concepts suggest functionally specific persons of prominence, influence and skill. There are therefore at least two fundamental and contradictory senses of elite. The strong or extreme conception is that of an integrated cohesive group of like-minded persons who effectively monopolize general decision-making, by virtue of access to political institutions and/or wealth. In contrast, the weak conception of elite is that of sector-specific minorities of key decision-makers, functionally delimited in role, and not integrated with other such function- or task-related elites. The former is a view tending to be found in political sociology, merging concepts of the political and the social. It is a view that is marginally reconcilable with Marxian theory and the ruling class concept, in which literature one finds the notion of a dominant economic class and fractions (elites) of that class acting and contending in the long-term interests of the ruling class. The weaker conception is represented in the discipline of political science by the liberal pluralist orientation that reiterates the openness and democratic character of constitutional politics. The notion of plural elites suggests a view of dispersed, balanced and stable power, organized in a complex and permeable system. On the other hand, the extreme concept of elite is more comprehensive, for it tends to be more simplistic, a truism. In a sense, the extreme concept explains everything, premised as it is on the view that all pertinent political decisions derive from the ruling elite.[8] These contrary conceptions of elite pervade and are often merged or confused in the research literature.

LEVELS OF ANALYSIS: COMMUNITY AND NATION

There are two well-established levels of elite research. In the first instance, there is the long tradition of social science research in community structure and leadership. This work is closely wedded to the study of social stratification, and can be found illustrated in early and influential works such as the Yankeetown series of W. Lloyd Warner[9] or Middletown by the Lynds.[10] Incorporating a methodological tradition familar to social anthropologists, these and similar works depended on an amalgam of reported or printed material, as well as observation and interview, to piece together a view of class structure and leadership in towns and small cities.

The extremely provocative work of Floyd Hunter was a direct heir to this tradition.[11] Hunter's study of the power structure in the city of Atlanta stimulated numerous approving and critical researchers, intent on replicating or repudiating his findings. Robert Dahl's study of New Haven,[12] and a companion volume by Nelson Polsby[13] representing the latter. The books by Hunter and Dahl are examples of community-level leadership or elite research. But they differ in very important ways, in research method and in interpretive ideology, and are ideally representative of the elitist-pluralist disagreement. While Hunter, a sociologist, concluded that there was a cohesive and well-defined power elite, Dahl rejected such a view and, in his own work, which came to be representative of such study in the discipline of political science, argued that there were several specialized decision-making groups.

A second level of elite analysis involves the entire nation. National elite analysis is most clearly in the tradition of the European social theorists whom we earlier designated the Machiavellians. The most influential such work in modern social science was C. Wright Mills', *The Power Elite*.[14] Like his fellow sociologist Hunter, Mills insisted that a dominant elite characterized American society, occupying the "command posts" of vital decision-making. Rather than a democratic society of effective interest groups and voluntary associations, with open and representative decision-making, the United States was, he argued, a mass society, with a citizenry helpless before the power elite. To Mills, power was vested in the principal institutions of the society. As his critics, such as Dahl[15] and the sociologist Daniel Bell saw it,[16] Mills thereby contrived to avoid the reality of decision-making and politics. As Bell put it, Mills produced "a book which discusses power, but rarely politics",[17] a view aptly summarizing the pluralist objection.

In Canada, John Porter produced a monumental contribution to the tradition of national elite analysis. In *The Vertical Mosaic*,[18] Porter reveals the influence of C. Wright Mills. But unlike Mills, Porter developed a thorough and carefully documented view of the class structure of Canada. And although Porter wrote of elites, he was disinclined to interpret his data as proving there was a unitary ruling class, leaving the question of the degree of integration of the several Canadian elite groups open to further research. Thus, although Porter worked in the tradition of elite analysis after the fashion of the Machiavellians and Mills, he stopped short of their conclusions, and reported findings akin to the pluralist model.

RESEARCH METHODS AND BIASES

At both the community and national levels of analysis, but especially the former, a wealth of research findings has been accumulated in the disciplines of political science and sociology. Along with this mass of research has emerged evidence suggesting a bias in research strategy and findings by discipline, such that findings reinforce elitist or pluralist predispositions.

The two distinct theoretical or ideological approaches to the nature and location of power and leadership tend to affiliate with the social science disciplines of sociology and political science: the elitist model tends to be associated with sociology, and the pluralist tends to be associated with political science. These contrary theoretical predispositions are taught succeeding generations of students in the two disciplines, and the outlooks are reinforced and perpetuated. These learned views, in turn, orient the definition of the research problem, of the appropriate data, and of the correct interpretation of the data. The disciplinary preconceptions thereby tend to result in elite findings in sociology, and multiple elite findings in political science. This shows not deliberate distortion but how the real process of research is shaped by theoretical inclination and preferred research method.

In general there have been three methods developed to investigate power structures. Finer distinctions may be made, but most elite research will use a variant of one or more of the positional, the reputational or the decision-making methods.[19] Each is associated with disciplinary preference; political scientists favor the decision-making method, and sociologists the positional or the reputational. Each realizes findings consistent with the theoretical preconceptions of the researchers. Accordingly, several social scientists have been led to conclude that the only way in which valid empirical results are to be had is by triangulation, that is, the use of the several research approaches in the same research project.[20] Yet, as we shall consider, the disparity in research findings seems as much a matter of data interpretation as of data collection. That is, the theoretical position from which the researcher begins, as well as the method used, govern the conclusions, leading one to be satisfied, or not satisfied, that the data are sufficient to confirm the existence of a ruling elite.

The Positional Method

The most prominent example of a positional approach is the work of Mills. In *The Power Elite*, he argued the existence of an American national elite on the basis of the key roles or positions existing in the United States.[21] That is, certain positions such as the presidency, the military chief of staff, or the chairman of the board of directors of a major corporation such as General Motors, were obviously deemed positions of power and their incumbents, therefore, people of power. Accordingly, the power elite was comprised of those in the "command posts" of American society who "share decisions having at least national consequences."[22] Similarly, in a less well known work, Mills had identified a labor elite, the "new men of power", on the basis of occupancy of key positions of power in labor organizations.[23]

The positional method to this point is rather straightforward, and certainly not a social science innovation insofar as it depends on citing formal or institutionalized positions of significant power and the people who fill these positions. But the power elite concept implies much more than some number of individuals who are in positions of power; an elite is a group exercising coordinated power and collective decision-making. Mills insisted that this collective group character of key decision-makers existed in the United States. He took the view that the demands and skills associated with decision-making in one top command post were much the same as in another, whatever the institutional setting. Thus the individuals who filled these positions were interchangeable, in theory and in practice. Individual men of power had had careers in which mobility from one sector of power to another was usual, thereby negating any possibility of institutional checks or balances of power.

Mills distinguished three important sectors of power in American society: the economic, the political and the military. He claimed that the three were interdependent in interests and in personnel. Military officers moved to directorships in major corporations, or into politics and even the presidency, or corporate heads ran for and won political office, or politicians would move from Capitol Hill to the corporate boardrooms. Not surprisingly, corporate, military and political interests coincided. Government policies and expenditures related to the magnitude of the military establishment; military expenditures on personnel and especially on innovative and more elaborate technology were good for big business and not infrequently for politicians whose constituencies were dependent on a military base or a big business, such as Boeing, locked into military production; and politicians depended on business largesse for their compaign funds and perhaps some personal income, as well as postpolitical careers.

In addition to this interchangeability and interdependence, Mills noted that the men of power shared a social class background and experience. They went to the same or similar schools, lived in the same or similar neighborhoods, played at the same or similar clubs. In short, they shared an interaction set and life style. Thus, they thought alike, had similar attitudes and decision predispositions and, Mills thought, they did collaborate. Because of these features—the interchangeability of roles, the interdependence, and the similarity of outlook and experience—Mills spoke not of isolated men of power but of an elite. Thus, the positional method, as exemplified in the work of Mills, consisted of identifying power positions and the people occupying them. But, additionally, he spoke of an elite on the basis of reasonable inference of frequent contact and interaction.

The Reputational Method

The reputational method requires similar indication of collusion, but a different technique is used to identify the men of power. The method is premised on the view that leadership in important decision areas is not necesarily, perhaps not even usually, to be found in the formal roles or offices of major institutions. Rather, there are powerful people who influence and make decisions in the absence of such office, and such people may not operate in a publicly visible manner. But they will be known to people in key positions in a community or society, if not to the general public. The method that one adopts, therefore, is to poll a number of key informants who, in turn, may suggest other informants, in order to compile a list of these people who by reputation are most influential, whether holding office or not. The initial interviews lead the researcher in snowballing fashion to additional interviewees until a reputational consensus becomes apparent. The list of leaders may then be resubmitted, if the researcher wishes, to a panel of key informants to determine priority of power, probably already indicated by the number of times a person of power was cited. Quite literally, then, the reputational method entails eliciting the names of people who have a reputation for guiding important decisions in a community or a society.

This method is obviously best suited for small systems, such as towns or moderately sized cities. However, it is quite conceivable that a panel of informants could identify at a national level those people in or out of formal office whom they deem of pre-eminent power. In fact, political journalists often do make such judgments. It is the case, though, that the method has been associated mainly with community-level analysis.

The principal innovator in reputational method was Floyd Hunter. In his *Community Power Structure*,[24] Hunter pioneered the method and identified a clear consensus on the people dominating decision-making in the city of Atlanta. He found that they tended to be associated with business and that they appeared to be not isolated individuals but an effective group. They shared not only a similarity of interest but also of social background, socialization, residence and recreation. And although in business and not elected office, they tended to maintain close ties with the state legislature. Thus, as in the positional method, once the men of power were identified, they were judged to constitute an elite by virtue of some indication and some inference of interaction and collusion.

The Decision-Making Method

As we indicated previously, many social scientists took exception to such elitist conclusions. Reacting initially to Hunter and then to Mills, the opposition was best represented by Robert Dahl. Dahl set out to demonstrate an alternative method, and he subsequently generated quite different conclusions. The decision-making method, as the designation implies, was premised on the argument that if one is identifying decision makers, then one must avoid reputations and suspicions and deal in real decisions. To Dahl and to other critics such as Bell,[25] the trouble with researchers like Hunter was that they accepted statements about power, but did not look at or analyze the real execution of power by demonstrating who really made specific decisions.

In his work in New Haven, Dahl set out to recreate, on the basis of documentary records and the recollections of witnesses and participants, the decisions made in the community over a period of years. Those people found to have been active in forming decisions were considered the leaders. Dahl found that the leadership structure was pluralistic. Different kinds of decision situations engaged different people, leading Dahl to conclude that there were several specialized leadership groups rather than one powerful elite.

Different Methods and Different Findings

The New Haven study and similar findings were not convincing to the elitists, who scoffed that Dahl was merely dealing in superficialities and trivial decisions. They did not concede that the "front men" in elected office, such as city council, were the real power in a community. Nor could public records ever disclose the true decision-making interaction and the impact of informal participants. To the elitists, the decision-making method, given its focus, could only identify lower-level or secondary leaders, and its advocates were naive in viewing such leaders as the real men of power.

Conversely, to those working in the pluralist mode and using a decision-making method, the reputational and the positional approaches must inevitably suggest an elite, whether one existed or not. The elitist conclusions were thus viewed as conspiratorial fantasy, ignoring the reality of political interaction.

Both parties to the issue have a point. The theoretical models and the methods with which they are associated do, to a considerable degree, predefine the research outcomes, rendering the findings a function of the researcher's preconceptions and investigative technique. In the 1960s several social scientists published works empirically indicating that researchers selected a research method on the basis of their training in a discipline, political science or sociology, and that the method seemed almost to guarantee the findings.[26] It seemed that pluralist or elitist conclusions were artifacts of the methods used and the methods a function of the orienting model prevailing in the discipline. Terry Clark further suggested that even where the methods produced valid findings, there was a biasing preselection of target communities.[27] That is, sociologists tended to select communities with elitist or pyramidal power structures, while political scientists tended to select communities with pluralist or dispersed power structures. Thus, for example, the dispute was dealing in apples and oranges, as in Hunter's industrial Atlanta and Dahl's university town of New Haven.

Further complicating the research findings, Nelson published the results of his re-analysis of community power-structure studies, and the analyses of critics of the studies, Walton, and Curtis and Petras. Nelson's data, based on correspondence with community power researchers, suggest that the confusion in findings is a matter of "poorly communicated ideas" or ambiguously stated conclusions on the nature of the leaders or elite identified, whether they are one or plural.[28] The ambiguity is compounded by the predisposition of the critics, who expect to find sociologists preferring a reputational method and political scientists preferring a decision-making method. Accordingly, Nelson concludes that the bias reported by Walton, and by Curtis and Petras, is as much their bias as that of the primary researchers.[29]

The dispute lives on, in theory and in empirical findings. It is unlikely that the existence or nonexistence of a ruling elite will ever be conclusively established in a modern complex liberal-democratic society such as the United States or Canada. One can point to privileged and powerful people, whether at the community or the national level. But it seems inevitable that there will always remain reasonable doubt about the extent of deliberate collaboration among such men of power. The idea that such people form an active and cohesive group seems doomed to remain at best a matter of conjecture and circumstantial evidence, especially on the national level. Stated otherwise, whatever the theoretical and research bias or objectivity, the confirmed data are unlikely ever to take one beyond the finding of a plurality of elites, whatever one's suspicions to the contrary. The Canadian research data illustrate this conclusion.

CANADIAN FINDINGS: THE LOCAL LEVEL

The American tradition of investigation into community leadership does not have a strong counterpart in Canada. But there are some comparable data, usually dealing with single-industry company towns, agricultural communities, and communities in economically depressed regions subject to government intervention, as in the Newfoundland outports or the Manitoba interlake fishing villages.[30] The methodologies used in such studies were similar to those previously described, although much of the work was not exclusively directed to the leadership structure but to the character and organization of the total community.

Reminiscent of the American research, a clear generalization that emerges from the Canadian community-level research, and that we will rediscover in the national studies in Canada, is the strength of the economic variable. The leadership of communities in Canada tends to be associated with economic success and business status. For example, a study of the Manitoba interlake communities and the fishing industry found that the economic success of individual fishermen was generally translated into overall leadership status. In the communities and the fishermen's association, leadership, both by formal position and by reputation, was in the hands of the most successful and prosperous fishermen. Yet these were still secondary leaders. As in company towns, the owners and managers of the companies, in this instance the fish-packing and marketing companies who even owned the boats used by the fishermen, were conceded the obvious dominance in decision-making. Similarly, in his very thorough survey of community studies, Lucas notes that small businessmen and a few professionals dominate formal positions of decision-making and tend to be viewed as most influential.[31] Even in company towns, where by definition the company runs things, the nearest thing to a countervailing influence or opposition elite was found not among company workers, but among the few independent merchants and professionals in the towns. Similar findings are reported in prairie agricultural regions. In his study of Biggar, Saskatchewan, Richard Laskin reports that businessmen and professionals dominate community organizations.[32] In Alberta, Bennett finds that the reputational and formal leaders are the wealthy ranchers, the prosperous element of these mixed farming-ranching districts. These are characteristically the people engaged in provincial politics, making the big decisions, leaving overt local politics to their lesser neighbors, the farmers.[33]

An additional empirical generalization of note emerges from the Canadian community-level research. In small communities, the pre-eminence of people from "correct" ethnic backgrounds is consistently noted. With very localized exceptions, such as the high status of the Icelanders in the Manitoba interlake region,[34] people of United Kingdom origins have been found in dominant leadership positions. Most researchers remark on the pattern of ethnic stratification in their communities, with Anglo-Scottish Canadians at the pinnacle, in wealth and in power.[35]

A study of the power structure in a large Canadian city also confirmed the business and ethnic pattern of dominance. Kelner's Toronto data led her to distinguish a primary or core elite level, and a lesser or strategic elite, both business-dominated. At the lesser level of corporate leadership, persons were demonstrated to have achieved or earned access to their functionally important roles; consequently there was access by ethnic minorities. For example there was some penetration by the Jews and the Irish. But she reports the core elite of inherited wealth and position closed, and consisting of old monied families of British descent.[36] Like American sociologists, therefore, Kelner's findings, reminiscent of Hunter's work, distinguish a more accessible "democratic" level of secondary decision-making from a superordinate and closed minority of top decision-makers.

The community-level empirical generalizations prove to be very consistent with national power-structure research findings. They constitute strong confirmation of John Porter's conclusions on ethnic advantage and power in Canada, and of the domination of national elite groups by people of British descent.

CANADIAN FINDINGS: THE NATIONAL LEVEL

The most influential work dealing in Canadian elites remains John Porter's *The Vertical Mosaic*. As we noted earlier, although probably influenced by C. Wright

Mills, Porter's work is far more thorough theoretically and empirically than *The Power Elite*. Porter's conclusions can most aptly be termed as qualified elitist; he does not deny, as the pluralists do, the possibility of a ruling elite, but empirically he can only demonstrate a plurality of elites.

Porter cites the critical sectors of power in Canada as being the economic, political, bureaucratic, ideological and labor, and attaches the greatest importance to the economic. Like Mills, he examines the social class origins and life styles of people in positions of power in these sectors and finds sufficient coincidence of background, interaction and interest to suggest similar or complementary decision-making. But rather than insist that there is a unified and cohesive ruling elite dominating the nation, Porter resists such an inference and instead concludes that in Canada the several elites do not fully merge. Despite the degrees of identity among the powerful in the several elite sectors, they may, because of the specializations of the elites, not only cooperate but also compete. Porter persisted in this view ten years after the publication of *The Vertical Mosaic* and wrote

> In *The Vertical Mosaic* I adopted what might be called a plural elite model which, very simply, stated that the power of economic, political, bureaucratic, military and other institutions tend to be separated because they perform different tasks for a society and, in so doing, become specialized, and hence there is always a tendency for power also to be separated. At the same time the overall coordinating and guidance needs of the society require interaction between the various elite groups. It therefore becomes a matter of empirical investigation to discover the extent to which these coordinating and guidance needs lead to an aggrandizement of power, to the creation of what might be called a power elite.[37]

In his research, Porter found, as reaffirmed by later researchers, that the more privileged and more powerful Canadians tended to be people of United Kingdom descent. This was especially so in the economic sector. The political elite proved an exception, largely because of the structure of formal political organization in Canada, that is, federalism, and regional patterns of immigration. Canada has regionally specific ethnic concentrations, approximately coincident with provincial boundaries. The obvious example is the French in Québec, but in addition, there are the Scots in the Maritimes, the Anglo-Irish in Newfoundland, the Anglo-Scots in Ontario, and the central Europeans in the Prairies. Within the structure of local, provincial and federal politics, local ethnic representation, especially that of French Canadians, was inevitable by force of number, despite the economic privilege of Anglo minorities. Thus we find that the political elite is more ethnically heterogeneous than other elite sectors. Middle-class professional occupations lead to electoral success and cabinet positions,[38] but, significantly, for people of many ethnic groups. There is a class advantage, but an ethnic bias or advantage, which is a marked feature in nonpolitical sectors, especially the economic elite, is not an important factor in gaining access to the political elite except regionally, as described above.

Porter also remarked on the pattern of ethnic privilege in the federal bureaucracy. This finding was later supported in Beattie's work when he clearly demonstrated that francophones had only slight access to middle range executive positions, although there were indications that senior positions were becoming increasingly accessible to francophones.[39] In general, the bureaucratic elite has been a stable influence in Canadian politics, not subject to the turnover characteristic of elected political office, and thereby very often the object of the attention of corporate interest groups.

Olsen, who worked with John Porter and employed a positional method, also finds that the "state elite", that is, politicians such as federal cabinet ministers, provincial premiers, justices of the Supreme Court of Canada, and provincial chief justices, tend to be middle class in origin. He also finds that people of British descent still dominate the judiciary, although the proportion of francophones has been increasing.[40] Olsen reports that except for Québec, where francophone politicians are obviously well represented, people of British descent dominate, especially in Ontario, British Columbia and Alberta.[41] Olsen also looks at federal and provincial bureaucrats at the rank of deputy or assistant deputy minister and heads of Crown corporations or regulating bodies in the provinces. Again he finds people of middle-class origins and, by ethnicity, the British, very much overrepresented, with the francophones moderately underrepresented and all other ethnic groups considerably underrepresented.[42]

Clement, also a student of Porter's, attempted to replicate and update Porter's work. Concentrating on the economic or corporate elite, Clement confirms the ethnic pattern of representation but comes to quite different conclusions from Porter on the degree of access or mobility into the elite and the extent of elite integration.[43] Clement attaches major importance to the Anglo-dominated corporate and media elites that control the economy and the ideology of the nation, and thereby effectively dominate or rule Canadian society. Distinguishing by economic sector, Clement finds that there are significant variations in the extent of foreign penetration of corporate ownership in Canada. The mass media, transportation networks, financial institutions and utilities are Canadian-owned, and Clement hence speaks of an indigenous Canadian elite. Noting that the degree of foreign control of Canadian industry will have increased dramatically from the early post-World War II period of Porter's research, Clement distinguishes a second elite group of considerable importance, the comprador elite. These are the directors of foreign-owned corporations, residents in Canada and dominating the resource and manufacturing industries. He also identifies a third group, the parasite elite, non-residents of Canada usually located in the United States, who direct the multinational corporations active in Canada. Both of the latter are associated with the branch-plant companies operating in Canada. Clement concludes that the members of the indigenous Canadian elite have essentially been go-betweens *vis-à-vis* the American and other foreign interests, and have thus developed a complementarity of interest and benefit, sanctioned and furthered by the state, that is, the Canadian government.[44]

Related to this division of function in the elite, Clement finds that access to and mobility into elite positions have become increasingly restricted since

Porter's research. Although Clement is willing to speak of an effective ruling elite, he does not lose sight of the class basis of Canadian society and observes that the elite, with rare exceptions, now consists of people of upper-class social origins and is thereby more homogeneous and better integrated than in the earlier post-World War II period.[45]

> The existence of a powerful Canadian commercial elite, controlled by the upper class and of a predominantly foreign elite in production means that Canada remains a "low mobility" society. Concentration and centralization in commercial sectors has been the result of indigenous forces while these same processes in the productive sectors have been imposed from outside. The result is an economy which is highly structured with few mobility avenues for those outside the upper class.[46]

Clement very explicitly seeks to distinguish his analysis from the pluralist conviction of representative politics in which interest groups contend with one another, effectively check one another, and in which their activities tend to be mediated by the federal and provincial governments. He is particularly critical of the work of Robert Presthus,[47] the major pluralist contributor to the Canadian literature on elite structure.[48] Unlike Porter who insists on the existence of such an elite, Presthus perceives countervailing elites. His model might be described as an interest-group concept of elites in Canada, much like that of Engelmann and Schwartz who write of economic, political, administrative and ideological subsystems and elites.[49]

Presthus deals in three components of the political elite: legislators, bureaucrats or public servants and interest-group leaders. His analysis seeks to relate the activities of elite groups in the economy to the provincial and federal bureaucracies, legislatures and cabinets. Although he finds considerable corporate influence, an influence much greater than that of organized labor as an interest group, and some coincidence of corporate and government interest, Presthus insists on the effective autonomy of the state and that corporate interest groups and elites have not merged or integrated. This insistence upon the separation of elites is a feature of the pluralist interpretation, despite the fact that the pluralists are as aware as the elitists of some degree of harmony of interest and outlook between elites. In Canada we know that particular interests are associated with particular parties. For example, in his study of party financing, Paltiel reports that the Liberal party and the Progressive Conservative party are largely financed by big business, while the New Democratic Party tends to be supported by organized labor.[50] Few of us find such a relationship remarkable. As the pluralists would suggest, such financial connections are altogether reasonable and expected features in interest-group politics.

Presthus holds the view that elite competition and bargaining are essential in a viable political system. In the process of elite accommodation, he argues, contending interests reach a degree of accord that creates equilibrium in society and deters "disintegrative tendencies". Thus "elite accommodation may be regarded as a structural requisite of any democratic society."[51]

It is this theoretical premise that enables Presthus to come to quite different conclusions about the importance of elites in Canadian society. Like Clement and Porter, Presthus finds that, with the exception of the relatively open political elite, the economic-based elite groups are quite homogeneous insofar as class, ethnic background and experience are concerned.[52] But the accommodation and cooperation among the socially homogeneous elite subgroups is vital to the stability of the socially heterogeneous society of Canada. Like other political scientists, such as Arend Lijphart and Kenneth McRae, Presthus believes that some measure of elite collaboration or rule must exist.[53] To the elitist, such "consociational democracy" is not democracy and deters necessary social change, while to the pluralist such elite accommodation ensures the continued existence of the national society. One thereby finds in the Canadian literature the essence of the elitist-pluralist dispute, rooted not so much in diverging empirical findings as in the theoretical meaning and importance attached to the empirical findings.

The Scope and Relevance of Elite Research

Investigation of elites is an area of study that extends over two academic disciplines: sociology and political science. The question of whether or not there are elites is of long standing and of fundamental theoretical interest, for it addresses the very nature of society and of power and government. It addresses the question of who rules, and for whom, a question elemental to and in a sense synonymous with political analysis. In the older literature in political science, the question was often taken up in terms of the existence, nature and influence of oligarchies. The modern inclination is to substitute the concept of elite for oligarchy, but the end, determining the nature and process of the exercise of power, remains the same.

Elite analysis in the modern literature in political science and political sociology is in no part unique to Canadian scholarly research. Rather, as we have attempted to make clear, its origins and its cross references are to be found in European social and political theory as well as in American empirical research. To take two prominent examples, we know that John Porter was much influenced by C. Wright Mills and his work in the elitist tradition, while Robert Presthus is an American who brought his pluralist outlooks with him when he took up a university appointment in Toronto, and applied them in his Canadian research. To understand empirical research and interpretations of research on elites in Canada, one must be aware of the non-Canadian history and context of the work.

In addition to the general ties to fundamental social and political theory, research on elites in Canada and elsewhere also relates to specific subfields or traditions of enquiry in social science. The best examples in sociology are to be found in the area of social stratification research where the matter of elites is of intrinsic interest and, in political science, in the study of interest group politics where researchers must inevitably come to terms with the question of elites. Once again, we may revert to the examples of John Porter and Robert Presthus: Porter, a sociologist, works in the subfield of social stratification, while Presthus orients his interest in elites within the broader subfield of interest-group politics.

Another growing area of social science research which involves elite analysis is especially pertinent to Canada; this is the study of multi-ethnic society and politics and, in particular, the popular concept and model of consociational democracy.[54] The reformulation of the long-standing academic interest in the bases of social and political stability is a defining feature of the consociational model, and it cannot avoid coming to grips with the nature and role of elite groups. Other obvious links to subfields in political science and political sociology would include the study of political socialization, political ideology and culture, mass politics and political movements, political mobilization, and political development. It is all but impossible to conceive of a field of political enquiry that does not at some point have to deal with the question of elites, given that the study of politics is the study of the exercise of power.

We must not, however, lose sight of the fact that analysis of elites is but a fraction of the important research in political science or political sociology. The so-called elites, or the ruling class, are but minorities of the mass of Canadian people and organization. They represent vast wealth and power, but not autonomous power. Above all else, the one important matter with which elite analysis does not deal involves the degree of autonomy of such men of power or, conversely, the extent and manner in which a ruling elite or a plurality of elites is influenced by non-elite Canadians. It is not satisfactory to assume that in the study of political elites we have the essence of social and political explanation. Such an emphasis ignores mass behavior, fails to demonstrate the elite's manipulation of public behavior, attitudes, ideologies or political cultures, and does not clearly demonstrate effective control of agencies of socialization in Canada or any society.

In sum, the greatest weakness of elite analysis has been the widespread assumption that elites, integrated or plural, really run things, be it in collusion or in competition. In fact, however, all that is demonstrated is that elites are people of wealth or positional influence who make many important political decisions. But they do not do so in a social vacuum. Elites, too, exist in a larger society and are subject to influences. If we hope to gain anything close to a full understanding of society, of politics, and of sociopolitical change, we must study not only elites but also the interaction between elites and non-elites; anything less will be incomplete and inadequate.

CONCLUSIONS

It is apparent when we consider the cumulative research findings dealing with the subject of elites that there is a fundamental theoretical divergence in the outlooks of people working with the concept. It is doubtful, given that the divergence is more theoretical than empirical, that the disputants can be reconciled. On the one hand, the theoretical or ideological predisposition of elitists stems from a critical and pessimistic view of modern capitalist democracies. The pluralist view, on the other hand, derives from an essentially satisfied view of the same socio-political systems. Research by each finds elite groups, but in the former instance these groups constitute an effectively integrated and ominously powerful ruling elite. In the latter instance, the several elite groups maintain a measure of subautonomy, and to the degree that they cooperate and share outlooks and interests, such cooperation is functionally necessary to maintain our society. Each school of elite analysis invokes the call to political realism, the reality of extreme power or the reality of political exchange. Finally, and conceptually important, both seem to concede, at times explicitly, that the ruling elite or the several specialized elites, are representatives of some larger social body, a privileged and influential upper or ruling class. In particular, the elitists are willing to make this explicit, perhaps because they are more apt to initiate their elite analyses from the broader theoretical and empirical standpoint of stratification on class analysis that is such a prominent interest in the discipline of sociology. Thus ultimately Clement not only makes clear that the thrust of his analysis is to point to a ruling class,[55] but also suggests that the concept of elite may therefore be of subordinate importance and a mere methodological tool.[56]

The elitist pessimism and the pluralist optimism fundamentally relate to the necessity for and the prospects of change in society. To the extent that one concludes that liberal democratic-capitalist societies such as Canada are desirable and even admirable social systems, whatever their imperfections may be, then one may logically emphasize structures and processes that maintain that kind of society. Given that point of view, such change as is desired must be gradual, allowing a stable evolutionary transition. We find such a sentiment in the work of John Porter who seems to bridge the elitist and pluralist extremes. Although Porter has explicitly decried the excesses and inequalities of stratified Canadian society, he rejects calls to change in Canada that are premised on radical or violent transformations.[57] His meritocratic Canada of equal opportunity is an ideal that he considers to be an achievable target, and one that will presumably not utterly eliminate privileged and powerful groups or elites.

Elite analysis is ubiquitous to the study and explanation of politics. In fact, though, the two contending concepts of elite have different implications for conclusions regarding the nature of political behavior. Elitists emphasize that politics are closed to all but a minority, and therefore the prevailing politics are deplorable; pluralists find coordinating elite groups to be broadly representative and open, the basis of political stability. To expect a synthesis of these divergent views would be a naiveté of the magnitude of which each of the protagonists accuses the other. In Canada, as elsewhere, the conclusions one reaches about elites are largely the result of the theoretical and ideological convictions one holds; again we realize that no science, and certainly not a social science, is ever fully objective and value free.

SUMMARY

1. In the social sciences, the analysis of elites has generally focused on ways in which elites affect the limits and operations of democratic societies, the extent to which political power is concentrated or diffused.

2. The elitists, represented by Robert Michels, argue that in society a small and cohesive minority garners information, develops expertise, makes the important decisions and gets the major rewards. The pluralists, represented by John Meisel, argue that in a democracy there is at the very least competition between groups of elites. The elitist model has tended to be associated with sociology and the pluralist with political science.

3. Elite research has tended to deal with two areas: community structure and leadership (Floyd Hunter) and national structure and leadership (C. Wright Mills, John Porter).

4. Researchers in elite studies have tended to employ one of three approaches: the decision-making, the positional, or the reputational method.

5. A researcher's basic orientation affects the type of research he undertakes, his findings and his conclusions.

6. Leadership in Canadian communities is influenced greatly by the economic variable as well as ethnicity, with United Kingdom origins generally prevalent.

7. At the national level in Canada the economic factor is very important as is ethnicity; additionally, regional ethnic concentrations are reflected in elite structures. Given Canada's political system it is not surprising to discover that the political elite is more ethnically heterogeneous than other elite sectors. An economic class advantage seems to pervade all elite sectors.

8. Some writers, such as Robert Presthus, hold the view that elite competition and bargaining are essential in a variable political system; elite accommodation provides equilibrium in society and tends to deter disintegration.

9. It is all but impossible to conceive of a field of political inquiry that does not somehow deal with the question of elites, or a ruling class. However, elite analysis is not, in itself, adequate. Elites do not operate in a vacuum—they are subject to various pressures and influences.

10. In Canada, as elsewhere, the conclusions one reaches about elites are largely the result of the theoretical and ideological convictions one holds; again we realize that no science, and certainly not a social science, is ever fully objective and value free.

STUDY QUESTIONS

1. To what extent is elite analysis similar to Marxist analysis of society?
2. Why have certain writers on elitism been called "the Machiavellians"?

3. How valid is Robert Michels' "iron law of oligarchy"?

4. Which of the major research models—decision-making, positional or reputational—seems to you to be most useful? Why?

5. What is the difference between the "strong" and the "weak" conception of the elite?

6. Why are John Porter's conclusions termed "qualified elitist"?

7. Explain and contrast Wallace Clement's categories of "indigenous Canadian elite", the "comprador elite", and the "parasite elite".

8. What is meant by "consociational democracy"?

9. What major aspects of Canadian politics are anti-elitist?

10. In future decades is Canadian society likely to become less or more elitist? Why?

ENDNOTES

1. Peter Newman, *The Canadian Establishment* (Toronto: McClelland and Stewart, 1974).

2. James Burnham, *The Machiavellians: Defenders of Freedom* (New York: John Day, 1943).

3. John Meisel, *The Myth of the Ruling Class: Gaetano Mosca and the Elite* (Ann Arbor: The University of Michigan Press, 1962).

4. Robert Michels, *Political Parties: A Sociological Study of the Oligarchical Tendencies of Modern Democracy* (New York: Collier Books, 1962).

5. Murray Edelman, *The Symbolic Uses of Politics* (Urbana: University of Illinois Press, 1964).

6. David Riesman, *The Lonely Crowd* (New Haven: Yale University Press, 1961).

7. Geraint Parry, *Political Elites* (London: George Allen & Unwin Ltd. 1969).

8. Meisel, *op. cit.*

9. W.L. Warner and P.S. Lunt, *The Status System of a Modern Community* (New Haven: Yale University Press, 1947).

10. Robert S. Lynd and H.M. Lynd, *Middletown: A Study in Modern American Culture* (New York: Harcourt, Brace and World, 1929).

11. Floyd Hunter, *Community Power Structure* (Chapel Hill: University of North Carolina Press, 1956).

12. Robert Dahl, *Who Governs? Power and Democracy in an American City* (New Haven: Yale University Press. 1963).

13. Nelson Polsby, *Community Power and Political Theory* (New Haven: Yale University Press, 1963).

14. C. Wright Mills, *The Power Elite* (New York: Oxford University Press, 1956).

15. Robert Dahl, "A Critique of the Ruling Elite Model," *The Search for Community Power*, ed. W. Hawley and F. Wirt (Englewood Cliffs, NJ: Prentice-Hall, 1968), pp. 151-8.

16. Daniel Bell, *The End of Ideology: On the Exhaustion of Political Ideas in the Fifties*, rev. ed. (New York: Collier Books, 1962).

17. *Ibid.*, p. 74.

18. John Porter, *The Vertical Mosaic* (Toronto: University of Toronto Press, 1965).

19. Arnold Rose, *The Power Structure: Political Process in American Society* (New York: Oxford University Press, 1967), pp. 255-97; Wendell Bell et al., *Public Leadership* (San Francisco: Chandler, 1961), pp. 1-120; Delbert Miller, *International Community Power Structures: Comparative Studies of Four World Cities* (Bloomington: Indiana University Press, 1970), pp. 3-29; Ted Goertzel, *Political Society* (Chicago: Rand McNally, 1976), pp. 119-32.

20. Terry Clark, "Community or Communities," *Community Structure and Decision-Making: Comparative Analyses*, ed. Terry Clark (San Francisco: Chandler, 1968), pp. 83-90; Michael Nelson, "Community Power Structure: Fact or Artifact?" M.A. Thesis, Carleton University, Ottawa, 1972.

21. Mills, *op. cit.*

22. *Ibid.*, p. 18.

23. C. Wright Mills, *The New Men of Power* (New York: Harcourt, Brace and World, 1958).

24. Hunter, *op. cit.*

25. Wendell Bell, *op. cit.*

26. John Walton, "Substance and Artifact: The Current Status of Research on Community Power Structure," *American Journal of Sociology*, 71 (1966), pp. 430-8; Terry Clark et al., "Discipline, Method, Community Structure and Decision-Making: The Role and Limitations of the Sociology of Knowledge," *The American Sociologist*, 3 (August, 1968), pp. 214-7; James Curtis and John Petras, "Community Power, Power Studies, and the Sociology of Knowledge," *Human Organization* (Fall, 1970), pp. 204-18; Michael Nelson, *op. cit.*

27. Terry Clark, *op. cit.*, pp. 83-90.

28. Michael Nelson, "The Validity of Secondary Analyses of Community Power Studies," *Social Forces*, 52 (June, 1974), p. 535.

29. *Ibid.*, pp. 531-7.

30. Richard Laskin, *Organizations in a Saskatchewan Town* (Saskatoon Centre for Community Studies, 1961); Rex Lucas, *Minetown, Milltown, Railtown; Life in Canadian Communities of Single Industry* (Toronto: University of Toronto Press, 1971); Dennis Forcese, "Leadership in a Depressed Primary Industry," M.A. Thesis, University of Manitoba, Winnipeg, 1964.

31. Lucas, *op. cit.*

32. Laskin, *op. cit.*

33. John Bennett, *Northern Plainsmen: Adaptive Strategy and Agrarian Life* (Chicago: Aldine, 1969).

34. Forcese, *op. cit.*

35. Lucas, *op. cit.*

36. Merrijoy Kelner, "Ethnic Penetration into Toronto's Elite Structure," *The Canadian Review of Sociology and Anthropology*, 7 (May, 1970), pp. 128-37.

37. John Porter, "Foreword," in *The Canadian Corporate Elite*, by Wallace Clement (Toronto: McClelland and Stewart, The Carleton Library, 1975), p. xiv, reprinted

by permission of The Canadian Publishers, McClelland and Stewart Ltd., Toronto.

38. Dennis Forcese and John deVries, "Occupation and Electoral Success in Canada: The 1972 Federal Election," Department of Sociology and Anthropology, Carleton University, Ottawa, 1974; Dennis Forcese and John deVries, "Occupation and Electoral Success in Canada: The 1974 Federal Election," *The Canadian Review of Sociology and Anthropology*, 14 (1977), pp. 331-40.

39. Chris Beattie, *Minority Men in a Majority Setting: Middle-Level Francophones in the Canadian Public Service* (Toronto: McClelland and Stewart, The Carleton Library, 1975).

40. Dennis Olsen, "The State Elites," *The Canadian State*, ed. Leo Panitch (Toronto: University of Toronto Press, 1977), pp. 199-224.

41. Olsen, *op. cit.*

42. *Ibid.*

43. Wallace Clement, *The Canadian Corporate Elite: An Analysis of Economic Power* (Toronto: McClelland and Stewart, The Carleton Library, 1975); "Continental Capitalism: Corporate Power Relations Between Canada and the U.S." Ph.D. Thesis, Carleton University, Ottawa, 1976.

44. Clement, *The Canadian Corporate Elite, op. cit.*, pp. 344-66; "Continental Capitalism," *op. cit.*

45. Clement, *The Canadian Corporate Elite, op. cit.*, pp. 172-223.

46. *Ibid.*, p. 357, reprinted by permission of The Canadian Publishers, McClelland and Stewart Ltd., Toronto.

47. *Ibid.*, pp. 358-61.

48. Robert Presthus, *Elites in the Policy Process* (London: Cambridge University Press, 1974).

49. Frederick Engelmann and Mildred Schwartz, *Political Parties and the Canadian Social Structure* (Scarborough: Prentice-Hall, 1967), pp. 76-90.

50. Khayyam Paltiel, *Political Party Financing in Canada* (Toronto: McGraw-Hill, 1970).

51. Presthus, *op. cit.*, p. 34.

52. *Ibid.*, pp. 238, 394.

53. Kenneth McRae, *Consociational Democracy* (Toronto: McClelland and Stewart, The Carleton Library, 1975).

54. *Ibid.*

55. Clement, *The Canadian Corporate Elite, op. cit.*, pp. 357-8.

56. Clement, "Continental Capitalism," *op. cit.*

57. John Porter, "Foreword," *The Canadian Corporate Elite, op. cit.*, pp. ix-xv.

SELECTED REFERENCES

Bell, Wendell, R. Hill, and C. Wright. *Public Leadership* San Francisco: Chandler, 1961. A thorough critical review of the several approaches to elite investigation, with a comprehensive pre-1960 bibliography.

Clark, Terry, ed. *Community Structure and Decision-Making: Comparative Analyses.* San Francisco: Chandler, 1968. A good collection of comparative community decision-making analyses, attempting to represent the several methodological approaches.

Clement, Wallace. *The Canadian Corporate Elite: An Analysis of Economic Power.* Toronto: McClelland and Stewart, The Carleton Library, 1975. A detailed attempt to update John Porter's analysis of the corporate elite, with evidence of increased concentration of power. The book includes a good bibliography.

Dahl, Robert. *Who Governs? Power and Democracy in an American City.* New Haven: Yale University Press, 1961. The pathfinding work in the decision-making approach, and as such a "classic" work.

Hunter, Floyd. *Community Power Structure.* Chapel Hill. University of North Carolina Press, 1956. The empirical study of elites in North America effectively begins with this work in the reputational tradition.

Meisel, John. *The Myth of the Ruling Class: Gaetano Mosca and the Elite.* Ann Arbor: The University of Michigan Press, 1962. A detailed critique of the work of Mosca, and what Meisel considers the error of elite analysis.

Michels, Robert. *Political Parties: A Sociological Study of the Oligarchical Tendencies of Modern Democracy.* New York: Collier Books, 1962. The most famous, and oft-cited work in the European tradition of empirical elite analysis.

Miller, Delbert. *International Community Power Structures: Comparative Studies of Four World Cities.* Bloomington: Indiana University Press, 1970. A comparative analysis of power structure in America, England, and Latin America.

Mills, C. Wright. *The Power Elite.* New York: The Oxford University Press, 1956. This work was the ideological spur that prompted the spate of counter-efforts in elite analysis, and remains the most famous book in North American sociology.

Mosca, Gaetano. *The Ruling Class.* New York: McGraw-Hill, 1939. Along with Michels, this work is the usually cited European theoretical reference for elite analysis.

Nelson, Michael. "Community Power Structure: Fact or Artifact?" Unpublished M.A. Thesis, Department of Sociology and Anthropology, Carleton University, Ottawa, 1972. A very detached analysis of disciplinary and methodological bias in elite investigation, with an extensive bibliography.

Porter, John. *The Vertical Mosaic.* Toronto: The University of Toronto Press, 1965. The most influential work in Canadian social science, Porter's analysis offers systematic evidence of concentrated power in Canada.

Presthus, Robert. *Elites in the Policy Process.* London: Cambridge Press, 1974. A comparative analysis of elites and interest groups in Canada and the United States.

_____ . *Elite Accommodation in Canadian Politics.* Toronto: Macmillan, 1973. An analysis of interest group politics and elites in Canada, with considerable empirical detail.

Rose, Arnold. *The Power Structure: Political Process in American Society.* New York: Oxford University Press, 1967. An explicit attempt to speak against the pluralist interest group conception of elite behavior in the United States.

14

The Group Basis of Politics

Mildred A. Schwartz*

INTRODUCTION

To the contemporary social scientist, the call to a "group basis of politics" seems self-evident. Politics is inherently a group process since it involves the definition of collective goals, particularly those affecting the allocation of scarce resources. Politics does not concern isolated individuals; the political process gets underway only when collective existence leads to the development of political leadership, institutions and organizations. Yet to the extent that groups in politics may no longer connote anything special, we risk missing the innovative potential of the group approach, and the battles fought and won that gave the group approach much of its lasting impact as well as its inability to excite us now.

An intellectual history of the group approach must give pre-eminence to the rejection of nineteenth century views of sovereignty, in which the locus of authority was confined to the state.[1] Among the major figures producing a shift in emphasis was the German exponent of historical jurisprudence, Otto von Gierke (1841-1921), who argued that the state had many similarities to other social groups, and in particular, shared with other groups in making and enforcing laws. In other words, he treated law and authority as general social processes, operating in the life of all organized collectivities, rather than just exclusive attributes of the state.[2] Translated into English, von Gierke's work influenced a broad range of scholars, including Harold Laski (1893-1950), in

*Professor of Sociology, University of Illinois at Chicago Circle. Author's Note: My colleagues Paul Pross, Fred Engelmann, and Léon Dion kindly reviewed this chapter, though time did not permit adding specific suggestions. They are not responsible, however, for my interpretations. For the second edition, Paul Pross contributed additional insights and suggestions.

turn highly influential in his early writing in furthering the "pluralist theory of the state", in which power was conceptualized as lying in a number of associations, of which the state is but one.[3]

This new emphasis, attuned to the spread of popular sovereignty and growing limits on the authoritarian state, was also attractive to political thinkers in the United States, but even more important there was a concern with how government actually operated. This is the origin of the "behavioral revolution", which began with a shift away from juridic and institutional emphases to a focus on how governments work. The crucial figure was Arthur Bentley, whose *The Process of Government,* published in 1908, was the American version of a group emphasis.[4] For Bentley, the task was straightforward: to explain political behavior we cannot spend time dissecting laws, constitutions or treatises; nor can we concern ourselves with individual psychological qualities.

> The raw material [of government] can be found only in the actually performed legislating-administrating-adjudicating activities of the nation and in the streams and currents of activity that gather among the people and rush into these spheres.[5]

In the United States as well, the move to a group approach, describing things as they were, found an outlet in the writings of "muckrakers", those concerned with exposing political corruption and venality to the public. The relation between the study of groups and the muckrakers lay in their revelations of how special group interests affected the course of governmental decisions.[6] This direction is found as well in the work of economic historians, in particular Charles Beard, who placed a new emphasis on the impact of business interests on party politics.[7] To the extent that these various threads can be brought together, they have in common a concern with the place of the individual in his social and political milieu, and constitute an affirmation of the liberal, democratic state. The contemporary view is stated most carefully by the eminent Laval University political scientist Léon Dion, in his two-volume work.[8] This view is not primarily concerned with the dominance of the state, nor with the rather simple-minded solutions suggested by Bentley, that defining groups and their interests tells us everything we need to know about politics, nor does it have the conviction that a plurality of interests protects the individual from the tyranny of any one of them. Yet it does recognize that groups serve to buffer the isolated individual from his vulnerability to the manipulations of elites. It questions the arguments of neo-rationalists such as Mancur Olsen,[9] who give preeminence to the individual as the unit of political analysis, but omit collective experiences and aspirations. From the perspective of political theory, then, we can begin with Dion's contention that the group approach is not all there is about politics; but to ignore groups is to ignore the fundamental issues raised by the liberal society concerning the role of the individual and his place in the polity.

Canadian political thought was not engaged by the issues of historic concern to the originating theorists, even though Harold Laski taught at McGill

University during World War I. Nor were there notable followers of Bentley here, such as David Truman or V.O. Key in the United States. Certainly Canadian students are now unusually fortunate to have available Dion's impressive work on the subject. But Dion is too comprehensive in his review of the literature and too fair-minded in his assessment to be characterized as a whole-hearted group theorist. Dion doubts whether the study of groups can even be termed a theory. Moreover, his two-volume work is relatively thin on Canadian material, and in that sense one would be hard-pressed to describe him as a theorist of Canadian groups. None of these points, however, detracts from our debt to Dion, whose work provides the framework for this chapter.

In the one major political science text which takes seriously the group approach, Van Loon and Whittington begin their relevant chapter with an assertion on the pervasiveness of groups in Canada.

> Wherever government turns its hand, there it will find some kind of organized group operating—and whatever groups operate they find that government activities overlap their own. [10]

Nevertheless, they still indicate considerable reservation about the effectiveness of the group approach, and its applicability to Canada. We will not be looking, then, for Canadian group theorists. Our main concern is with how the group approach has contributed to the study of Canadian politics.

THE MANY MEANINGS OF GROUPS

One of the most irritating experiences in reading Bentley's now classic work is a vagueness of language, an unwillingness to define concepts, and a lack of guidelines for those who would follow him. He could say, with alarming inclusiveness, "When the groups are adequately stated, everything is stated. When I say everything I mean everything," [11] and yet not tell us what an adequately stated group is, or even more precisely, what is not a group. Bentley's diffuseness contributed to a comprehensive, all-encompassing way of conceptualizing the political process, in which the life of groups, in whatever form, is treated as the essence of politics.

It is simply not useful to consider all groups. At most, we need take into account only those groups that pursue political interests. A useful working definition of the elements characterizing such political interest groups is derived largely from Dion. [12] An interest group is first of all an association in which members are organized in more or less stable relationships with assigned roles. It is here that Dion differs with some other students of interest groups, who are prepared to include unorganized entities in their definition, recognizing their potential for political action. [13] But if interest groups are going to perform their task they must be able to act, and while individuals can act together without prior organization, as in a mob, such action is too uncertain to be part of our concern.

The central task of interest groups is the promotion or defence of the group's welfare. An interest group comes into being when some number of individuals with shared characteristics recognize an identity of concerns and unite to further them, either because of perceived threat from others in the society, or because they believe they can, through organization, enhance their share of or access to valued goods and services. The collective objectives or goals which develop in this way may be simple or complex, few or many, and may involve a great deal or little organized activity: the goals remain as the group's *raison d'être*.

Interest groups are more or less voluntary associations. Why "more or less"? They are voluntary in the sense that they are not the result of some ascribed status, and require some positive act of joining. However, those who are members may have little choice about joining. This can be illustrated in the case of trade union membership in a closed shop. The union is a voluntary association, and membership is a positive act, but refusing to join may preclude the possibility of employment. Membership in business or professional associations may not have this fully coercive character, yet it too may be essential for establishing contacts with clients, providing specialized services (as in the case of physicians who are dependent on referrals), conforming to licensing regulations, and achieving substantial success in a given field. Given these limitations, one may wonder why it is still so important to stress the voluntary nature of interest groups. The answer lies in their comparison with similar groups that have a totally involuntary membership. These are generally termed corporate groups. They are found in many undemocratic societies, and are indeed the hallmark of fascist-style politics. Under fascism, all major interests in the society, e.g. farmers, industrial workers, owners, students, are organized and those with the appropriate characteristics are automatically a part of them. This organization has a political goal, enabling the authoritarian regime to control these interests. However, it is true that in democratic societies there are also corporate groups, in which membership is essentially automatic. The instance already cited of trade union membership in a closed shop situation would be a case in point. Such corporate groups differ from the fascist example in not being organized by some central political authority and existing independently of it. Moreover, they may be called upon to cooperate with other organized interests, as business and labor might do in agreeing on voluntary wage restraints. We follow the tradition here of speaking of interest groups and not of corporate groups since the latter are involuntary or ascribed, while the voluntaristic nature of the former is always present as an essential characteristic, even if not empirically present in all instances. Finally, they differ from corporate groups in not always having a recognized place in the political process.

Interest groups are distinguished from other groups in the society by their primary orientation to the political system, coupled with a separate and distinct organizational existence. It is in this sense that we argue that interest groups are different from corporate groups, at least when the latter are creatures of the political authorities. They are also distinct from political parties. Parties exist to attain power, whatever other purpose they may pursue, but interest groups do not. The political concerns of interest groups are expressed through pressures on decision-makers, not through direct participation in the political decision-making process.

Interest groups may take many forms. Pross suggests that we treat interest groups as organizations that can be located along a single continuum, ranging from institutionalized groups to issue-oriented ones.[14] One could, more precisely, divide his single dimension into two, since it encompasses both the objectives of the groups and their organizational make-up, but in either case this does not affect the usefulness of his approach. The most institutionalized groups are those with well-developed organizational structures that enable them to retain stable memberships and maintain ready access to government. They tend to have a range of concerns, be adept at bargaining, and place strong emphasis on the maintenance of the organization itself. In contrast, issue-oriented interest groups are loosely organized, and are often dependent on volunteer and intermittent assistance for carrying out their activities. They often have a single issue as their focus, and it is this which determines their activities, not any particular concern for the continuity of their organization.

This typology aids in classifying, and hence understanding, existing groups, although no single group may exactly conform to either extreme. At the institutionalized end we can locate the Canadian Manufacturers' Association, the Consumers' Association of Canada, and the Canadian Federation of Agriculture. We can also find examples of institutionalized groups among local ratepayers' associations and neighborhood businessmen's groups. Groups which have a less coherent organizational structure and greater focus on particular issues include those which operate on the local level, inspired by concerns with housing, education, transportation or environment. A famous Toronto example is the Stop Spadina group. Nationally, issue-oriented groups may come into being in response to an equally broad range of issues. Among recent examples are the abortion rights and right to life groups.

The conception of groups used here is a limiting one, in which there are clear, if permeable, boundaries between groups and other elements of the political environment. This departure from the Bentleyan conception of groups is in keeping with the approach of Canadian scholars, as well as being more systematic and, I would argue, more useful.

RELATIONS WITH GOVERNMENT

The principal justification for studying the role of groups in the political process lies in their relations to government. In the Canadian setting, there are several loci of possible influence: Cabinet, legislative bodies, the public bureaucracy and other official agencies. Agreement on these loci has not produced similar judgments, however, on the location of greatest contact between interest groups and government, the level at which efforts to influence are most effective, or the modes by which these efforts can be made influential.[15] Some of the disagreements, or perhaps more properly, differences in emphasis, are associated with the difficulties of obtaining information on the processes of contact and in evaluating outcomes.

Cabinet

Institutionalized interest groups maintain contacts with the cabinet through the submission of annual briefs. According to Helen Dawson, whose work on interest groups represents one of the few long-standing commitments to the topic among Canadian political scientists, Canadian cabinets (at both federal and provincial levels) are readily accessible to interest groups, and even welcome contacts as a means of obtaining information on public demands and possibly counterweighing the demands of their own public servants.[16] Probably more significant than formal briefs are regular contacts with individual cabinet ministers. Such contacts are evident not only with ministers responsible for departments that are directly relevant to a particular group, but also with ministers from the same region as the affected interest group. The importance of such contacts comes into perspective when studying groups without easy access to cabinet. Thus Chant argues, in studying efforts to bring about pollution control, that pressure on cabinet is one of the necessary ingredients for the success of issue-oriented groups.[17] Dawson suggests that cabinets in minority governments are more vulnerable to pressure from interest groups than they may have been under circumstances of a strong majority.

Engelmann and Schwartz question just what impact interest group tactics in fact have. Interest groups by definition present their own concerns; even where individual cabinet members have a strong commitment to the same goals, the cabinet as a whole, charged with governing the country, will always be hard-pressed to satisfy all groups which place demands on it.[18] Yet even if this is generally true, Pross argues that these same governing pressures turn ministers away from their local constituents and make them responsive to special interests. Ministers' policy responsibilities give advantages to interest groups with the information resources and the organizational skills to make a persuasive case.[19] Still, in that most critical arena of Canadian political life, negotiations between the federal and provincial governments at the ministerial level, interest group participation is virtually absent.[20]

Legislature

Until recently, there was general consensus that interest group contacts with individual members of Parliament were not likely to lead to productive interchanges. Some reevaluation has occurred, partly through the success of issue-oriented groups which are dependent on the publicity they can achieve, either through broad-gauged contacts through members of Parliament, or the indirect pay-off from favorable publicity through the mass media. For example, agitation by organized pensioners appears to have led to changes in provisions of the Canada Pension Plan, and subsequent pension policy.[21] As Van Loon and Whittington point out, one could easily overlook the possible impact of interest groups on Parliament, in the sense that we are speaking of two analytically distinct sources of political action, when many MPs, either themselves or through their families, are also members of interest groups. This means that, for example, spokesmen for consumer interests are not solely concentrated in the Consumers' Association, but find many allies and even members among MPs. Robert Presthus also requires us to consider the impact of relatively frequent contact between MPs and interest group representatives with whom there was already some affinity of interest.[22] As a result of recent changes in the committee structure and powers in Parliament, Dawson predicts that we may see more direct contacts with MPs, and a lessened impact on cabinet. At present, however, interest groups rarely supply information to Parliamentary committees and continue to have a somewhat touchy relationship with MPs.

Even more contradictory are assessments of contact with the Senate. Dawson states that her research gives little support to the notion that strong lobbying of Senators is influential, and indeed, sees little point to such efforts by interest groups, unless government plans to introduce more legislation through Senate initiative become significant. Senators, however, cannot be dismissed so readily, if Van Loon and Whittington's judgments are accepted. They see the most effective lobbyists to be those with strong connections with the executive and administrative levels of government. Among those with such contacts are included current members of the Senate, opening a whole new avenue of access for interest groups.[23] Campbell takes an even stronger line, portraying the Senate as a "lobby from within", representing business interests.[24]

Public Service

The downgrading of members of Parliament as targets of interest groups inheres in the operation of the Canadian parliamentary system. When legislation is introduced in Parliament, it is already too late for much influence to be exerted. Moreover, the ordinary member is unlikely to introduce significant legislation, which remains the prerogative not just of the party in office, but of the cabinet. In a real sense, then, even lobbying cabinet members can come too late to influence legislation where the government has already made a policy commitment. It is for these reasons that the public service is a prime target for interest groups. At this locus the opportunity exists for influencing both pending legislation and its eventual implementation. Presthus considers access to the bureaucracy as the most important activity for interest groups.[25] Efforts to influence include direct contacts and briefings. These are helped by the tendency of both civil servants and interest group officials to hold office for a long time which increases the likelihood that personal ties will develop. Barriers still exist against employing formal representatives of interest groups in the higher echelons of the public service since this would hardly be in keeping with the spirit of an impartial bureaucracy, let alone with the bureaucracy's demands for employee commitment which could easily run counter to the interest group. This is contrary to Presthus's interpretation of the pressure for a "representative bureaucracy".[26]

Interest groups often appear to have special legislative advantages because, once they are identified as interested parties yet prepared to be constructive in their advice and criticisms, they can be shown drafts of instructions for legislation (not the same as the legislation itself). After a bill has gone through first reading in the House, they may also be sent a pending bill and solicited for comments.

Many factors enter into an interest group's success in accomplishing policy goals. Membership size, control over financial resources, monopoly over important technical knowledge, and the prestige of its leaders all bear on whether the group will be taken seriously. A willingness to cooperate and avoid outright confrontation and personal criticism also appear to be important elements in success, if not on a particular issue, at least on the chances of continued easy access to the loci of power. Regional centers of support can help interest groups where they are effective in first convincing provincial authorities of their cause, and where these in turn are prepared to help argue their cause nationally. Bucovetsky, for example, demonstrates how mining and oil interests with a strong provincial base were able to make their case counter to apparent government intentions on tax reform.[27] As Bucovetsky demonstrates, the public bureaucracy is not a monolith, but incorporates a diversity of perspectives and goals. The autonomy of government departments is then an important independent element in an interest group's successful challenge. Where there is not sufficient evidence of overwhelming public support and hence political expediency, bureaucratic interests are able to sustain their position against a challenging interest group. Thus Barry shows how, despite concerted efforts on the part of an issue-oriented group founded to aid the plight of Biafrans, and aided by such institutionalized groups as the Presbyterian Church and the Canadian Red Cross, the Department of External Affairs was able to sustain its definition of the situation. Barry judges that this was possible because the government did not feel there was sufficient public pressure to warrant a change in policy on Biafra.[28]

Other Agencies

Interest groups also have scope for influence in such official bodies as royal commissions, task forces, regulatory agencies and advisory councils. These kinds of agencies provide what appear to be the ideal set of partners for interaction with organized interests: their membership composition is largely or entirely apart from government, their mandate requires the collection of information, and they recommend policy. Yet even such apparently auspicious factors do not always lead to advantages for interest groups. For example, the Royal Commission on Health Services had four of its seven commissioners from the health professions. Local, provincial and national health-related bodies presented formal submissions, appeared before the Commission, and provided assistance to the Commission's own research facilities. The research itself, however, was under the direction of social scientists, and the Commission's recommendations for governmental involvement in health care were not a reflection of the views of the medical establishment.

Since systematic reviews of interest group participation in public bodies have not been done, it is not possible to assess fully the impact of interest groups. Lowi's judgment that regulatory agencies in the United States quickly became coopted by the interests they were intended to control is not so apparent for Canada.[29] For example, Brown-John's survey of contacts between trade unions in Ontario and regulatory agencies indicated cases where agencies ruled for unions against employers, or ruled in favor of both against a third party, generally a foreign competitor.[30] Altogether the most conclusive evidence of the influence of interest groups comes from their participation in advisory councils, where, as in the National Research Council and the Medical Research Council, members chosen to fill advisory roles to the government tend to reflect the policy positions of their constituents.[31]

Assessing Relations

Perhaps the most telling factor preventing a full assessment of interest group relations with government and, in particular, with the bureaucracy, is the cloak of secrecy under which these activities are conducted. This is not to say that there is anything illegal or even of questionable legitimacy in what occurs, but it is a reflection of the style of Canadian government, and the manner in which the bureaucracy operates. This has made judgments difficult and the most careful students of this topic cautiously avoid explicit conclusions without much more empirical evidence.

We have enough information to recognize that relations between interest groups and government are really reciprocal. Neither is passive and both try to influence each other. We have already suggested that cabinet members will make use of information supplied by interest groups in deliberate efforts to thwart the control of their own bureaucracies. Members of Parliament also appear to welcome interest group contacts as a means of obtaining information they can use for their own purposes. If interest groups try to obtain places on regulatory agencies and Royal Commissions, government agencies actively recruit them as members of advisory committees. These may then become "tame" experts, tools of a government department. Governments see a real value in interest groups which provide information and demands through recognized channels, and where they do not exist, may even aid in setting them up. It is certainly no secret that many such interest groups accept government grants as a necessary bulwark to their continuity. While this does not necessarily make them tools of government, their independence can more readily be compromised. In this sense, we see how the thin line separating voluntaristic interest groups from centrally organized corporate groups is easily bridged. It has led some Canadian interests to be at least reluctant to locate in Ottawa, where chances for cooptation are greatest, if only through flattering appeals for their appearance and the ties they forge with governmental agencies.[32]

As more students of politics turn their attention to the policy-making process, it is likely that the role of interest groups will be given new scrutiny. This is suggested by Pross's identification of policy configurations, in which government departments, interest groups and key politicians interact in specific policy areas. To the extent that these configurations exist, Pross finds them troublesome, undermining our usual understanding of representative democracy and giving interest groups a new centrality.[33]

RELATIONS WITH POLITICAL PARTIES

Any discussion of the relation between interest groups and political parties is affected by the conceptual problems of adequately distinguishing between the two. Presthus, for example, is prepared to subsume political parties under interest groups.[34] Many political scientists are more comfortable with Almond's distinction on the basis of function. "Interest groups articulate political demands," that is, they raise demands, seek support for them and attempt to influence policy-makers to satisfy them. "Political parties...are aggregative," that is, they combine articulated interests and assign priorities in ways that permit the selection of political authorities and the making of policy decisions.[35] Empirically, the distinctions between the two may not always be clear-cut, but analytically their separation is a necessary part of understanding the political process in any system where there are competitive parties. Unless we wish to give unnatural flatness to our political analysis, we must emphasize that parties, unlike interest groups, are exclusively engaged in politics, and exist to acquire direct governing authority.

The form and character which relations between parties and interest groups take is related to the social and political milieu of their existence. The closest ties occur where the politicization of an interest group leads to the development of an organizational arm specifically devoted to political action. Instances of such cohesion existed between trade unions and the British Labour Party and the founding of confessional parties in the Netherlands.

In Canada, it is alleged that the relation between parties and interest groups is very tenuous, with one notable exception.[36] That one exception, and even it is not of the character of its British counterpart, concerns the connection between organized labor and first the CCF and then the NDP.[37] For the most part, reasons for assuming a non-partisan stance seem overwhelming. Most crucially, overt attachment to a single party will preclude much governmental favor when that party is out of office. Some groups, notably the Wheat Pools, experienced political difficulties when their party, the United Farmers, went into oblivion. As a result, many interest groups follow a policy of avoiding partisan attachments. In the past, for example, the Canadian Manufacturers' Association (CMA) and more recently, the Retail Manufacturers' Association (RMA) have revealed strong proclivities for the Conservative party. Yet they have still been restrained by the necessity of continued dealings with a Liberal government. The more usual policy has been the traditional one of making financial contributions to both major parties.

One can find close relations between interest groups and parties only if a loose definition of interests is used. For example, the Liberal Party may be said to include corporate interests among its leaders if the business background of these individuals is considered sufficient evidence of interest group involvement.[38]

Pross predicts that the rising importance of interest groups, functionally organized and adapted to the modern economy, will contribute to a parallel decline in political parties, which are tied to the representation of individual and local interests.[39] But it is also possible to predict that, if these interest groups become more potent, the political machinery will adapt to restrain them. That potential lies, for example, in an expanded role for MPs as ombudsmen for their constitutents, not only in dealing with the bureaucracy, but also in confronting interest groups.[40]

Normative restraints on admitting the possibility of interest group-party interrelations have left us with sparse evidence. According to Engelmann and Schwartz,

> Both actors in, and observers of Canadian political life hesitate to face up to the realities of interest-party relations; until recently, they tended to maintain strongly that these were illegitimate, or non-existent.[41]

From the evidence available, it is clear that interrelations are much more modest than is true in other Western democracies, yet we still feel a sense of dissatisfaction at the sketchy information we have.

SOCIAL AND POLITICAL MILIEU

The very existence of interest groups, their scope of operation, and their possible impact are closely intertwined with the nature of the society in which they operate. It is in this context that the role of Canadian interest groups appears to differ from the role of those in other countries. For example, Van Loon and Whittington consider interest groups in both the United States and Britain to have greater impact on political parties. Presthus, who has done a systematic comparison of interests in the United States and Canada, rates those in Canada as less active and less effective. His findings lead him to make a number of judgments about differences between the two societies.

> In the United States the system of interest group politics is more fully developed. Explanations include a more participative political culture; the separation-of-

powers apparatus which provides more, and more effective, points of group access; and greater wealth and occupational differentiation which encourage a more intensive and well-supported interest group structure. As a result, lobbying activities are more common and group effectiveness seems to be generally higher, particularly regarding business and welfare groups. Although labor is only marginally effective in the American system, it is clearly more effective than its Canadian counterpart. American directors [of interest groups] tend to have more political resources, which apparently rest upon a generally higher level of felt political efficacy. Since several of their hard resources—for example, directors' education and occupation, experience, age, organization—are often no greater than those of Canadian directors, one must attribute this condition to cultural differences, including American optimism, contrasted with the somewhat pessimistic strain apparent in Canadian thought and literature.[42]

Societal Factors

Prior to evaluating the impact of the social setting we need to know whether groups have a legal basis for existence (not a problem in Canada though it has been elsewhere); whether sizable portions of the population affiliate with them; and whether members attach importance to groups as a means of exerting influence on the political system. For Canada we have information only for membership and not on public evaluations of its significance. The United States has often been viewed as a nation of "joiners", but comparative research now calls into question its uniqueness. Specifically, as Curtis has recently demonstrated, there is little difference between Canada and the United States in the proportions who belong to voluntary associations, and this is also true when considering multiple group affiliation.[43] While French and English speakers join associations in similar proportions, the former are much less likely to affiliate with civic associations.[44]

For interest groups, the major question concerns the legitimacy accorded their efforts to influence government. By legitimacy we do not refer to the legal right to organize but to the more subtle, yet every bit as essential, recognition that interest groups can appropriately engage in activities which result in pressure on political authorities. It is legitimacy which is typically problematic, since it immediately calls into question the role and independence of political representatives, the political insulation of the public bureaucracy, and the protection of the public generally from those subgroups which have the organization and other resources to make their positions politically dominant. Everyone who writes about interest groups in Canada faces a situation where interest group activities in the political sphere are questioned, presented as non-existent, or dimissed as illegitimate. "Lobbying", it is alleged, is an American experience, foreign to Canada. We have, in fact, seen that this is not the case, yet we must still recognize these reactions as reflections on the legitimacy of interest groups. One consequence has been a relatively small number of studies on interest groups, only recently changing, and as indicated in the discussion of relations with government and parties, considerable difficulty in breaking through the secrecy that surrounds their actions. One should not assume, however, that questions of legitimacy are raised only in Canada. These are general problems, endemic in all societies where interest groups exist. For example, Presthus calls attention to the absence of all political science writing on interest groups in Britain until 1955 as an indication of low legitimacy there.[45] Even in the United States, a so-called paradise for interest groups, serious questions remain. As indicated at the outset of this paper, the whole tradition of "muckraking" literature in that country was premised on the dangers interest groups posed to the viability of American democracy. Dion also documents the range of literature demonstrating the continuing distaste for interest groups in the United States, and the pressures that exist for interest groups to keep out of politics.[46] Without better comparative data, we can only suggest that their legitimacy remains questionable in many societies, and this in itself does little to explain cross-national differences in the presence or effectiveness of interest groups.

One question raised by the concept of legitimacy relates to the role and independence of political representatives. From the perspective of theories of representation, the question is: Whom do legislators represent, and how do group interests enter into their selection and deliberations? An answer that has recently received attention in Canada is based on the theory of consociational-ism. Elaborated by Arend Lijpart from his analysis of the Netherlands, the theory postulates that the stability of political systems, riven by deep social and economic cleavages, is maintained through the cooperative activities of elites representing the principal cleavages. The cleavages are themselves insulated from contact, while members are sufficiently trusting of their leaders to permit them to bargain on their behalf.[47] The applicability of consociationalism to Canada was first picked up by Noel,[48] and applied to the realm of interest groups by Presthus. MacRae notes that consociationalism is probably present, to a degree, in all societies with major social cleavages, but having said this it becomes necessary to establish empirically the degree in any particular society. The special features of Canadian society, with its complex, sometimes overlap-ping, system of cleavages include the comparative lack of clear-cut organization along lines of greatest segmentation; an electoral and party system which does not divide along lines of cleavage; and a system of accommodation which takes place primarily, though not always successfully, within the federal cabinet.[49] In this sense, consociationalism is not a particularly apt model for Canada.

Another theory of representation that is gaining attention is based on models of corporatism, particularly as applied to the liberal state.[50] Liberal democratic corporatism differs from consociationalism in stressing the functional represen-tation of socio-economic interests, the close ties between these interests and the state, and the reciprocal impact of the state on corporate groups. Panich sees few corporatist elements in Canada,[51] though one aspect of corporatism, where the state calls on representatives of critical interests for purposes of consultation, may be present, and corporatist approaches appear to be increasingly attractive.

Political Factors

If we move now to more narrowly political factors as these affect the emergence and operation of interest groups, Dion draws our attention to four. They include federalism, the nature and dispersion of power, the proliferation of governmental activities and agencies, and the constitutional separation of powers. In each instance, where there is more governmental activity Dion hypothesizes greater scope for interest groups.

Most attention has been given to the impact of federalism. Major interest groups, with some national focus, normally adopt a federal structure, mirroring the structure of government.[52] This is a necessary characteristic, enabling interests to mobilize their membership and effectively deal with different governments with jurisdiction over them.

According to Dawson, this federal structure of interest groups themselves, as well as the need to involve themselves in the federal structure of the government, is generally a source of considerable strain on the potential impact of interest groups.

> The fact that the national organization's executive or board of directors or both is often composed of regional or provincial representatives (usually branch presidents), means that the achievement of consensus on desirable national, as opposed to regional or provincial, policies often verges on the impossible. Consequently the national headquarters is frequently unable to present a vigorous, consistent, or sometimes even united front to the federal government. Furthermore, for reasons that are not always clear, provincial branches and other affiliates tend to keep re-electing the same personnel to the national executive, board of directors and committees. Not surprisingly, many organizations have the same personnel for years at a stretch. This has two consequences: an ageing executive body and difficulty in initiating policy changes.[53]

Dawson goes on to say that the national executive is largely dependent on the popularity of provincial components, who in turn need to make their appeals in terms of their local membership or clientele. All of this has consequences for consistent and united policy-making, and contributes to a frequent lack of unity among the components of the organization. Moreover, when the interests served are covered by more than one governmental jurisdiction, the ability of the national executive to deal with the federal government can be impeded by local considerations. Where uniformity in regulations is sought, the organization becomes a victim of the political maneuvering characteristic of federal-provincial relations in Canada. All these symptoms contribute to and enhance the likelihood of financial weaknesses, fed by the resentment of members at the costs of financing a national headquarters. Indeed, because some interest groups rely on federal grants, they may be reluctant to have a national headquarters, or at least one in Ottawa, where, it is feared, the executive would come under the sway of the federal government.

Not all students of interest groups in Canada echo this essentially negative assessment of the consequences of federalism. They see more positive advantages, reflecting an assessment made earlier in the context of the American federal system by David Truman.

> Groups that would be rather obscure or weak under a unitary arrangement may

hold advantageous positions in the State governments and will be vigorous in their insistence upon the existing distribution of powers between State and nation. As the advantage of access shifts through time, moreover, groups shift from defenders to critics of the existing balance.[54]

Bucovestky, for example, records the ways in which the mining industry as an interest group took advantage of its crucial role in the economies of the western provinces to further the bargaining power of the provinces themselves in affecting federal tax legislation. Kwavnick presents case study material from two interest groups, associated with students and labor, to argue that the means available under a federal system enable interest groups to enhance their position. This is demonstrated through the rivalries between the Canadian Union of Students (CUS) and the Union Générale des Etudiants du Québec (UGEQ). The latter was able both to become an independent organization and to promote its bargaining position when the federal government in effect defined the interest of French-speaking students as lying solely under the jurisdiction of the Québec government. There was then no major need for participation in a national organization. Perhaps illustrating even more clearly the impact of federalism were efforts by the Canadian Labour Congress (CLC) and the Québec-based Confederation of National Trade Unions (CNTU) to increase their roles through two opposing approaches. The CLC attempted to alter the balance of power between provincial and federal governments by pressing for more centralizing policies. In contrast, the CNTU was concerned with enhancing the position of the provincial governments as a means of consolidating its own position.[55]

Of the remaining political factors, Dawson provides a useful checklist of the ways in which interest groups in the Canadian political system have differed in their impact from either Britain or the United States. In Canada, there is considerably less contact with parliamentary committees than in the other two countries, taking into account differences in their political systems and in the procedures of contact. There is also less contact with and effort to influence private members of Parliament. In Britain, interest groups maintain considerable contact with former cabinet ministers; in Canada, this is virtually non-existent. This contrast is also evident in the case of parliamentary secretaries. When comparison is made with the United States, Dawson finds little scope here for the kind of venal lobbying that has characterized the worst abuses of interest group politics, although perhaps this has something to do with our own ignorance. With fewer appointments available outside the civil service, there is also less consultation with Canadian interest groups on personnel. The one exception to generally lower interest group activity in Canada, tied by Dawson to differences in political structure, are the greater contacts made by Canadian interests directly with the Prime Minister. In Britain, such contacts are highly unusual. Thompson and Stanbury confirm this analysis, arguing that "both the restricted role of Canadian interest groups and the weaker explanatory power of interest group theory are in large part attributable to the constitutional structure of the Canadian government and its decision-making process."[56]

LIMITATIONS AND CONTRIBUTIONS

The perspective taken here is one that rejects the claim of those group theorists who argue that political processes need only a focus on groups to illuminate them. In an effort to explain everything through one approach or one framework, we could find ourselves explaining nothing, and be left with conclusions too general, and analyses too descriptive, to advance the study of politics in any significant way. Instead we consider the world of politics a multi-faceted arena, comprising struggles among social cleavages and the organized interest groups that emerge to participate directly in that struggle, conditioned by issues and events, and shaped by the existing political machinery. We find greatest value in a group approach that confines itself to organized interests with political goals.

In its most general form, the group approach tends to slight the effects of issues and events on the political process. In this respect we found the work of Paul Pross particularly useful, especially the emphasis on issues and events in his concept of "issue-oriented groups". Issues and events, however, not only have an impact on specific interest groups whose goals are directly tied to them, but are also involved in the life of institutionalized interest groups. They provide the circumstances to which interests must respond, and the setting that shapes their daily lives and the direction of their organizations. In the example cited of the mining industry, proposed tax changes were the crucial stimulus to mobilizing an interest group. In Kwavnick's study of labor unions, changes in the market, in particular industries, and the nature of the provincial and federal governments all affect the course of interest group development.

Allied with this lack of concern for issues and events is a parallel absence of attention to the impact of individual actors. Garson, in his critique of the group approach, makes a strong objection to this omission in Bentley. He attributes it partly to Bentley's aversion to psychological interpretations, but this in itself is not of major importance. What is more significant is Bentley's lack of differentiation between elites and the mass of followers or members. Yet even an emphasis on elites does not always result in the conception of a differentiated group life, in which members have unequal access to decision-makers, both within the interest group itself and in government. Again we have to turn to specific case studies, as in Kwavnick, to obtain a more effective measure of the role of individuals and the ways in which specific members of interest groups, along with individual members of government, make a difference to outcomes. the relation between group structure, the interaction between interest groups and government, and the effect of individual actors is also brought home by Van Loon and Whittington in at least two ways. They note, for instance, the low level of influence exerted through mass write-ins to government, attributable in part to the undifferentiated quality of mass pressure. This observation is confirmed in another way by Chant's study of Pollution Probe, an issue-oriented group that was aided by its connection with an existing university organization, and the high status and good contacts of its leader. At the elite level, Van Loon and Whittington attribute prime importance to the network of relations between interest groups and government necessary for effective influence, and confirm the particularly advantageous position of specific individuals.

The rationale for group approach to politics was a more effective way of describing and explaining how politics really works. One of the ironies of its development has been an underestimation of political factors, as some practitioners of the approach have turned away from concern with the role of political parties and government itself. As Dion points out, the structure of interest groups and their scope of action is largely dependent on the structure of government, and hence to ignore the political system leads only to an imperfect understanding of interest groups themselves.

We are concerned by tendencies to ignore the distinctions between interest groups and political parties. The principal goal of interest groups is to influence political agencies and decision-makers in ways favorable to the existence of the group, in contrast to political parties, which exist to gain governmental power. To the extent that some small parties see their role as primarily one of influencing existing governments, they fall much more in the category of interest groups than of parties. All organizations have, by definition, continuing structures, with a life of their own, and a set of organizational imperatives that become independent of other, even primary, goals for their existence. This does not make party organization an interest group; all it means is that both parties and interest groups have similar structures simply because they are organizations. Yet, for the most part, we can say that the reason for ignoring political parties in the study of Canadian interests has to do with the low level of contact and impact that one has on the other. To the extent that this has not been true with regard to organized labor and the CCF and NDP, it has also been carefully recognized by most students of the topic.

If downplaying political parties can be rationalized in Canada by the apparently minor role of party-interest group relations, although there is no conclusive evidence on this, the same cannot be said where government is given a minor role. Government is simply not just a reflection of a variety of interest groups, either contending for greater access to resources, as the pluralists might describe, or reflecting the dominance of particular interest groups, as class analysts would allege. It may be this, it is true, but it is also much more. Just as we said in the case of political parties, government as an institutional area, once in existence, continues largely in response to its own imperatives. Members of Parliament are elected, government departments organized, cabinets formed, the day-to-day business of government met, even crises faced, through the structural mechanisms which exist to meet these exigencies. Interest groups may have an impact on them, but governmental activities are still independent of interest groups in the most essential ways. Not to recognize this explicitly and not to take this into account in the study of interest groups, results in an apolitical, if not mindless, analysis. We must also acknowledge what students of interest groups tell us about the difficulty of ascertaining the actual impact of interest groups' efforts. We do know that prime ministers and cabinet members weigh some of the pressures they perceive, reject some, and are always mindful of their own special powers. It is instructive that a neo-Marxist theory of the state now argues that government must necessarily be autonomous if only to carry out the interests of the bourgeoisie.[57]

CONCLUSION

The above criticisms do not deny the profound contributions of the group approach, including the most general form. Wherever it has been applied, it has made us confront the political world as it is, stripped of idealized conceptions about how it should work. It turns us away from inhibiting concerns about the legitimacy of interest groups to more illuminating ones about the nature and impact of interest group activities.

Garson's assessment of the challenges to group theory over the past two decades in the United States have led him to a sweeping dismissal of its current relevance.[58] But we, in turn, need to evaluate the bases of Garson's judgments. For one thing, we note that his objections are to the claims of group theory, and there we can agree that, as a theory, it could not be sustained. However, as a perspective on the political world it has been important, and continues to be so. Moreover, his comments are directed to the state of the field in the United States. While they are instructive, they have only limited applicability to Canada, since the group approach never had the same kind of dominance here. Even if the theoretical pretensions of the group approach have been superceded, an overextended rejection of the group approach can still be interpreted as a reflection of the dynamism of the field, always looking for new and better paradigms, theories and methods, rather than a faithful representation of reality. The continuing importance of the group approach lies in the fundamental questions it raises about the process of policy-making,[59] the strains on representative democracy associated with the rise of the bureaucratic state and the alleged decline of political parties, and the still unexplored possibilities of democratic corporatism.

SUMMARY

1. Though politics is inherently a group process, we must be careful not to overemphasize its significance in Canadian politics.
2. Initially the American writings on group politics were associated with the writings of muckrakers and a rejection of the traditional institutional approach to politics.
3. The central task of interest groups is the promotion or defence of the group's welfare.

4. Generally we think of interest groups as voluntary associations but in many instances individuals have little choice but to join.

5. The main difference between political parties and political interest groups is that the former seek political office and, if successful, operate the institutions of government while the latter do not seek public office but attempt to influence policies.

6. In Canada, interest groups seek to achieve their political goals by maintaining contacts with cabinet members, by interacting with members of the legislature, by attempting to influence the civil service, by "utilizing" appointments to regulatory and other quasi-political agencies, and by seeking to influence public opinion.

7. Generally it is difficult to assess the significance of interest group activity in Canada, partly because of the climate of secrecy and partly because there has been relatively little research based on empirical evidence.

8. In Canada, it seems that apart from the close connection between organized labor and the NDP, the relation between parties and interest groups is very tenuous. Most major interest groups give financial support to both major parties and work with whichever party is in power.

9. In general, interest group politics is more fully developed in the US than in Canada probably because in the US there is a more participative culture, there are more access points in the political system, there is greater wealth and there is greater occupational differentiation.

10. In Canada the major national interest groups tend to take their concerns directly to the head of government, the Prime Minister.

11. If taken to an extreme, the group approach tends to slight the effects of issues and events on the political process and to underrate the significance of individual actors and political parties.

12. Despite its weaknesses and ambiguities, the group approach has made profound contributions to the study of politics in Canada and elsewhere.

STUDY QUESTIONS

1. Is the importance of group activity in Canadian politics likely to increase or decrease? Why?

2. Is the expansion of group political activity in a free society a sign of political health or political illness?

3. Is group activity in Canada likely to expand more at the provincial or national level? Provide a rationale for your view.

4. Assess the importance of the following in the development of Canadian political group activity: political culture, political institutions, affluence.

5. Why, according to conventional wisdom, is there not much point in groups putting pressure on individual backbenchers in the House of Commons?

6. What factors make groups relatively powerful? With reference to the major Canadian political interest groups, is the effect of the factors increasing or decreasing?

7. Would growth in media influence likely increase or decrease the influence of Canadian political interest groups?

8. What tactics or practices might Canadian interest groups adopt in order to enhance their effectiveness?

9. Why are some interest groups more effective than others in achieving their political goals?

10. What policies should be adopted by Canadian governments to facilitate pressure group activity and what policies should be adopted to regulate and control pressure group activity?

ENDNOTES

1. David B. Truman, "Political Group Analysis," *International Encyclopedia of the Social Sciences*, Vol. 12 (1968), pp. 241-5; Earl Latham, "The Group Basis of Politics: Notes for a Theory," *American Political Science Review*, 46 (June, 1952), pp. 376-97.

2. John D. Lewis, "Otto von Gierke," *International Encyclopedia of the Social Sciences*, Vol. 6 (1968), pp. 177-80.

3. Herbert A. Deane, "Harold J. Laski," *International Encyclopedia of the Social Sciences*, Vol. 9 (1968), pp. 30-33; G. David Garson, "On the Origins of Interest-Group Theory: A Critique of a Process," *American Political Science Review*, 68 (December, 1974), pp. 1509-11.

4. Arthur F. Bentley, *The Process of Government* (Evanston, Ill.: Principia Press, 1935), originally published 1908 by The University of Chicago Press; Garson, "On the Origins of Interest-Group Theory," pp. 1511-14; Richard W. Taylor, "Arthur F. Bentley," *International Encyclopedia of the Social Sciences*, Vol. 2 (1968), pp. 58-62.

5. Bentley, *op. cit.*, p. 180.

6. Louis Filler, *The Muckrakers: Crusaders for American Liberalism* (Chicago: Regnery, 1968).

7. See, for example, Charles Beard, *The Economic Basis of Politics* (New York: Vintage, 1957), originally published 1922.

8. Léon Dion, *Société et politique: La Vie des groupes* (Québec: University of Laval Press, 1971), Vol. 1, *Fondements de la société libérale*, Vol. II, *Dynamique de la société libérale* (1972).

9. Mancur Olson, *The Logic of Collective Action*, rev. ed. (New York: Schocken Books, 1971).

10. Richard Van Loon and Michael Whittington, *The Canadian Political System*, 2nd ed. (Toronto: McGraw-Hill Ryerson, 1976), p. 286.

11. Bentley, *op. cit.*, pp. 208-9.

12. We use "interest group" throughout, but it should be considered synonymous with "pressure group", "political group", or "lobby". Dion, *Société et politique*, Vol. I., pp. 98-108.

13. For example, David B. Truman, *The Governmental Process*, 2nd ed. (New York: Knopf, 1971), pp. 511-15; V.O. Key, Jr., *Politics, Parties and Pressure Groups*, 5th ed. (New York: Crowell, 1964), p. 116.

14. A. Paul Pross, "Pressure Groups: Adaptive Instruments of Political Communication," *Pressure Group Behaviour in Canadian Politics*, ed. A. Paul Pross (Toronto: McGraw-Hill Ryerson, 1975), pp. 9-12. I use "institutionalized" rather than "institutional" to stress both the patterned and regulative aspects of interest group organization and the process by which they become established in their ties with major institutional areas.

15. Interest group efforts to influence government are often termed "lobbying". I have avoided the term whenever possible because of its pejorative connotations.

16. Helen Jones Dawson, "National Pressure Groups and the Federal Government," in Pross, *op. cit.*, pp. 36-8.

17. D.A. Chant, "Pollution Probe: Fighting the Polluters with Their Own Weapons," in Pross, *op. cit.*, p. 66.

18. F.C. Engelmann and M.A. Schwartz, *Canadian Political Parties: Origin, Character, Impact* (Scarborough: Prentice-Hall, 1975), pp. 154-6.

19. A. Paul Pross, "The Canadian Public Service and the Special Interest State," *The Administrative State: Canadian Perspectives — Essays in Honour of J.E. Hodgetts* (Toronto: University of Toronto Press, forthcoming).

20. Richard Simeon, *Federal-Provincial Diplomacy* (Toronto: University of Toronto Press, 1972), pp. 144, 281-3.

21. Kenneth Bryden, *Old Age Pensions and Policy-Making in Canada* (Montreal: McGill-Queen's University Press, 1974), pp. 196-7.

22. Robert Presthus, "Interest Groups and Parliament: Activities, Interaction, Legitimacy and Influence," *Canadian Journal of Political Science*, 4 (December, 1971), p. 460.

23. Van Loon and Whittington, *op. cit.*, p. 298.

24. Colin Campbell, *The Canadian Senate: A Lobby from Within* (Toronto: Macmillan of Canada, 1978).

25. Robert Presthus, *Elite Accommodation in Canadian Politics* (London and New York: Cambridge University Press, 1973), p. 211.

26. *Ibid.*, p. 197.

27. M.W. Bucovetsky, "The Mining Industry and the Great Tax Reform Debate," in Pross, *op. cit.*, pp. 89-114.

28. Donald Barry, "Interest Groups and the Foreign Policy Process: The Case of Biafra," in Pross, *op. cit.*, pp. 117-47.

29. Theodore Lowi, *The End of Liberalism* (New York: Norton, 1979).

30. Lloyd Brown-John, "The Regulatory Policy Process: The Role of Ontario Trade Unions as Intervenors," paper prepared for the Canadian Political Science Association annual meeting, Halifax, 1981.

31. Peter Aucoin, "The Role of Functional Advisory Councils," *The Structures of Policy-Making in Canada*, eds. G. Bruce Doern and Peter Aucoin (Toronto: Macmillan of Canada, 1971), pp. 154-78.

32. Dawson, *op. cit.*, p. 34.

33. Pross, "The Canadian Public Service," *op. cit.*

34. Presthus, *Elite Accommodation, op. cit.*, p. 60.

35. Gabriel Almond, "Interest Groups and the Political Process," *Comparative Politics: Notes and Readings*, ed. R.C. Macridis and B.E. Brown (Homewood, Ill.: Dorsey Press, 1961), pp. 129-30.

36. Van Loon and Whittington, *op. cit.*, p. 295.

37. David Kwavnick, *Organized Labour and Pressure Politics* (Montreal: McGill-Queen's University Press, 1972); Gad Horowitz, *Canadian Labour in Politics* (Toronto: University of Toronto Press, 1968).

38. John McMenemy and Conrad Winn, "Party Personnel-Elites and Activists," *in Political Parties in Canada*, eds. C. Winn and J. McMenemy (Toronto: McGraw-Hill Ryerson, 1976), p. 163.

39. Pross, "The Canadian Public Service," *op. cit.*

40. David Hoffman, "Liaison Officers and Ombudsmen: Canadian M.P.s and Their Relations with the Federal Bureaucracy and Executives," *Apex of Power*, ed. Thomas A. Hockin (Scarborough: Prentice-Hall of Canada, 1971), pp. 146-62.

41. Engelmann and Schwartz, *op. cit.*, p. 166.

42. Robert Presthus, "Interest Group Lobbying: Canada and the United States," *Annals of the American Academy*, 413 (May, 1976), p. 57. See also Robert Presthus, *Elites in the Policy Process* (New York: Cambridge University Press, 1974).

43. James Curtis, "Voluntary Association Joining: A Cross-National Comparative Note," *American Sociological Review*, 36 (October, 1971), pp. 872-89.

44. Dion, *op. cit.*, Vol. I, pp. 243-44.

45. Presthus, "Interest Group Lobbying," *op. cit.*, p. 45. See also *Interest Groups on Four Continents*, ed. Henry Ehrmann (Pittsburgh: University of Pittsburgh Press, 1958), p. 183.

46. Dion, *op. cit.*, Vol. I, pp. 294-7, 303-4.

47. Arendt Lijphart, "Consociational Democracy," *World Politics*, 21 (1969).

48. S.J.R. Noel, "Consociational Democracy and Canadian Federalism," *Canadian Journal of Political Science*, 4 (1971), pp. 15-8.

49. K.D. McRae, "Consociationalism and the Canadian Political System," *Consociational Democracy*, ed. K. McRae (Toronto: McClelland and Stewart, 1974), pp. 238-61.

50. Philippe Schmitter, "Still the Century of Corporatism?" *The Review of Politics*, 36 (January, 1974), pp. 85-131.

51. Leo Panitch, "The Development of Corporatism in Liberal Democracies," *Comparative Political Studies*, 10 (April, 1977), pp. 61-90.

52. Engelmann and Schwartz, *op. cit.*, p. 146. Apparent disagreement with Presthus's findings (*Elite Accommodation*, p. 113), is tied to his sampling methods, and his criteria for defining interest groups. These procedures result in the inclusion of many local, minor interest groups.

53. Dawson, *op. cit.*, p. 30.

54. Truman, *The Governmental Process, op. cit.*, p. 323.

55. David Kwavnick, "Interest Group Demands and the Federal Political System: Two Canadian Case Studies," in Pross, *op. cit.*, pp. 70-86.

56. Fred Thompson and W.T. Stanbury, *The Political Economy of Interest Groups in the*

Legislative Process in Canada (Montreal: Institute for Research on Public Policy, 1979), p. 14.

57. Leo Panitch, "The Role and Nature of the Canadian State," *The Canadian State*, ed. Leo Panitch (Toronto: University of Toronto Press, 1977), pp. 3-27.

58. G. David Garson, *Group Theories of Politics* (Beverly Hills: Sage Publications, 1978).

59. Peter Aucoin, "Pressure Groups and Recent Changes in the Policy-Making Process," in Pross, *Pressure Group Behaviour, op. cit.*, p. 174.

SELECTED REFERENCES

Bentley, Arthur F. *The Process of Government.* Evanston, Ill.: Principia Press, 1935. Originally published by the University of Chicago Press in 1908, this is the classic statement on the group approach in the United States.

Canada, Library of Parliament, Research Branch. "Pressure Groups in Canada." *The Parliamentarian* LI (January, 1970), pp. 11-20. A useful compilation of pressure groups in Canada.

S.D. Clark. *The Canadian Manufacturers' Association.* Toronto: University of Toronto Press, 1939. An early study, with continuing relevance, of one of the major interest groups in Canadian society.

Dawson, Helen Jones. "An Interest Group: The Canadian Federation of Agriculture," *Canadian Public Administration*, III (June, 1960), pp. 134-49. Dawson is the major student of farm organizations in Canada.

_____. "The Consumers' Association of Canada." *Canadian Public Administration*, VI (1963), pp. 92-118. An analysis of organized consumers as an interest group.

Dion, Léon. *Société et politique: La Vie des groupes.* Vol. I, *Fondements de la société libérale* (1971); Vol. II, *Dynamique de la société libérale* (1972). Québec: Les Presses de l'université Laval. These two volumes present an analysis of the group approach and a thorough review of the literature, covering both Europe and North America. The extensive bibliography is a major source for further study of interest groups and the group approach.

_____ *Le Bill 60 et la société québécoise.* Montreal: Editions HMH, 1976. Educational change in Québec and the impotence of interest groups.

Engelmann, F.C., and M.A. Schwartz. *Canadian Political Parties: Origin, Character, Impact.* Scarborough, Ont.: Prentice-Hall, 1975. Chapter 7 discusses the relations between interest groups and political parties.

Garson, G. David. "On the Origins of Interest Group Theory: A Critique of a Process." *American Political Science Review*, 68 (December, 1974), pp. 1505-19. Critical of the group approach and useful in summarizing the positions of its early exponents, as well as reviewing work in the United States up to the 1970s.

Kwavnick, David. *Organized Labour and Pressure Politics.* Montreal: McGill-Queen's University Press, 1972. A major study of trade unions as pressure groups.

McRae, Kenneth, ed. *Consociational Democracy.* Toronto: McClelland and Stewart, 1974. A collection of essays on consociational democracy, with direct relevance to the group approach in Canada.

Meynaud, Jean. "Groupes des pression et politique gouvernementale au Québec," *Reflexions sur la politique au Québec*, ed. André Bernard. Montreal: Sainte Marie, 1968, pp. 69-96. A review of the position of interest groups in Québec politics.

Presthus, Robert. *Elite Accommodation in Canadian Politics*. London and New York: Cambridge University Press, 1973. A comparative study of interest groups in Canada that has been subject to critical attention and merits careful reading.

Pross, A. Paul, ed. *Pressure Group Behaviour in Canadian Politics*. Toronto: McGraw-Hill Ryerson, 1975. If one were to read only one book on Canadian interests, this would suffice.

Truman, David B. *The Governmental Process*, 2nd ed. New York: Knopf, 1971. This has been the major text on American government devoted to an elaboration of the group approach.

Van Loon, Richard, and Michael Whittington. *The Canadian Political System*, 2nd ed. Toronto: McGraw-Hill Ryerson, 1976. Chapter 13 presents the role of interest groups in Canadian politics.

15

Political Economy and Class Analysis: A Marxist Perspective On Canada

Philip Resnick*

INTRODUCTION

Classical political economy has fallen into disrepute in recent decades. Where political economists like Smith, Ricardo or Mill tried to uncover the laws of production, distribution and consumption in relationship to the public as well as private spheres of capitalist society, twentieth-century economics and political science have gone their separate ways. Each of the social science disciplines— political science, economics and sociology—at least in North America, has defined a specific subject matter, usually emphasizing technical, at times microscopic, problems at the expense of what may be called global, interdisciplinary concerns.

It is precisely these global questions that Marxist political economy raises and that this chapter will seek to explore. What has been Canada's place in a larger world capitalist system? What are the social classes in advanced capitalist society, and the implications of class relations for the political, no less than economic, process? What is the role of the state in contemporary and earlier capitalist development? What is the significance of nationalism, both in multinational societies such as Canada and between smaller and larger powers? What relationship exists between political ideology, educational curricula, or the mass media and the capitalist mode of production?

Those operating within a Marxist framework, to be sure, are not the only ones concerned with interdisciplinary questions. In the Canada of the 1920s and 1930s, for example, an important school of liberal political economists, principally Harold Innis, Donald Creighton and their associates, sought to chart Canada's economic history in a broad, macroscopic perspective. Some of the

*Associate Professor of Political Science, University of British Columbia.

themes they developed have been taken over by recent authors. Themes such as the role of metropolitan powers like France and Britain in stimulating staple production—cod, fur, wood, wheat—in the Canadian hinterland; the role of the state in fostering capitalist development for projects like canals and railways; or the shift in the early part of the twentieth century from a British to an American orientation in Canada's political economy, have attracted the interest of Kari Levitt, Mel Watkins, Cy Gonick and Tom Naylor, all of whom write from a Marxist or neo-Marxist perspective. This renewed interest now provides an important foundation to the current revival of Canadian political economy.

The major strand in Marxist political economy, however, owes nothing to this earlier liberal tradition, which tended to a geographical determinism in which men and women were but secondary actors to the rivers and resources of a half-continent. Where Marxism breaks with liberal political economy is in positing class relations, in conjunction with material forces, as the determining factor in historical development, grounding political and social institutions in them.

> The history of all existing society is the history of class struggle.[1]
>
> The mode of production of material life conditions the social, political and intellectual processes in general. It is not the consciousness of men that determines their being, but, on the contrary, their social being that determines their consciousness.[2]

From these basic insights, Marx and Engels go on to postulate certain theses about the capitalist mode of production in particular: the role of the state as an instrument of bourgeois domination; the exploitation of labor power as the basis for capitalist accumulation; the tendency of the system to chronic and repeated crises of production and distribution; increasing polarization of society between that class owning the principal means of production, the bourgeoisie, and a class with only its labor power to sell, the working class.

CANADIAN MARXIST ANALYSIS IN THE TWENTIETH CENTURY

Not every aspect of Marx's or Engels' analysis of nineteenth-century capitalism, with England as their model, holds good for twentieth-century capitalism. Nor is there universal agreement among twentieth-century Marxist writers on various developments in the political economy of capitalism, let alone the theory and practice of socialism. But if there is no single Marxist orthodoxy, and indeed it may be more accurate to speak of Marxisms in the plural, there is a kernel of Marxist political economy that holds good and which for the purposes of this essay I would thus define: *Marxist political economy posits an integrated social science grounded in material relations and forces of production and embracing political, ideological and social phenomena. Further, it looks beyond the parameters of capitalism to a classless society and world system in which unequal property relations and the institutions these give rise to will have disappeared.*

The utility of Marxist political economy to the study of Canadian politics has been relatively untested for the very simple reason that until recently very few researchers have been working in the Marxist tradition. Unlike continental Europe and later Asia, Latin America and Africa which developed Marxist parties and movements of major importance, Canada, like Britain and the United States, did not. The Canadian Communist Party, for all its trade union and related activity from the 1920s through the 1940s, had relatively little impact on the mainstream of Canadian society and, with exceptions such as Stanley Ryerson, produced few intellectuals of note. The CCF/NDP, being staunchly Fabian, has had little use for Marxism, opposing the latter's vision of class conflict and revolutionary transformation with its own emphasis on gradualism and legislative reform. Most Canadian intellectuals calling themselves socialists in the last forty years have been social democrats, not Marxists.[3] This tendency was reinforced during the period of the Cold War (1945-1965 [?]), when, for many, Marxism came to be identified with Stalinism and the Soviet Union, further undermining its legitimacy in Canadian intellectual life.

The waning of the Cold War, the success of the Chinese, Cuban and Vietnamese revolutions, the weakening of American imperialism and simultaneously of Soviet hegemony over the international communist movement, the radicalization of the student movements of the 1960s, and the emergence of a left-leaning variant of English-Canadian nationalism, have all played their part in making Marxism more attractive to English-Canadian students and intellectuals over the last one and one-half decades. Simultaneously, the breakdown of the old order in Québec following the death of Duplessis, the so-called Quiet Revolution and rise of a modernizing nationalism and separatism, increasing university exchanges between Québec and France, and the radicalization of the trade union movement, gave Marxism a constituency in French Canada where it had had almost none before. The result has been a veritable outpouring of articles, collections, theses and books exploring Canadian and Québec reality from a Marxist perspective.

CONTRIBUTIONS OF MARXIST ANALYSIS

Some of the principal themes of Marxist analysis have already been suggested in the opening paragraphs. While some of these touch on our interpretation of Canadian history, others directly concern contemporary questions. For the moment, let me stress three major contributions that Marxist political economy can make to the study of Canadian and Québec politics.

Firstly, in positing an integrated social science, it breaks with the jurisdictional boundaries erected among such disciplines as political science, sociology and economics, stressing instead the underlying unity of capitalist development. It sees little use in discussing political institutions such as parliament or the party system divorced from the functions these have played and continue to play in maintaining capitalist relations of production. Similarly, it finds little point in economic discussions that leave out the state, class conflict or imperialism in their fanciful search for perfect equilibrium between demand and supply.

Secondly, in bringing to bear a larger international perspective on Canadian development and looking at capitalist and imperialist relations as part of a world process, it transcends the parochialism into which so much of the discussion of Canadian politics and economics descends. While there are certainly features of Canadian development that are unique, most are not: Canada is a capitalist society like many others; the mechanisms of accumulating wealth and exploiting labor are scarcely different; external capital is prominent here as in many Latin American countries; the Canadian state is not some neutral agency but, like all capitalist states, historically an instrument of bourgeois rule; and our contemporary class structure is analogous to that of other advanced capitalist societies. Once these facts are accepted, we can get down to the business of charting what is peculiar to Canada's political economy.

Thirdly, Marxist political economy does not share the system-defending focus of mainstream Canadian political science.

> The philosophers have only *interpreted* the world in various ways; the point, however, is to *change* it.

So Marx argued in this eleventh thesis on Feuerbach. This commitment finds precious little support in most writings on Canadian government. That is quite natural given the liberal biases of Dawson, Ward, Corry and Hodgetts, Smiley, Mallory, or Van Loon and Whittington, to cite some of the major textbook authors of recent decades. For them, the real is the rational, and with timely reforms the Canadian political system is an ideal system extending into the future indefinitely. A Marxist perspective cannot but look beyond the limits of a class-bound political system to a social order in which those who work with hand or brain exercise the dominant political and economic power. It is this commitment to revolutionary change, or at the minimum to radical transformation in class and power relations, that differentiates Marxist political economy from other approaches to Canadian politics. At the same time there is a vastly different interpretation of what is *important* in the political sphere. Mainstream political scientists dwell on political institutions or electoral behavior as independent variables in themselves, something which Marxism categorically rejects.

A MARXIST ANALYSIS OF CANADA

The starting point for a Marxist analysis of Canada is twofold: on the one hand it recognizes the position that Canada, or its component parts, has occupied within a world capitalist system with its international division of labor among core states, semiperipheral states and peripheral states;[4] and on the other hand it recognizes the economic relations of production within Canadian capitalism, in particular the domination the Canadian capitalist class or bourgeoisie, and more marginally in Québec a small capitalist class and petty bourgeoisie, has over other social classes and over the political system as a whole.

As far as the first assertion is concerned we need to understand that New France and what was later to become Canada sprang up on the periphery of a world system centered in Europe, for several centuries playing the role of staple producer and resource supplier to that continent. The political systems of New France and the British colonies depended quite directly on those of France and Britain, while the mode of capitalist production favored mercantile pursuits over industrial into the late nineteenth century. Although in Québec agriculture showed vestiges of feudal organization in the seigneurial system, it is more correct to speak of petty producers as the key group in Canadian agriculture through to the twentieth century.[5] Ideologically speaking, as befitted peripheral outposts of empire, Québec and Canada resisted the revolutionary currents of the late eighteenth century, the American and French revolutions, coming instead to find in counterrevolutionary values and hinterland production the base for a regionally splintered state. As time went by, manufacturing, often foreign-controlled, came to play an increasing role, while the Canadian political economy, reflecting shifting international patterns, moved from the British to the American empire. The origin of the Canadian state in dependency *vis-à-vis* core areas continued to dog Canadian development into this century, while the unequal union of Québec and English Canada undermined the possibilities of a Canadian nation.[6]

As far as the second assertion is concerned, we cannot hope to understand Canadian politics without an understanding of class. Canadian capitalism, like all capitalist societies, has been based on unequal property relations between those who own the principal means of production, usually called the bourgeoisie, and those with only their labor power to sell, the working class. However, these have not been the only two classes in Canada. Farmers long played a crucial role in the politics and economics of the country; small proprietors have also been not unimportant; while self-employed professionals, joined in recent decades by large numbers of salaried professionals such as teachers, civil servants, scientists, and the like, have also played an important role.

There is still good reason to underline the role of the bourgeoisie as the dominant class in Canada. To be sure, the Canadian bourgeoisie has been more regionally divided than that of more centralized states in Europe or Japan; consider the friction between the regional bourgeoisies of Western Canada and the Maritimes and those of central Canada over the tariff, or more recent divisions over resource pricing and revenue. The existence of a separate national group in Québec with a class structure parallel to, but in most respects separate from, that of English-speaking Canada further undercuts the national character of this class. Notwithstanding this, the Canadian bourgeoisie in its various guises, from the Family Compact and fur merchants through the railway syndicates and industrial and financial corporations of a later date, has controlled the Canadian economy, at least those parts not owned and controlled from the outside, and, in conjunction with the metropolitan bourgeoisies of Britain and the United States, set the priorities for the political system.

Those priorities have been geared to rapid accumulation of capital, intensive exploitation of resources, and repression of untoward dissent. As the muckraker, Gustavus Myers, argued as early as 1914, the state was the basis of the great Canadian-derived fortunes from the Hudson's Bay Company to the Catholic Church to the CPR.[7] Capital accumulation in a peripheral area was too risky to attract capitalists without major support from the state. If Canada has had an interventionist policy through much of its history, it has been applied to help socialize the costs of capitalist development, such as transportation systems, by subsidies and pilfering from the public purse.

It is symbolic that the godfathers of Confederation were the Baring Brothers of London with their large loan commitments to the Grand Trunk and other colonial railways,[8] and that Canadian capitalism and Canadian governments at all levels have, since Confederation, relied heavily on outside capital to meet their most pressing needs. Most importantly, this capital has not come without a price, namely, long-term Canadian specialization in staple production and resource extraction for international markets. The image of Canadians as hewers of wood and drawers of water for the outside world is a somewhat exaggerated depiction of the late nineteenth-century situation (else why the National Policy?), and is even more so for the twentieth. Nonetheless the mark of Cain that Jacques Cartier discerned on the landscape of this country is an apt metaphor for the minerals and primary resources that for so long defined Canada's position in the international capitalist system.

Bourgeois domination of the political system has been most evident in the repression of political dissent. The essentially petty bourgeois revolts of the 1830s in both Lower and Upper Canada ended in defeat as the Château Clique and Family Compact, in effect the commercial bourgeoisie of the day, rallied against revolt all that was most conservative in both Canadas. Confederation was an arrangement between British imperialism and colonial capitalist spokesmen such as George Etienne Cartier and John A. Macdonald aimed against the United States, but aimed no less definitely against an independent Québec,[9] and against any radical challenge to property relations.[10]

As far as French Canada is concerned, Canadian history from the Riel Rebellion, to the Manitoba schools question, to the conscription crises of both World Wars, to contemporary Québec nationalism, has often reflected diverging interests between the Canadian bourgeoisie, committed to a united predominantly English-Canadian state at almost any price, and more nationalist forces in Québec. To be fair, however, Québec history is not restricted to this conflict and the traditional Québec ruling class—lawyers, professionals and French-Canadian entrepreneurs—has by and large collaborated with the Canadian bourgeoisie, sharing the latter's ideological commitment to capitalism. How else is one to interpret the procapitalist policies of successive Québec governments from Honoré Mercier, to Alexandre Taschereau, to Maurice Duplessis, to Robert Bourassa, and to which the accession to power of René Lévesque has brought only very limited modifications?

Where threats to property are concerned, the century since Confederation has seen the use of state force, both the militia and army and in more recent years the police, against striking workers, and state intervention by executive, legislative and judicial means against class-conscious trade unionism. Mackenzie King made things crystal clear in his 1903 Report on Industrial Disputes in British Columbia:

> With regard to these [radical] organizations we think they ought to be specially declared to be illegal, as their leaders have shown that they care nothing about the obligation of contracts or about the interests of their employers, against whom they are ever fomenting discontent;...that they at all times preach the doctrine of confiscation of property without compensation, and that society is divided into two classes, the toilers and the spoilers; that they justify the boycott and the sympathetic strike; that they do not disapprove of violence and intimidation.[11]

And from the mining and railway strikes of the early 1900s to the Winnipeg General Strike of 1919, from Duplessis's Padlock Law and anti-labor legislation to Mitchell Hepburn's opposition to the Committee for Industrial Organization (CIO), there is a long history of repression in the policy of the Canadian state toward labor.

Where farmers were concerned, brutal class repression was less common. But tariff and railway policy largely did the trick, and it was only for a brief interregnum between the two world wars that farmers were able to organize themselves into protest parties with some limited effect on the political system. The dominant political parties since Confederation, the Liberals and Conservatives, have served the interests of commercial and industrial capitalism well, and though their policies toward different classes have varied over time, both have been resolutely committed to the defense of private property.

It is worth underlining how little attention mainstream political scientists pay to such phenomena. For them, the substance of Canadian politics resides primarily in Parliament, especially the Prime Minister and Cabinet, secondarily in the provinces, but *not* in the workings of the class system. The musings of Mackenzie King to his diary, the idiosyncracies of Maurice Duplessis or W.A.C. Bennett as provincial premiers, the formal debates of Parliament or its committees, take precedence over structural developments within Canadian capitalism. The attitudes and interests of capital—the Canadian Manufacturers' Association, Boards of Trade, Chambers of Commerce—get scanty attention, as does the changing constellation of outside capital in the development of the Canadian or regional bourgeoisies.

CANADIAN CAPITALIST DEVELOPMENT SINCE THE
SECOND WORLD WAR

Yet Capitalism evolves, and capitalist political economy in the post-World War II period has a number of specific features on which I would like to dwell. The most striking are the following: the rise and relative decline of American imperialism over a thirty-year period; the changing class structure of advanced capitalist society; the changing role of the state; the eruption of nationalism in industrialized, no less than Third World, countries; and the greatly increased importance of education and mass communications in the political economy of advanced capitalism.

Let us examine the implications of these features more carefully for Canada and Québec.

Where American imperialism is concerned, the roots of American economic domination in Canada go back well before the turn of the century.[12] The Canadian bourgeoisie and Québec petty bourgeoisie, like those of Latin America, welcomed American branch plants, while links with the United States gained in importance as British imperialism weakened between the wars. The crucial turning point came with the Second World War and the forging of a full-fledged military and political alliance at Ogdensburg in August 1940.[13]

As American investment in the Canadian economy, especially in the resource sector, skyrocketed in the postwar period, the strategic importance of Canada to the United States increased. The simultaneous development of the Cold War turned Canada into a neocolonial appendage of the United States in both foreign and defense policy. A series of bilateral and multilateral agreements, such as the radar lines in the Canadian North, the North Atlantic Treaty Organization, the North American Air Defense Agreement, and the Defense Sharing Agreement, all reflected the shrinking margin of Canadian sovereignty, while the practitioners of quiet diplomacy lent support to American foreign policy, from containment of the Soviet Union to imperialism in Vietnam.[14]

In the heyday of the American empire, roughly 1945-65, the United States was the determining factor for much of the Canadian political economy. Through the branch plants, American capitalists were active coparticipants in shaping Canadian economic priorities; through radio and television programs, magazines, films and the like, American culture set the tone for mass culture in this country; in the academic world, American universities were magnets for tens of thousands of Canadian graduate students, while American techniques and approaches spilled over into Canada, for example, behavioralism in the social sciences. If the Canadian political system, both federal and provincial, enjoyed formal autonomy through this period, the *quid pro quo* was a close alignment by governing parties, most notably the Liberals, with American positions. The one instance of hesitation, by the Diefenbaker government over nuclear weapons in 1962-63, ended in open American political, though not military, intervention and that government's quick demise.

Yet imperialism is not a once and forever proposition and in the decade since

1965 there has been evidence of a significant weakening in American hegemony over allies and client states. The rise of nationalism in the Third World and in such advanced capitalist countries as France under de Gaulle was one important factor; massive opposition within the United States to the Vietnam War was a second; the revival of Western Europe's and Japan's economic power a third; the increased influence of both the Soviet Union and China in world politics yet a fourth. The result, since the early 1970s, has been an American capitalism beset by balance-of-payments problems, bedevilled by the growing independence of energy-producing states, defeated in Vietnam, and generally less able to get its way in international forums.

This tendency has been no less operative in American-Canadian relations. If Canadian foreign policy has shown marginally greater independence in recent years, for example, the so-called third option in Canadian foreign policy, and if nationalism has become a more important force, then the chief explanation lies in the relative weakening of American power. I stress relative, for I certainly do not want to imply a wholesale reduction of what remains the major external operating force on the Canadian political economy. It is the shifting position of the United States within the international capitalist system and the structural changes to that system itself, which may well decide the future of Canadian capitalism.

THE IMPORTANCE OF CLASS ANALYSIS

Class is a crucial variable where Marxist analysis is concerned. Defined as the relationship of people to the means of production, it has often led Marxist theorists to stress two main classes: the big bourgeoisie, who own the principal factories, resources and pools of capital on the one hand, and the working class, who have only their labor power to sell, on the other.

Marx and Engels proposed such a two-tiered class model in the *Communist Manifesto,* though Marx himself in such a work as *The 18th Brumaire of Louis Bonaparte* seriously modified it, talking of different types of capitalists, for example, financial and industrial, the peasantry, and the petty bourgeoisie, as well as the working class in nineteenth-century capitalism. A similar sophistication is required in any analysis of the class structure of twentieth-century capitalism.

Where contemporary Canada and Québec are concerned, I would suggest that the chart in Figure 1 shows a comprehensive class model. There are two distinct, though parallel class systems, similar in most respects, though with a stronger capitalist class in the case of English Canada than of Québec.

The exact numbers of the big bourgeoisie in Canada as a whole are difficult to determine, though Corporations and Labor Unions Returns Act (CALURA) data for 1972 show 669 nonfinancial corporations with assets in excess of $25 million, some 63.2% of the assets of all nonfinancial corporations.[15] Throwing in

Figure 1
The Class Structure of English Canada and of Québec American Imperialism

	Canada		
	English Canada		Québec
Big Bourgeoisie: *(assets in excess of $25 million)*	Foreign-control—manufacturing, resources Indigenous-control—manufacturing, finance, transportation	Big Bourgeoisie: *(assets in excess of $25 million)*	Foreign control—manufacturing, resources English-Canadian control—manufacturing, finance, transportation, resources Indigenous control—some manufacturing, finance, transportation
Smaller bourgeoisie: *(assets under $25 million)*	Foreign control as above Indigenous control as above	Smaller bourgeoisie: *(assets under $25 million)*	Foreign control as above English-Canadian control as above Indigenous control as above
Traditional petty bourgeoisie:	Farmers, i.e., independent commodity producers self-employed business self-employed professionals	Traditional petty bourgeoisie:	Identical to English Canada
New petty bourgeoisie:	Teachers, professors civil servants other salaried professionals	New petty bourgeoisie:	Identical to English Canada
Working class:	white collar blue collar unemployed	Working class:	Identical to English Canada

Source: Philip Resnick, *The Land of Cain: Class and Nationalism in English Canada 1945-1975*, (Vancouver: New Star Books 1977), chap. I.

the large financial corporations such as banks and insurance companies would give us a range of at least ten to twenty thousand principal directors and executives in the contemporary Canadian bourgeoisie. This is a good deal more than the roughly one thousand souls Porter and Clement describe in their books,[16] but then Marxist analysis, unlike the elite theory, does not see the Canadian big bourgeoisie as a conspiratorial handful of individuals defined more by their prep schools and private clubs than by their structural relationship to the means of production. Some of these big capitalists are in the foreign-owned sector, some in the indigenous, yet both share a common allegiance to an open, expanding capitalist system.

The smaller bourgeoisie, that is, firms with assets under $25 million, are also important employers of labor, though at its lower levels this class shades over into the petty bourgeois entrepreneur, usually self-employed, and employing at most only a handful of laborers. Business proprietors and investors have constituted a stable 8.2% of all occupations, according to tax returns, since 1946.[17] Politically speaking, the influence of the big bourgeoisie, through such organizations as the Canadian Manufacturers' Association and the Canadian Chamber of Commerce, or directly on the major political parties and the state, is enormous, usually carrying smaller business in its wake. The smaller and even petty bourgeois entrepreneurs, however, also have their influence, particularly at the provincial and municipal levels, and do not always see eye to eye with the big bourgeoisie. Consider, for example, the activities of the Canadian Federation of Independent Business in recent years, or the campaign waged by small businessmen and farmers for public ownership of electricity in Ontario in the 1900s.[18]

A class whose importance has declined are the farmers, almost 50% of the labor force in the late nineteenth century, down to 25% at the beginning of World War II, and to under 6% today.[19] Clearly, their political influence was greater in an earlier day, though even then the big bourgeoisie called the shots at the national level, than in the urban industrialized Canada of the 1980s.

Conversely, there has been a sharp rise in the number of professionals, especially salaried, in recent decades, to at least 12% of the total labor force.[20] With the new demands that capitalism makes in the scientific and technological fields, with the tremendous development of the educational system, witl the increased importance of communications, and with the takeoff of the state sector, salaried professionals from research scientists to journalists, from academics to civil servants, have become an important force. From the Marxist point of view, they can be termed the new petty bourgeoisie; though not self-employed, they occupy a position between capital and labor, absorbing through their high salaries and other prerequisites part of the surplus value extracted by capital from labor.[21]

Elements of the new petty bourgeoisie have access to both ideological and political levers of power, and for all their vacillation, have at times attempted to redefine the political system in their own interests. Such, for example, is one interpretation of the Quiet Revolution in Québec, the coming to power of a new urban French-Canadian middle class.[22] In English Canada as well, nationalist politics in recent years has been much influenced by members of this class, for example, the Committee for an Independent Canada or the Waffle. This is not to say that the new petty bourgeoisie in fact dominates the political system. But there is the possibility of class friction between the new petty bourgeoisie and members of the big bourgeoisie over the size of the state sector, the nature of state intervention, and so on; and doubtless such conflict will play an increasingly important role in late capitalism.

The working class, those who have only their labor power to sell, remain the vast majority of the population, though increasingly in white-collar rather than blue-collar occupations. While theoretically this class could challenge the big bourgeoisie for power, in practice the Canadian working class has seldom been class-conscious in the Marxist sense, especially not since World War II. Furthermore, only a third of the working class is unionized, and the influence of American business unionism in the Cold War years coupled with conservative currents within the Canadian trade union movement, has had a dampening effect on radicalism. It is significant that the major exception to this has been Québec where radical trade unionism has taken root in recent years.[23] It remains to be seen whether a similar radicalization, spurred on by measures such as wage controls, will characterize the English-Canadian working class in coming years.

The analysis of the state should be at the very heart of political science, yet it is remarkable how little serious reflection there has been on this subject in Canada over the last thirty-five years. From the White Paper on Income and Employment of 1945 to Wage and Price Controls in 1975, the trend has been to ever-greater government involvement in the economy. Nor is this trend by any means confined to Canada.[24]

Marxist theory would argue that state intervention becomes necessary as capitalism fails to function, either through crises of overproduction or under-consumption. To be sure, the state has been involved in fostering capitalist accumulation for centuries, but in the period since the 1930s its role has become a good deal more one of planning and coordinating capitalist development as a whole. Left to individual capitalists, the system is too prone to generate crises.

Simultaneously, the broadening of the franchise since the nineteenth century means that the state has been forced to meet some of the demands of other classes, most notably the working class. The system must be made to appear legitimate to different classes in society, hence the legitimizing function of various social and economic programs.[25] It follows that the state in advanced capitalist society, if it is "a committee for managing the common affairs of the whole bourgeoisie," as Marx and Engels argued in *The Communist Manifesto*, must have a certain degree of autonomy to fulfill its role.

How great that autonomy is, is another matter. In Canada, the greatest part of the economy remains in private hands, and government intervention, from monetary and fiscal policy to funds for regional development or research, or to price and wage controls, is grafted onto a predominantly capitalist structure.

The economic policies of Canadian governments, federal and provincial, are greatly circumscribed by the likes and dislikes of those who dominate the corporate sector, the big bourgeoisie, though that class does not always get its way. The state has a commitment to make the capitalist system function as a system, and this may take it into areas of activity that many individual capitalists may oppose, such as pensions or price controls. To use Rousseau's terminology for a moment, the state may be said to articulate the "general will" of capitalism rather than the "particular wills" of individual capitalists.

At the same time, the state must seek to accommodate other classes. This explains the move toward accommodation and integration, rather than overt repression, in the policies of both the federal government and most provincial governments toward labor since 1945. Labor relations boards, labor codes, and the like can be important carrots in winning labor support, though the stick of repression, physical no less than judicial, is always there. Similarly, social programs, from family allowances, to unemployment insurance, to Medicare, to the Canada Pension Plan, are ways of humanizing capitalism, without calling the underlying capitalist structure into question.

The figures on the growth of the state sector in postwar Canada are remarkable, though no more so than for other Western societies. They show an overall rise in combined government revenue (i.e. federal, provincial and local) from roughly 25% of Gross National Product in the late 1940s to 40% of GNP by the late 1970s. What they reflect is not a move toward socialism, as critics on the right are prone to suggest, but a move to statism, to ongoing involvement by the state in the running of the capitalist economy. This is, of course, a reversal from an earlier liberalism's commitment to the noninterventionist or "night-watchman" state, but it does not necessarily spell the beginnings of a transition from capitalism to socialism. It may be more correct to call it monopoly state capitalism, suggesting a partnership between the state and the largest corporations.

Even this is not the whole story. In some important ways those who work for the state or in state-financed institutions are, as I have argued above, salaried professionals or workers with class interests different from those of the big bourgeoisie. With some 22% of the labor force working in the state sector in Canada today, though not all of these, by any means, are new petty bourgeois, with many more people dependent on the state's social and welfare programs, the possibilities of a drastic weakening of the state's role are slight.[26]

A MARXIST VIEW OF STATE AND NATION

A further consequence of these structural changes in capitalist political economy is that the state is relatively little affected by whichever political party is in power. The changes that a new government at either the federal or provincial level is likely to introduce are only marginal, for the factors affecting state behavior are secular and long-term. Within the limits of a capitalist economy, then, the areas of difference among such political parties as the Conservatives, the Liberals, the NDP or Social Credit are far less important than the sound and fury in the public arena might lead one to believe. All are forced to practise a greater or lesser measure of state intervention, while none is pledged to eradicate capitalist power. In Western societies with stronger Marxist traditions, such as France or Italy, it is theoretically possible to envisage more structural changes in the nature and operation of the state. Whether this will happen in practice if governments of the left come to power in those countries is another matter.

The specificity of the Canadian state — the federal system — reflects both the regional character of English Canada and the binational character of Canada as a whole. The main consequence has been that class differences at the national level have been less clear-cut than in more centralized polities, such as those of Western Europe. Federalism has also served to weaken the power of the central state and of the provinces *vis-à-vis* foreign capital, the so-called balkanization effect, though conversely it has tended to give state actions greater credibility and support in the different regions than would be the case under a more centralized scheme. For Marxist theory, federalism points to the underlying importance of the national question in Canada, and to the regional splintering of classes within the Canadian political economy. It does not, however, detract from the underlying capitalist character of that economy.

The national question in Canada principally involves Québec's relationship to English Canada and Canada's relationship to the United States. Applying Marxist theory, we have little difficulty in recognizing that by the criteria of geography, history, language and culture, both Québec and English Canada constitute national entities and that, as a political consequence, each must enjoy the right to self-determination.

Marxism, however, does not separate the issue of nationalism from that of class. Rather, it recognizes that nationalism has a class basis and that as often as not, in advanced capitalist societies, this will give nationalism a reactionary rather than a progressive character. Evidence of national oppression in much of Québec history would for the Marxist, certainly bolster the case for Québec's right to self-determination. Still, the Marxist would have to distinguish carefully between the clerico-conservative nationalism of the Abbé Groulx, Maurice Duplessis, and much of the traditional petty bourgeoisie that long ruled Québec; the economic and political nationalism of the new petty bourgeoisie in recent years, such as the Parti Québécois, tending toward a technocratic capitalist state; and a more working-class-based nationalism putting socialism first on the agenda.[27] Clearly, Marxism would favor the third.

Where English Canada is concerned, Marxist theory would be hesitant to speak of an oppressed nation. Not only was there general support by Canada's bourgeoisie and by other social classes for Canada's ties, first with Great Britain, then with the United States, but in recent years Canadian capitalists themselves have become important participants in imperialist ventures in Third World countries.[28]

Nonetheless, Marxist analysis would recognize the subordinate role Canada came to play within the American empire after World War II, and would support an anti-imperialist form of nationalism aimed at weakening American domination in this country. In class terms, an anti-imperialist nationalism would have to embrace the Canadian working class and probably a significant component of the petty bourgeoisie, especially those new petty bourgeois salaried professionals who have been so important to the nationalist movements of the last ten years. On the other hand, the Canadian big bourgeoisie, ever more integrated into American and world capitalism, ever more interested in multinational ventures of its own, cannot but be the chief enemy of any progressive nationalism in this country.

Having acknowledged all this, Marxist analysis, in my opinion, would remain wary of forms of English-Canadian nationalism that did not place socialism first. In particular, it would reject the position that nationalism provides some kind of shortcut to socialism, or that one should downplay the latter in the name of some common national goals. Bourgeois and petty bourgeois nationalists would like nothing better. Important as the national question may be, it is not removed from class and class conflict, least of all in advanced capitalist countries. Anti-imperialism, while important, is only one part of what a Marxist analysis of Canadian political economy must stress.

"The ideas of the ruling class are in every epoch the ruling ideas, the class that is the ruling material force of society is at the same time its ruling intellectual force."[29] Marx and Engels wrote that back in 1845. In the capitalist mode of production, then, one would expect these ruling ideas to be those of the bourgeoisie, and that has indeed been the case throughout Canadian history. The "peace, order and good government" tradition enshrined in the BNA Act can be interpreted as a capitalist bill of rights, while the parliamentary tradition that our history and political science textbooks revere came out of centuries of struggle for power by the bourgeoisies of Europe and America. The bourgeois concept of representation reduces politics to the parliamentary arena at the expense of more direct and participatory forms of government.[30] Consider the overwhelming emphasis on electoral studies in contemporary Canadian political science.

The hegemony of bourgeois and prebourgeois values in Canada and Québec has been fostered through religious and educational institutions, as well as through the mass media. In Québec, until recently, the church, through its control of educational and other institutions, effectively eliminated all critical points of view. In English Canada, while the churches and school system were somewhat less monolithic, the results were much the same. The Canadian intelligentsia has been what John Porter aptly called a "clerisy,"[31] a group of establishment intellectuals strongly supportive of the state and state institutions:

> Our concern is with the deeply embedded beliefs that support and justify present day democratic [i.e. liberal] government, and with the rejection of these beliefs [e.g. Marxism] that has brought modern dictatorship to the fore.[32]

That this clerisy in important respects has been a branch-plant intelligentsia *vis-à-vis* Britain and the United States has only reinforced its native conservatism.

In the case of the mass media, much the same class that owns the principal means of production, the big bourgeoisie, owns the newspapers, private radio and television stations, theater chains, and so on. The capitalist state exercises very effective behind-the-scenes control over such institutions as the CBC, for example, the CBC directive cautioning against criticism of the government during the October Crisis. McLuhan notwithstanding, content is still the crucial feature of mass communications in advanced capitalist society. In the words of Ralph Miliband:

> It does not seem extravagant to suggest that radio and television in all capitalist countries have been consistently and predominantly agencies of conservative indoctrination and that they have done what they could to inoculate their listeners and viewers against dissident thought. This does not require that all such dissent should be prevented from getting airing. It only requires that the overwhelming bias of the media should be on the other side. And that requirement has been amply met.[33]

To return to the educational system, it remains, despite changes from an elite to a mass institution, particularly at the higher levels during the last three decades, firmly geared to capitalist values. As Harold Innis, no Marxist, recognized in a prescient passage: "The descent of the university into the market place reflects the lie in the soul of modern society."[34] The lie does not begin with university, but with the socialization that sets in from kindergarten on. The predominant values instilled by the educational system, individualism, consumerism, and so on, are bourgeois liberal to the core, while the bias of history and social studies, no less than literature and language texts, is toward middle- and upper-middle-class conceptions of the world.

To be sure, there are countervailing currents in the schools, as in the media; there are some radical teachers and journalists and a few left-wing periodicals and small publishing houses. There are slightly larger numbers of critics in Canadian universities and colleges today than was the case twenty or thirty years ago. The student movement of the 1960s has left some small imprint on university structures, such as student and faculty representatives on boards of governors, while the fiscal crisis of the 1970s is bringing salaried professionals closer to unionization. But these countercurrents are fairly weak and have failed to alter the class nature of educational institutions. Teachers and professors rarely identify with the working class against the big bourgeoisie, though here again there has been slightly more of this identification in Québec recently than in English Canada.[35] At best, educational institutions, like the mass media, are potential arenas for class conflict. The tasks of any would-be Marxist intelligentsia in moving these institutions to the left or mapping alternatives to mainstream, for the most part bourgeois, Canadian culture and ideology are enormous.

LIMITATIONS OF MARXIST ANALYSIS

It should be evident to the reader that there are limitations to a Marxist analysis of Canadian politics. The first difficulty stems from the ambitious character of the Marxist project, which attempts to explain the larger forces at work often at the expense of detailed investigation. This danger is compounded by the fact that Marxism as a theory first developed in reference to Europe, and its expansion to deal with capitalism in other parts of the world is not without its problems. Capitalism for the semiperiphery is not identical to capitalism for the center, and though Canada is a developed and not a Third World country, a Marxist political economy of Canada must take her position within the world capitalist system into account.

A second danger in Marxist analysis is dogmatism, a tendency to be more concerned with what Marx, Lenin, or other founding fathers wrote, than with what has actually been happening in twentieth-century capitalism. Certain of Marx's predictions have simply not come true, for example, the growing pauperization of the working class; other parts of his analysis, for example, the withering away of the state, are inadequate. Moreover, the distortions to which Marxist theory has been subjected in such ostensibly socialist societies as the Soviet Union (wholesale suppression of civil rights, establishment of work camps, retention of the worst features of the capitalist division of labor) make it all the more imperative to apply Marxist theory creatively and in a new way to those societies for which it was originally intended—the developed industrial nations.

Thirdly, there is the need yet again to underline the internationalist dimension of Marxism. There has been a tendency in English Canada for some spokesmen to reduce Marxism to a form of Canadian nationalism, or to attempt to graft Marxist political economy wholehog onto the liberal writings of the 1930s.[36] While there are features of the early political economy tradition worth retaining, the latter differs from a Marxist approach in terms of theory no less than practice. Similarly, nationalism may well have provided the environment in which Marxist analysis began to put down new roots in English Canada and in Québec. But Marxist, political economy is not simply a form of nationalism! While recognizing the reality of imperialism in the contemporary world, Marxist analysis does not dwell narrowly on the Canadian-American relationship at the expense of larger trends in the world capitalist system. Nor does it exaggerate the dependency factor in Canadian-American or Québec-Canadian relations over the indigenous class structure of each, a class structure that bears close analogy to that of other capitalist societies. While, as I have just argued, Marxist political economy must pay close attention to Canadian specifics, it must be careful not to stress Canadian uniqueness at all costs. The road to hell is paved with such assertions.

CONCLUSION

I have intended to stress the differences marking Marxist political economy off from other approaches to Canadian politics, though acknowledging some similarities with the earlier liberal political economy tradition. Marxism poses an integrated social, political and economic theory. It poses such large questions as imperialism, the class nature of Canadian and Québec society, the nature of the state, and national question, and education and ideology, and addresses them in an integrated fashion. It looks beyond the limits of an existing capitalism and the political and ideological structures to which it gave birth, to a more egalitarian and democratic political and economic order. It is this combination of revolutionary commitment with cogent analysis of Canadian society that explains its growing attraction to younger people doing political and social science in Canada today. If Marxist political economy is gaining adherents, is it not because competing paradigms have been found wanting?

SUMMARY

1. Political economy attempts to tie together political science and economics as well as such disciplines as sociology and history. In Canada, it was associated with the school of Harold Innis and the staple theorists. In recent years, there has been a significant revival of political economy under Marxist auspices.

2. Marxism posits the importance of material relations in explaining political and social reality. It stresses the importance of class, and the domination of those who control the principal means of production in any society. In a capitalist society such as Canada, that class is the bourgeoisie.

3. Marxism places relatively little emphasis on parliament or political personalities as independent focal points for study. Rather, it stresses structural developments both internal to Canada or in the larger world economy to which Canada is linked.

4. Marxism underlines class exploitation and domination as key themes in Canada's political development. It pays attention to external imperialism, both British and American, as well as to the evolving class structure of Canada. It has done much to make the theme of the state a central one in Canadian political science, emphasizing the interventionist role the state plays in advanced capitalist societies, as well as its ongoing role in the maintenance of the capitalist structure. Marxism has paid careful attention to the national question in Canada, and to regionalism as well. Nor does it neglect the role of ideology, education and culture in shaping the type of politics we have in this country.

5. It is fair to say that some of the most innovative and exciting work in Canadian political science of the last decade has been done by those operating within the Marxist paradigm.

STUDY QUESTIONS

1. How does class impinge on the study of politics?
2. What have been the long-term consequences for the Canadian political economy of dependence on large-scale foreign investment?
3. What explains the increased economic role of the state of Canada since the 1930s?
4. How does the existence of different regional capitalist interests affect the operation of the political system?
5. What are the implications of monopoly concentration and control of the mass media for the transmission of political values?
6. How would you explain the role of nationalism in Québec and in English Canada over the last twenty years?
7. Can the Canadian economy escape from dependence on staples? Should it seek to do so?
8. What are the implications for Canada of shifts in the international political economy to new centers such as Japan and the Pacific?
9. Why has the Canadian working class been less radical politically than the working class of most European countries? Is this likely to change in the coming years? If so, under what conditions?
10. Is the function of political science to be "value free" or should it seek to change society and the world?

ENDNOTES

1. Karl Marx and Friedrich Engels, "Manifesto of the Communist Party," *Selected Works* (London: Lawrence and Wishart, 1968), p. 35.
2. Marx, "Preface to A Contribution to the Critique of Political Economy," in Marx and Engels, *op. cit.*, p. 182.
3. See, for example, League for Social Reconstruction, *Social Planning for Canada*, repr. of 1935 ed. (Toronto: University of Toronto Press, 1961), for two examples of social democratic thought.
4. See Immanuel Wallerstein's brilliant theoretical work, *The Modern World System* (New York: Academic Press, 1974), for a discussion of these three types of states and their relationship to the larger international system of capitalism.
5. See Denis Moniére, "L'utilité du concept de mode de production des petits prodocteurs pour l'historiographie de la Nouvelle France," *Revue d'Histoire de L'Amérique Francaise*, 29, No. 4 (mars, 1976). See also C.B. Macpherson's classical study, *Democracy in Alberta* (Toronto: University of Toronto Press, 1953) for an analysis of the "independent commodity producer" in Western Canada.
6. See Stanley B. Ryerson, *Unequal Union* (Toronto: Progress Books, 1968).
7. Gustavus Myers, *A History of Canadian Wealth*, 2nd ed. (Toronto: Lorimer, 1972).

8.   Alfred Dubuc, "The Decline of Confederation and the New Nationalism," *Nationalism in Canada*, ed. Peter Russell (Toronto: McGraw-Hill, 1966), pp. 112-32; Tom Naylor, *The History of Canadian Business 1867-1914*, Vol. 1 (Toronto: Lorimer, 1976).

9.   For a discussion of the opposition of Dorion and the *Rogues* to Confederation, see Jean-Paul Bernard, *Les Rouges: French Canadian Liberalism, Nationalism, and Anticlericism in the 19th Century* (Montreal: University of Quebec Press, 1971).

10.   See John A. Macdonald's 1861 comment: "Unless property were protected, and made one of the principles upon which representation was based, we might perhaps have a people altogether equal, but we should cease to be a people altogether free." Cited in Ryerson, *op. cit.*, p. 355.

11.   Canada, Royal Commission on Industrial Disputes in the Province of British Columbia, *Report* (Ottawa: King's Printer, 1903), p. 68.

12.   H. Marshall, F.A. Southard and K.W. Taylor, *Canadian-American Industry*, repr. of 1936 ed. (New York: Russell and Russell, 1970), for a history of American investment since the early nineteenth century. See also Kari Levitt, *Silent Surrender* (Toronto: Macmillan, 1970), for a more radical and up-to-date analysis.

13.   See Frank H. Underhill, "North American Front," *Forum - Canadian Life and Letters 1920-70; Selections from the Canadian Forum*, ed. J.L. Granatstein and Peter Stevens (Toronto: University of Toronto Press, 1972), pp. 191-3.

14.   See Jack Warnock, *Partner to Behemoth* (Toronto: New Press, 1970); Charles Taylor, *Snow Job: Canada, the United States and Vietnam, 1954 to 1973* (Toronto: Anansi, 1974); or Philip Resnick, "Canadian Defense Policy and the American Empire," *Close the 49th Parallel, etc.*, ed. Ian Lumsden (Toronto: University of Toronto Press, 1970), pp. 94-115.

15.   "In 1972 foreign controlled corporations with assets of over $25 million in the non-financial industries numbered 372 or about 6 percent of the total number of non-resident controlled corporations. They held $40 billion in assets or 71 percent of the assets of all non-financial foreign controlled corporations. The 297 Canadian controlled non-financial corporations in this asset size group represented less than 1 percent of the total number of domestically controlled corporations and had assets of $62 billion or 63 percent of the total assets under Canadian corporate control." CALURA, *Report for 1972*, Part 1, Corporations, 1975, p. 19. My 63.2% figure represents the share these 669 corporations have of the assets of both foreign and Canadian controlled corporations, including the many smaller corporations CALURA lists as "unclassified."

16.   See John Porter, *The Vertical Mosaic* (Toronto: University of Toronto Press, 1965), Ch. 8 and Appendix II; and Wallace Clement, *The Canadian Corporate Elite* (Toronto: McClelland and Stewart, 1975), Ch. 4.

17.   See Philip Resnick, *The Land of Cain* (Vancouver: New Star Books, 1977), Table 2.9.

18.   H.V. Nelles, *The Politics of Development* (Toronto: Macmillan, 1974), Ch. 6.

19.   See "Population in Nonagricultural and Agricultural Pursuits, 1881-1941," *Historical Statistics of Canada*, ed. M.C. Urquhart and Kenneth A.H. Buckley (Toronto: Cambridge University Press, 1965), p. 59; and *The Canada Year Book 1973* (Ottawa: Queen's Printer, 1973), Table 8.5, p. 356.

20.   See discussion of the statistical size of the "new petty bourgeoisie" in Resnick, *op. cit.*, Ch. 2.

21. For a theoretical discussion of the new petty bourgeoisie, see Christian Baudelot, Roger Establet and Jacques Malemort, *La petite bourgeoisie en France* (Paris: Maspero, 1974); and G. Carchedi, "On the Economic Identification of the New Middle Class," *Economy and Society*, IV, No. 4 (November, 1975).

22. See Hubert Guindon, "Social Unrest, Social Class and Quebec's Bureaucratic Revolution," *Queen's Quarterly*, 71 (1964), pp. 150-62; Jacques Brazeau, "Les nouvelles classes moyennes," *Le pouvoir dans la société candienne-française*, ed. Fernand Dumont and Jean-Paul Montminy (Quebec: Laval, 1966), pp. 153-63; Gilles Bourque and N. Laurin-Frenette, "Social Classes and Nationalist Ideologies in Quebec, 1870-1970," *Capitalism and the National Question in Canada*, ed. Gary Teeple (Toronto: University of Toronto Press, 1972), pp. 186-210.

23. See D. Drache, ed., *Quebec-Only the Beginning* (Toronto: New Press, 1972); Dianne Ethier, Jean-Marc Piotte, and Jean Reynolds, *Les travailleurs contre l'état bourgeois* (Montreal: L'Aurore, 1975).

24. For an excellent discussion of the growth of the state sector in all Western societes, see Ian Gough, "State Expenditure and Advanced Capital," *New Left Review*, No. 82 (July-August, 1975), pp. 53-92.

25. For a discussion of the legitimation function see James O'Connor, *The Fiscal Crisis of the State* (New York: St. Martin's Press, 1973); and for a Canadian application, Leo Panitch, "The Role and Nature of the Canadian State," *The Canadian State*, ed. Leo Panitch (Toronto: University of Toronto Press, 1977).

26. This figure is derived from Hugh Armstrong's excellent study, "The Patron State of Canada," M.A. Thesis, Carleton University, 1974, Table 5.9, p. 149.

27. See Bourque and Laurin-Frencette, *op. cit.*, pp. 186-210; and Stanley Ryerson, "Quebec: Concepts of Class and Nation," in Teeple, *op. cit.*, pp. 211-27.

28. See, for example, John Deverell and the Latin American Working Group, *Falconbridge: Portrait of a Canadian Mining Multinational* (Toronto: Lorimer, 1975); Daniel Jay Baum, *The Banks of Canada in the Commonwealth Caribbean* (New York: Praeger, 1974); "The Brascan File," *The Last Post* (March, 1973), pp. 28-39. For a somewhat dogmatic argument, see Steve Moore and Debi Wells, *Imperialism and the National Question in Canada* (Toronto: Author, 1975).

29. Karl Marx and Friedrich Engels, *The German Ideology*, ed. C.J. Arthur (New York: International Pubs. Co. Inc., 1970), p. 64.

30. See Philip Resnick, "The Political Theory of Extra-Parliamentarism," *Canadian Journal of Political Science*, VI, No. 1 (March, 1973), pp. 65-88.

31. Porter, *op. cit.*, pp. 491-494*ff.*

32. J.A. Corry and J.E. Hodgetts, *Democratic Government and Politics*, 3rd ed. (Toronto: University of Toronto Press, 1959), p. 23.

33. Ralph Miliband. *The State of Capitalist Society* (London: Weidenfeld and Nicholson, 1969), p. 224.

34. Harold Innis, *Political Economy in the Modern State* (Toronto: University of Toronto Press, 1946), p. 76.

35. See, for example, the document published by the Quebec Teachers' Federation, the CEQ, "Ecole et lutte de classes au Québec," 1974.

36. This is my reading of the article by Daniel Drache, "Rediscovering Canadian Political Economy," *Journal of Canadian Studies* (August, 1975).

SELECTED REFERENCES

GENERAL

Baran, Paul and Paul Sweezy. *Monopoly Capital.* New York: Monthly Review Press, 1966. An important updating of Marxist theory with particular reference to the United States.

Frank, Andre Gunder. *Capitalism and Underdevelopment in Latin America.* New York: Monthly Review Press, 1969. An analysis of metropolis-periphery relations with respect to Latin America.

Gamble, A., and P. Walton. *Capitalism in Crisis, Inflation and the State.* London: Macmillan, 1976. A discussion of the current economic crisis and its significance for the international capitalist system.

Magdoff, Harry. *The Age of Imperialism.* New York: Monthly Review Press, 1966. An updating of the Marxist theory of imperialism to the age of the American empire and multinational corporation.

Miliband, Ralph. *The State of Capitalist Society.* London: Weidenfeld and Nicholson, 1969. A theoretical discussion of the role of the state in twentieth century capitalism.

Wallerstein, Immanuel. *The Modern World System.* New York: Academic Press, 1974. An important work in Marxist historiography examining capitalist development between 1450-1650.

CLASSICAL CANADIAN POLITICAL ECONOMY

Creighton, Donald. *The Empire of the St. Lawrence,* rev. ed. Toronto: Macmillan, 1970. A paean to the Montreal merchants of the eighteenth to mid-nineteenth centuries and to the political economy of the St. Lawrence River system.

Innis, Harold. *Essays in Canadian Economic History.* Toronto: University of Toronto Press, 1956. Essays by the key exponent of staple theory.

Nelles H.V. *The Politics of Development.* Toronto: Macmillan, 1974. A discussion of the political economy of Ontario between 1850-1940.

Smiley, Donald, ed. *The Rowell-Sirois Report.* Toronto: McClelland and Stewart, Carleton Library, 1963. A classical treatment of federal-provincial relations up to World War II from a political economy perspective.

RADICAL AND MARXIST CANADIAN POLITICAL ECONOMY

Bourque, Gilles. *Question nationale et classes sociales du Québec, 1760-1840.* Montreal: Parti pris, 1970. A class analysis of the national question in Québec from the Conquest through to the Act of Union.

Clement, Wallace. *The Canadian Corporate Elite.* Toronto: McClelland and Stewart, Carleton Library, 1975. An extension of Porter's 1965 study of the Canadian power structure with particular reference to the corporate elite.

Gonick, Cy. *Inflation or Depression.* Toronto: Lorimer, 1975. A discussion of Keynesianism and its long-term failure to resolve some of the principal contradictions in Canadian and Western capitalism.

Jamieson, Stuart. *History of Industrial Strife in Canada,* Study No. 22. Task Force on Industrial Relations. Ottawa: Queen's Printer, 1970. A treatment of twentieth-century Canadian labor history which underlines the pervasiveness of industrial conflict and, at times, class consciousness.

Kealy, Gregory S., and Peter Warrian, eds. *Essays in Canadian Working Class History.* Toronto: McClelland and Stewart, 1976. Essays, principally on the nineteenth century, by some of the younger labor historians in Canada.

Levitt, Kari. *Silent Surrender.* Toronto: Macmillan, 1970. A strong critique of the Americanization of Canada through the multinational corporation.

MacPherson, C.B. *Democracy in Alberta.* Toronto: University of Toronto Press, 1953. A classical study of Social Credit in Alberta, underlining the role of the petty bourgeoisie as a social class in Canada.

Milner, Henry. *Politics in the New Quebec.* Toronto: McClelland and Stewart, 1977. A good analysis of political developments in Québec since 1960.

Naylor, Tom. *The History of Canadian Business, 1867-1914,* Vols. 1 and 2. Toronto: Lorimer, 1976. A carefully documented foray into Canadian business history between Confederation and World War I.

Panitch, Leo, ed. *The Canadian State.* Toronto: University of Toronto Press, 1977. A major collection of essays on the Canadian state by some of the younger Marxist political economists in Canada.

Porter, John. *The Vertical Mosaic.* Toronto: University of Toronto Press, 1965. An application of C. Wright Mills's power elite analysis to Canada.

Pratt, Larry and John Richards. *Prairie Capitalism.* Toronto: McClelland and Stewart, 1979. A foray into regional capitalist analysis of contemporary Alberta and Saskatchewan.

Resnick, Philip. *The Land of Cain: Class and Nationalism in English Canada, 1945-1975.* Vancouver: New Star Books, 1977. A class analysis of English-Canadian nationalism since 1945.

Ryerson, Stanley. *Unequal Union.* Toronto: Progress Books, 1968. A work in Marxist historiography of Canada between 1837-1871.

Teeple, Gary, ed. *Capitalism and the National Question in Canada.* Toronto: University of Toronto Press, 1972. A collection of essays focusing on class structure, labor history and the national question in Canada.

Subject Index

Name Index